OFFICIAL
CATALOGUE THE
EGYPTIAN
MUSEUM
AIRO

Verlag Philipp von Zabern
Mainz · Germany

Mohamed Saleh
and Hourig Sourouzian
Photographs: Jürgen Liepe

OFFICIAL
CATALOGUE

THE
EGYPTIAN
MUSEUM
CAIRO

Published by the Organisation of Egyptian Antiquities

THE ARAB REPUBLIC
OF EGYPT

268 pages with more than 300 illustrations, 290 in full colour

Frontispiece: The Egyptian Museum Cairo

Translations by Peter Der Manuelian and Helen Jacquet-Gordon

All photographs by Jürgen Liepe, Berlin
except cat. nos. 174, 176, 177, 178, 188, 189, 193
(Margarete Büsing, Berlin)
and 218, 223, 240 (Jim Jardine, Vancouver)

© 1987 Verlag Philipp von Zabern, Mainz
Alle Rechte, insbesondere das der Übersetzung in fremde
Sprachen, vorbehalten. Ohne ausdrückliche Genehmigung des
Verlages ist es auch nicht gestattet, dieses Buch oder Teile
daraus auf photomechanischem Wege (Photokopie, Mikro-
kopie) zu vervielfältigen.
ISBN 3-8053-0942-2
ISBN 3-8053-0952-X (Museumsausgabe)
Satz: Setzerei Hurler, Notzingen
Lithos: Witzemann & Schmidt, Wiesbaden
Papier: Papierfabrik Scheufelen, Lenningen
Printed in Germany/Imprimé en Allemagne
Gesamtherstellung: Verlag Philipp von Zabern,
Mainz am Rhein.
Printed on fade resistant and archival quality (PH 7 neutral)

Contents

Preface

Through informative, thoroughly researched text and highest quality illustrations, this new catalog should meet the needs of the countless visitors who come to marvel at the masterpieces housed in the Egyptian Museum of Cairo. Translations in English, French, German and Arabic will render it accessible to the widest possible audience of visitors from many nations.

The Egyptian Museum houses the largest and most important material source on ancient Egyptian civilization, with works of art as well as objects of invaluable historical and religious significance, to which this guide is now a necessary introduction.

It is a privilege and a pleasure to gratefully acknowledge here all those who have contributed to the production of this important volume: the scholars, the photographer, and last but not least the publisher and his press, all of whom have done so much to give us a handsome guide in every way worthy of the unparalleled collection which it describes.

Dr. Ahmed Kadry
Chairman of the Egyptian
Antiquities Organization

Preface
to the reedition

Since its first appearance this catalogue has been an invaluable companion and guide for inumerable people from all over the world visiting the unique collection of fascinating archaeological objects exhibited in the Egyptian Museum of Cairo.

More than 100 000 objects bear testimony to the history of ancient Egyptian culture from prehistoric down to Graeco-Roman times.

With its marvellous photographs of the highest standard and numerous scholarly explanations this catalogue allows for visitors to gain a better understanding of the culture and civilization of ancient Egypt.

I would like to take this opportunity to once again express my thanks to all those who contributed towards the creation of this appealing and successful catalogue, the scholars as well as the photographer and the publisher.

Finally, may it please the visitor to be reminded that Egyptian antiquities are more delicate than it would appear. For this reason may I voice an urgent appeal for everyone to please assist us in preserving this cultural heritage for later generations, by refraining from touching the objects on show.

Prof. Dr. Sayed Tawfik
President of the Egyptian
Antiquities Organization

◁ The Egyptian Museum Cairo. Hall (Inner Court)

The Facade of the Museum (drawing in red chalk), by Zépur Sourouzian, 1984

Introduction

Ancient Egyptian civilization is one of the sources of modern culture. It attracted and influenced other peoples of the ancient world, especially the Greeks and the Romans. Scientists, artists, and historians visited Egypt to study in its temples. They transferred the knowledge they gained in science, fine arts, religion, and mythology to their homelands. The Arabs received this knowledge from the Greeks and Romans and in turn transmitted it to Europe during the Middle Ages, where it helped to stimulate the European Renaissance.

Great interest in ancient Egyptian civilization arose again in modern times following Bonaparte's expedition to Egypt in 1798, which stimulated such scientific studies of Egypt as the *Description de L'Egypte* (1809–1828), written by French scholars who accompanied Napoleon's army, *Manners and Customs of the Ancient Egyptians* (1837) by John Gardiner Wilkinson, and *Denkmäler aus Aegypten und Aethiopien* (1849–1859) by Richard Lepsius and other German scholars. The progress towards the decipherment of the hieroglyphic script made by such European scholars as Silvestre de Sacy, Akerblad, and Thomas Young enabled Jean François Champollion to establish its correct reading (1822), and the information gathered from the ancient inscriptions and papyri resulted in a better understanding of the history and culture of ancient Egypt.

The enormous quantity of Egyptian monuments is itself proof of the richness of the ancient civilization. A visit to one of the many temples scattered all over Egypt is sufficient to convince one of this cultural wealth, for each is extravagantly decorated with reliefs and inscriptions and adorned with various types of columns and statues. The tombs of kings and nobles are covered with beautiful paintings, reliefs, and inscriptions, and were originally provided with large amounts of funerary furniture and equipment. This quantitative richness reflects the fondness of the ancient Egyptian for the multitudinous in all aspects of life, from deities in their temples to the seemingly endless number of hieroglyphic signs, and from the variety of forms and poses in which gods and people were represented in reliefs and statues to the precise depiction of the objects making up the environment of this world and the next. The quantity and variety of objects in the Egyptian Museum is a further testimony to the multifaceted mind of the ancient Egyptian and his skill in producing tangible manifestations of it.

Most of the objects in the museum are on exhibition to the public. On the first (ground) floor, the arrangement follows the chronological order of ancient Egyptian history. On the upper floor groups of objects found undisturbed are displayed along with collections of objects of the same type or with the same function.

In 1835, the Service des Antiquités de l'Egypte was established. The authorities intended to prevent the plundering of archaeological sites by local and foreign treasure-hunters as well as by consuls representing foreign countries and their agents. For the first time, Egyptian artifacts were collected by the Egyptian government and stored in a small building in the Azbakiah garden in Cairo. This collection of artifacts was later transferred to another building in the Citadel of Saladin. When the Austrian Archduke Maximilian visited Egypt in 1855, the whole collection was presented to him as a gift by Abbas Pasha, the ruler of Egypt. In 1858, another museum was prepared at Boulaq by Auguste Mariette. Later he worked very hard to establish a great museum suitable for Egyptian monuments, especially after the flooding of the first Boulaq museum in 1878, when many objects were washed away or stolen. In 1890, the contents of the Boulaq museum were transferred to an annex of the Giza palace of Ismail Pasha, where they remained until the present museum was opened in 1902. The present museum was designed by the French architect Marcel Dourgnon in the neo-classical style thought suitable for ancient monuments. Two main floors are reserved for exhibitions open to the public and for study galleries. It now contains more than 120 000 objects dating from the various eras of ancient Egyptian civilization. The most important groups of objects are the following:

1. The jewellery of Queen Ah-hotep, wife of Seqenen-re and mother of both Kamose and Ahmose, who liberated Egypt by expelling the Hyksos invaders from the country at the end of the 17th Dynasty. Her tomb was found in Thebes in 1859.

2. The mummies of some of the 18–20th Dynasty kings and their coffins gathered together by the priests of the 21st Dynasty and hidden in the so-called Deir el-Bahari cachette in Thebes. These were found between 1875 and 1881 (in the tomb of Queen Inhapi, no. 320) and consist of the mummies of Seqenen-re, Ahmose I, Amenophis I, Tuthmosis I, Tuthmosis II, Tuthmosis III, Seti I, Ramses II, Ramses III.

3. The funerary equipment from the tomb of Sennedjem and his family (tomb no. 1 in Deir el-Medina, Thebes), which was discovered in 1886. Part of it is now in the Metropolitan Museum in New York and in Berlin.

4. Mummies and coffins of the priests of Amon found in Deir el-Bahari in 1891. Of the 153 coffins dating from the 21st and 22nd Dynasties which were recovered, many were given as gifts or sold abroad by the Egyptian government.

5. Artifacts from the tombs of kings and members of the royal families of the Middle Kingdom (Hor, Nub-hetepti-khered, Khnumit, Sat-Hathor, Ita, Merit, Sat-Hathor-Yunet) found at Dahshur in 1894.

6. Artifacts from the tomb of Prince Maherperi of the 18th Dynasty, which was discovered in 1898 in the Valley of the Kings.

7. Artifacts and royal mummies found in the tomb of Amenophis II in 1898 in the Valley of the Kings (the mummies are those of Amenophis II, Tuthmosis IV, Amenophis III, Merenptah, Seti II, Siptah, Ramses IV, Ramses V, Ramses VI, three women and a child).

8. The funerary equipment from the tomb of Yuya and Thuya (the maternal grandparents of Akhenaten) and the remains of the contents of the royal tombs of Tuthmosis III, Tuthmosis IV, Amenophis III and Horemheb, all found before 1906.

9. Artifacts from the tomb of Tutankhamon, discovered in 1922. There were more than 3500 pieces, of which 1700 are exhibited in the museum; the rest are in storerooms in Cairo and Luxor.

10. Artifacts from the tomb of Hetep-heres, mother of Khufu, which were found to the east of the great pyramid at Giza in 1925.

11. Artifacts from the Amarna period made for Akhenaten and members of his family and some high officials. These were found in Tell el-Amarna, Hermopolis, Thebes and Memphis between 1912 and 1933.

12. Monuments from the tomb of Hemaka, chief administrator from the time of King Udimo of the 1st Dynasty. These were found between 1931 and 1936 at Sakkara.

13. Objects from some royal and private tombs at Tanis (east Delta) dating from the 21st and 22nd Dynasties. These were found in 1939.

14. Artifacts discovered by Egyptian and foreign expeditions in Giza, Sakkara, Helwan, Abu Bello, Athribis, Bubastis, Heliopolis, Aswan, Nubia, the eastern and western deserts, and Sinai.

15. Collections of artifacts from the royal palaces, seized for, purchased by, or donated to the museum.

Dr. Mohamed Saleh
General Director of the
Egyptian Museum

The beginnings of the Egyptian Museum. Boulaq (chromolithograph from *Views in Egypt* by Luigi Mayer, London 1804)

GENERAL INFORMATION

Museum hours: The museum is open every day from 9 a.m. to 4 p.m. except from 11.^{15} a.m. to 1.^{30} p.m. on Fridays. During the Muslim month of Ramadan, the museum closes at 3 p.m.

Notice to visitors: Visitors who have more than two hours at their disposal, or who intend to visit the museum more than once, are advised to see the objects of the Early Dynastic period at the main entrance of the museum (hall 43) and then proceed in a clockwise direction until they reach the entrance again. They should then go upstairs to visit the Tutankhamon collection and the other galleries. Visitors who are limited to a single two-hour tour are advised to see the objects of the Early Dynastic period at the main entrance, proceed in a clockwise direction to the end of the western corridor and then go upstairs to visit the Tutankhamun collection in the northern and eastern galleries.

Numbering system of the objects

In order to simplify the numbering system in the Museum, visitors using our catalogue may recognize the objects described in it by a brown label placed either close to each object or on the outside of the case.

The exhibition numbers written in black on white labels refer to the Brief Description of the Monuments available at the entrance to the Museum.

To assist the specialist who would like to pursue further research we also have included in this catalogue certain Museum reference numbers. These are:

— the museum entry number: *Journal d'Entrée du Musée* (JE); this number is usually marked directly on the monument in black;

— the number of the *Catalogue Général* (CG), publications, a list of which is given in our Bibliography; it is marked in red or white directly on the exhibit;

— the number of a temporary register (*Registre Temporaire* RT), which appears, written within a cross, on the exhibit itself;

— and finally, in special cases the number of the *Special Register* (SR) which appears in white on a black label; it refers to the inventory list drawn up by the curator of a particular section of the museum's collections.

Outline of Ancient Egyptian History

Ancient Egyptian civilization was certainly one of the most longlived and durable in all of world history. Among the factors contributing to its longevity are the Nile river, its naturally protected valley, and the stable weather conditions. The Nile valley is enclosed by the Mediterranean Sea on the north; the Arabian desert and Red Sea on the east; the Libyan desert on the west, and in ancient times danger seldom came from the south.

By the Neolithic Period (ca. 5000 B.C.), the Egyptians already enjoyed a sedentary and stable existence. The annual inundation of the Nile induced them to construct dykes and dams to protect their settlements, and to dig canals to better irrigate and cultivate their fields. They began to store harvest crops against times of famine, and they learned how to gauge the rise and fall of the inundation waters. One might even say that the regular annual rhythm of the river was the primary catalyst underlying the organization and political unification of the country. In this sense, then, Herodotus, the "father of history", was surely correct when he wrote in 449 B.C. that "Egypt is the gift of the Nile".

NEOLITHIC CULTURE

(5000 B.C.) Egyptian civilization at this period is known as the "Nagada culture", which can be divided into three phases. The culture first arises in the Fifth Millennium B.C. in Upper Egypt between Abydos in the north and Armant in the south, and subsequently spread over the rest of Upper Egypt. The first – or Nagada I – phase achieved trade relations with the Kharga oasis, reached the Red Sea to the east, and the First Cataract to the south. The process of consolidating the country, which resulted in historical times in a unified Egypt, may have begun under the Nagada II phase. Both trade relations and conflicts between Upper and Lower Egypt are attested at this time. Especially noteworthy during this period are the fascinating early mural paintings discovered in a tomb at Hierakonpolis (ca. 3500 B.C.), and the ceramic decorations displaying human and animal figures, as well as ships complete with oars and cabins.

The third and most advanced Nagada III phase seems to reveal influence both from Lower Egypt and other cultures in the Near East. Autonomous provinces were established and consolidated until two separate kingdoms eventually came into being: one in Upper Egypt with its capital at Nekheb (El Kab, near Edfu), and the other in Lower Egypt, with its capital at Buto (Tell el Farain, near Desouq).

THE HISTORICAL PERIOD

(ca. 3000−332 B.C.)   was divided into thirty-one dynasties, or royal families, by the Egyptian priest Manetho, who lived between 323 and 245 B.C. Manetho wrote his history of Egypt beginning with Menes of the First Dynasty and ending with Alexander the Great in 332 B.C. We can divide his dynasties further into several discrete eras.

THE EARLY DYNASTIC (THINITE) ERA

(ca. 3000−2705 B.C.)   consists of the first two dynasties, and derives its name from the town of origin of the earliest kings: Thinis. The first capital of the newly unified country to be established − by Hor-Aha (Menes), the fourth king of the First Dynasty − was at Memphis. Hieroglyphic writing also came into use at this time in moderate scale for simple economic and other types of documents. These early jottings mostly served to list names, places or objects. A few experiments with stone as a building material, instead of mud brick, were also undertaken. Royal tombs were constructed at both Sakkara and Abydos. Among the famous representational works from this period is the Narmer palette, which commemorates the defeat of the Lower Egyptians at the hands of the Upper Egyptians, and the unification of the two halves of the country.

THE OLD KINGDOM

(ca. 2705−2155 B.C.)   Pyramid Age.
This period includes Dynasties 3−6. Memphis remained the political capital, but Heliopolis grew as the most important religious center. The pharaohs were buried in the great pyramid necropoleis of Sakkara, Giza, Abusir and Dahshur (to the southwest of Cairo). The Old Kingdom was characterized by a highly bureaucratic and organized central administration. In the transition period from the Fifth to Sixth Dynasties, the corpus of religious mortuary literature known as the Pyramid Texts makes its first appearance inside the burial chambers of the pyramids. Members of the royal family and high officials were interred in *mastabas*, or in rock-cut tombs. The officials' sepulchres were located either around the pyramids of the pharaoh they had served, or in their own administrative province. The walls were richly decorated with painted reliefs of scenes of daily life and religious (mortuary cult) activities. The most famous kings of this era include Djoser (Netjer-Khet) of Dynasty 3, owner of the Step Pyramid at Sakkara, which was constructed by the great architect Imhotep; King Sneferu of the Fourth Dynasty built one pyramid at Medum and two at Dahshur. His successors Khufu, Khafre, and Menkaure constructed theirs at Giza; these last three are considered one of the seven wonders of the ancient world. In the Fifth Dynasty, the cult of the falcon-headed sun god Rê exerted tremendous influence over the country. Sun-temples were erected near the pyramids north of Sakkara and at Abusir.

THE FIRST INTERMEDIATE PERIOD

(ca. 2155–2134 B.C.)   Towards the end of the Old Kingdom, as central authority disintegrated, what contacts had existed between Egypt and Nubia, Phoenicia and Palestine were broken off. The officials in charge of the many Egyptian provinces struggled to gain their own independence, and political and economic chaos resulted. The period from Dynasties 7 to 10, also known as the Heracleopolitan Period, was one of civil war and starvation. Two weak ruling houses are attested: one at Thebes in the south, and the other at Heracleopolis in the north (Ehnasia near the Fayum). This was the classical period of the Egyptian language, and several descriptive accounts tell of the woes of the age, which lasted more than a century and a half.

THE MIDDLE KINGDOM

(ca. 2134–1781 B.C.)   Dynasties 11–12 come under this heading. The country was finally reunited under the Theban princes whose capital in the south became the religious center for all of Egypt. It was here at Thebes that King Mentuhotep II built his famous mortuary temple of Deir el-Bahari. In the Twelfth Dynasty, however, the capital shifted to the north, near El-Lisht, and the pharaohs were buried in mud-brick pyramids (Dahshur, Fayum, Beni Suef). The older Pyramid Texts evolved into the Coffin Texts, now no longer restricted to use by the king alone. They adorned the inside and outside of coffins, and are later attested in the tombs of certain high officials.

Provincial "nomarchs" and other independent high officials were allowed to excavate or construct their tombs in their own districts. These were provided with beautiful mortuary equipment and decorated with vivid scenes of both daily life and life in the next world (Beni Hasan, El Bersheh, Thebes, Aswan).

Great irrigation projects were undertaken during the Twelfth Dynasty. Attempts were made to irrigate the Fayum, and reservoirs and canals were constructed under Sesostris (Senusret) II, Sesostris (Senusret) III and Amenemhat III.

THE SECOND INTERMEDIATE PERIOD

(Dynasties 13–17, ca. 1781–1550 B.C.)   After a period of political and economic turmoil, most of the country was overrun for about a century by a Near Eastern people known as the Hyksos, or "rulers of foreign Lands" (Dynasties 15–16). Composed of immigrant tribes of Syrians, Palestinians and Hurrians, the Hyksos found refuge in the fertile Nile valley. They introduced into Egypt the horse and horse-drawn chariot, as well as new types of daggers, swords and composite bows, all of which were to play a large role later on in Egyptian military history. In terms of artistic achievement or economic prosperity, the Hyksos domination was a relatively decadent and impoverished era.

The Hyksos worshipped the deity Seth (Sutekh), god of strength and confusion. Avaris in the eastern Delta between Tanis and Qantir served as their capital. During the Seventeenth Dynasty, however, the Theban princes had been consolidating their own power in the south, and eventually moved to oust the foreigners from their homeland. Finally, under the leadership of Seqenenre, Kamose and Ahmose, the Thebans expelled the Hyksos, reunited the country and initiated a new dynasty.

THE NEW KINGDOM

(ca. 1550–1070 B.C.)   The Empire Period.
This period includes Dynasties 18–20, and is considered by many to be the golden age of Egyptian civilization. In the Eighteenth Dynasty, Thebes was both the political and religious center of the realm. Magnificent temples were erected there for the state god Amon-Rê. The temple of Karnak functioned not only as the major religious center, but also the political, economic and diplomatic focus for everything, from the delivery of local taxes from across the river to foreign tribute from provinces such as Nubia, Syria-Palestine and Phoenicia, and from countries such as Punt (Somalia?), Libya, Crete, the Aegean islands and Mesopotamia. Famous rulers of Dynasty 18 include:

Queen Hatshepsut (1488–1470 B.C.), the best-known queen-cum-pharaoh of Egypt. Her relatively peaceful reign, trade relations with Punt and building activities at Thebes (Deir el-Bahari and Karnak) are especially noteworthy.

Tuthmosis III (1490–1436 B.C.), whose military exploits in the north, northeast and south earned him the title of creator of the Egyptian empire. He also conducted an active building campaign, especially at Thebes (Karnak, Luxor).

Amenophis III (1403–1365) B.C.), with his prosperous and peaceful reign, and friendly diplomatic relations with many foreign countries in western Asia. Egyptian art and culture reached a zenith during his rule.

Amenophis IV (Akhenaten) (1365–1348 B.C.), the first to establish a form of monotheism in Egypt. Akhenaten's great religious revolution involved the replacement of the state god Amon-Rê with the solar deity Aten. Artistic conventions and political traditions were also totally restructured. The king moved the capital to a completely new city in Middle Egypt (Akhetaten, now Tell el-Amarna). Many of the Egyptian holdings in Syria-Palestine which Tuthmosis III had secured, were nearly lost under Akhenaten's reign.

Tutankhamon (1347–1337 B.C.), a successor of Akhenaten, restored the cult of Amon-Rê, and abandoned Tell el-Amarna in order to return to tradition. The discovery of his nearly intact tomb in 1922 revealed the wealth and prosperity of the Eighteenth Dynasty.

Horemheb (1332–1305 B.C.), who served as generalissimo and then king after the death of Tutankhamon, and protected the country from foreign intruders.

In Dynasty 19 (ca. 1305–1196 B.C.), Egyptian influence in Syria-Palestine was partially restored during the reigns of Seti I and Ramses II. The capital was moved once again, this time to Pi-Ramesse in the eastern Delta, the origin of the Ramesside family and a more strategic location vis à vis Syro-Palestinian affairs. The Hittites in Asia Minor were Egypt's chief rival at this period; both sides struggled for control of the Syro-Palestinian region (Battle of Kadesh).

In the reign of Ramses III (ca. 1196 B.C.), Aegean tribes known as the Sea Peoples threatened to infiltrate the Egyptian Delta region. Economic and cultural decline, coupled with the threat of foreign invasion, contributed to the weakening of central authority; strikes and cases of corruption are documented in the ancient sources. At Thebes, the priesthood of Amon achieved ever greater political influence.

THE THIRD INTERMEDIATE PERIOD

(1070–750 B.C.)   Dynasties 21–24 are generally ascribed to this era. In Dynasty 21, Egypt was divided once again into two regions. In the south, the theocratic state was ruled by the priesthood of Amon-Rê at Karnak, while the north was controlled by the priests of Tanis. The Twenty-second to Twenty-fourth Dynasties were of Libyan origin.

THE LATE PERIOD

(750–332 B.C.)   The ruling house of Nubia succeeded in founding the Twenty-fifth Dynasty. Egypt was reunited under King Shabaka, and the capital was moved to Napata near the Fourth Cataract in the Sudan. At the end of this period, the Assyrians conquered Egypt (671 B.C.).

The Twenty-sixth, or Saite, Dynasty achieved a renaissance of Egyptian civilization. Art, language and many other aspects of traditional Egyptian culture were resurrected from bygone classical ages. The dynastic capital was at Sais in the western Delta, until the Persians under Cambyses conquered Egypt in 525 B.C.

During Dynasties 27–30, Egypt remained under Persian rule, occasionally succeeding in placing native Egyptian rulers on the throne.

GRAECO-ROMAN PERIOD

(332 B.C.–A.D. 395).   In 332 B.C. the country was again invaded, this time by Alexander the Great, who founded the city of Alexandria in the following year. After his death in 323 B.C., Egypt fell under Ptolemaic rule until the death of Antony and Cleopatra VII in 30 B.C. The country then became a Roman province until A.D. 395. Christianity then arose and Alexandria became a theological center of the new religion.

The Byzantine Period began in A.D. 395 in the time of Arcadius, the Emperor of the East.

In the year A.D. 640, Amr ibn el-As, the muslim general of Caliph Omer ibn el-Khattab, conquered Pelusium (near Suez) and defeated the Byzantines at Heliopolis. His conquest was completed in 646 with the taking of Alexandria, and Egypt then became an Islamic province.

Mohamed Saleh

The Style and Conventions of Egyptian Art

Art in the works of man is the expression of an aesthetic ideal. All art, no matter what historical period it derives from, is distinguished by its own aesthetic, rules and manner of expression; in other words, its own style. In each artistic endeavor, the process of representation has a stimulating motive, and the object or theme reproduced has its own significance, for a representation aspires to fix an idea, a real or imaginary situation by means of pure figuration, of symbols or of abstraction. Even in modern art, the most abstract artist entitles his work, and freely explains to all who care to learn the sense, image or hidden concepts behind even a completely empty canvas.

Egyptian art, like all other art, was aware since its inception of its own aesthetic, its conventions and objectives. If we understand art in this sense, then such statements as: "Art for its own sake did not exist in Egypt;" "Egyptian art is exclusively funerary;" or even: "It was intended only as a tool to serve the requirements of eternity," become unnecessary. For if a concern for aesthetics, as we define art today, had not existed from the beginning, then Art itself would never have existed at all in Egypt.

The Egyptian art which we are considering is certainly the fruit of a religious belief which explained the cosmic order, and of a funerary belief based on the survival of the components of this order. It is thus similar to other manifestations of art born of an ideology, illustrating a religious belief, or participating in an aesthetic research. Egyptian art envelops all of these things. It would never have taken place if "art for art's sake" had not existed, just as the entire development of civilization in Egypt would never have evolved if the Egyptians had resigned themselves to death after merely living to the rhythm of the seasons, or if Pharaoh had been content with a simple tombstone and his retainers with a simple pit in the earth.

These beliefs created a concern to reproduce for the next life an eternal world, thus the Egyptians chose the imperishable material stone in order to transpose their daily surroundings into the eternal one; it is this work in stone which has survived. But it would be incorrect to say that Egyptian art is essentially funerary in nature, because the temples provide immutable testimony to a religious art as well. They have survived down to the present day because they were constructed of stone, but quite numerous were the brick sanctuaries of which we only know the location or the foundations. However, let us take care to avoid the pitfall of claiming that Egyptian art is merely an "instrument" for serving the requirements of eternity. Judging from what we can glimpse, furtive as it might be, of life on earth, we know, for example, that the officials' houses at Tell el-Amarna were as richly decorated as the Theban tombs, whose painted walls we admire so much. Furthermore, the workmen's village of craftsmen and artists at Deir el-Medina, far from being an agglomeration of huts, contains comfortable houses built of stone, decorated with paintings, and provided with altars for the worship of the gods. We know that the royal palaces gleamed every bit as brightly as the divine temples, whose archaeological remains permit us to reconstruct their original splendor.

It is true that of the Old Kingdom, we only know the funerary aspect of Egyptian art. The divine temples disappeared under a burst of reconstruction during the Middle Kingdom, a burst which was repeated in both the New Kingdom and the Late Period. Settlements of unbaked brick have left only traces; we must not forget that a thousand years already separate the constructions of the Old Kingdom from those whose remains are better known to us. All that is left are the great necropoleis, with the royal pyramid in the center of a field of mastabas; the latter reproduce in stone the dwellings of brick, peopled with inhabitants in the form of statues of stone or, as the need arose, of wood, stuccoed and painted.

But the origins of Egyptian art reach back to the Fourth Millennium, revealing all the facets of artistic creativity. Ceramics are attested in an extraordinary range: red polished ware with metallic sheen, dull red ware with traced white decoration, buff colors with painted decoration in purplish red, containing geometric motifs in addition to schematic figures, animals, plants and human beings. There are innumerable stone vases and moulded vessels, whence originate little theriomorphic ceramics. Cleverness and skilled technique are combined with a creative sense of taste. Lithic tools reach the height of perfection at this time. The countless palettes, whether for actual use or purely votive purposes, attest to the grinding of pigments as well as to a concern for style and ornament. Jewellery consisted of bracelets in the form of rings of copper, of ivory or bone, and there were necklaces of strings of beads, pendants and colored stone amulets as well as shells. Egyptian "faience", quartz paste with a vitrified surface, had already been invented by this time; toilet articles, combs or pins in bone or ivory, are attested. Sculpted ivories show beautiful votive knife handles, providing the first masterpieces of the art of bas-relief. The first mural painting, at Hierakonpolis, reproduces in four natural colors (red ochre, yellow ochre, white from chalk and black from soot) the daily routines of hunting, farming and navigating, which at this time were the primary occupations of the Egyptians. Figures of dancers and images of idols combined in the decoration imply the birth of the cult. The same dancers and idols occur in sculpture in the round, modelled in clay, along with schematic human figurines in ivory or stone, and statuettes of animals in clay or stone. If we are dealing, for the majority of these objects, with funerary or religious themes, they no less reflect the daily preoccupations of the inhabitant of the Nile valley, and they prove that he consciously made use of artistic expression.

When the two halves of the country were in the process of unification around 3100 B.C., the same period that writing made its first appearance, the conventions of Egyptian art were already initiated. Religious architecture in brick is attested by representations of primitive sanctuaries on cylinder-seals. Funerary architecture, consisting of a pit covered by a brick superstructure, prepared the way for the arrival of stone pyramids and

the mastabas of private individuals. In three dimensions, the corpus of votive figurines includes delightful female statuettes in ivory. They are shown either naked, the body reproduced with an exquisite naturalism, or clothed in a pleated robe, covered in turn by a garment which leaves one shoulder exposed. They display carefully arranged coiffure. All this testifies to the production of fine linen, pleated from the earliest times on with a care for elegance, and to the use of combs, numerous examples of which have been discovered. Other votive objects, in faience, limestone or clay, represent all kinds of animals, revealing the Egyptians' close observation of nature. The pottery corpus is enriched both with jars of large dimensions and smaller vessels of various shapes. Vases cut from diverse types of stone imitate contemporary ceramics, sometimes even going so far as to reproduce patterns borrowed from basketry, trilobate leaves, or the body of a duck whose wrung neck forms the vase's rim. Jewelry very early on develops past a simple collection of shells and strung pendants to include harmonious assemblages of polished stones of selected colors, arranged with care to form necklaces or bracelets. Gold is introduced early on either in the form of beads, or intended to serve as fasteners or simply as symbolic ornament. Far from merely functional implements, toilet articles are refined works of art in themselves. Some of the examples known from the prehistoric period include: cups in the form of tiny basins, cosmetic spoons, kohl sticks and hairpins terminating in animal forms or symbolic designs. Furniture is ornamented with ivory legs imitating bull's or lion's feet. Palettes decorated with various themes take on such importance that they become votive gifts of great size deposited in divine temples. Examples of inlay work appear on disks of schist with central perforation.

At the end of the Second Dynasty, the royal tomb is already a complete complex in which the facade of the palace, the royal apartments and the numerous magazines are represented. Royal sculpture reveals its first masterpieces. Funerary equipment ranges from provisions of oil in terra cotta jars to delightful little unguent vessels in alabaster, schist or carnelian, and includes funerary vessels of all types and shapes using all kinds of stones.

At the beginning of the Old Kingdom, in the Third Dynasty, monumental architecture in stone is successfully attempted. The pyramid makes its appearance at this time and was to remain a dominant architectural

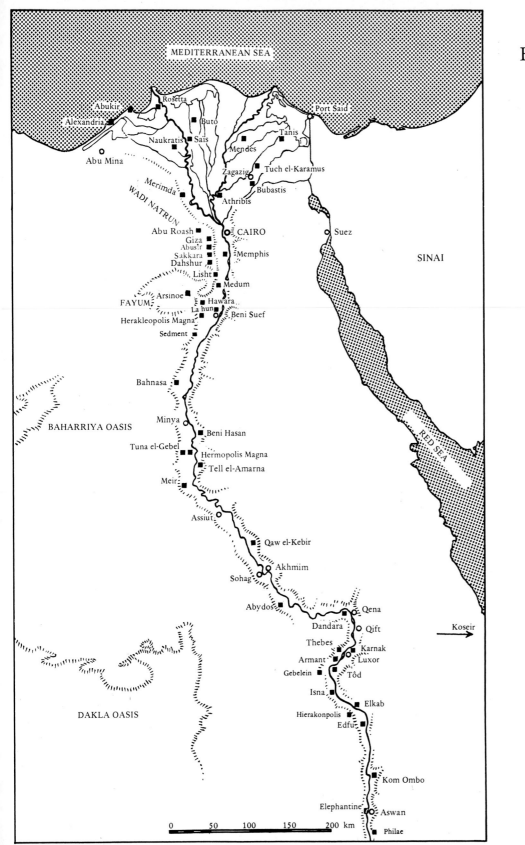

Egypt

MEDITERRANEAN SEA

Abukir
Rosetta
Alexandria
Buto
Naukratis   Saïs
Tanis
Port Said
Mendes
Merimda
Zagazig   Tuch el-Karamus
Bubastis
Athribis
WADI NATRUN
Abu Mina
Abu Roash
CAIRO
Suez
Giza
SINAI
Abusir
Memphis
Sakkara
Dahshur
Lisht
Medum
Arsinoe
Hawara
FAYUM
La hun   Beni Suef
Herakleopolis Magna
Sedment
Bahnasa
BAHARRIYA OASIS
Minya
Beni Hasan
Tuna el-Gebel
Hermopolis Magna
Tell el-Amarna
Meir
Assiut
Qaw el-Kebir
Akhmim
Sohag
RED SEA
Abydos
Qena
Dandara   Qift
Thebes
Koseir
Karnak
Armant   Luxor
Gebelein   Tôd
Isna
Elkab
Hierakonpolis
DAKLA OASIS
Edfu
Kom Ombo
Elephantine   Aswan
Philae

0   50   100   150   200 km

form. In unrestrained devotion to immortality on the part of the Egyptians, the pyramid would reach its most glorious culmination at Giza. In the plastic arts during this time, the conventions inherited from the archaic period become solid rules which the Old Kingdom will now develop.

It follows that the principal concern of a work of art is its representative ability. In three dimensions, the statue is frontal, combining all of the characteristics of a living person. The poses are not numerous: the subject is seated or standing; the king traditionally appears thus in majestic pose. Women are shown with feet together, the men standing with left leg advanced. Occasionally, the figures are represented kneeling, but the crouching "scribal" pose found great favor among private individuals.

The ultimate distinction of this representative ability is perhaps to be found in the rather exceptional bust which appears in the Fourth Dynasty. More numerous are the contemporary three-dimensional heads known as "reserve heads," which might be said to derive from this category, although their function seems to relate more to that of the funerary mask.

Sculpture in relief displays its own set of conventions. Here the figure appears in profile, but the different elements of which it is composed are viewed from the front. In order to represent several men, animals etc., one simply aligned them behind each other. Instead of superposition and subtleties of real perspective, which could contradict the idea that the Egyptians made use of representative figuration, viz. giving the maximum number of characteristic and recognizable components, Egyptian relief sculpture preferred to use an original code of perspective. That which was intended to be on both sides of a figure was represented above and below it. Or both the plan and the section of an object were successfully combined into a single composition. Scenes are generally divided into registers, with a particular code for "reading;" the term is apt even when no hieroglyphic text is provided. Registers are generally read from the bottom up; but we also find that within one register simultaneous action can occur both from right to left and from left to right.

Both sculpture in the round and bas-relief are almost always covered with a fine layer of stucco and enlivened with color. The representations merely painted upon stuccoed walls follow the same rules as apply to painted bas-relief.

The style of the Old Kingdom may be characterized in sculpture in the round by the idealization of the modelling. Even here, where realism emerges, the works remain tinged with idealism in the majority of cases. If by the force of convention the artists fell into formalism, there were many who even within the confines of these conventions succeeded in individualizing their subjects. Old Kingdom sculpture is generally on a modest scale, but a certain natural grandeur exists from the time of Djoser onward. Dimensions larger than even nature itself surface in the Fourth Dynasty; colossal statues themselves are rare, or have perhaps simply not survived. The statuary is static, even rigid for works representing the king and the high officials, but animated for all that constitutes their entourage, especially the servants. The same applies to relief sculpture and painting: the lord appears fixed, represented always at a much larger scale than other individuals. Gathered around him are his fishermen, boatmen, artisans, butchers and bakers.

During the First Intermediate Period, while the Memphite ateliers maintained the artistic tradition, a provincial art style flourished in the various autonomous centers far from the capital. There was naïveté and clumsiness, but also a new freshness which brought about a certain disregard for tradition. Forms were elongated, colors were enlivened; a new canon of proportions replaced the classical canon; and a new ideal of beauty emerged. It was at this period that wooden models appeared instead of more traditional sculpture; eventually they all but replaced mural representations.

With the arrival of the Eleventh Dynasty, and the rise to power of the Theban princes, a provincial style was promoted at the new capital (Thebes) in which power became the ideal. Far removed from the finesse of the Memphite style, it was force and vigor which manifested themselves in these new works of realism.

The art of the Twelfth Dynasty, during which the capital alternated between the Memphite region and the Fayum, combined both of these previously conflicting styles. On the one hand, we find the fruits of the Memphite tradition, with its careful study of proportion and purity of forms, features characteristic of raised and sunk relief sculpture, as well as of royal and private portraits at the outset of the dynasty. On the other hand, we can observe the results of the Theban innovations, which endow powerful works of art with extreme realism, as is represented by the royal portraits at the end of the dynasty, in the north, in the Fayum and at Thebes. The fusion of the two styles engendered masterpieces equal to those discussed above, such as the double statue of Amenemhat III as a Nile god, also known as "the offering-bearers of Tanis."

The Middle Kingdom invented a type of statuary known as the block-statue, examples of which continue all the way down to the Late Period. From the Middle Kingdom come also tiny statuettes, as well as royal colossi and Osiride statues backed against the pillars of portico courts in mortuary temples. Painting displays vivid colors animating the walls of rock-cut tombs and sarcophagi.

A perceptible decline from the Thirteenth Dynasty on caused an impoverishment of the arts during the Second Intermediate Period, an impoverishment explained first by internal political chaos and secondly by the Hyksos "invasion" and domination of the Delta.

However, nothing was irretrievably lost. At the end of the Seventeenth Dynasty, an actual cultural rebirth revealed the survival of the artistic tradition with such pieces as the stela of Ahmose, which adds the beauty of hieroglyphic text to the finesse of relief sculpture. This period also achieved fame with several artistic innovations. Among them are *rîshi* coffins, adorned with feather patterns; some of these were huge anthropoid boxes, enveloping with their feathers the magnificent mummiform coffins of female members of the royal family.

In the Eighteenth Dynasty at Thebes the path to glory once again begins. Under the dynasty's first rulers, the institution of the Royal Tomb commences a long line of impressive sepulchres. The artistic creations which began under the reign of Hatshepsut reach a technical perfection and harmonious aesthetic of rare elegance by the time of Tuthmosis III, and culminate in its apogee under Amenophis III. At the same time, the almost imperial conception of the temple of Hatshepsut at Deir el-Bahari awakens the new taste for monumentality: there followed the temples of Karnak, as well as those on the west bank of the Nile, the tombs, and royal statues reaching colossal proportions under Amenophis III. In relief sculpture, relatively animated scenes depart from pictorial rigidity and even from the hieroglyphic conception of linear arrangement as early as the reign of Hatshepsut, in order to provide veritable narratives of particular expeditions or festivals. Moreover, the decoration of private tombs, whether carved in relief or merely painted, gradually liberates itself from strict pictorial conventions. Towards the middle of Dynasty 18, under Amenophis II, but especially under Amenophis III, the period during which the Theban tombs display their most successful examples of mural decoration, narrative representation is animated and reaches its highpoint under the reign of Akhenaten. Nevertheless, in both artistic conception and style, a sharp break took place, provoked by a brutal change in religious belief. With a new manner of representing the unique god, his intermediary upon earth (i.e. the king), and all creation, Akhenaten initiated the "Amarna style" in a halo of spirituality. The tormented faces and deformed bodies, animated under the omnipresent rays of the Aten, clash completely with previous tradition. However, this mannerist ecstasy eventually levels off and reaches in its own way a purity of synthesis.

After this brusque disorder of rather short duration, the return to orthodoxy engendered an original, expressive art style, in which tradition resurfaces, but contains persistent vestiges of the Amarna heresy. The arts of relief sculpture and mural painting long continue to bear the imprint of the Amarna taste for motion and love of nature. Statuary becomes enriched with a reflective expression and, imbued with a spirit of piety, produces new themes in royal iconography, and new poses in the iconography of private individuals.

The art of the Eighteenth Dynasty also discovered, no doubt through contact with Asia, its taste for luxury, reflecting the contemporary mentality and revealing to us the changes in fashion. Costume now becomes elaborate; sumptuous dress emerges for the first time. The simple garments in use since the archaic period give way to abundant fabrics of transparent, pleated linen wrapped around seductive silhouettes. The overlapping kilts worn by men display loose panels and long pleated belts, terminating in fringed edges. Both masculine and feminine hairstyles reach a highpoint of refinement: enveloping wigs with long locks, curls, or tresses, encircled with floral diadems and surmounted by fragrant cones, form works of art all by themselves. Intricate jewelry adorned its wearer from the ankles up to the wig, including the ears. A profusion of toilet articles in the most inventive forms imaginable, for both the living and the deceased, was manufactured now for more than just the upper classes. Everywhere we find this concern for luxury, refinement and beauty.

The art of the beginning of the Nineteenth Dynasty,

under the short reign of Ramses I, prolonged the preferences current at the end of Dynasty 18, as is clear from the royal tomb and civil statuary. Nevertheless, already under the following reign of Seti I there occurred a concerted return to tradition. The plastic arts are characterized by a serene beauty; relief sculpture returns to purity of line, elegance and perfection; architecture leans once again toward gigantic proportions. A Ramesside art style proper then develops, with grand architectural projects initiated by Seti I and Ramses II. In royal statuary, iconographic themes diversify, depicting the king slaughtering his enemies on the one hand, but on the other hand stretching out prostrate to present a royal offering before a deity. Personal piety on the part of private individuals goes hand in hand with the devotion displayed by pharaoh. Private statuary multiplies in the temples, including naophorous and stelophorous statues, and other types showing the individual in the company of a divinity. In this way, these privileged Egyptians could participate in the offerings of the temple. A new repertoire adorns the private tombs; the scenes of daily life are replaced with religious themes based on life in the netherworld. The academism eventually dominates until, by the last Ramessides, just the royal tombs seem to be noteworthy exceptions.

However, throughout the New Kingdom, thanks to both the unfinished state of certain tombs, and more importantly to countless fragments bearing artists' preliminary sketches, we can discover the beauty and spontaneity of design, as well as the Egyptian artist's exquisite mastery of his craft.

The Third Intermediate Period developed its own style, inherited from the New Kingdom, but lacking in creative attempts to break new ground. All we can cite here is the abundance of decorated coffins for the priesthood, and the multitude of small stelae, figurines and amulets, evidence of personal piety and even popular superstition.

The Twenty-fifth Dynasty, of Kushite origin, adapted and added to the Egyptian legacy with the contribution of artistic realism from the south. This contribution was, however, of short duration. The indigenous Twenty-sixth Dynasty researched and rediscovered the grandeur of the past. Vast tombs for high officials were adorned with relief sculpture copied from the ancient corpus. Archaizing statuary acquires an extraordinary sophistication. Private representations or divine statuettes in stone or bronze, display a remarkable technical perfection. Male portraits, such as those of priests with clean-shaven heads, appear at this time. They are admirably polished, with meditative expressions, and radiate a high spirituality. Their style could in fact be related to the realistic portraits of the Middle Kingdom, while their spiritual expression is reminiscent of pre- and post-Amarna art.

The Thirtieth Dynasty strove to imitate the Twenty-sixth. In a passion for authenticity, monolithic chapels to the greater glory of Nectanebo were donated to the temples. Between these two dynasties, diverse foreign influences, among them a Persian interlude, gradually infiltrated Egyptian art and altered it temporarily, until the Hellenistic age introduced new winds of change altogether. The result is a mixed artistic sensibility, where the foundation remains Egyptian, but the aesthetic is Greek. However, the effort to maintain native traditions manifests itself down to the Roman Period with the construction of great temples in which the facades of the pronaos, formed of columns with lower intercolumnar walls, replace the massive pylons. Furthermore, columns with composite capitals began to diversify the traditional lotiform, papyriform and palmiform types. If architecture gained in airiness, the plastic arts imbued with a new aesthetic were now devoid of their pharaonic vigor. A multitude of sculptors' models prove that technique and proportion could still be learned. But eventually even a funerary mask, an Egyptian element par excellence, winds up in the Roman Period as a portrait painted in Roman fashion on a wooden board.

Be that as it may, the conventions and rules of representation which surfaced at the start of pharaonic history nevertheless survived the many changes in style down to the Roman Period. From the quarrymen to the illustrators, the same techniques were at work. The same instruments were used in construction and sculpture, the same ores ground and then diluted in the painters' palettes. The same teams divided into phyles alternated under the surveillance of the chief architect; teams which cut the stone, others which polished the surfaces; teams for drawing and others for sculpting the walls; master draftsmen for correcting; expert sculptors for chiseling, and painters for coloring. The successive construction projects were always achieved by means of the same collective work.

If the Egyptian artist remains for the most part anonymous, his creative spirit, his soul, is nevertheless there, present in each masterpiece he created throughout the millennia. And if the chief sculptor works a team of men, or the head draftsman his painters, his hand is present for all to see in the perfection of the completed work, even if the patron involved is the king himself.

It is irrelevant that the ancient work itself was rarely signed. The title of a man such as Imhotep, preserved on the statue of his king, informs us that he was the architect of King Djoser. The statues and private tombs of the Old Kingdom fairly often reveal the name of those responsible for the project, such-and-such a master sculptor, or chief draftsman. In the beautiful mastaba of Ptahhotep at Sakkara, we see the chief sculptor, Ny-ankh-Ptah, represented with his name and title carefully inscribed next to him. He cuts a venerable figure, well-advanced in years. He sits in a barque which goes for a sail, and receives the food and drink which a servant respectfully brings to him.

Middle Kingdom stelae provide us with the names and titles of these master artists. From the New Kingdom we have the vivid picture of daily life in the workmen's village at Deir el-Medina. We know Senenmut, chief architect under Hatshepsut; Amenophis son of Hapu, who held the same position under Amenophis III; and also Men and Bak, sculptors whose careers continued into the reign of Akhenaten. Two sculptors signed the statue of Sennefer; the workshop of Tuthmosis, Akhenaten's chief sculptor, revealed for us its most famous pieces at Amarna, where Iutu, sculptor for Queen Tiye, portrayed himself at work, on the wall of a private tomb.

The Egyptian artist knew how to perpetuate pharaonic thought and aesthetic, from the prehistoric period all the way down to the Roman era. It was only with the arrival of Christianity that this artistic production of more than 4000 years expired, in order to manifest itself under a new aspect, namely, the rise of Coptic art.

Hourig Sourouzian

Egyptian Religion

The considerable number of temples erected throughout Egypt for countless deities attests to the polytheistic nature of Egyptian religion. However, we can observe certain tendencies within particular nomes or localities which to us seem monotheistic. These were most likely originally independent tribal settlements whose god had remained the sole local patron, even after the unification of the realm. The abstract concept for "divinity," *netjer*, was known since the time of the earliest sanctuaries; we can observe a constant tendency to unite within a single deity the names and functions of two or three divine forces. Seen in this light, the reforms of Akhenaten are no more than the institutionalization of a monotheistic concept which was already in existence. The important difference here is the fact that the "great god" is thus truly the unique god, both named and visible, and imposed upon all the populace, whereas formerly each nome could support its own unique deity without suffering conflation with that of its neighbor.

The hundreds of deities which in the historical period appear in human, animal or vegetable form as emblems, scepters or fetishes, are at the beginning of time the sentient divine forces in the universe and in nature. These forces gradually had to take visible, if not tangible forms of appearance in order to be accessible to mankind.

Polytheism in Egypt may be explained by a preference early on for seeing a superhuman force behind each element in nature. Sometimes we can return to the associative origins between the divine force and its form of appearance upon earth. That the falcon personifies the celestial deity because of its agility in the sky and keen eyesight is quite clear. It is also easy to comprehend the association of the bull or the ram with a god of fecundity and with reproductive forces; similarly, one will readily concede that the crocodile came to be venerated because of the dangerous power dwelling within it.

Other associations, however, remain unexplained to us, such as the incarnation of the God Thoth, father of science, as an ibis or a baboon.

Egyptian polytheism is characterized by a formidable flexibility. The three properties which constitute a divine force, viz. its name, incarnation and function, are interchangeable from one god to the next, sometimes even within the same locality.

Communal forms: Under the same incarnation, deities with different names have different functions. See, for example, the falcon which stands for the god of heaven named Horus at Edfu, the solar god named Rê-Horakhty at Heliopolis, the chthonic god Sokar at Memphis, and the god of the Theban nome, Montu. These deities differ from one another in that the first two bear the solar disk, the third takes a mummiform shape, and the fourth adds two uraeus cobras to its disk, along with two tall feathers.

Communal function: The funerary god at Memphis is Sokar who appears as a falcon. At Abydos, it is Osiris in anthropomorphic mummiform. In several necropoleis it is Anubis the jackal.

Identical names: Hathor, mistress of heaven, can appear as a woman at Giza. Hathor, goddess of the necropolis, takes the shape of a cow at Thebes. At Dendera, her principal cult focus, where she combines all of her possible Hathoric functions, she is also worshipped in the form of her emblem, the sistrum with the goddess's head and ears of a cow.

Identical function, identical name: The god of science, Thoth, can appear indiscriminately as a baboon or an ibis, both forms coexisting at Hermopolis.

Identical form, identical function: The funerary jackal god is called in one case Anubis, in another Wepwawet. The same is true of the wrathful lioness goddess Sekhmet and/or Pakhet.

Identical name, identical form, but with different surnames, attributes and functions: Horus (*Hor* = "the distant one") as a falcon or with falcon head, is the deity of heaven. By way of example, among the numerous incarnations of Horus throughout all of his cults, from the Delta to Nubia, he is the one of Behdet (Edfu) and of Mesen, the name of a town in the Delta where he is considered to have battled Seth with a harpoon. He wears the solar disk in association with the sun god. Under this form he is also Horus of the Horizon (Horakhty) at Heliopolis; as a god for the king and patron of the monarchy, he wears the double crown and two feathers. After the myth of Osiris was devised, Horus was described with the surname, among several others, of "He who unifies the Two Lands" (Harsamtous), or as the "Son of Isis" (Harsiese). He wears the double crown and, according to the place in question, might appear in the triad of Horus the Great (Haroëris at Edfu or Kom Ombo), or in that of Osiris (Abydos, Philae).

The three factors, form, function and name, are themselves subject to variation within the same deity.

Multiplicity of forms. The form of appearance does not always remain fixed. The anthropomorphic Amon, bearing a headdress with tall feathers, might also appear under the ithyphallic form of the fecundity god Min, or in the guise of either of his sacred animals, the ram or the goose. Similarly, Rê can manifest himself as a falcon or a ram, or in anthropomorphic form with the falcon's or ram's head, and so forth. These are all merely visible effigies, conceived as hieroglyphs, intended to allow recognition of the deity throughout his numerous characteristics and attributes. In the same manner, the sacred animals are not the gods themselves, but function rather as "receptacles," or material supports, for the divine force.

Diversity and evolution of functions. A single divinity can have several functions, either simultaneous or progressive. By herself, Hathor combines an extraordinary variety of functions and activities: mistress of heaven, mistress of life, mother of mothers, celestial nurse, goddess of truth, love, cheerfulness, of music and dance; mistress of gold, of mines and gems; guardian of the entrances to the wadi: eye of Rê: bloodthirsty goddess who returns only after being appeased, bestowing fertility; and even funerary deity, worshipped in the arid necropoleis . . .

Khonsu, a young lunar divinity and originally destroyer of mankind, evolves gradually into a patron of the life-span. He cures man's illnesses, protects him against harmful animals, and is eventually considered an effective oracle.

Elasticity of names. A divine force may bear several different names, in addition to its numerous surnames. Thus the sun is known as Khepri in the morning, Rê during the day, and Atum in the evening. Taweret, the hippopotamus goddess, is also called Reret, "the sow," or Hedjet, "the white one."

Associations. Numerous deities come in pairs, without the one forcibly assimilating the other. Certain associations originate from a communal function or action, such as Hathor and Isis, mother goddesses par excellence; Atum and Rê, deities which embody the sun; Isis and Nepthys, the two mourners of the Osirian legend. In other cases, the association derives from a conflict between two separate cults which in earliest times opposed one another: Horus and Seth, the Two Lords, who since the First Dynasty are simultaneously embodied in the person of the king. Wadjet and Nekhbet, the cobra and the vulture, are goddesses of Lower and Upper Egypt respectively who become the Two Ladies, protectresses of the king, after the unification of the realm. Rê and Osiris function as both the visible diurnal sun and the nocturnal sun which illuminates the darkness.

Syncretism. These associations may lead to the fusion of two or three divinities into one powerful and universal force. At Heliopolis, Horus and Rê are united as the solar god Rê-Horus of the Horizon (Rê-Horakhty). At Memphis, the union of Ptah, Sokar and Osiris forms a divinity which bears all three names at once. At Abydos, Osiris and the local god Khentamentiu are fused into Osiris-Khentamentiu, the "foremost of the westerners." And finally at Thebes, the most important syncretistic fusion is that of the local god Amon with Rê, thus forming the most universal god in existence: Amon-Rê.

Assimilation. The association of two deities may result in the total assimilation of one by the other. For example, at Busiris, the local god Anedjty becomes associated with Osiris and is eventually supplanted by him.

Theological systems. With the passage of time, as a result of the complex affiliations, fusions and syncretisms, as well as simple geographical proximity between deities, Egyptian theology created Dyads, Triads, the Ogdoad and the Ennead. More than just divine families, these are assemblages of complimentary deities, or members of a hierarchy, organized into systems which tended to explain the cosmic order and creation of the world. Hence the difference between cosmic gods and local gods; the latter could, by political coincidence, be promoted to the status of the former.

The two most important theological systems originated at Heliopolis, with the formation of the Ennead, and at Hermopolis, with the creation of the Ogdoad.

Heliopolis. Out of the primordial ocean, *Nun* ("chaos"), the god Atum created himself. Atum, whose name means "the undifferentiated one," normally takes anthropomorphic shape, wearing the double crown. However, as a pre-existent being, he can also appear in the form of a serpent or scarab beetle. This androgynous being begets by itself the first divine couple, Shu, the air, and Tefnut, the moisture. Shu is represented anthropomorphically, crowned with a feather, while Tefnut appears as a woman or a lioness. This couple engender Geb, the earth-god, and Nut, the sky-goddess. Shu separates the heavens from the earth, while Nut, as a woman whose naked body is adorned with stars, is shown stretched over the earth, which in turn is represented by Geb as a recumbent male. Nut brought into the world the four gods of the Osirian cycle, in two couples: Osiris and Isis, Seth and Nepthys. These nine gods comprise the Ennead of Heliopolis. Osiris was considered the first sovereign on earth after the departure of the gods for heaven, and the transition period between the creation of the earth and the rule of men was mythologically explained through his reign. Each king became the son of Osiris, and was himself the living Horus. At Heliopolis, a small ennead assembled gods of lesser importance, at whose head stood Horus.

Alongside the Ennead, the Heliopolitan theology developed the cult of the sun during the Old Kingdom. This heavenly body, which appeared from the heart of a lotus flower at the moment when Shu raised the heavens above the earth, enjoyed − under the name of Rê − a continuous cult which was to exert extraordinary influence.

Hermopolis. According to the (much later) Hermopolitan theology, it was Thoth, the local god and patron of science, who created by means of his voice a council of eight primordial deities, the Ogdoad. Spontaneous creatures, frogs for the males and serpents for the females, these divinities came in couples which constituted the elemental forces. There were Nun and Nunet, the primordial waters; Heh and Hehet, spacial infinity; Kek and Keket, the darkness; and Amon and Amonet, the

nothingness or emptiness. These four couples took refuge on the primordial mound, and emerged from the abyss in Hermopolis itself. They then created the egg out of which the sun came forth. Thereupon the sun created and organized the world by itself, after having defeated its enemies.

The other theologies merely vary on or result from these two systems. Each Egyptian temple was thought to be constructed on the primordial mound. The formation of a group of deities or a triad in each locality was accomplished by the association of the local and neighboring gods, or of the local and (preferably) supreme deities who were invited or otherwise attracted to join the formation.

Memphis. The local god Ptah was also god of earth and of materials. He is shown in mummiform, wearing a tight-fitting sort of skull cap. The god of the capital, Ptah was soon considered a demiurge, and venerated as the patron of artists and craftsmen. In the New Kingdom, he was included in a triad with Sekhmet, "the powerful one," and Nefertum, "the beautiful complete one," a young man sporting a lotus flower upon his head, since he personified the primordial lotus, symbol of the birth of the sun. Thus three heterogeneous entities came to form a divine "family."

From the Old Kingdom onward, however, Ptah was associated with Sokar, the local funerary god, with Tatenen, "the emerging earth," and with the bull Apis, fecundity god at Memphis. The introduction of the cult of Osiris there resulted in the union of Ptah, Sokar and Osiris, worshipped both individually and as a single divine entity.

Abydos. Here the triad is a veritable family. As a deceased god Osiris, who was originally not the local deity here, was naturally drawn to Abydos, where the first rulers of the unified realm were buried. Having assimilated Khentamentiu, the local funerary god, Osiris became in the Old Kingdom the god of the dead and the "foremost of the westerners." Along with Isis, his wife, and Horus, his son, he formed an "imported" triad here at this burial place of the first king of Egypt, and of the coronation of his successor. For according to the Osirian legend, Seth killed his brother Osiris, the first mythical sovereign, out of jealousy, in order to gain the throne of Egypt. Osiris' dismembered corpse was thrown into the Nile, only to be rescued and reassembled by his sister and wife, Isis, with the aid of Nepthys. Having restored Osiris, Isis conceived Horus, whom she raised secretly in the Delta marshes. Horus avenged his father and regained the throne. Thus is explained ingeniously how a god-king can perish and be replaced by his son; consequently the identification of the country's first historical ruler with Osiris was established. Isis, who was originally a mother-goddess and a personification of the throne, became quite naturally the mother who begets Horus, as well as the widow of Osiris. Horus, who had existed well before Osiris, is himself duplicated in order to be born as the avenger of his father, and the sovereign of the Two Lands, whom every Egyptian king personifies. Finally, each deceased king will become deified and identified with Osiris.

Other gods, such as Wepwawet, "he who opens the ways," the jackal-deity of Assiut, are likewise worshipped at Abydos, and in the New Kingdom, the supreme deities Ptah of Memphis, Rê-Horakhty of Heliopolis, Amon-Rê of Thebes, and all their companions duly received their own cults.

Thebes. Amon, "the hidden one," was at the beginning some kind of celestial deity of the Theban region who (since the Eleventh Dynasty) was promoted to the rank of supreme god. United with Rê, Amon-Rê came to be the most universal god Egypt ever produced. Despite the existence of his feminine counterpart Amonet, it was Mut, "the mother," an anthropomorphic goddess with double crown, and Khonsu, a lunar child-deity, who made up and remained his family both in the New Kingdom and beyond.

At Karnak the Great Heliopolitan Ennead joined with Montu, the god of the Theban nome, Horus, Sobek, and goddesses invited from neighboring regions, Hathor of Pathyris, Tanent and Iunyt. Thus the Egyptians created here a council of fifteen deities.

But other cults existed at Thebes as well. Montu and his companions Râttawy and Horus; Ptah of Memphis with Sekhmet "his beloved;" Osiris under a number of different surnames; Opet, hippopotamus-goddess, and nursing mother; and Maat, the incarnation of truth and justice. In addition, the Egyptians worshipped on the western side of the river a primordial female serpentine creature; a cow named Hathor at the heart of the necropolis; Anubis, the patron of mummification; and Imentet, the goddess of the west. Neither should we forget the deified kings, or the multiple aspects of Amon, who on either side of the river, from one temple to the next, included Amon-Rê of Karnak, king of the gods; Amon who hears prayers at East Karnak; Amon of Opet at Luxor; the ithyphallic Min-Amon-Kamutef; Amon the good ram and last but not least, the Amon of the king, or the King-Amon, in the funerary temples.

In this complex and complicated pantheon, the gods or groups of gods were not invented successively, but were perceived, experienced and worshipped, sometimes simultaneously, throughout all regions. It is therefore difficult to trace the history of Egyptian religion. One could, however, follow the ascent of one or the other deity, according to the importance acquired in the course of history by a given religious center. For example we might mention Ptah, who raises himself (since the Old Kingdom) to the status of supreme deity because he was the principal god at the capital. The rise of the cult of Rê, from the Fourth Dynasty onward, became irreversible from the moment the kings of Dynasty 5 adopted the Heliopolitan belief as official doctrine. The dynastic god Horus was identified with the supreme deity of the Ennead under the name of Horakhty, and the kings of this period proclaimed themselves sons of Rê in an effort to be united with the heavens.

Thereafter, all sorts of associations with Rê were created as the need arose: Montu-Rê, Sobek-Rê, Khnum-Rê, and later Amon-Rê, the most important one. Only Ptah and Osiris escape the ascendancy of the sun; Ptah because he is a chthonic deity, and Osiris because his particularly popular legend, which was incorporated with the cult of the deceased-as-Osiris, reserved for him a completely different destiny. However, despite the evident incompatibility of these opposing forces, the cults of Rê and of Osiris both became predominant ones, evolving parallel to one another, and by the Late Period Osiris enjoyed even a certain precedence.

All deities, whether they represented the Nile, heaven or earth, the sun or the moon, and depicted thereby the predominance of one over the other, existed simultaneously. This posed no conflict with the concept of the demiurge, whose name was Atum at Heliopolis, or with the creator who was called Khnum at Elephantine.

Such was the system of coexistence when the religious reform of Akhenaten suppressed all the gods in order to replace them *all* with a *single* universal deity. No more question about primordial gods, demiurges or gods of the underworld. The unique deity was now the visible sun which had always existed. It was omnipresent, and the entire earth lived, rejoiced and flourished in its light. Gone were the closed sanctuaries; the god could now be worshipped everywhere and by everyone. The rupture with all preceding forms of adoration was complete. But after this shortlived schism, when the ancient cults were restored, the gods gained increasing universal acceptance; the individual became possessed with devotion. Nevertheless, the concept of the absolute being, of the anonymous universal force which all the gods strove to attain from this period on, was not a new one. Beginning with the Old Kingdom the *wisdom literature* speaks of it in these terms: "These are not the inclinations of man which come into being, but are instead the designs of God" (Ptahhotep); or: "One does not know which events the God creates when he punishes" (Kagemni). In an inscription of a nomarch of the Middle Kingdom, we read: "I appeased the God with that which he loves, remembering that I will come to him on the day of my death." At the end of the New Kingdom, the wisdom of Amenemope tells us that "Man is mud and straw; God is his manufacturer." Finally, in the Late Period, Petosiris expresses it thus: "Happy is he who proceeds on the path of God."

The divinities are known to us by the representations and inscriptions accompanying them. The former reveal their characteristic attributes, the latter theological formulae giving the name, epithets and surnames of the divine power. In the temples, where the deities could dwell, numerous priests maintained their cults; thanks to the priestly titles mentioned we are able to discern the characteristics of each particular god.

Sacred writings which codify, explain or impose a dogma do not exist in ancient Egypt. It is the hymns which instruct us on the nature of each divine entity. The religious texts proper are on the one hand cult rituals, known since the Thinite period, and on the other hand funerary compendia which appeared in the Fifth Dynasty, the period during which the formation of a specialized clergy was taking shape. The earliest example of such compendia are the *Pyramid Texts,* which appear for the first time inscribed on the walls inside the pyramid of Unas. We find there a repertoire of independent formulae, some of which seem to have been composed at a much earlier period. They are intended for the use of the deceased king, whose goal is to attain the heavens. In the First Intermediate Period and Middle Kingdom, the netherworld was firmly located in the

west, and the posthumous journey of Osiris could now be shared by all. The *Coffin Texts* make their appearance at this time. They comprise more than a thousand prophylactic and other beneficent spells; the older Pyramid texts are mixed with new popular creations. In addition, a *Book of the Two Ways* attempts to locate topographically the netherworld and the place of Osiris. In the New Kingdom was composed for each individual a *Book of the Dead,* which partially reproduced the repertoire of the coffins. The spells here are divided into "chapters," and illustrated with "vignettes." The king himself benefits from the creation of homogeneous writings, guides to the netherworld, displayed on the walls of his sepulchre. These "books" are veritable descriptions of the underworld, where the sun regenerates while it traverses this region. The books invite the deceased king to participate forever in the journey of the renascent sun.

It is the *Book of the Am-Duat,* or "the writing of the hidden chamber," which describes the twelve domains corresponding to the twelve hours of the night across which the solar barque sails. There follow the *Book of Gates,* where the twelve domains are separated by portals, the *Book of Caverns,* which counts six caverns successively illuminated by the sun, and the *Book of Day* and the *Book of Night,* which describe the diurnal and nocturnal skies. All of these richly illustrated books serve to acquaint the deceased with the stations of the solar barque, and to provide the name and characteristics of the divinities and genii who abound there. From the end of the New Kingdom on, these texts become in turn available to private individuals.

This repertoire additionally contained the rituals of funerary liturgies for the *Opening of the Mouth* and the *Embalming.* When placed in the tombs, they secured the effectiveness of the necessary funerary practices there. Finally, there were later rituals for the cult of Rê, for the deceased, and even writings for animating certain deities.

The official religion was practiced in the temples. The king who, depending upon the period, was called either the great god, the good god or the chosen one, was theoretically the sole officiant. This was true regardless of whether he appeared as the incarnation of Horus, as the son of Rê, or as the intermediary of the Aten. It was always the king who was charged with constructing the divine temple among men, to provide for the cult and maintain it, to insure the rule of the order and justice of

Rê in the temple, and to manage and perpetuate its institution. The clergy played the role of substitute for the king in all the temples.

The populace, which was denied access to the temple sanctuary, seems to have glorified in its own way its "popular deities," its genii, deified kings and heros, fetishes and grigris (which bordered on superstition and magic). But on festival days, of which there were many, the common people were indeed allowed to approach the temple, witness the appearance of the divine bark, take part in the procession, and worship their god through the intermediary of the divine statue hidden in the barque shrine. Certain special individuals were even permitted to enter into the temple's first court, where the privileged had (since the Middle Kingdom) acquired the right to deposit their statues. With these statues acting as intermediaries, these individuals not only participated in the offerings of the temple, but proclaimed themselves able to intercede with the god on behalf of those lacking this privilege.

Individuals were able to approach the supreme being by means of the "ear stelae" in the chapel courts of the "gods who listen to prayers," accessible stand-ins for those who dwelt in the inaccessible great sanctuaries. In the Late Period, when large numbers of people marched behind the barque procession on festival day, they could see the divine image represented on the exterior wall of the sanctuary, an image closely based on the one which was hidden away in the holy of holies. Finally, it was by means of the particular sacred animal, whose entire species eventually ended up officially representing the local divinity in each nome, that the common man was able to see, worship, offer to or thank his god.

In one way or another the people gained the right to their share of the god. After all, the divine representations displayed on the walls of the sanctuaries were themselves merely transitional appearances of the deity. Even the sacred image, guarded in the holy of holies, was in the last analysis nothing more than a terrestrial effigy of the god.

Hourig Sourouzian

Glossary

Akh beneficent spirit, one of the elements which constitute the human personality. 117

Amulet small object or prophylactic figurine providing magical protection for its owner. 266

Ankh hieroglyphic sign for life. 33

Atef crown worn by Osiris and by the king, composed of a central mitre mounted upon two ram's horns, surmounted by a sun disk and flanked by two ostrich feathers. 252

Ba soul or spiritual element of an individual which appears in the form of a human-headed bird. 216

Block statue schematic representation of a crouching individual with hands drawn up over the knees. 132, 247

Blue crown → *Khepresh*

Canopics four funerary jars containing the viscera of the deceased, placed under the protection of the four sons of Horus, whose heads are represented on the jars' stoppers. 97, 171, 176

Cartouche oval-shaped ring in which the birth and coronation names of pharaoh are inscribed. 24, 87 etc.

Cavetto cornice architectural element (primarily Egyptian) consisting of an incurvate cornice stylized after palm fronds. 68, 109, 110, 216

Cenotaph commemorative (false) tomb. 10, 91

Colossus divine or royal colossal statue. 173

Criosphinx sphinx with the body of a lion and head of a ram.

Crook, or *heqa* scepter crooked scepter serving as part of royal insignia. 202, 252

Djed hieroglyphic sign of a pillar, symbol of stability and duration. 17

Double crown combination of the respective crowns of Upper and Lower Egypt. 173

Dromos processional way leading to the temple entrance; in Egypt an alleyway of sphinxes.

Dyad group of two divine or royal entities. 104

Ennead group of nine deities; the most important one was the Great Ennead at Heliopolis.

Faience in Egypt: quartz paste with vitrified surface. 17, 82–84

False door funerary architectural element imitating a door through which the deceased could communicate with the world of the living. 57, 58

Flabellum fan with a long handle and ostrich feathers. 186, 195, 225

Flagellum → Flail

Flail, or *nekhakha* scepter composed of a handle and three loose strands serving as part of the royal insignia. 28, 116

Heb-Sed	jubilee festival which the king celebrated theoretically after thirty years of rule. 19	Maat	universal order established by the gods, symbol and hieroglyphic sign (a feather) of the goddess who personifies it. 257
Hyksos	Hellenized form of the Egyptian term designating the Asiatic nomads who infiltrated Egypt during the Middle Kingdom, and eventually dominated the northern half of the country in the Second Intermediate Period. 104, 118	Mandrake	round fruit possessing qualities of an aphrodisiac; decorative symbol of life and love. 118, 219
		Mastaba	Arabic word meaning "bench," used to designate the private tombs of the Old Kingdom whose superstructures bear a bench-like form.
Ibes	round and curled royal wig, encircled with a diadem. 202, 227	*Menat*	beaded necklace of gold whose counterpoise bears the image of the goddess Hathor; attribute of the goddess. 152, 196, 209, 251
Isis knot, or *tit*	hieroglyphic sign and symbol for protection. 185, 248		
Jubilee	→ *Heb-Sed*	Naophorous	statue of an individual holding a naos.
Ka	one of the elements constituting both human and divine personality, a sort of double representing vital force. The hieroglyphic sign portrays a pair of arms uplifted toward the heavens. 117	Naos	small divine sanctuary or chapel; holy of holies. 178, 257
		Nekhakha	→ Flail
		Nemes	royal headdress with two side lappets and knotted in the back in the form of a cadogan. 31, 86, 211
Khat	royal headdress enveloping the hair completely and terminating in back with a thick appendage. 131, 139, 177, 180	Nine Bows	symbol of the foreign ethnicities who made up the traditional enemies of the king of Egypt. 87, 133, 201
Khekheru	elements making up a frieze which resemble the tops of stalks tied into bundles; they usually adorn the uppermost reaches of decorated walls. 138, 268	Nomarch	governor and administrator of a nome.
		Nome	Egyptian province or administrative district.
Khepesh	scimitar or battle-axe of victory; a type of sword with incurvate blade which symbolizes royal valor. 212	Ogdoad	group of eight primordial gods.
		Ointment cone	cone of scented fat placed on top of wigs to serve as perfume. 215, 243
Khepresh	blue crown with tiny curls, often called (for no reason) a "war helm." 143, 160, 230	Ostracon	limestone flake or pottery sherd used as a surface for writing or sketching. 169, 220, 230, 231
Kherep	scepter of authority.		
Kohl	cosmetic with a base of ground galena, serving to protect the eyes.	Palermo Stone	fragment of a stela of the Fifth Dynasty, preserved in the Archaeological Museum of Palermo, upon which are listed the names of the kings of the Old Kingdom, as well as the important events of their respective reigns.
Labyrinth	term used by the Greeks to designate the vast mortuary temple of Amenemhat III at Hawara.		

Pectoral	trapezoidal pendant adorning the breast at the height of the pectoral muscles. 55, 93, 109, 110
Pharaoh	word transmitted from the Bible, derived from the Egyptian *Per-âa*, "the great house," designating the royal palace and, in the New Kingdom, the master of the palace, i.e. the king.
Phyle	Greek term designating the division of a group of priests, or members of a work gang.
Poem of Kadesh	epic account glorifying the alleged "victory" of Ramses II against the Hittites in year 5 of his reign.
Primordial ocean	waters of chaos preceding the creation of the world.
Pylon	massive double edifice with battered walls flanking the entrance to Egyptian temples.
Pyramid	Greek word designating the royal mortuary monument.
Pyramidion	capstone of a pyramid or, in the New Kingdom, a small pyramid surmounting a chapel or a stela.
Red crown	red headdress in the form of a mortar, symbolizing the sovereignty of the king over Lower Egypt. 35, 192
Rekhyt	lapwings with human arms originally symbolizing the conquered inhabitants of Lower Egypt; in the New Kingdom representing all subjects. 143, 178
Rosetta Stone	trilingual decree of Ptolemy V, discovered at Rosetta in 1798, which Champollion used to decipher Egyptian hieroglyphs in 1822; preserved in the British Museum (the Cairo Museum possesses a replica exhibited on the ground floor, hall 48).
Royal titulary	collection of five names borne by Pharaoh, includes those of: Horus, Horus of gold, the Two Ladies, birth and coronation.
Scepter	baton or insignia of authority; → Crook, Flail, *Was*, *Kherep* . . .
Scribe	literate Egyptian. 43
Sekhem	scepter of power. 87
Sema-tawy	Union of the Two Lands. 31, 87, 190
Senet	board game divided into thirty squares. 189, 215, 216
Serdab	enclosed room built within a mastaba to house the statues of the deceased.
Serekh	facade and plan of a palace represented in combined perspective with decorative patterns, surmounted by a falcon and bearing the Horus name of the king. 9, 10
Shawabti	mummiform funerary figurine or statuette intended to perform menial tasks in the next world. 150, 151, 172, 182
Shen	circular buckle symbolizing power and universal duration. 33, 193
Shendjyt	royal pleated kilt with central tab. 28, 31, 33 etc.
Sistrum	ritual musical instrument, emblem of the goddess Hathor. 264
Sphinx	Greek word derived from the Egyptian *shesep-ankh*, "living image," designating a statue with the body of a lion and head of the king, symbolic of sovereignty. 102, 134
Staff of millions of years	hieroglyphic sign for year, symbolic of the eternal existence which the god bestowed upon the king. 121, 212
Standard	sacred staff whose "shield" bears the emblem or head of a divinity. 225
Standard-bearing statue	type of royal or private statue representing the individual bearing a divine emblem. 225
Stela	inscribed rectangular or rounded slab of wood or stone serving as a commemorative or funerary monument. 91, 92, 118, 143, 197, 212, etc.
Stelophorous	statue of an individual holding a stela.

Tit	→ Isis knot
Titulary	→ Royal titulary
Torus moulding	architectural element in the form of a cylindrical roll which runs along the edges of buildings and just under the cavetto cornice. 185, 258
Triad	group of three deities.
Udjat	beneficent amulet and decorative ornament for false doors and sarcophagi; represents the eye which Horus is considered to have lost during his combat with Seth. The eye was saved and healed by the magic of Thoth; generally a lunar symbol, but also a solar symbol when referring to the uninjured right eye of Horus. 68, 94, 193
Uraeus	term derived from the Egyptian word for "cobra," i.e. the female cobra goddess adorning the brow of the king and certain deities. 108
Was	scepter with a canine head, common attribute of the gods. 243
Wesekh	"broad" collar of beads. 114
White crown	tall conical mitre with a bulbous terminus, symbolizing the sovereignty of the king over Upper Egypt. 33, 88, 133
Winged sun-disk	symbol of the solar deity of Edfu, and sign of protection. 118

Key to the Bibliography and Selected Works

ABBREVIATIONS TO THE BIBLIOGRAPHY

ASAE   Annales du Service des Antiquités de l'Egypte, Cairo.
BIFAO   Bulletin de l'Institut Français d'Archéologie Orientale du Caire, Cairo.
BMMA   Bulletin of the Metropolitan Museum of Art, New York.
JEA   The Journal of Egyptian Archaeology, London.
MDAIK   Mitteilungen des Deutschen Archäologischen Instituts, Abteilung Kairo, Wiesbaden, Mainz.
MIFAO   Mémoires publiés par les Membres de l'Institut Français d'Archéologie Orientale du Caire, Cairo.

CATALOGUES, GUIDES AND DESCRIPTIONS OF THE MUSEUM'S COLLECTIONS

CG Catalogue Général des Antiquités Egyptiennes du Musée du Caire:
CG 1–1294 – L. Borchardt, Statuen und Statuetten von Königen und Privatleuten I–V, Berlin 1911–36
CG 1295–1808 – L. Borchardt, Denkmäler des Alten Reichs I–II, Berlin, Cairo 1937–64
CG 1308–1315 & 17001–17036 – Ch. Kuentz, Obélisques, Cairo 1932
CG 2001–2152 – F. W. von Bissing, Tongefäße, Bis zum Beginn des alten Reiches, Vienna 1913
CG 3426–3587 – F. W. von Bissing, Metallgefäße, Vienna 1901
CG 3618–4000, 18001–18037, 18600, 18603 – F. W. von Bissing, Fayencegefäße, Vienna 1902
CG 4798–4976 & 5034–5200 – G. A. Reisner, Models of Ships and Boats, Cairo 1913
CG 5218–6000 & 12001–13595 – G. A. Reisner, Amulets I–II, Cairo 1907–58
CG 6001–6029 – E. Chassinat, La Seconde Trouvaille de Deir el-Bahari (Sarcophages), Leipzig 1909
CG 7001–7394 & 8742–9200 – J. Strzygowski, Koptische Kunst, Vienna 1904
CG 8001–8741 – W. E. Crum, Coptic Monuments, Cairo 1902
CG 8742–9200 – s. CG 7001–7394
CG 9201–9304 – H. Munier, Manuscrits Coptes, Cairo 1916
CG 9201–9400, 26001–26123 & 33001–33037 – J. G. Milne, Greek Inscriptions, Oxford 1905
CG 9401–9449 – G. Daressy, Textes et Dessins Magiques, Cairo 1903
CG 10001–10869 – B. P. Grenfell and A. S. Hunt, Greek Papyri, Oxford 1903
CG 11001–12000 & 14001–14754 – J. E. Quibell, Archaic Objects I–II, Cairo 1904–05
CG 12001–13595 – s. CG 5218–6000

CG 17001–17036 – s. CG 1308–1315
CG 18001–18037 – s. CG 3618–4000
CG 18065–18793 – F. W. von Bissing, Steingefäße, Vienna 1904–07
CG 18600 & 18603 – s. CG 3618–4000
CG 20001–20780 – H. O. Lange and H. Schäfer, Grab- und Denksteine des Mittleren Reiches I–IV, Berlin 1902–25
CG 22001–22208 – Ahmed Bey Kamal, Stèles Ptolémaïques et Romaines I–II, Cairo 1904–05
CG 23001–23256 – Ahmed Bey Kamal, Tables d'Offrandes, I–II, Cairo 1906–09
CG 24001–24990 – G. Daressy, Fouilles de la Vallée des Rois 1898–99, Cairo 1902
CG 25001–25385 – G. Daressy, Ostraca, Cairo 1901
CG 25501–25832 – J. Černý, Ostraca Hiératiques I–II, Cairo 1935
CG 26124–26349 & 32377–32394 – C. C. Edgar, Greek Vases, Cairo 1911
CG 27425–27630 – C. C. Edgar, Greek Sculpture, Cairo 1903
CG 28001–28126 – P. Lacau, Sarcophages Antérieurs au Nouvel Empire I–II, Cairo 1904–06
CG 29301–29323 – G. Maspero and H. Gauthier, Sarcophages des Epoques Persanes et Ptolémaïque I–II, Cairo 1914–39
CG 29501–29733 & 29751–29834 – C. Gaillard and G. Daressy, La Faune Momifiée de l'Antique Egypte, Cairo 1905
CG 30601–31270 & 50001–50165 – W. Spiegelberg, Demotische Denkmäler, Leipzig, Berlin 1904–32
  I: Die demotischen Inschriften, 1904
  II: Die demotischen Papyrus, 1908
  III: Demotische Inschriften und Papyrus, 1932
CG 31271–31670 – A. E. P. Weigall, Weights and Balances, Cairo 1908
CG 32001–32367 – C. C. Edgar, Greek Moulds, Cairo 1903
CG 32377–32394 – s. CG 26124–26349
CG 33101–33285 – C. C. Edgar, Graeco-Egyptian Coffins, Masks and Portraits, Cairo 1905
CG 33301–33506 – C. C. Edgar, Sculptors' Studies and Unfinished Works, Cairo 1906
CG 34001–34068 – P. Lacau, Stèles du Nouvel Empire I–II, Cairo 1909–26
CG 34087–34189 – P. Lacau, Stèles de la XVIII. Dyn., Cairo 1957
CG 36001–37521 – P. E. Newberry, Scarab-Shaped Seals, London 1907
CG 38001–39348 – G. Daressy, Statues des Divinités I–II, Cairo 1905–06
CG 41001–41041 – A. Moret, Sarcophages de l'Epoque Bubastite à l'Epoque Saïte I–II, Cairo 1913
CG 41042–41072 – H. Gauthier, Cercueils Anthropoïdes des Prêtres de Montou I–II, Cairo 1913
CG 42001–42250 – G. Legrain, Statues et Statuettes des Rois et des Particuliers I–III and Index, Cairo 1906–25
CG 44001–44102 – G. Bénédite, Miroirs, Cairo 1907

CG 44301–44638 – G. Bénédite, Objets de Toilette I, Cairo 1911
CG 46001–46529 – H. Carter and P. E. Newberry, Tomb of Thutmosis IV, London 1904
CG 46530–48575 – P. E. Newberry, Funerary Statuettes and Model Sarcophagi I–III, Cairo 1930–57
CG 50001–50165 – s. CG 30601–31270
CG 51001–51191 – J. E. Quibell, The Tomb of Yuaa and Thuiu, Cairo 1908
CG 52001–53855 – E. Vernier, Bijoux et Orfèvreries I–II, Cairo 1927
CG 57001–57023 – A. Moret, Monuments de l'Ancien Empire III, 1, Autels, Bassins et Tables d'Offrandes, edited by Dia' Abou-Ghazi, Cairo 1978
CG 57024–57049 – Dia' Abou-Ghazi, Denkmäler des Alten Reiches III, 2, Altars and offering tables, Cairo 1980.
CG 58001–58036 – W. Golénischeff, Papyrus Hiératiques, Cairo 1927
CG 59001–59800 – C. C. Edgar, Zenon Papyri, I–IV, Cairo 1925–31
CG 61001–61044 – G. Daressy, Cercueils des Cachettes Royales, Cairo 1909
CG 61051–61100 – G. Elliot Smith, The Royal Mummies, Cairo 1912
CG 63001–64906 – Ch. T. Currelly, Stone Implements, Cairo 1913
CG 67001–67359 – J. Maspero, Papyrus Grecs d'Epoque Byzantine I–III, Cairo 1911–16
CG 69201–69852 – H. Hickmann, Instruments de Musique, Cairo 1949
CG 70001–70050 – G. Roeder, Naos I–II, Leipzig 1914
CG 70501–70754 – F. Bisson de la Roque, Trésor de Tôd, Cairo 1950
A Brief Description of the principal monuments, Cairo 1927–1930.
Brève description des principaux monuments, Cairo 1927–1938.
J. P. Corteggiani, L'Egypte des Pharaons au Musée du Caire, Paris 1979, 1986. English edition: The Egypt of the Pharaohs in the Cairo Museum, 1987. German edition: Kunst des Alten Ägypten im Kairo Museum, 1979, 1987.
G. Daressy, A Brief Description of the principal monuments exhibited in the Egyptian Museum of Cairo, Cairo 1924.
S. Donadoni, Le Musée Egyptien, Les Musées du Monde, Paris 1971. English edition: The Egyptian Museum, Great Museums of the World, New York 1969. German edition: Ägyptisches Museum Kairo, Berühmte Museen, 1976.
E. Drioton, Le Musée Egyptien, Cairo 1939.
E. Drioton, Encyclopédie Photographique de l'Art, Le Musée du Caire, Paris 1949.
Egyptian Museum, Brief description of the principal monuments, Cairo 1950–1986. French edition: Musée du Caire, Description sommaire des principaux monuments.
W. Forman, M. Vilimkova, M. H. Abd-ur-Rahman, Egyptian art, London 1962. German edition: Ägyptische Kunst, Hanau/Main 1962.
G. Grimm and D. Johannes, Kunst der Ptolemäer- und Römerzeit im Ägyptischen Museum Kairo, Mainz 1975.
A. Hermann, Führer durch das Museum der Ägyptischen Altertümer zu Kairo, Cairo 1935.
J. Leibovitch, Ancient Egypt, Cairo 1938.
A. Mariette, Notice des principaux monuments exposés dans les galeries provisoires du Musée d'antiquités de S.A. le vice-roi à Boulaq, Alexandria 1864, Paris 1872, Cairo 1874–1879.
A. Mariette, Album du Musée de Boulaq, Cairo 1871.
A. Mariette, Monuments divers recueillis en Egypte et en Nubie, Paris 1889.
G. Maspero, Guide du visiteur du Musée de Boulaq, Boulaq 1883.
G. Maspero, Notice des principaux monuments exposés au Musée de Guizeh, Cairo 1895.
G. Maspero, Guide du visiteur au Musée du Caire, Cairo 1902–1915.

English edition translated by J. E. and A. A. Quibell: Guide to the Cairo Museum, Cairo 1903–1915. German edition revised by G. Roeder: Führer durch das Ägyptische Museum zu Kairo, Cairo 1912.
G. Maspero et alii, Le Musée Egyptien I–III, Cairo 1890–1924.
R. P. Riesterer and K. Lambelet, Das Ägyptische Museum Kairo, 1980.
E. L. B. Terrace, H. G. Fischer, Treasures of the Cairo Museum, London 1970.

EXHIBITION CATALOGUES OF OBJECTS OF OUR COLLECTIONS

Archaic Egypt, Cairo 1982.
Centenaire de l'Institut Français d'Archéologie Orientale, Musée du Caire, Cairo 1981.
Cinquante années à Saqqarah de J. P. Lauer, 13. 4. 1980 – 15. 3. 1981, Cairo 1982.
5000 ans d'art égyptien, Brussels 1960. German edition: 5000 Jahre Ägyptische Kunst, Essen, Konstanz, Zurich, Vienna, 1960–62.
The Egypt Exploration Society, Centenary Exhibition 1882–1982, Cairo 1982.
The Egyptian Museum in Ten Years 1965–1975, Cairo 1976.
Exhibition of the 25th anniversary of Czech Excavations 1959–1984, Cairo 1985.
Götter Pharaonen, in Germany, (Mainz) 1978–79.
Nofret – Die Schöne, Die Frau im Alten Ägypten, German edition (Mainz) 1985. French edition: La Femme au temps des Pharaons, Brussels, (Mainz) 1985.
Nofretete Echnaton, in Germany, (Mainz) 1976.
Le Règne du Soleil Akhnaton et Nefertiti, Brussels 1975.

Catalogues of Tutankhamon exhibitions:
USA Tutankhamun Treasures 1961–63.
Japan Tutankhamen exhibition in Japan, 1965–66.
Paris Toutankhamon et son temps, 1967. Petit Palais.
London Treasures of Tutankhamun, British Museum 1972.
USSR Temporary exhibition, 1974.
USA/Canada Treasures of Tutankhamun, 1976–79.
Germany Tutanchamun 1980–81.

Ramses II:
Ramsès Le Grand, Grand Palais, Paris 1976.
Le grand pharaon Ramsès II et son temps, Montreal 1985.
Ramses II, catalog of exhibitions in USA/Canada, 1985–88.

GENERAL WORKS

LÄ Lexikon der Ägyptologie, edited by W. Helck, E. Otto and W. Westendorf, Wiesbaden 1972–1986.
PM B. Porter and R. L. B. Moss, Topographical bibliography of Ancient Egyptian hieroglyphic texts, reliefs and paintings I–VII, Oxford 1927–1981. Vol. I–III: revised edition.
G. Posener, S. Sauneron and J. Yoyotte, Dictionnaire de la civilisation égyptienne, Paris 1959.

HISTORY AND CIVILIZATION

J. Baines and J. Málek, Atlas of Ancient Egypt, Oxford 1980. German edition: Weltatlas der Alten Kulturen, Ägypten, Munich 1980.
J. von Beckerath, Abriß der Geschichte des Alten Ägypten, Munich 1971.
The Cambridge History of Africa, Cambridge 1978–1982. Vol. I: P. G. Trigger, B. J. Kemp; vol. II: D. O'Connor, R. C. C. Law, P. L. Shinnie.

E. *Drioton* and J. *Vandier*, L'Egypte, Les Peuples de l'Orient Méditerranéen II, Paris 1962. Revised edition 1976.

A. *Eggebrecht* et alii, Das Alte Ägypten, Munich 1984.

Egypt's Golden Age: The Art of Living in the New Kingdom 1558–1085 B.C. Museum of Fine Arts Boston, 1982.

A. *Erman*, Life in Ancient Egypt, reprint, New York 1971.

A. *Erman* and H. *Ranke*, Ägypten und ägyptisches Leben im Altertum, Tübingen 1923. Reprint Hildesheim 1981. French edition: La Civilisation Egyptienne, Paris 1963.

A. H. *Gardiner*, Egypt of the Pharaohs, Oxford 1962. German edition: Geschichte des alten Ägypten, Stuttgart 1965.

W. *Helck*, Geschichte des Alten Ägypten = Handbuch der Orientalistik I, 3, Leyden 1968.

W. *Helck*, Wirtschaftsgeschichte des Alten Ägypten, Wiesbaden 1975.

E. *Hornung*, Grundzüge der ägyptischen Geschichte, Darmstadt 1978.

E. *Otto*, Ägypten. Der Weg des Pharaonenreiches, Stuttgart 1966.

P. *Posener-Kriéger*, Les Archives du Temple funéraire de NeferirkarêKakai (Papyrus d'Abousir) I–II, Cairo 1976.

B. G. *Trigger*, B. J. *Kemp*, D. *O'Connor* and A. B. *Lloyd*, Ancient Egypt, A Social History, Cambridge 1985.

J. *Yoyotte*, L'Egypte, dans: Encyclopédie de la Pléiade, Histoire Universelle I, Paris 1961.

ART AND ARCHITECTURE

Ägyptisches Museum, Berlin 1967.

Ägyptisches Museum, New edition, Berlin 1985. English edition: Egyptian Museum. French edition: Musée Egyptien.

C. *Aldred*, Old Kingdom Art in Ancient Egypt, London 1949.

C. *Aldred*, Middle Kingdom Art in Ancient Egypt, London 1950.

C. *Aldred*, New Kingdom Art in Ancient Egypt During the Eighteenth Dynasty, London 1961.

C. *Aldred*, Jewels of the Pharaohs, New York 1971. German edition: Die Juwelen der Pharaonen, Munich 1972.

C. *Aldred*, Akhenaten and Nefertiti, New York 1973.

J. *Assmann* and G. *Burkard*, 5000 Jahre Ägypten, Genese und Permanenz Pharaonischer Kunst, Speyer 1983.

A. *Badawy*, Le Dessin architectural chez les anciens Egyptiens, Cairo 1948.

B. V. *Bothmer*, Egyptian Sculpture of the Late Period, The Brooklyn Museum, New York 1960.

H. *Carter* and A. *Mace,* The Tomb of Tut-ankh-Amen I, London 1923.

H. *Carter*, The Tomb of Tut-ankh-Amen II–III, London 1927, 1933.

Ch. *Desroches-Noblecourt*, L'Art Egyptien, Paris 1962.

Ch. *Desroches-Noblecourt*, Vie et Mort d'un Pharaon, *Toutankhamon*, Paris 1963–67. English edition: Tutankhamen; Life and death of a Pharaoh, New York 1963. German edition: Tut-ench-Amun. Leben und Tod eines Pharao, Frankfurt–Berlin 1963.

I. E. S. *Edwards*, The Pyramids of Egypt. Revised edition, London 1985. French edition: Les pyramides d'Egypte, Paris 1967. German edition: Die ägyptischen Pyramiden, Wiesbaden 1967.

I. E. S. *Edwards*, Tutankhamun; His Tomb and its Treasures, New York 1976. German edition: Tutanchamun, Das Grab und seine Schätze, Bergisch Gladbach 1978.

L'Egypte avant les Pharaons, IVᶜ millénaire, Grand Palais, Paris 1973.

H. G. *Evers*, Staat aus dem Stein, Denkmäler, Geschichte und Bedeutung der ägyptischen Plastik während des Mittleren Reiches, I–II, Munich 1929.

G. A. *Gaballa*, Narrative in Egyptian Art, Mainz 1976.

W. C. *Hayes*, The Scepter of Egypt, A background for the study of Egyptian antiquities in the Metropolitan Museum of Art I–II, New York 1953–59.

M. *Hirmer* and E. *Otto*, Ägyptische Kunst I–II, Munich 1971.

B. *Hornemann*, Types of Ancient Egyptian Statuary I–VII, Copenhagen 1951–69.

E. *Iversen*, Canon and Proportions in Egyptian Art, Warminster 1975.

T. G. H. *James*, Egyptian Painting, British Museum, London 1985.

T. G. H. *James* et W. V. *Davies*, Egyptian Sculpture, British Museum, London 1983.

M. *Kayser*, Ägyptisches Kunsthandwerk, Braunschweig 1969.

K. *Lange* and M. *Hirmer*, Ägypten, Architektur, Plastik, Malerei in drei Jahrtausenden, Munich 1967. French edition: L'Egypte, Sculpture, Architecture, Peinture, Paris 1956. English edition: Egypt, Architecture, Sculpture, Painting in three thousand years, London 1968.

J.-Ph. *Lauer*, Histoire monumentale des Pyramides d'Egypte, Bibliothèque d'Etudes, Cairo 1962.

J.-Ph. *Lauer*, Saqqara, The royal Cemetery of Memphis. Excavations and discoveries since 1850, London 1976. French edition: Saqqarah, La nécropole royale de Memphis, quarante siècles d'histoire, cent vingt-cinq ans de recherches, Paris 1977. German edition: Saqqara. Die Königsgräber von Memphis. Ausgrabungen und Entdeckungen seit 1850, Bergisch Gladbach 1977.

J. *Leclant* (éditeur) et alii, Les Pharaons I–III, Univers des Formes, Paris 1978–79. German edition: Ägypten I–III, Munich 1979–81.

The Luxor Museum of Ancient Egyptian Art, Mainz 1979.

K. *el Mallakh* and A. C. *Brackman*, The Gold of Tutankhamun, New York 1978.

Meisterwerke Altägyptischer Keramik, exhibition catalogue, HöhrGrenzhausen 1978.

A. *Mekhitarian*, Egyptian Painting, Geneva 1954, 1978. French edition: La Peinture Egyptienne. German edition: Ägyptische Malerei.

Das Menschenbild im alten Ägypten, Porträts aus vier Jahrtausenden, Hamburg 1982.

G. *Möller*, Die Metallkunst der alten Ägypter, Berlin 1924.

H. W. *Müller*, Alt-Ägyptische Malerei, Berlin 1959.

H. W. *Müller*, Ägyptische Kunst, Frankfort 1970.

W. H. *Peck* and J. *Ross*, Drawings from Ancient Egypt, London 1978. German edition: Ägyptische Zeichnungen aus drei Jahrtausenden, Bergisch Gladbach 1979.

Propyläen Kunstgeschichte 15, Das Alte Ägypten. Edited by C. Vandersleyen, Berlin 1975.

E. R. *Russmann*, The representations of the King in the XXVᵗʰ Dynasty, Brussels 1974.

H. *Schäfer*, Von ägyptischer Kunst, Eine Grundlage. Revised edition, Wiesbaden 1963. English edition: Principles of Egyptian art, Oxford 1974.

W. S. *Smith*, A history of Egyptian sculpture and painting in the Old Kingdom, Oxford 1949.

W. S. *Smith*, The Art and Architecture of Ancient Egypt, revised by W. K. Simpson, Harmondsworth 1981.

R. *Stadelmann*, Die ägyptischen Pyramiden. Vom Ziegelbau zum Weltwunder, Mainz 1985.

J. *Vandier*, Manuel d'Archéologie Egyptienne I–VI, Paris 1952–78.

D. *Wildung*, Sesostris und Amenemhet, Ägypten im Mittleren Reich, Munich 1984. French edition: L'âge d'or de l'Egypte: le Moyen Empire, Paris 1981.

D. *Wildung*, Ägypten vor den Pyramiden, Munich exhibition catalogue, Mainz 1981.

A. *Wilkinson*, Ancient Egyptian Jewellery, London 1971.

W. *Wolf*, Die Kunst Ägyptens, Stuttgart 1957.

J. *Yoyotte*, Treasures of the Pharaohs, Geneva 1968. French edition: Les trésors des Pharaons. German edition: Kunstschätze der Pharaonen.

RELIGION

J. *Assmann*, Ägyptische Hymnen und Gebete, Zurich–Munich 1975.

P. *Barguet*, Le Livre des Morts des anciens Egyptiens, Paris 1967.

P. *Barguet,* Les textes des sarcophages égyptiens du Moyen Empire, Paris 1986.

H. *Bonnet,* Reallexikon der ägyptischen Religionsgeschichte, Berlin 1952.

H. *Brunner,* Grundzüge der Altägyptischen Religion, Darmstadt 1983.

E. *Hornung,* Ägyptische Unterweltsbücher, Zurich–Munich 1972.

E. *Hornung,* Der Eine und die Vielen, Ägyptische Gottesvorstellungen, Darmstadt 1973.

E. *Hornung,* Das Totenbuch der Ägypter, Zurich–Munich 1979.

R. O. *Faulkner,* The Ancient Egyptian Pyramid Texts, Oxford 1969.

R. O. *Faulkner,* The Ancient Egyptian Coffin Texts I–III, Warminster 1973–80.

R. O. *Faulkner,* The Ancient Egyptian Book of the Dead, London 1985.

H. *Frankfort,* Ancient Egyptian Religion, New York 1948.

H. *Kees,* Totenglauben und Jenseitsvorstellungen der alten Ägypter, Grundlagen und Entwicklung bis zum Ende des Mittleren Reiches, Berlin 1956.

H. *Kees,* Der Götterglaube im alten Ägypten, Berlin 1977.

S. *Morenz,* Ägyptische Religion, Stuttgart 1960, 1977.

M. *Saleh,* Das Totenbuch in den thebanischen Beamtengräbern des Neuen Reiches, Mainz 1984.

J. *Vandier,* La religion Egyptienne, Paris 1949.

LITERATURE

H. *Brunner,* Grundzüge einer Geschichte der altägyptischen Literatur, Darmstadt 1966.

E. *Brunner-Traut,* Altägyptische Märchen. Dusseldorf–Cologne 1976.

A. *Erman,* Die Literatur der Ägypter, Leipzig 1923, reprinted in 1971.

E. *Hornung,* Meisterwerke altägyptischer Dichtung, Zurich–Munich 1979.

C. *Lalouette* and P. *Grimal,* Textes sacrés et textes profanes de l'ancienne Egypte, Paris 1984.

Leben im Ägyptischen Altertum, Literatur, Urkunden, Briefe, aus vier Jahrtausenden, Staatliche Museen zu Berlin, Papyrus-Sammlung, Berlin 1977.

Naissance de l'écriture, cunéiformes et hiéroglyphes, Grand Palais, Paris 1982.

G. *Posener,* L'enseignement loyaliste, Sagesse égyptienne au Moyen Empire, Geneva 1976.

M. *Lichtheim,* Ancient Egyptian Literature I–III, Berkeley 1975, 1976, 1980.

A. *Roccati,* La littérature historique sous l'Ancien Empire égyptien, Paris 1982.

W. K. *Simpson,* The literature of Ancient Egypt, New Haven–London 1973.

1 Head of a deity (?)

Painted terra cotta   JE 97472
H. 10.3 cm; W. 6.7 cm
Merimda-Benisalama, excavations of the German Archaeological Institute, Cairo, 1982
Predynastic period, end of the 5th Millennium B.C.

This oval shaped head is the oldest sculpture in the round known from Egypt, if not from all of Africa. It derives from one of the earliest Neolithic settlements, located at the western edge of the Delta, whence originates the designation "Merimda culture."
Excavations here revealed several stratigraphic levels dating from the sixth and fifth Millennia. Characteristic lifestyles of these early cultures included hunting, fishing, husbandry and stock farming. It was in one of the relatively younger strata that this sculpture, recently came to light.
The summarily executed features of the man represented have been modelled into a compact mass of pinkish clay. The eyes are deep recesses, the nose a gentle protrusion and the mouth a contracted crevice. Traces of ochre pigment are visible. Numerous holes are distributed throughout the skull and around the face, perhaps originally for securing tufts of hair. In spite of its ancient fractures, this remarkable sculpture lacks neither expression nor originality. A deep hole under the chin suggests that it was once fastened to a post. The piece thus probably served as a ritual object either mounted on a post or borne aloft during cult ceremonies.

Bibliography: J. Eiwanger, in: MDAIK 38, 1982, p. 74 and pl. 10; A. Eggebrecht, Das Alte Ägypten, München 1984, p. 37.

Black-topped red-ware ceramics

Double vase with convex base   JE 41247
H. 7.6 cm; W. 6.5 cm
Abydos; discovered by Ayrton in 1909

Three-legged goblet with white-painted decoration   JE 26530
H. 13.2 cm; Diam. 5.7 cm   = CG 2008
Gebelein; discovered in 1885

Pot with rounded rim and flat base   JE 41251
H. 7 cm; Diam. 6.6 cm
Abydos; discovered by Ayrton in 1909
Predynastic period, Nagada I, 4000−3500 B.C.

Widespread throughout Egypt and even into Nubia, ceramics with red bodies and black tops and interiors appear in several common forms during the entire course of the Predynastic. Among them are tulip-form goblets, double vases and bulging pots and bowls. These vessels were mass produced in varying dimensions, sometimes standing as tall as half a meter. The Egyptian potter first molded the clay into shape, then set it out in the sun to dry. Before the sun had completed its work, however, the pot was polished with a smooth stone and occasionally coated with an ochre slip. It was this polish which gave the vessel its red hue after a good firing. The black top and interior color was obtained by carbonization when the red-hot vessel was placed upside down in a bed of smouldering chaff. This process produced a dark metallic sheen which could then be enhanced with painted geometric patterns such as chevrons, checks or cross-hatches.

Bibliography: S.: Von Bissing, Tongefäße (CG), p. 21, pl. 1; A. Lucas/J. Harris, Ancient Egyptian Materials and Industries, London 1962, pp. 376–81; Vandier, Manuel I (1), pp. 299–300; J. Bourriau, Umm el-Ga'ab, Pottery from the Nile Valley before the Arab Conquest, Fitzwilliam Museum, Cambridge 1981, pp. 44–50.

3   Ground floor, room 43

Bowl with crocodiles and geometric design

Reddish-brown polished clay, white paint   JE 38284
H. 11 cm; Diam. 19.5 cm   = CG 18804
Gebelein (?), purchased in 1906
Predynastic period, Nagada I, 4000–3500 B.C.

This bowl forms but a single example from an immense corpus of white-painted, red-polished ware sporting geometric decorations: chevrons, triangles, lozenges and schematic animal or plant motifs are all typically occurring patterns. Less common is applied plastic decoration, such as figures of hippopotami or crocodiles.

Our bowl shows a flat rim and softly rounded base, with four diagonal bands of interlocking white chevrons which separate four modelled figures of painted crocodiles. The interior pattern consists of additional chevrons and two triangles pointing inward towards the center of the bowl.

The rim, too, is ornamented with chevrons. On the inside two checkered triangles are separated by a band, also checkered, which diminishes toward the center of the vessel.

Bibliography: Von Bissing, Tongefäße (CG), p. 23, pl. 7.

3

4   Ground floor, room 43

Vase with painted decoration

Buff terra cotta with red paint   JE 64910
H. 22 cm; Diam. 15 cm
Provenance unknown
Predynastic period, Nagada II, 3500–3100 B.C.

During the second phase of the Nagada culture new developments in ceramic colors, forms and decorative motifs become evident. The base color is no longer polished red but a flat buff. Decorations now occur in red paint, and the older broken lines give way to curves and spirals. Multi-oared boats make their first appearance, as do female dancers with upraised arms; to the faunal repertoire are added ostriches and flamingos, and to the floral, aloes.

This oval vase displays a flat rim, tubular pierced lug handles, and a slightly convex bottom, thus typifying the salient characteristics of this form of pottery. The decoration consists primarily of a boat equipped with forty oars and two cabins, one of which is topped by a standard. A wooden post marks the prow; an anchor hangs directly beneath it. The same type of boat appears on the other side of the vase, but bears a slightly different standard. In the open space below the boats are stylized ostriches — four on one side, five on the other — all aligned in a row. On either side of these appear two aloes, each clearly planted in a pot. Wavy lines representing water run around the foot of the vessel, while others cover the base and the lug handles. The shoulder area, below each of the handles, is occupied by four lines broken in the middle which might possibly represent clouds.

One finds these motifs not only on countless vases of this period, but also in the earliest known Egyptian wall painting: the so-called "painted tomb of Hierakonpolis", dating to the middle of the second phase of the Nagada culture (a fragment of this painting is on exhibit at the entrance to this hall).

Bibliography: Cf.: Vandier, Manuel I (1), pp. 332–65; J. Bourriau, Umm el-Ga'ab, Pottery from the Nile Valley before the Arab Conquest, Cambridge 1981, pp. 26–29; F. El-Yahky, in: BIFAO 85, 1985, pp. 187–95, pls. 33–34.

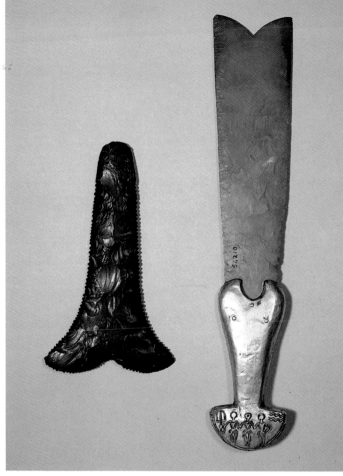

5

5
Lithic implements

1 Spearhead   JE 56606
Obsidian
L. 16.3 cm; W. 9.5 cm
Purchased in 1931

2 Knife with gold handle   JE 34210
Flint, gold leaf   = CG 64868
L. 30.6 cm; W. 6 cm
Gebelein (?), purchased in Qena in 1900
Predynastic period, second phase of Nagada II, 3370–3240 B.C.

In the Predynastic period Egyptian flint-working techniques reached a zenith unparalleled by any later stage in its long history. Polished blades were prepared on one or both sides by knapping off thin flakes to achieve the desired shape. The cutting edges were then retouched in a sharp, serrated pattern. The gleaming black spearhead consists of a shaft rounded at one end and forked at the other. The individual teeth protrude at regular intervals; only the rounded end, where blade and shaft would have joined, lacks denticulation. One generally finds such spearheads and knife blades made of local flint (see the specimens on view in this case); examples in imported materials such as obsidian are much less common.

The no less stylish flint knife with gold handle shows a unique form. The forked blade is encased in a handle with a rounded edge composed of two joined golden leaves and fastened on a plaster base with three rivets. The engraved decoration of the handle depicts on one side (illustrated here) three dancers in a multi-oared boat. The leftmost figure holds a fan or parasol. Two water lines, visible at right, continue around to the other side of the handle, which shows a boat with two cabins and standards. An aloe fills the righthand part of the scene. These designs resemble those found on Gerzean vases (see no. 4).

Bibliography: J. E. Quibell, in: ASAE 2, 1902, p. 130, pl. 1; Curelly, Stone Implements (CG), p. 272, pl. 47; Massoulard, Lances fourchues, in: Revue d'Egyptologie II, 1936, p. 135 ff. Cf. also: Leclant, Les Pharaons I, p. 50.

6

6

Theriomorphic vessel and oval-shaped vase

1 Vessel in the form of an antelope	JE 66628

Hard pink limestone
H. 8.5 cm; L. 14 cm; W. 5 cm
Provenance unknown; purchased in 1936

2 Oval-shaped vase	JE 31437
Diorite	= CG 14347

H. 9.5 cm; W. (with handles) 10 cm
Gebel Taref
Predynastic period, 4th Millennium B.C.

As early as the Predynastic period the Egyptian craftsman had mastered the art of cutting and polishing every type of stone, from the softest to the hardest. Neither finely sculpted miniature vases nor towering storage jars stood outside his repertoire; the most important point was to create a durable work of eternity.

The corpus includes flat, oval, spherical and cylindrical forms, many patterned after ceramic examples, or taken directly from nature, for the Egyptians were conscientious observers of their environment. Theriomorphic vessels occur, with rounded bellies in harmonious imitation of the weighty form of a hippopotamus or elephant. In our example, the slender form of an antelope is treated as an elliptical cup, completely hollowed out and opening along the animal's back. The result is successful: one can still identify the beast despite the schematic rendering of the head with inlaid eyes. The legs are extremely abbreviated to merely two curving appendages, insufficient to hold the piece upright. Perhaps it was originally suspended by means of the four carefully pierced holes at the top, as was the case with other vessels lacking flat bases.

The second pot takes the more classical oval form with two pierced lug handles, flat rim and small, flat base. Although perfectly polished on the exterior, the piece revealed some marks of the recently invented stonecutter's drill on the interior.

Such vessels accompanied the deceased in his tomb and served either as equipment for his funerary repast, or as containers of precious unguents and perfumes. They were costly and difficult to manufacture; their diversity and great numbers therefore underline the Egyptians' preference for beautiful luxury items.

Bibliography: J. E. Quibell, Archaic Objects (CG), p. 253 and pl. 53; Corteggiani, no. 2. Cf. also: Vandier, Manuel I, pp. 306–17; Ali El-Khouly, Egyptian Stone Vessels Predynastic Period to Dynasty III, Mainz 1978.

7

"Libyan" palette, or palette showing the foundation of cities

Schist	JE 27434
H. 19 cm; W. 22 cm	= CG 14238

Abydos
Protodynastic period, c. 3100–3000 B.C.

Palettes were originally used for grinding malachite and galena. Just before the beginning of the First Dynasty, however, they developed into display monuments intended to commemorate a royal victory, a successful hunt or a foundation ceremony. Some were deposited as ex-votos in the temple of that deity responsible for the good fortune being commemorated.

Only the lower portion of this palette survives, carved on both sides in raised relief (a plaster copy in room 42 of the upper floor reproduces the other face of the palette). Above we see defiles of animals divided into three registers, and below, groups of trees. The topmost register contains oxen with large eyes surmounted by several ridges, and strong, stylized musculature bulging at the shoulders and feet. Donkeys fill the second register and rams the third. These beasts decrease in size

7a   7b

towards the end of each defile and eventually even overlap each other. The last ram turns his head to the rear; in breaking the monotony of the scene, it displays a feature which continued throughout Egyptian art. Similarly the division into registers and the representation in profile introduce us to the beginnings of artistic conventions which were to enjoy a long and uninterrupted tradition.

In the lowest register, to the right of the (olive?) trees, we find a group of hieroglyphs: the throw-stick and the earth or land sign (⬭). This gives us the name *Tjehenu*, a region located at the western edge of the Delta, which in earliest times included parts of Libya. A very fertile area, *Tjehenu* provided Egypt with cattle and oil, whether as tribute or in times of mutual trade.

The opposite side of the palette depicts a falcon, a lion, a scorpion and an additional pair of falcons (symbolic of royal power), equipped with hoes and participating in a foundation ceremony, just as the king was later to be represented. The structures in question are fortified towns. Inside the enclosure walls, some of the buildings are accompanied by hieroglyphs naming localities in the western Delta, one of which may be the well-known Buto.

Bibliography: PM V, p. 105 (6); Quibell, Archaic Objects (CG), pp. 232−33; Vandier, Manuel I, pp. 590−99; Terrace/Fischer, no. 1; Corteggiani, no. 3.

8   Ground floor, room 43
The Narmer Palette

Greywacke (schist)   JE 32169
H. 64 cm; W. 42 cm; thickness 2.5 cm   = CG 14716
Hierakonpolis (Kom el Ahmar); discovered by Quibell in 1894
Protodynastic period, c. 3000 B.C.

This palette commemorates the victories of Narmer, whom tradition identifies with king Menes, the unifier of Upper and Lower Egypt. The upper part of the palette is decorated on both sides with the bovine heads of the goddess Hathor flanking the royal name. Written with the hieroglyphic signs for the fish, *(nar)*, and for the chisel, read *(mer)*, this name is inscribed within the serekh, or rectangular enclosure wall and panelled facade of the royal palace.

The main decoration on the reverse represents the king on a grand scale, wearing the White Crown of Upper Egypt and an ornamented ceremonial costume complete with hanging animal tail. Followed by his sandal-bearer, he brandishes a mace, poised to smite the kneeling prisoner who probably represents an inhabitant of Lower Egypt. This theme showing the king smiting his enemies will from now on symbolize the triumph of order over chaos and continue throughout ancient Egyptian history. In front of Narmer, the Horus falcon, pro-

8a   8b

tector of kingship, holds a prisoner by a rope through the nose
and stands on a bundle of plants symbolizing the submission
of the Delta. In the lower register are shown two slain
enemies, accompanied by the hieroglyphic signs for their
countries.

The obverse shows in the upper register a triumphal procession in which the king, wearing the Red Crown of Lower
Egypt, followed by this sandal-bearer and escorted by officials
and standard-bearers, approaches the temple of Horus and
inspects the bound and beheaded corpses of enemies lying in
two rows before him. The central part of the palette contains
a circular depression surrounded by the intertwined necks of
two marvelous beasts which are held on leashes by two at-
tendants. They represent the two rival halves of the land now
subdued and held at bay. At the bottom, the king is portrayed
as a bull destroying a captured fortress and trampling on its
slain rebels.

The historical events commemorated here, which seem to have
led to the unification of the country, the beginnings of official
hieroglyphic writing, the divine representations and royal ico-

nographic themes all combine to render this palette one of the
most famous and important pieces in our collection.

*Bibliography: PM V, p. 193; Quibell, Archaic Objects I (CG), pp.
312−15; Smith, Art and Architecture, p. 34, figs. 13−14; Vandier,
Manuel I, pp. 595−97; Lange/Hirmer, pls. 4−5.*

9   Ground floor, room 43

Plaque of Aha (Menes)

Ivory   JE 31773
H. 4.8 cm; W. 5.6 cm   = CG 14142
Nagada, 1897; additional fragment discovered by Garstang in 1904
Thinite period, 1st dynasty, reign of Aha (Menes), c. 3000−2965 B.C.

This ivory plaque preserves one of the oldest examples of
Egyptian hieroglyphic writing. It is pierced in one corner and
forms part of a series of plaques discovered in the royal tombs
of the First Dynasty apparently serving as jar labels. Smaller
labels bear the names of products, places or numbers, while

larger ones might also include the king's name, types of oil, and a date of issue marked by some important festival or historical event. The plaques are thus to be associated with the manufacture of oils, which the Egyptians considered at this early period one of the most valuable products in the land.

The plaques represent an important documentary source on a system of writing already fairly advanced, whereas earlier royal inscriptions of the protodynastic period merely contain isolated hieroglyphs (see Narmer, no. 8). Nevertheless it remains no easy task to read these texts, and many of the signs pose constantly recurring problems for the translator.

On this particular plaque, found in the tomb of one of King Aha's wives, one reads the name of Aha, "the Fighter," first king of Dynasty 1, in the second group of hieroglyphs from the right in the topmost register. The name is written with the ideogram for doing battle (two arms holding shield and mace) within a Serekh, or palace facade motif surmounted by the Horus falcon; "Aha" is the king's Horus name.

The first group of signs at the right seems to reproduce the so-called Two Ladies name of the king, MEN (i.e. Menes in Greek) written with the gaming board pronounced "Men" and placed inside a booth under the aegis of the goddesses Nekhbet, the vulture of Upper Egypt, and Wadjet, the cobra of Lower Egypt. King Aha must therefore be identical to Menes, the pharaoh whom tradition credits with the original unification of the country. But the gaming board may also be taken as the verb "to endure, be firmly established", in which case we would have here the name of a structure founded by the king called "The Two Ladies endure". Further to the left a boat, set in the water and equipped with a cabin surmounted by a falcon, commemorates a visit to this very structure by the king in the form of Horus. The poorly preserved hieroglyphs at left most likely relate one of the Horus-king's battles, the foundation of a fortress or the opening of a canal.

The second register depicts a ceremony attended by the king (at right), who strides out of his palace accompanied by three courtiers. In the center, two men flank a large supported vessel, either stirring its contents or pouring a liquid, perhaps oil, into it. On an identical plaque now in the Liverpool museum, an inscription underneath this scene seems to describe the deliverey of "provisions of Lower Egypt and food supplies of Upper Egypt." Ritual sacrifices on the left of the plaque include crouching prisoners, bound or decapitated oxen, sealed jars, and a loaf of bread placed upon a mat (the hieroglyphic sign for offerings).

In the lowest register, four advancing figures seem to accompany the royal cortege. On the left, the hieroglyphic text mentions a type of oil.

Bibliography: PM V, p. 118; Vandier, Manuel I, pp. 827–30; W. Helck, Handbuch der Orientalistik I, 1975, pp. 23–25. Cf. also Naissance de l'ecriture, catalogue de l'exposition au Grand Palais, Paris 1982, no. 20.

10   Ground floor, room 43

Bracelets from the tomb of Djer

Gold, turquoise, lapis lazuli, amethyst   JE 35054
Max. L. 18 cm   = CG 52008–52011 and 53835
Abydos, tomb of King Djer; excavations of F. Petrie, 1901
Thinite period, 1st dynasty, reign of Horus Djer, c. 2964–2912 B.C.

Petrie discovered these bracelets fastened onto a detached forearm, probably of a female mummy, within the enclosure wall of the royal tomb.

Tasteful jewellery appears early in Egypt and is distinguished from the first dynasties onward by a concern for harmonious

9

10

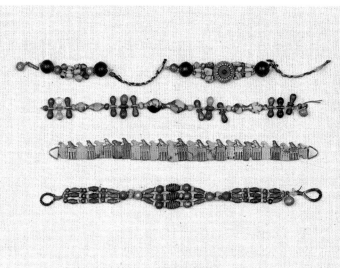

11

forms and color combinations. To these qualities was added superior craftsmanship, and the result is readily apparent in the group of bracelets illustrated here.

The two semi-circular elements, which consist of gold filigree and twisted animal hair (perhaps giraffe tail), are fastening ties which serve to connect the two halves of the first bracelet. This is made up a central golden rosette, irregularly shaped beads of perfectly polished turquoise, round beads of lapis lazuli and little golden balls.

The second bracelet mixes vertically arranged beads of amethyst, gold or brown stone with turquoise shaped into lozenges or little balls and connected by gold coupling pieces. Alternating gold and turquoise representations of the Horus falcon perched upon a palace facade make up the third bracelet. The facade motif was termed *serekh* and generally framed the king's name. Two threads passing through the two holes present in each *serekh* are bounded on either side by triangular end-pieces of gold.

The fourth and final bracelet consists of elongated beads of coiled gold filigree and similarly shaped lapis lazuli beads. These two varieties are interspersed with balls of turquoise, lapis lazuli and gold, all of varying shapes. The bracelet is securely fastened by means of two rings and a ball of gold.

The tomb of Djer, surrounded by a large number of sepulchres belonging to his courtiers, was located, like those of all the First Dynasty kings, at the site called Umm el-Gaab at Abydos. This was the necropolis of the Thinite nome whence these kings originated. They resided, however, in the capital near Sakkara, and here they also erected tombs. Which of the two series of tombs were merely cenotaphs (dummy tombs) remains to be clarified.

Djer's sepulchre at Abydos was robbed already in the Old Kingdom. It was most likely after one such violation and subsequent rearrangement that the mummified forearm of a member of the royal family came to light within the masonry of a brick wall.

In the Late period tradition this monument was considered the resting-place of Osiris become lord of Abydos and patron god of all the deceased.

Bibliography: PM V, p. 79; W. M. F. Petrie, The Royal Tombs of the earliest dynasties II, London 1901, pl. 1 and p. 173 ff.; Vernier, Bijoux et Orfèvreries (CG), pp. 10–15 and 513, pls. 5–6; Aldred, Jewels, pl. 1; Corteggiani, no. 4.

11
Ground floor, room 43

Animal figurines

Faience, limestone, rock-crystal	JE 36123
Max. H. 5 cm; max. L. 7.2 cm	JE 38174
Abydos; Abusir el Melek; Nagada	JE 31776
Thinite period, c. 3000 B.C.	= CG 14044

Clay or flint animal figurines were frequently deposited in tombs during the Predynastic period. This practice expanded during the First Dynasty to include ex-voto figurines placed in the courts of the earliest sanctuaries. The falcon, crocodile, hippopotamus and frog, all in faience, were discovered by Petrie in the archaic temple of Khentamentiu at Abydos dating to the First Dynasty. The rock-crystal lion derives from the tomb of one of Aha's wives at Nagada, while the limestone monkey was found by Möller in a tomb of the early cemetery at Abusir el Melek.

These figurines, statuettes or amulets served in some cases as gaming pieces as the lions, (see no. 12) and in others as votive objects depicting divine forces which had to be appeased (such as the hippo or crocodile), or alternatively whose protection was sought (such as the falcon or the monkey, symbol of ancestors in this remote age). Yet another purpose, best exemplified by the frog, was to answer prayers for fertility. But regardless of their numerous functions, they preserve for us the first examples of animal sculpture in the round, a genre which was to claim many artistic masterpieces over the long course of Egyptian history.

Bibliography: Petrie, Abydos II, London 1903, pls. 6 and 7; de Morgan, Recherches sur les Origines de l'Egypte II, Paris 1897, p. 163, fig. 700; Möller/Scharff, in: Wissenschaftliche Veröffentlichungen der Deutschen Orient-Gesellschaft 49, 1926, pl. 39, fig. 436. Cf. also: G. Dreyer, Elephantine VIII, Der Tempel der Satet, Archäologische Veröffentlichungen 39, Mainz 1985.

12

13
"Basket" in stone

Schist   JE 71298
H. 4.8 cm; W. 13.8 cm; L. 22.7 cm
North Sakkara; excavations of Emery, 1937
Thinite period, 2nd dynasty, ca. 2830–2705 B.C.

The reproduction in more durable materials of objects destined for use in the afterlife became such a persistent phenomenon that even basketry was eventually "translated" into stone. But Egyptian art would hardly have succeeded if, from the beginning, an aesthetic sensibility had not existed side by side with the desire to merely produce durable objects, nor if the Egyptian artist had lacked the courage to tackle the hardest stones. Many examples of schist plates have been found which imitate large trilobate leaves, the underside revealing a meticulously crafted network of veins. Such plates, often displaying extremely delicate carving, anticipate by some five millennia the metal and faience objects of the turn of the Twentieth Century which receive so much attention today.
This dish is a perfect example of "basketry" in schist. The indication of gold carved on one side suggests that the piece may have held jewellery or gold ingots. In a particular New Kingdom tomb we see the wife of Sennefer offer her husband a golden collar placed upon a similar sort of plate. Our basket may be a purely utilitarian object, but nevertheless illustrates the skill and taste of the stonecutter with regard to form and material.

Bibliography: W. B. Emery, Archaic Egypt, pl. 39 b; Terrace/Fischer, no. 3; Ali El-Khouly, Egyptian Stone Vessels Predynastic Period to Dynasty III, Mainz 1978, Vol. II, no. 5604 and Vol. III, pl. 160; Corteggiani, no. 7.

12
Game pieces

Ivory   JE 44918 A-F
Max. H. 3.5 cm; max. L. 6.5 cm
Abu Roash, tomb M. VIII; excavations of the Institut Français
d'Archéologie Orientale du Caire, 1913–1914
Thinite period, 1st dynasty, c. 3000–2830 B.C.

Games of luck or skill remained among the most valued forms of entertainment in ancient Egypt, and even accompanied the deceased in his tomb with no less significance than his funerary offerings. More than mere recreation, these games came to play an important religious role as well. The serpent game, from which our pieces derive, was commonly played in the Thinite period and Old Kingdom; Thinite tombs have revealed numerous examples.
In Egyptian the game was called Mehen, or "coil", and was played upon a circular sort of plate in the form of a coiled serpent with head in the center and body divided into square sections (see the plate on view in the same case). The pieces include white and red marbles, three recumbent lionesses with decorative collars, and three recumbent lions with beautifully incised manes. The precise rules of the game remain unclear, but it seems that the lionpieces moved according to the position or number of marbles thrown by each player into the center of the game board.

Bibliography: Montet, in: Kêmi VIII, 1946, pp. 186–89, pl. 7; Centenaire de l'Institut Français d'Archéologie Orientale, Cairo 1981, no. 1.

13

14 King Khasekhem

Ground floor, room 43

Green schist   JE 32161
H. 56.5 cm; W. 13.3 cm; profile 30 cm
Hierakonpolis (Kom el-Ahmar); discovered by Quibell in 1898
Thinite period, 2nd dynasty, reign of Khasekhem, c. 2740–2705 B.C.

Royal statuary from the earliest periods of Egyptian history remains modest in scale but nonetheless quite competent in the use of hard stone. As early as the end of the Second Dynasty it attains a technical perfection to complement its pure and sensitive style.

This is one of two statues which King Khasekhem deposited in the temple of Hierakonpolis. The king sits upon a throne, the legs and back of which are simply defined in raised relief upon a cube of schist. He wears the white crown of Upper Egypt and an enveloping sleeved garment which folds over the breast and extends down to the shins. Starting at the sleeve, a large band forms the border of the garment wrapped around in front. Such clothing was worn by the king during the Sed festival, celebrated after thirty years of rule. The right hand is closed and rests on the thigh while the left arm bends across the body with left fist placed upon right forearm. Each fist is provided with a hole for the insertion of insignia. The naked feet rest flat upon the base.

The entire right hand portion of the statue, including the nose, is unfortunately broken away. Yet what little remains of the face reveals an excellent piece of portraiture: both the eye and the facial musculature are masterfully rendered.

Around the periphery of the base, both here and on this statue's mate in Oxford, sprawl outlined figures of Lower Egyptian rebels smitten by the king. According to the inscription on the base, the number of rebels reached 47,209! The practice of commemorating major events with votive objects, initiated during the protodynastic period, thus continued into the Thinite era.

Khasekhem, last king of the Second, or Thinite, Dynasty is in fact known to have suppressed a revolt in Lower Egypt. Following his successful reconquest of the north he seems to have changed his name from Horus Khasekhem ("the powerful one appears") to Horus-Seth Khasekhemwy ("the two powerful ones appear"), thus placing the two realms of south and north under the respective protection of these two deities. However, it should be mentioned that the second name may be that of a successor.

Bibliography: PM V, 193; Quibell, Hierakonpolis I, London 1900, p. 11, pls. 40–41; Quibell/Green, Hierakonpolis II, London 1902, p. 44; Propyläen Kunstgeschichte 15, pl. 115; Leclant, Les Pharaons I, p. 175, fig. 174; Corteggiani, no. 8.

15 Two sealed vessels

Ground floor, room 43

a) Carnelian and gold
H. 4.2 cm; Diam. 6.5 cm   JE 34941
b) Dolomite and gold
H. 7.2 cm; Diam. 10.5 cm   JE 34942
Abydos, Umm el-Gaab, tomb of King Khasekhemwy, excavated by Petrie, 1900–1901
Thinite period, 2nd dynasty, reign of Khasekhemwy, c. 2740–2705 B.C.

The funerary equipment from the tomb of Khasekhemwy at Abydos included more than two hundred stone vases, of which six of dolomite and one of carnelian possessed covers of gold. The latter consist of thick gold leaf fitted to the form of the vessel's rim and attached to its mouth by a golden chain stamped with a clay seal.

These precious materials were selected for use in the next world, hence their imitation of objects normally found in other media. The gold leaf represents the piece of cloth generally used to close unguent vessels; the chain imitates a simple braid or string. The clay seal, originally stamped, served to perpetuate the name of the owner.

The extraordinary polish and harmony of form and color indicate a concern for beauty over and above the more mundane desires for longevity and conservation of the vessels.

Bibliography: PM V, p. 87; Petrie, The Royal Tombs of the earliest dynasties II, p. 27, pl. 9.

15a

15b

King Djoser (Horus Netjery-Khet)

Painted limestone   JE 49158
H. 142 cm; W. 45.3 cm; L. 95.5 cm
Sakkara, funerary complex of Djoser. Excavations of the Egyptian
Antiquities Service, 1924–25
Old Kingdom, 3rd dynasty, reign of Djoser, 2690–2660 B.C.

This statue is thought to be the oldest life-size statue known
from Egypt. It represents King Djoser seated in an archaic attitude, his body enveloped in a jubilee mantle. The statue was
entirely covered with a coat of white plaster and painted. The
king wears an ample black striated wig surmounted by the
royal headdress called the *nemes* made of a pleated material.
A false ceremonial beard is attached to the lower part of his
face which is clean shaven except for a thin moustache on his
upper lip.

The deep-set eyes were once inlaid, and still retain a far-away
look. But the face is enlivened by the slightly disdainful
expression of the mouth which emphasizes the distance that
separated the King from ordinary mortals in those days.

The king is seated on an elevated throne with a high back. A
carefully engraved hieroglyphic inscription on its base mentions the royal Horus name Netjery-khet. The statue was
found in a small chapel built against the north face of the step
pyramid, in the funerary complex of King Djoser which is
considered to be the earliest known monumental construction
of dressed stone. The chapel, commonly designated by the
Arabic word *serdab*, had two small 'windows' in its façade
which permitted the dead king, buried in the pyramid, to look
out, through the eyes of his statue, and perceive the offerings
placed before him. He could likewise behold the northern sky
and the never setting circumpolar stars where, according to
Old Kingdom beliefs, the world of eternal life was situated.

Bibliography: PM III, 2, p. 414; Vandier, Manuel I, pp. 987–88;
C. Aldred, Old Kingdom Art in Egypt, p. 28; Lange/Hirmer,
pp. 16–17; Leclant, Les Pharaons I, p. 179, fig. 175; R. Stadelmann,
Die Ägyptischen Pyramiden, Mainz 1985, pl. 8.

17

Panel of blue faience tiles

Limestone and faience
H. 181 cm; W. 203 cm
Sakkara, funerary complex of Djoser, excavations of the Egyptian Antiquities Service, 1928
Old Kingdom, 3rd dynasty, reign of Djoser, 2690–2660 B.C.

JE 68921

It was during the time of Djoser and his ingenious architect Imhotep that stone replaced the lighter materials previously employed in funerary and religious architecture. Within the bounds of King Djoser's funerary complex we witness the translation into stone of such elements as brick chapels, daub and wattle constructions, plant ornaments, and even of wooden beams and pillars.

King Djoser's funerary chamber, situated at the bottom of a pit 28 meters below the step-pyramid, was surrounded by a network of subterranean galleries including royal apartments and store-rooms for his funerary equipment. The western walls of the royal chambers were of dressed stone inlaid with blue faience tiles, the whole imitating a wattle construction made with reeds. J. Ph. Lauer has reconstructed a panel here from one of these walls, using original elements found in the apartment. The panel is surmounted by an arch supported on *djed*-pillars, symbols of stability. The rows of plaques are held in place by means of a plaster mortar sunk into the furrows in which they are embedded. The plaques are also sewn like buttons with a vegetable thread which through channels pierced in the stone and through the tenons of a series of four to eight plaques. One of the other walls was decorated in the semblance of a palace façade with its windows and doors; the latter are closed and the door leaves ornamented with admirable scenes in low-relief depicting the king performing various rites.

Walls similarly decorated with inlaid faience tiles had previously been found in the underground apartments of a second tomb called 'the southern tomb', cut into the southern massif of the enclosure wall around the step-pyramid.

Bibliography: J. Ph. Lauer, La Pyramide à Degrés I, Cairo 1936, pp. 34–37; Lauer, Saqqara, p. 94, pl. 102; Propyläen Kunstgeschichte 15, pl. 20; Leclant, Les Pharaons I, p. 64, fig. 73; Corteggiani, no. 11; R. Stadelmann, Die Ägyptischen Pyramiden, pl. 7 and see also pls. 9 and 13.

18

Offering- or libation tables

Alabaster CG 1321
H. 38 cm; L. 89 cm; W. 42 cm
Sakkara, mortuary complex of Djoser;
excavated by Mariette around 1860
Old Kingdom, end of the 2nd dynasty – beginning of the 3rd dynasty,
c. 2705 B.C.

A pair of identical tables depicts a lion motif, found on many examples of pharaonic furniture. Two lions side by side support a tray which slopes gently downward towards the back. Their tails curl around a vessel with a deep cavity intended to catch the liquid, in this case blood, which drained through a small gutter or trench.

The two tables were discovered in one of the chambers of a subterranean tomb, along with two alabaster slabs and some pottery beside a limestone bench. On top of the bench were human skeletal remains. The burial should date prior to the reign of Djoser because it was located underneath the fill of the terrace erected by this king to the north of his mortuary temple. The tomb probably did not belong to a private individual, given the rudimentary form of offering and libation tables normally deposited in private tombs during the Old Kingdom. A royal burial seems much more likely, unless these tables are a deposit from a mortuary temple.

Beds and tables of this type are known, albeit during later pe-

riods, to have been used during the embalming of the body and viscera. To judge from their small dimensions, these two tables appear better suited to the viscera. However, the bones deposited bare in the tomb, without bandages or shroud, prevent any hasty conclusions on this hypothesis, which would imply a fairly advanced stage in the practice of mummification for such an early age. Furthermore, the earliest known canopic chest belongs to Queen Hetep-heres, dating to about a century after our two tables.

On the other hand, a royal altar surrounded with lion's heads (on view in corridor 42) derives from the entrance colonnade of Djoser's mortuary complex. Another example, depicting a lion whose sharply inclined back forms a table which pours into a vase, was discovered among the funerary equipment of King Sahure at Abusir. Finally, New Kingdom versions of tables similar to ours were found in the tomb of Horemheb at Thebes. All of these examples concern monuments for the cult of the dead king. They are either libation tables, as Mariette originally believed, or sacrificial altars, fashioned to catch the dripping blood which could not be allowed to desecrate a holy place.

Bibliography: PM III, 2, p. 415; Mariette, Les Mastabas de l'Ancien Empire, pp. 83–86; Borchardt, Denkmäler des Alten Reiches (CG) I, pp. 9–10, pl. 3; Firth, in: ASAE 28, 1928, p. 82; Lauer, La Pyramide à Degrés I, Cairo 1936, p. 186; Götter Pharaonen, no. 3. Cf.: Borchardt, Das Grabdenkmal des Königs Sa3-hu-rec I, figs. 144–45.

Stone vessels

Bowl: gneiss H. 5.7 cm; Diam. 11.9 cm;   JE 64886

Pot: amethystine quartz H. 9.2 cm; Diam. 7.2 cm;   JE 65416

Vase: speckled schist H. 16.5 cm; Diam. 8.2 cm   JE 65422

Sakkara, Step Pyramid of Djoser, subterranean galleries.
Excavations of the Egyptian Antiquities Service, 1932–33
1st and 3rd dynasties, c. 3000–2700 B.C.

The thousands of vases, bowls, goblets and pots buried in the subterranean galleries of Djoser's pyramid demonstrate a wealth of form and material, and a perfection of craftsmanship rarely equalled elsewhere. This cache, from which three of the most beautiful specimens are selected here out of the many on display, represents the best of the royal ateliers not only of Djoser's reign, but of the two preceding dynasties as well. It seems that Djoser chose out of piety to preserve what remained of the funerary equipment from the pillaged royal tombs of Abydos and Sakkara in his own pyramid, which he must have considered inviolable.

Bibliography: Cf.: Lauer, La Pyramide à Degrés III, Cairo 1939, pp. 1–31, pls. 4–18; Lauer, Histoire Monumentale des Pyramides d'Egypte I, Cairo 1962, pp. 91–94; Ali El-Khouly, Egyptian Stone Vessels Predynastic Period to Dynasty III, Mainz 1978.

Heb-Sed vase

Alabaster   JE 64872
H. 37 cm; Diam. 28 cm
Sakkara, funerary complex of Djoser, subterranean galleries
Excavations of the Egyptian Antiquities Service, 1932–33
Old Kingdom, 2nd dynasty, c. 2730 B.C.

Two of the subterranean galleries below the Step Pyramid revealed a total of about 40.000 vessels of all types of stone in a multitude of shapes and styles. This vase, of relatively large proportions, bears an original relief decoration composed of ritual symbols. The crouching figure of the god of eternity, who also represents the hieroglyphic sign for "million," supports a tall pedestal flanked by staircases, upon which rests a double pavilion sheltering the thrones of Upper and Lower Egypt. This is the pavilion of the Heb-Sed, or royal jubilee, generally held after thirty years of rule. The representation symbolizes in this case eternal jubilees which the king hoped to celebrate in the next world. At the top of the fluted handle a scarab, symbol of eternal renewal, serves to prolong the deceased king's life in the hereafter.

Bibliography: Firth/Quibell, The Step Pyramid, Cairo 1935, I, p. 135, II, pl. 104; J. Ph. Lauer, La Pyramide à Degrés I, pp. 64–65; Lauer, Saqqara, pl. 104.

Hesire

Wood   JE 28504
H. 114 cm; W. 40 cm; thickness 8 cm   = CG 1427
Sakkara; discovered by Mariette in mastaba A.3
Old Kingdom, 3rd dynasty, c. 2700 B.C.

Hesire was a high official of the Third Dynasty whose important titles included "chief of royal scribes," "greatest of the Tens of Upper Egypt," "chief of Buto," and "chief dentist." His *mastaba* (the Arabic word for "bench" used to designate the private tombs of the Old Kingdom due to their rectangular form and battered walls) was found at Sakkara to the north of the funerary complex of king Djoser in the extension to the archaic cemetery of the first two dynasties. Conceived as a grand house with numerous subterranean elements, this tomb already contains all the features found in later mastabas: an underground chamber to house the mummy, and a shaft relating it to the superstructure with a *serdab* (statue-chamber) and offering room with a niche (later a false door). In Hesire's tomb this room takes the form of a long interior passage decorated with painted matting and friezes of funerary equipment. Eleven niches cut in the west wall of this passage once displayed a lining of wooden panels sculpted with the figure of the tomb-owner. Only six of these panels were still preserved upon discovery; they are now in the Museum. They show Hesire in various costumes and poses at different stages in his life. The beautiful hieroglyphs included give the name, titles and functions of this important dignitary. One can see the care and precision with which sculpture was executed at this remote period.

On our panel, Hesire is shown standing with his left leg advanced. The torso is particularly long, the musculature skilfully modelled. On the face, the eyebrow, upper eyelid and moustache are carved in light relief. Hesire wears a long wig with wavy locks and a belted kilt with a plaited edge. In his left hand he holds a staff and his scribal equipment, consisting of a palette with two inkwells (generally containing the colors red and black), a long pen case and a small leather bag for supplies. He holds the Kherep-scepter, symbol of power and authority, in his right hand.

Following the conventions of Egyptian art, concerned with showing the best view of each of the body's elements, the figure is seen in profile, with eye and shoulders straight on, legs and arms in profile but hands straight on. The leg farthest away from the viewer is extended and both feet are shown from the inside (this view was to be abandoned in the New Kingdom).

Bibliography: PM III, 2, p. 438; Mariette, Les Mastabas de l'Ancien Empire, Paris 1882–1889, p. 81; Borchardt, Denkmäler des Alten Reiches (CG) I, p. 109, pl. 27; Quibell, Tomb of Hesi, 1929, pp. 4–5, pl. 29; Terrace/Fischer, no. 4; Lange/Hirmer, pl. 18–19; Corteggiani, no. 12.

22

Ground floor, room 43

Hetepdief

Speckled red granite
H. 39 cm; W. 18 cm; profile 20 cm
Discovered at Memphis, 1888
Old Kingdom, end of the 3rd dynasty, c. 2650 B.C.

JE 34557
= CG 1

This piece is one of the earliest known examples of Egyptian private statuary. For the first time, the figure is shown kneeling with both hands resting on the thighs, in the attitude of prayer. Hetepdief wears a round wig with tiered locks and a short kilt which covers him only sparingly.

While royal stone statuary had, by the middle of Dynasty 2, already attained the purity of line and perfected modelling techniques for which it is customarily known, private statuary on the other hand continued to display an archaic quality. The present example is both thick-set and compact. The proportions are none too successful: the large head, rendered even heavier by the full wig, seems to sink into the shoulders. The limbs are rigid and angular, the knees flat, the legs awkwardly folded. The face on the other hand is more carefully worked, and one recognizes the attempt at an idealized portrait intended to commit forever a particular self-image to an imperishable material.

Also visible in this statue are the major principles, developed as early as the 4th Millennium, which were to form Egyptian artistic convention all through its long history: frontality, symmetry and "representativity", all serving to faithfully perpetuate the moment. Likewise toward this end, we find the name and titles of the individual inscribed in raised relief on the statue's base slab, as well as his father's name: Mery Djehuty. Hetepdief's titles are in some cases difficult to interpret; one seems to call him "great of incense in the red house." The Horus names of the first three kings of the Second Dynasty, Hetepsekhemwy, Raneb und Nynetjer, whose cults Hetepdief probably served as priest, are carved behind his right shoulder, preceded by a phoenix perched atop a pyramidion, perhaps already the symbol of eternal resurrection.

Both the stylistic similarity to a securely dated statue of one Metjen in West Berlin, and the raised relief techniques used for the hieroglyphs allow us to date our piece to the end of Dynasty 3.

Bibliography: PM III, 2, p. 864; Borchardt, Statuen und Statuetten (CG) I, pp. 1–3, pl. 1; Terrace/Fischer, no. 2; Corteggiani, no. 9.

23

Golden shell

Gold leaf   JE 92656
L. 5.3 cm
Sakkara, excavated by the Egyptian Antiquities Service, 1950
Old Kingdom, 3rd dynasty, reign of Sekhemkhet, c. 2660−2655 B.C.

Discovered in the unfinished funerary complex of the Horus Sekhemkhet, to the southwest of Djoser's Step Pyramid, this delightful little container faithfully reproduces the form of a seashell. It swings open on a tiny hinge and clasps shut by means of two little exterior hooks, which may also have allowed the shell to be hung from a chain and worn as a pendant. Its primary function, however, was perhaps as a receptacle for cosmetics and pigments.

The piece was found among the other objects of jewellery displayed in the same case: gold bracelets and rings, and necklaces of either gold, blue faience or carnelian beads. Not far from this cache, Goneim discovered a multitude of hard stone and alabaster vessels, as well as pottery jars whose clay stoppers were stamped with the name of Sekhemkhet, the probable successor to (and possible son of) King Djoser. The restrained forms of such jewellery and vessels bear witness to the high quality of Egyptian artistic craftsmanship.

Bibliography: Z. Goneim, Horus Sekhem-Khet. Vol. I, Cairo 1957, p. 13, pl. 32 a−c; J. Ph. Lauer, Saqqara, 1977, pp. 133−36; Leclant, Les Pharaons I, fig. 247.

24

Commemorative relief of Sneferu from Sinai

Red sandstone   JE 38568
H. 112.5 cm; W. 133 cm
Sinai, turquoise mines of Maghara
Old Kingdom, beginning of the 4th dynasty, reign of Sneferu, 2630−2585 B.C.

This relief once adorned the face of a cliff at Maghara, site of the ancient turquoise mines. Turquoise made its first appearance at the very beginning of pharaonic history and has been considered a precious stone ever since. From the Third Dynasty onward royal expeditions sent to the Maghara mines often commemorated a successful mission with reliefs and inscriptions carved on the cliff face, to the greater glory of their king. Pharaoh ist usually shown smiting an enemy, thus symbolically repressing the forces of chaos and restoring natural order.

Two such monuments are known from the reign of Sneferu. This extremely active founder of the Fourth Dynasty built no less than three pyramids at Medum and Dahshur, and the Palermo stone mentions his successful raids into Nubia and Libya. Even the later literary tradition labels him "a very good king." In the Sinai, Sneferu was considered the conqueror of the peninsula, and was in fact deified during the Middle Kingdom. He appears in the pantheon at the neighboring site of Serabit el-Khadim, exalted equally with Hathor, mistress of turquoise, Soped, lord of the east, and Thoth, lord of the foreign lands.

This particular bas-relief forcefully advertises the might of the king. Dressed in a plaited kilt and wearing a divine crown composed of double plumes and two double horns set upon a round wig with border curls, Sneferu brandishes his mace in his right hand. With his left he grasps a baton as well as the scalp of a defeated Asiatic prisoner who begs for mercy.

The inscriptions list the royal titulary, in particular the king's Horus name of Neb-Maat "Lord of Truth" − dominated by the figure of the falcon. The small cartouche gives the throne name of Sneferu, "the great god," which is followed by the epithet "who conquers the foreign lands," written vertically behind the king.

Other monuments from Maghara, recognizable by the use of the same reddish sandstone, are also on view in this room. To save them from destruction, Petrie carefully sawed them loose and transported them by both camel and ship to the Museum.

Bibliography: PM VII, p. 340; F. Petrie, Researches in Sinai, London 1906, p. 44, fig. 50; Gardiner/Peet/Černý, The Inscriptions of Sinai II, London 1955, p. 56.

Reliefs with paste inlays from the tomb of Nefer-Maat

Limestone, colored paste   JE 43809
H. (2 registers) 61.5 and 62 cm; W. 138.5 and 124 cm
Medum, mastaba of Nefer-Maat and Atet, excavations of Petrie, 1892
Old Kingdom, 4th dynasty, beginning of the reign of Sneferu, c. 2620 B.C.

The belief in the continuity of a material existence involves a concern not only for the preservation of the body, but also for the provisioning of the deceased with all items necessary for an eternal life in the next world. These items consist of all manner of offerings, and in order to perpetuate them as well as explain their origins, recourse was made early on to mural representations.

The principal aim in earliest times was therefore not merely to construct magnificent pyramids and tombs but to reproduce the world in which the deceased would live. Stone, with its highly valued durability, served as a medium for carved bas-relief scenes which were then completely painted for an enhanced sense of realism. In the cause of permanence certain techniques were developed, tested and, as was the case with painted bas-relief, retained. One particular technique, however, that of colored paste inlays fitted into hollowed-out forms, was attempted once and then abandoned forever.

The inventor of this process was the prince Nefer-Maat, son of Sneferu, who was buried in a large mastaba near the pyramid of Medum. From this mastaba derive the famous "Medum geese" painting (no. 26), as well as these two paste-inlaid wall fragments. One shows a desert hunting scene: a hunter approaches a leopard from behind while a dog attacks three foxes. The other fragment depicts fowling and agricultural work. As beautiful as this technique was, it had to be abandoned because the paste inlays dried out, cracked and ultimately fell to the ground.

Bibliography: PM IV, p. 93; F. Petrie, Meidum, London 1892, pl. 18.

The Medum geese

Painted plaster   JE 34571
H. 27 cm; W. 172 cm   = CG 1742
Medum, mastaba of Nefer-Maat and Atet,
Mariette's excavations, 1871
Old Kingdom, beginning of the 4th dynasty,
beginning of the reign of Sneferu, c. 2620 B.C.

This magnificent panel, on which three pairs of geese are shown feeding on the grass, gives us an excellent idea of the high quality and the technical ability of Egyptian painting. It comes from the mastaba of Nefer-Maat and Atet at Medum where it decorated the lower part of one of the walls in the passage giving access to Atet's chapel. Both chapels in this double mud-brick mastaba were faced with limestone and adorned with inlays of coloured paste (cf. no. 25), while the decoration of the passage was painted. The painting is in distemper, utilizing mineral pigments diluted with water and an added agglutinant such as egg-white or vegetable gum. The ground consists of a thin surface of a light coloured plaster (a clayey silt) covering a somewhat heavier mud coating which adheres to the brick walls.

The composition is symmetrical, grouping together three pairs of geese which the artist took care to sufficiently differentiate from one another so that the result is quite naturalistic. However, although the silhouette and the general attitude of each is faithfully depicted and the colours well chosen, the rendering of the plumage is very stylized and not to be found in nature.

Bibliography: PM IV, pp. 93–94; Borchardt, Denkmäler des Alten Reiches II (CG), pp. 167–68, pl. 97; A. Mekhitarian, La Peinture Egyptienne, Genève 1954, p. 9; Lange/Hirmer, pl. III; Propyläen Kunstgeschichte 15, pl. XVIII; Leclant, Les Pharaons I, fig. 158. Cf. also: T. G. H. James, Egyptian Painting in the British Museum, London 1985, pp. 20–21, fig. 18.

26

Rahotep and Nofret

Painted limestone
Rahotep H. 121 cm; W. 51 cm; L. 69 cm   CG 3
Nofret H. 122 cm; W. 48.5 cm; L. 70 cm   CG 4
Medum, discovered by Mariette in 1871 in the mastaba of Rahotep
and Nofret north of the pyramid of Sneferu
Old Kingdom, beginning of the 4th dynasty, beginning of the reign of
Sneferu, about 2620 B.C.

These two statues, which can be counted among the masterpieces of the Museum, represent a couple of courtiers who
lived at the time of the first pyramid builders. Prince Rahotep
was probably a son of King Sneferu. He held the titles of High
Priest of Re at Heliopolis, Director of Expeditions and Chief
of Construction. His wife Nofret was designated as 'one
known to the King'.
Rahotep is seated, his right arm bent across his chest while his
left hand is lying on his knee. He wears a knee-length kilt, a
short wig, and has a thin moustache. A heart-shaped amulet
hangs around his neck. On the statue's back slab a single column of hieroglyphs in sunk relief painted black gives his titles
and his name. Nofret, likewise seated with both arms crossed
on her breast, is enveloped in a long mantle underneath which
one can see the straps supporting her dress. She is wearing a
wide necklace composed of several concentric rings of different coloured beads. Under her heavy shoulderlength wig,
encircled by a diadem ornamented with rosettes, one catches a
glimpse of her natural hair. The inscription gives her name
and title.
In accordance with the artistic conventions adhered to
throughout Egyptian history, the man's skin is painted a reddish brown, and that of the woman a pale cream colour. The
inlaid eyes (the retina is made of opaque quartz and the pupil
of rock crystal), the perfectly realistic expressions of the faces,
and the admirably preserved colours confer on these statues
such a life-like appearance that Mariette's workmen, at the
moment of their discovery, took fright and fled. The solemn
attitudes of the two figures together with their imposing stature, and the realistic expressions of their countenances, are a
reflection of the dignity and authority of these personages.

*Bibliography: PM IV, p. 90; Borchardt, Statuen und Statuetten (CG),
pp. 3–5, pl. 1; Aldred, Old Kingdom Art in Egypt, p. 28; Vandier,
Manuel III, p. 28; Smith, Art and Architecture, p. 85; Yoyotte, Kunstschätze der Pharaonen, pp. 26–27; Leclant, Les Pharaons I, fig. 179;
Corteggiani, no. 13.*

28a

28b

28   Upper floor, hall 48
Statuette of King Cheops

Ivory   JE 36143
H. 7.5 cm; W. 2.5 cm; profile 2.9 cm
Abydos, excavations of F. Petrie, 1903
Old Kingdom, 4th dynasty, reign of Cheops, ca. 2585–2550 B.C.

This little figure remains by strange coincidence our only complete representation of the great King Cheops. The cartouche carved upon the left side of the throne is completely broken; if the king's Horus name were not preserved upon the right side, one might never have guessed that this diminutive sculpture actually depicts the builder of the greatest of the pyramids.

The piece preserves for us a royal portrait executed with a certain realism: the figure's age is visibly advanced, its pose serene and reserved, a fitting precursor to the immutable majesty apparent in King Chephren's diorite statue (see no. 31). On Cheops's face we find a hint of a smile which, while under certain lighting conditions seemingly disdainful, is hardly cruel, as the later legends of his character would claim.

The enthroned king wears the crown of Lower Egypt and the *shendjyt*, a short, pleated kilt with central tab. In his right hand, clenched firmly over the breast, he holds the ceremonial flail, finely carved here with much attention to detail. The left hand rests flat upon the left thigh.

The statuette was found in a temple at Abydos dedicated originally to the god Khentamentiu and from the end of the Old Kingdom onward to the god Osiris, who thus came to be associated with this local god of the dead. Located on a site which served as the Thinite royal cemetery, the temple of this "Lord of the West" was the beneficiary of a cult which continued almost uninterrupted from the First Dynasty down to the Late Period. Each new reign saw the site embellished or enriched with additional statues, stelae and other monuments.

When the statuette was excavated, three weeks elapsed between the discovery of head and body, which were subsequently reunited.

Bibliography: PM V, p. 46; F. Petrie, Abydos II, 1903, p. 30, pls. 13,14; Lange/Hirmer, pl. 23; Corteggiani, no. 15; Smith, Art und Architecture, fig. 80; Z. Hawass, in: Mélanges Gamal Moukhtar I, Cairo 1985, pp. 379–94, pls. I and III; R. Stadelmann, Die Ägyptischen Pyramiden, pl. 38.

29

29   Upper floor, room 2
Sedan chair of Queen Hetepheres

Wood, ebony (both modern), beaten gold   JE 52372
H. 52 cm; L. 206.5 cm; W. 53.5 cm
Giza, Harvard/Boston expedition, 1925
Old Kingdom, 4th dynasty, reign of Cheops, c. 2585 B.C.

The funerary furniture and other burial objects of the mother of Cheops and wife of Sneferu were discovered at the bottom of a secret tomb shaft on the east side of the Great Pyramid at Giza. The finely carved alabaster sarcophagus, however, was empty; only the canopic chest bore the resinous remains of the queen's viscera. Sneferu's name was found upon a large portable canopy of gilded wood, as well as on the curtain box which accompanied it. The rest of the furniture dates to the reign of Cheops.

The sedan chair displays both a remarkable simplicity of form and a high quality of workmanship. Unfortunately, the wood did not survive the millennia and had to be replaced. The two carrying poles terminate in elegant golden palmiform capitals. Strips of gold chased to resemble a pattern of woven matting cover the chair's edges and borders. A horizontal ebony panel at the front of the backrest and three more vertical ones at the rear are decorated with exquisite golden hieroglyphs, each sign meticulously crafted as an individual work of art. The four identical inscriptions reproduce the name and archaic titles of the queen: "Mother of the King of Upper and Lower Egypt, follower of Horus, controller of the butchers of the acacia house, one for whom everything she says is done, the god's bodily daughter, Hetepheres."

The sedan chair was the preferred mode of transport of the well-to-do. Those who could afford them enjoyed their promenades with knees drawn up to the chest, fan in hand, and a thick cushion for support and comfort. Such representations may actually be found in the relief of the official Ipy (see no. 62), or in the Sakkara tomb of Mereruka.

Bibliography: PM III, 1, pp. 180–81; G. A. Reisner/W. S. Smith, A History of the Giza Necropolis II, Cambridge Mass., 1955, pp. 33–34, pls. 27–29; Propyläen Kunstgeschichte 15, pl. 354. Cf. also: M. Lehner, The Pyramid Tomb of Hetep-heres and the Satellite Pyramid of Khufu, Mainz 1985.

30

Vessels of Hetepheres

Gold
Spouted cup H. 5.2 cm; Diam. 8.5 cm   JE 52404
Dish H. 2.4 cm; Diam. 8.2 cm   JE 52405
Giza, Harvard/Boston expedition, 1925
Old Kingdom, 4th dynasty, reign of Sneferu or Cheops, c. 2585 B.C.

Among the many objects found in the shaft tomb of the queen
were a bed, two chairs, a tubular leather case for walking
sticks, a box, a gilded chest containing silver bracelets inlaid
with precious stones, copper and stone vessels, copper uten-
sils, and a small box containing razors and three golden vessels. Here are two of these vessels, each showing an elegant
clarity of form: a cup with a long, graceful spout, and a small,
flat-bottomed dish.

*Bibliography: Reisner/Smith, A History of the Giza Necropolis II,
p. 45, pl. 40.*

31
Chephren

Diorite   JE 10062
H. 168 cm; W. 57 cm; L. 96 cm   = CG 14
Giza, found in 1860 by Mariette's workmen in the
favissa of Chephren's valley temple
Old Kingdom, 4th dynasty, reign of Chephren, about 2540–2505 B.C.

This extraordinary statue of King Chephren is indisputably a masterpiece of sculpture in the round. The majesty of its pose, the perfection of its modeling and polish and the subtle symbolism of its component parts, make it an ideal manifestation of the Old Kingdom theocratic monarchy. Chephren was the son of Cheops and builder of the second pyramid at Giza. The creation of the great Sphinx is also attributed to him.

The enthroned king rests one hand flat on his knee while in the other he holds a folded piece of material, the ends of which hang down on one side over his leg. He wears the *nemes* headdress with pleated lappets, against which the uraeus at his brow is visible in slightly raised relief. The ceremonial beard, symbol of his royal dignity, is attached to his chin. He is dressed in the short pleated kilt called *shendjyt*.

The throne is a seat supported by two lions whose heads flank the king on each side conferring on him both power and protection, while their paws form its legs. On each side of the throne a motif, sculptured in high relief, symbolizes the union of the Two Lands. It is known as the *sema-tawy* symbol because it consists of the hieroglyphic sign for 'union' *(sema)* around which are knotted the heraldic plants symbolizing the Two Lands *(tawy)*, the lily for the south (Upper Egypt) and the papyrus for the north (Lower Egypt).

Seen from the front, the king's gaze rests far away beyond the ken of those who look upon him and for whom he is a god. But if we go around behind the statue, we discover in the back of the royal headdress, the falcon Horus, god of the sky and dynastic divinity, perched on the back of the throne and protecting the sovereign with his wings. His head, which is slightly higher than the king's, is nevertheless invisible for a person standing in front of the statue. Thus there emerges a close relationship between the sovereign power and the god. The king is the representative of Horus on earth while the god manifests himself in the person of the king, the living Horus.

Bibliography: PM III, 1, p. 22; Smith, Art and Architecture, fig. 107; Lange/Hirmer, pls. 30–31 and IV; Terrace/Fischer, no. 6; Propyläen Kunstgeschichte 15, pls. 126–27; Corteggiani, no. 16; Leclant, Les Pharaons I, fig. 182; R. Stadelmann, Die Ägyptischen Pyramiden, pl. 44.

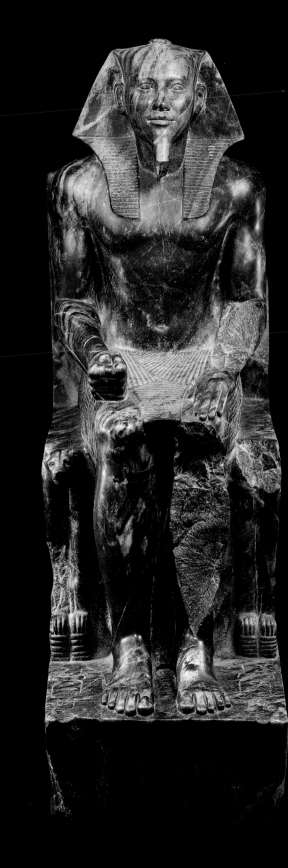

32

which connected it to the burial shaft of the mastaba. They display a natural grandeur, and are usually carved in limestone. They are all close-shaven, as if they wear skull caps, so that it is often difficult to distinguish between masculine and feminine portraits. Although idealized, these representations nevertheless display an individuality and mark the beginning of a tendency toward realism. The ears are usually broken, and lines are incised around the face and at the back of the skull.

One is tempted to see in this type of sculpture a substitute for the head of the deceased (or even the statue), a model after which the artist fashioned his funerary representations, or even a figure helping the spirit to identify the mummy. Perhaps the most plausible suggestion so far proposed is that the naturalistically carved heads were used as a mould for a funerary mask in plaster which would portray the features of the deceased after mummification (see the funerary masks on display in gallery 31). This suggestion would explain the care taken by the sculptor solely on the face itself, and the general absence of color. One might also thus explain the absence of ears (by omission or deliberate removal), as well as the incisions which would have been cut at the time of removal of the mask. The head chosen here, which represents a member of Chephren's family, is characteristic of this type of sculpture. The eyes continue towards the nose in deeply cut lines. The eyebrows are in raised relief, the cheek bones high. The atypical nose and the slightly frowning mouth add to the realistic character of this portrait of a self-assured member of the upper class.

Bibliography: PM III, 1, p. 134; G. A. Reisner, A History of the Giza Necropolis, I, 1942, pls. 50e and 55b, p. 482. Cf. also: A. Shoukry, Die Privatgrabstatue im Alten Reich, Cairo 1951, pp. 45–52; LÄ II, pp. 11–14; N. B. Millet, in: Essays in Honor of Dows Dunham, Museum of Fine Arts, Boston 1981, pp. 129–31.

32   Ground floor, gallery 47
"Reserve head"

Limestone   JE 46216
H. 25.5 cm; W. 18 cm
Giza, western cemetery, mastaba no. G 4240 A;
Harvard/Boston expedition, 1915–16
Old Kingdom, 4th dynasty, c. 2520 B.C.

The mastaba or tomb of a high official in the Old Kingdom was usually built near the pyramid of the king whom he served. The mastabas of the Fourth Dynasty grouped around the pyramids at Giza are constructed of stone. It was always believed that due to a reduced decoration scheme, one had recourse in certain mastabas – and particularly in the west cemetery at Giza – to a portrait of the deceased, or to what are called "reserve heads." These heads were placed at the entrance to the subterranean burial chamber, or in the passage

33   Ground floor, gallery 47
A triad of Mycerinus

Greywacke (schist)   JE 40679
H. 92.5 cm; W. 46.5 cm; L. 43 cm
Giza, Valley temple of Mycerinus, Harvard/Boston expedition, 1908
Old Kingdom, 4th dynasty, reign of Mycerinus, about 2500–2482 B.C.

Four similar group statues, in perfect condition, were found in the valley temple of the pyramid of Mycerinus at Giza. Three of them are on view in the Museum, the fourth and a fragment of a fifth are in the Boston Museum of Fine Arts. They represent Mycerinus accompanied by the goddess Hathor and the personification of a nome (province) of Egypt. It was formerly thought that at the time of Mycerinus there existed thirty or more of these groups one for each of the recognized nomes of the Old Kingdom. However, according to a recent study there would have been only eight groups, corresponding to the eight chapels in the front court of the temple, each triad comprising the statues of Hathor and the King accompanied by the personification of a nome or city in which Hathor was particularly venerated.

33

The triad depicted here represents king Mycerinus wearing the white crown of Upper Egypt, the ceremonial beard and a pleated *shendjyt* kilt. In each hand he holds a cylindrical object. His body is youthful and athletic, the torso delicately modeled, while the anatomy of the legs has been considerably elaborated.

Hathor, the goddess of the sky, of life and of love, standing to the right of the King, is here designated by her most usual epithet: 'Lady of the house of the sycamore', an epithet linked to her cult at Memphis. On her head she wears her characteristic emblem, the solar disk resting between two cow's horns, for as is well known, she can be represented likewise in the form of a cow (see nos. 8 and 138). In her right hand she holds the symbol *shen*, signifying durability and universal energy, while with her left arm she embraces the king. One can see her hand on the latter's left arm. The feminine figure on the other side of the king is the personification of the cynopolite nome (the 17th nome of Upper Egypt). She is identified by the emblem on her head: the jackal-god, patron god of the nome. The inscription on the pedestal in front of her feet specifies that this nome gives the king "all good things among the offerings of Upper Egypt".

Thus these triads represent Hathor associated with the king as guarantor of the fertile products presented by the various nomes for the royal cult.

These exquisitely modeled feminine figures, in their long, tightly-fitting robes, give witness to a substantial anatomical understanding, and the perfect execution of this beautifully curved and polished sculpture is an example of the excellence of the ancient craftsmen's art.

Bibliography: PM III, 1, p. 28; Reisner, Mycerinus, pl. 38, p. 109; Terrace/Fischer, no. 7; W. Woods, A Reconstruction of the Triads of King Mycerinus, in: JEA 60, 1974, pp. 82–93; Corteggiani, no. 17; Nofret – Die Schöne, no. 96.

34

Ground floor, gallery 47

Sarcophagus of a high official

Painted limestone
Total H. 110 cm; W. 97.5 cm; L. 210 cm
JE 54934
Giza, shafts of mastaba G 7340, to the east of the pyramid of Cheops;
Harvard/Boston expedition, 1924–31
Old Kingdom, 4th dynasty, c. 2550 B.C.

The Egyptian sarcophagus was conceived as an eternal mansion housing the body of the deceased. The first known stone sarcophagi derive from royal tombs and are of alabaster, without any decoration, such as the queens' sarcophagi from the funerary complex of Djoser (two sarcophagi identical to these

were discovered at Dahshur, and are on exhibit in gallery 41 of the ground floor), or the sarcophagus of Queen Hetepheres (room 2 on the upper floor). During the Fourth Dynasty at Giza, the king and members of the royal family possessed sarcophagi of granite or limestone whose exterior decoration was carved in imitation of palace architecture, with facade and enclosure wall equipped with gates, niches and open-work windows. The particularly well preserved layer of paint on our example displays the vegetal wattles which adorned the walls of palaces and houses.

A panther skin with some traces of paint has been carved in sunk relief upon the lid of this sarcophagus. Both the tail and the head have been unfolded to lie flat on the lid. The panther skin was generally worn by high priests. We do not know the occupation of the anonymous owner of this sarcophagus, but the second known example of this type belongs to a high official who was not a member of the priesthood. Perhaps the panther skin designates the deceased's wish to have the services of a priest available for all eternity, or even to be able to perform these services himself.

The contemporary sarcophagi from Giza which occupy this gallery are all monoliths. The limestone examples derive from Tura, on the opposite (east) side of the river, while those of granite come from Aswan. The unfinished sarcophagus of Djedefhor, placed just behind this one, tells us much about techniques of production. A rectangular block extracted from the quarry is rough-hewn in place, then rounded on one side to form the lid and hollowed on the other to produce what will become the coffin and so lighten the weight for purposes of transport. In order to avoid any accidents during the journey, the rounded portion is not detached from the base of the coffin until the entire block has arrived at its destination. This also explains why the sarcophagus lid always fits so snugly onto its coffin. The process is completed with the aid of wire saws taken to all four sides of the block simultaneously. It was only inside the finished tomb that the decoration was finally applied. The four tenons cut at the edges of the lid, which rests on two supports, allow it to glide onto the coffin with the aid of a lever, after the body had been placed within. Consequently, these tenons were theoretically intended to be removed.

Bibliography: PM III, 1, p. 192; Gauthier, in: ASAE 30, 1930, p. 177, pl. 3; Bonnet, Reallexikon der ägyptischen Religionsgeschichte, p. 581; Lange/Hirmer, pl. V; A. M. Donadoni Roveri, I Sarcofagi Egizi Dalle Origini Alla Fine Dell'Antico Regno, Roma 1969, pp. 87–89, 123, and pls. 24, 40.

35

35

King Userkaf

Ground floor, gallery 46

Greywacke (schist)   JE 90220
H. 45 cm; W. 25 cm; L. 26 cm
Abusir, solar temple of Userkaf, excavations of a joint expedition of the German and Swiss Institutes in Cairo, 1957
Old Kingdom, 5th dynasty, reign of Userkaf, about 2475–2467 B.C.

This royal head wearing the red crown of Lower Egypt is a striking example of the style marking the beginning of the 5th dynasty which so well succeeded not only in prolonging but likewise in enriching the illustrious heritage left by the preceding dynasty. Userkaf, like his predecessor Shepseskaf, the last king of the 4th dynasty, built his pyramid not at Giza but at Sakkara. In his funerary temple was found the head of the first colossal royal statue known from the Old Kingdom (on view in gallery 47), as well as a number of bas-reliefs of a very high artistic quality (cf. no. 36). Somewhat to the north of Sakkara, in the desert at Abusir, Userkaf built the first of a series of temples dedicated to the sun god, the importance of whose cult had increased considerably during the 4th dynasty. Our statue head, found in the precincts of the sun temple, follows the traditions established in the time of Mycerinus. Its execution exhibits the perfection already attained in the celebrated triads of that King (cf. no. 33) which were likewise sculptured in schist. We can observe in both the same rounded contours of the face and the same fleshy nose. However, the pleasing proportions of the eyes, elongated by a line of eye-paint in low relief (this device is already observable in some of Chephren's statues) and surmounted by prominent eyebrows which follow the curve of the lids, the smooth finish of the face and its beautiful proportions, make this head a work of art worthy of the great fifth dynasty.

At the moment of its discovery, it was suggested that this head was not that of a king but of the goddess Neith of Sais, who

can also wear the red crown. However, despite the unusual delicacy of the visage and the absence of a beard, attested on certain other statues such as those of Khasekhem (no. 14) and Cheops (no. 28), the presence on our head of a very lightly indicated moustache on the upper lip, proves that this is a royal portrait.

Bibliography: PM III, 1, p. 325; H. Ricke, in: Beiträge zur ägyptischen Bauforschung, 8, 1969, p. 139ff.; Terrace/Fischer, no. 9; Götter Pharaonen, no. 7; Leclant, Les Pharaons I, pp. 191–92; R. Stadelmann, Die Ägyptischen Pyramiden, pl. 62.

36
Ground floor, gallery 47

Birds in the marshes

Limestone, originally painted   JE 56001
H. 102 cm; W. 77.5 cm
Sakkara, funerary temple of Userkaf. Excavations of the Egyptian Antiquities Service, 1928
Old Kingdom, 5th dynasty, reign of Userkaf, c. 2475–2467 B.C.

For the first time in a royal funerary temple, scenes from nature form an important part of the wall decoration. Here is a delightful fragment of painted relief from the funerary temple of Userkaf at Sakkara depicting a flock of birds in a papyrus clump. The realistic style permits us without difficulty to recognize: a butterfly, a pied kingfisher hovering in the air and a green kingfisher perched on a flower opposite a night heron, a hoopoe turned towards a purple gallinule, a sacred ibis with his long curved beak and at the very bottom, the head of a bittern.
The details of the relief were line engraved, then plastered and covered with a thin coat of paint. Judging by the traces of the green and ochre colours remaining on the papyrus flowers at the bottom of the panel, the effect must certainly have been striking. It is supposed that the appearance in the royal funerary temple of scenes of this kind, inspired by nature, is linked with the triumph, now become absolute, of the cult of the sun god, the creator of all things.

Bibliography: PM III, 2, p. 398; Firth, in: ASAE 29, 1929, pl. 2, p. 66; Corteggiani, no. 19; Smith, Art and Architecture, pp. 126–27.

37
Ground floor, gallery 36

Divinities bearing offerings (detail)

Painted limestone   RT 6.12.24.9
H. of the register 68 cm; L. 96 cm
Abusir, mortuary temple of Sahure; excavated by L. Borchardt in 1907–8
Old Kingdom, 5th dynasty, reign of Sahure, ca. 2467–2453 B.C.

The mortuary complex of Sahure at Abusir, with its valley temple, ascending causeway and funerary temple adjacent to the pyramid, was without doubt one of the most impressive buildings of the necropolis. We can still admire the successful marriage of colors between the various materials there, such as basalt for the floor, alabaster for the sanctuary floor, limestone for the walls and red granite for the court with portico and papyriform columns. The complex also contained one of the richest programs of relief sculpture ever conceived. Borchardt may only have discovered in situ 2% of these scenes; the rest of them, estimated at some ten thousand square meters of sculpted decoration, have disappeared in the lime kilns of modern times. The remains nevertheless allow us to appreciate the richness and beauty of the decoration.

A suite of six Lower Egyptian fertility gods (three illustrated) once formed part of the procession of various divinities represented in the secondary entrance to the funerary temple. They approach under the starred vault of the heavens, bearing their offerings into the temple. In their outstretched arms they hold the sign of *hetep*-offerings, and the *was*-scepter, symbol of dominion; around their forearms hang several *ankh* signs, symbols of life. The horizontal inscription above the gods identifies them and mentions what they carry.

At the head of the procession, Mehy, "the Northern One," i.e. the personification of Lower Egypt, "giving all life and stability." His name is written with the symbolic Delta papyrus plant, which also serves as emblem above his head. Nekheb, "the budding one," follows, "giving life and dominion." The third figure is the most original: Wadj-wer, "the Great Green," personification of the sea, fresh water marshes and the Fayum lake, appears completely covered in green and blue

waves, while he "gives life." The deities which follow are Hetepet, "the offering," giving dominion; Neper "the Grain," giving life; and Aut-ib, "Joy," also giving life.

These defiles of deities occur in almost all Egyptian temples. Particularly common is Hapi, "the Nile," fertility god par excellence, who supplies the offerings which nourish the entire country.

The black grid-lines still visible on this relief aided the artists of the Late Period, when Sahure's temple was transformed into a sanctuary for the goddess Sekhmet, in copying these representations.

Bibliography: PM III, 1, p. 330; Borchardt, Das Grabdenkmal des Königs Sa3-hu-re^c II, pl. 30; Leclant, Les Pharaons I, fig. 137; J. Baines, Fecundity Figures, 1985, p. 84 ff., fig. 44.

38   Upper floor, hall 48

King Neferefre

Pink limestone   JE 98171
Total approx. H. 34 cm
Abusir, mortuary temple of Neferefre, excavations of the Czechoslovak Institute of Egyptology, 1984–85
Old Kingdom, 5th dynasty, reign of Neferefre, c. 2433–2428 B.C.

Recent excavations in the newly discovered mortuary complex of King Neferefre have proven most successful. They have not only revealed the unfinished pyramid and mortuary temple of unbaked brick, with all of its annexes, but also an important

38a

38b

archival deposit, an extraordinary ensemble of cult objects, collections of seals, and a completely unexpected number of statues providing the richest sample of royal statuary from the Fifth Dynasty.

This statue, which bears many traces of polychromy, is particularly well crafted. Neferefre is seated, his face turned slightly to the right. In his right hand he clutches a broken-headed *hedj* mace against his breast. His head is snugly enclosed with a round valanced wig whose regular waves form concentric circles around the skull, and upon which are incised stylized curls in a fishbone pattern. In the hole provided in front was once inserted the head of the uraeus, most likely of a precious material. Its body winds in four curves carved in low relief on the front of the wig. A false beard with fastening straps delineated in paint adorns the royal chin. The face is youthful with full cheeks. The slightly downcast eyes are bordered by a cosmetic line in black paint, and the folds of the upper eyelids are rendered by an incised line. The eyebrows are indicated in low relief; the naso-labial lines and the corners of the rather full lips fully accentuate the bulge of the muscles. The fleshy mouth is bordered by a delicate edge. The torso is rendered with youthful vigor.

Hidden behind the head of Neferefre, Horus the falcon surrounds the nape of the neck with his wings; his claws grasp two *shen*-rings, symbols of duration.

Despite the fragmentary condition of the lower part of the statue, one can clearly recognize the plaited kilt with central tab, tied around the king's abdomen. A small fragment preserves part of the cube-shaped throne, and an additional piece shows the base upon which the sovereign's feet rest.

Bibliography: M. Verner, in: BIFAO 85, 1985, pp. 272–73, pls. 45–48.

The Dwarf Seneb and his family

Painted limestone   JE 51280
H. 34 cm; W. 22.5 cm; L. 25 cm
Giza, tomb of Seneb. Excavated by H. Junker in 1926–27
Old Kingdom, 4th or beginning of the 5th dynasty, about 2475 B.C.

Two kinds of dwarfs are to be distinguished in ancient Egypt: those who suffered from a pathological deformity occur as early as the first dynasty. They were entrusted with particular tasks, such as the maintenance of the wardrobe, the care of domestic animals and the amusement of their masters. Several were sculptors, jewelers or artisans while others worked in the fields. The second kind are the African pygmies, of normal build though small-statured; these the Egyptians employed in the temples as "dancers before the god" (see no. 90).

The dwarf Seneb was an Egyptian who attained to a high position. He was chief of all the palace dwarfs charged with the care of the royal wardrobe. He was attached in a priestly function to the funerary cults of Kings Cheops and Djedefre of the 4th dynasty. We learn from the inscriptions on the false door of his tomb (exhibited behind the statue) that Seneb was well-off, possessing several thousand head of cattle! We see him there carried in a litter or sailing in a boat in the marshes of the Delta surrounded by his children like any other dignitary.

In this group statue, which was found in the small limestone naos (exhibited in the same showcase), Seneb is seated in the position of a scribe, legs and hands crossed. His deformity, a head and torso exaggeratedly large in proportion to his diminutive arms and legs, is clearly reproduced.

The gentle smile on the visage of his spouse, Senetites, who encircles him with her arms, seems to signify a sentiment of mingled affection and satisfaction. The lady, who is leaning slightly forward, wears a black wig over her natural hair, which remains partly visible, and a long, fitting robe with long sleeves. She was a great lady of the court and held the titles of priestess of Hathor and of Neith.

Seneb's chubby children, a boy and a girl, are depicted in accordance with the iconography established for infants. They are nude, each with a finger to the mouth and a plaited lock of hair hanging down on one side of the head. They are placed in front of their father where his legs would normally have been, thus masking his deformity while at the same time admirably preserving the unity of the composition.

The inscriptions placed on either side of the children and on the horizontal face of the socle give the names and titles of the members of the family.

Bibliography: PM III, 1, p. 102; Junker, Giza V, Vienna/Leipzig 1941, pp. 107–14, frontispiece and pl. 9; Smith, Art and Architecture, fig. 133; Terrace/Fischer, no. 12; Leclant, Les Pharaons I, fig. 197, pp. 200–201; N. Cherpion, in: BIFAO 84, 1984, pp. 34–54, pls. 1–11.

Ka-aper called the "Sheikh el Beled"

Sycamore wood   CG 34
H. 112 cm
Sakkara, mastaba C 8. Discovered by Mariette in 1860, near the pyramid of Userkaf
Old Kingdom, beginning of the 5th dynasty, probably reign of Userkaf, c. 2475–2467 B.C.

This statue is that of a chief lector-priest named Ka-aper. It is, however, more widely known as the "Sheikh el Beled" (in Arabic: "The Headman of the village"), Mariette's workmen having baptized him thus because he resembled the headman of their own village. It is no doubt the most celebrated private statue of the Old Kingdom. It is sculptured life size with a startling realism, which conforms entirely to the ancient Egyptian's wish to create for eternity a true image of himself. This statue is so completely characteristic that the priest seems indeed to live in it forever.
Ka-aper's remarkable physiognomy reflects exactly the degree of social success of a well-to-do and respectable dignitary. On his round head with its full cheeks, his short-cut hair is marked by a slight relief. His eyes are inlaid in copper frames, the white made of opaque quartz and the cornea of rock crystal in which the pupil has been drilled from behind and filled with a black paste visible through the transparent crystal. The medium-length, straight skirt is knotted over his plump stomach. The statue's arms are separately formed and attached to the body, a technique frequently used in wooden statuary; the left arm is made of two pieces joined together. The legs have been restored. The original cane and scepter held in his two hands had disappeared; the cane which he now holds is modern.

Bibliography: PM III, 2, p. 459; Borchardt, Statuen und Statuetten (CG) I, pp. 32–33, pl. 9; Aldred, Old Kingdom Art in Egypt, p. 34; Lange/Hirmer, pls. 58–59; Corteggiani, no. 18. Cf. also: Cl. Vandersleyen, La Date du Cheikh el-Beled, in: JEA 69, 1983, pp. 61–65.

Ka-aper's wife?

Wood   CG 33
H. 61 cm
Sakkara, Mastaba of Ka-aper (C 8). Mariette's excavations in 1860
Old Kingdom, beginning of the 5th dynasty, about 2475–2467 B.C.

This bust is all that was preserved of the standing feminine statue which was found at the entrance to Ka-aper's chapel (see no. 40) in his large brick mastaba at Sakkara. In a realistic style, the statue, originally covered with plaster and painted, is that of a young woman of good family with a serene expression and dignified mien. She wears a wide-spreading wig of medium length which covers her ears. This kind of wig, with parallel strands of hair ending in small curls, and parted in the center, is widely used in representations of

41

42

women during the Old Kingdom. The long, tight-fitting robe is supported by two wide straps sculptured in low relief. A broad collar was originally painted around her neck. The arms of the statue were sculptured separately and attached to the bust by tenons.

Bibliography: PM III, 2, p. 459; Borchardt, Statuen und Statuetten (CG) I, pp. 31–32, pl. 9; Nofret – Die Schöne, no. 20.

42

Ground floor, room 42

Bust of a male statue

Wood
H. 69 cm
JE 10177 = CG 32

Sakkara, discovered in January 1860
Old Kingdom, beginning of the 5th dynasty, about 2475 B.C.

Here is another example of the admirable wooden statuary contemporary with the statue of Ka-aper. The realistic face is

that of a young man, as is the tall slim body, simply and elegantly sculptured. It was originally plastered and painted. The inlaid eyes, and slightly asymmetrical face, the serious mouth and rather haughty bearing, give the portrait a very lively character.

This statue, the lower part of which has been completely destroyed, was found at Sakkara at the beginning of the same year in which the statue of the priest Ka-aper was discovered. Some forty years later, on the basis of other discoveries and without taking into account the circumstances of Mariette's excavations, it was suggested that this statue also came from the tomb of Ka-aper and represented that personage in his youth. This perfectly plausible and very seductive hypothesis has nevertheless remained without firm archaeological foundation; neither has a stylistic study been made to justify the assertion.

Bibliography: PM III, 2, p. 724; Borchardt, Statuen und Statuetten (CG) I, p. 31, pl. 8; J. Capart, in: JEA 6, 1906, pp. 225–33; Vandier, Manuel III, p. 125.

43
The Seated Scribe

Ground floor, room 42

Painted limestone   JE 30272 = CG 36
H. 51 cm; W. 41 cm; profile 31 cm
Sakkara, excavations of the Egyptian Antiquities Service, 1893
Old Kingdom, beginning of the 5th dynasty, about 2475 B.C.

The scribe is here sitting on the ground, his legs crossed. He has partly unrolled a papyrus on his knees, holding the remaining roll in his left hand while with his right he is about to write with a quill pen which has since disappeared.

This statue presents us with the ideal image of a perfect official. Doubtless because the position of scribe was one of the most envied functions in Ancient Egypt, a great many tomb owners from the time of Cheops until the Late Period had themselves represented in the scribal attitude, reading or writing.

We do not know even the name of this scribe, but the intensity of his attentive countenance enlivened by the inlaid eyes and the almost arrogant expression of his face full of realistic detail, make of him a personality as well known as his confrère in the Louvre.

The modeling of the body, painted orange-brown is rather summary and the position of the crossed legs not of the most felicitous. One feels immediately that all of the sculptor's attention was concentrated on the slightly asymmetrical face, its importance emphasized by the style of the wig, the locks of which thrown back over the shoulders leaving the face free.

Bibliography: PM III, 2, pp. 499–500; Borchardt, Statuen und Statuetten (CG) I, pp. 34–35, pl. 9; Lange/Hirmer, pl. 62 and V.

44

Ground floor, room 42

A sitting figure (detail)

Painted limestone   JE 30273 = CG 35
H. 61 cm; W. 21 cm; profile 31 cm
Sakkara, excavations of the Egyptian Antiquities Service, 1893
Old Kingdom, beginning of the 5th dynasty, about 2475 B.C.

This statue found not far from the seated scribe (no. 43), probably represents the same person.
Sitting rather stiffly on a cubical seat, one hand lying flat on his knee and the other holding a rolled object, the personage wears a round wig made up of small curls, and a kilt with the ends pleated and held in place by a belt. The modeling of the body is better than that of the scribe, perhaps because the limestone of which it is cut is of better quality. The head, somewhat too large for the body, is again the most carefully worked part of the statue. The admirable quality of the portrait brings out the individuality of the person. The eyes, made of quartz and rock crystal, are held in a copper framework. Likewise of metal, now very much corroded, were the ornaments attached to the ears.

Bibliography: PM III, 2, p. 500; Borchardt, Statuen und Statuetten (CG) I, pp. 33–34 and pl. 9; Corteggiani, no. 21.

45–46

Ground floor, gallery 31

Ranefer

Painted limestone
45 – H. 178 cm; W. 55.5 cm; L. 81 cm   JE 10063 = CG 19
46 – H. 186 cm; W. 52 cm; L. 90 cm   JE 10064 = CG 18
Sakkara, mastaba 40, excavated by Mariette in 1860
Old Kingdom, beginning of the 5th dynasty, about 2475 B.C.

The presence in the tomb of several representations of the deceased is a custom which we have already noted during the 3rd dynasty, on Hesire's sculptured panels. This practice is extended to sculpture in the round and the 5th dynasty particularly is noted for a series of tombs in which two, three or several statues of the deceased had been deposited. The two life-size statues of the High Priest Ranefer mark a high point in private statuary. They represent their model standing, supported by a back slab, the left leg advanced, and holding in his clenched fists what seem to be a reduced version of the scepter or staff of authority. The two statues differ only in two respects. In one of them Ranefer wears a wide-spreading wig and a short, partly pleated kilt, while in the other his hair is cut short and his skirt is of medium length and overlapping. Photographs of statue no. 46 on whose head a plaster cast of a wig has been placed, when compared with statue no. 45, show that a strong resemblance exists between the two portraits. We remark in these statues the same striving after realism and the same desire for lively expression which marks the statues of Ka-aper and of the scribe.
Ranefer, who was High Priest of Ptah and of Sokar at Memphis, also directed the artists and artisans of the royal workshops. These functions doubtless explain the high quality of his statues, which were found standing in the two niches prepared for them in the back wall of the chapel of his great mastaba at Sakkara. The same chapel also contained a seated statue of his wife Hekenu (exhibited in room 42).

Bibliography: PM III, 2, p. 462; Mariette, Mastabas, p. 123; Borchardt, Statuen und Statuetten (CG) I, pp. 19–20, pl. 5; Vandier, Manuel III, pp. 121–22; Smith, A History of Egyptian Sculpture and Painting in the Old Kingdom, Boston 1949, p. 49, pl. 18; Propyläen Kunstgeschichte 15, pl. 133; Terrace/Fischer, no. 10; Leclant, Les Pharaons I, p. 195.

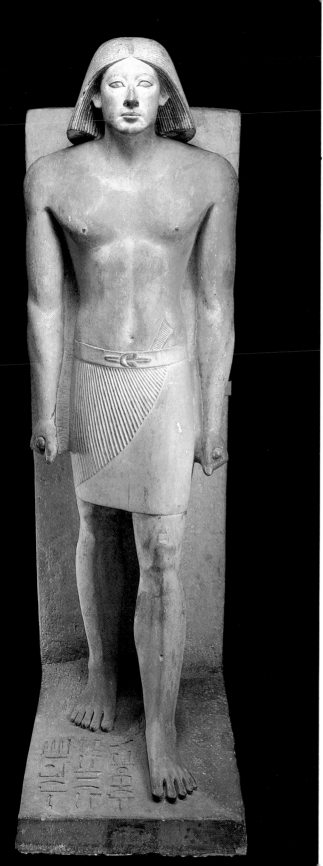

ance with a well-known technique. Here, the rock crystal often used for the pupils is replaced by opaque obsidian.

On the upper surface of the base are engraved the names and titles of the master and of his cult servant.

Bibliography: PM III, 2, p. 478; Borchardt, Statuen und Statuetten (CG) I, p. 91 and pl. 9; Aldred, Old Kingdom Art in Egypt, pl. 44; Leclant, Les Pharaons I, fig. 199.

48

Double statue of Nimaatsed

Painted limestone   CG 133
H. 57 cm; W. 29.5 cm; L. 17.5 cm
Sakkara, mastaba D 56 excavated by Mariette in 1860
Old Kingdom, 5th dynasty, not earlier than Niuserre, about 2428–2325 B.C.

Nimaatsed, who was attached to the cult of Re and of Hathor in the solar temple of Neferirkare, likewise held the positions of judge and prophet in the pyramids of Neferirkare, Neferefre and Niuserre.

His mastaba at Sakkara contained a number of statues, among which was this impressive group, composed of two portraits of Nimaatsed himself.

These two similar statues, united by a common back slab, differ only by a slight discrepancy in height. Nimaatsed is standing, his arms hanging at his sides, holding a small staff in each hand. As always in masculine statues, the left leg is advanced, giving a certain balance to the composition and an impression of movement.

He wears a wide stranded black wig divided by a central parting, which leaves the ears partly uncovered and falls onto the shoulders. The eyes, eyebrows and small moustache are painted black. Around his neck is painted a polychrome necklace. His skin is an ochre color. The firmly modeled torso is expressive of youth, but the legs, on the contrary, are delineated in a harsher style. The overlap of the white kilt which ends just above the knees is pleated and painted yellow and is secured by a tab outlined in black which passes under the belt.

The meaning of these double or sometimes triple effigies which we call "Pseudo-groups" is not clear. There is no doubt that we have here several representations of the same person grouped together on a single base. But if they were meant to depict the person at different ages, this distinction is not always perceptible to the eye, except possibly as a slight difference in height. Such a pseudo-group could also represent the person in company of his *ka* or *kas*. Whatever the solution, our two statues have the advantage of having preserved their marvelous colours which accentuate their beauty and their realistic quality and thus render the noble Nimaatsed doubly lifelike.

Bibliography: PM III, 2, pp. 584–85; Borchardt, Statuen und Statuetten (CG) I, pp. 99–100 and pl. 30; Hornemann, Types IV, pl. 1094; Vandier, Manuel III, pp. 85–89.

47

The Funerary Priest Kaemked

Plastered and painted limestone   CG 119
H. 42 cm; W. 15.5 cm; L. 22.5 cm
Sakkara, tomb of the treasurer Urirni (no. 62), excavated by Mariette in 1860
Old Kingdom, 5th dynasty, not earlier than Neferirkare, about 2453–2325 B.C.

Kaemked was the funerary priest of the noble Urirni, in whose mastaba were found a number of statuettes of women kneading dough, and of a servant cleaning a jar, which accompanied the rather conventional statues of Urirni himself.

Curiously enough, this statue of the funerary priest is more distinguished than those of his master. Kneeling with his hands crossed on his lap, Kaemked is wearing a wide wig composed of long locks, and a short kilt the overlap of which is pleated. The kilt, held in place by a belt, is ornamented over the front panel with four pendant strings of beads each finishing in a tassel.

The rather large head with heavy features gains a certain liveliness through the wide open eyes framed in copper, in accord-

the food offerings and incense brought by the priests each day, as is shown on each side of the slot cut in the wall in front of the statue. Ty appears in all his dignity, upright, with a youthful body, his left foot forward as if he is about to step out into life. He wears a round wig with tiers of small curls which covers the ears, and a starched kilt with front panel. In both hands he carries a short staff or rolled object. His skin, as well as the back pillar, is painted in ochre, the kilt is white.

This statue is exceptionally tall, but the quality of the sculpture is far from equalling that of the masterly bas-reliefs of his mastaba.

Bibliography: PM III, 2, pp. 477–78; Borchardt, Statuen und Statuetten (CG) I, pp. 20–21, pl. 5; Steindorff, Das Grab des Ti, Leipzig 1913, pl. 1, pp. 142–43.

50   Ground floor, gallery 47

Meresankh and his wife

Painted limestone   JE 66619
H. 49.5 cm; W. 28 cm; L. 18 cm
Giza, mastaba of Meresankh, excavated by Selim Hassan in 1929–30
Old Kingdom, end of the 5th dynasty, about 2325 B.C.

The statues from the tomb of Meresankh at Giza form an ensemble characteristic of private statuary of the end of the 5th dynasty. They represent the deceased in various ways: alone, as a double statue of himself, or accompanied by members of his family; also included are models of the servants of his household (see no. 52).

This charming couple, without inscriptions, found in one of the serdabs, probably represents Meresankh and his wife. They are standing side by side, the woman's hand resting delicately on the shoulder of her husband. The man wears a tight wig with small curls and a wide kilt with loose overlap; the woman has a flared wig and a long tight robe held up by two shoulder straps. Each one wears a wide collar of blue beads painted around the neck.

Their rounded visages are gentle and good-natured, and despite their conventional attitudes the couple appear full of life.

The good state of preservation of the polychrome painting enables us to realize to what extent such statues were endowed with a lifelike quality which permitted them to represent their models in the after-life and to have a claim to their part of the funerary offerings.

Bibliography: PM III, 1, p. 270; S. Hassan, Excavations at Gîza (I) 1929–30, Oxford 1932, pp. 115–16, pl. 73; Vandier, Manuel III, p. 74.

49   Ground floor, room 32

Ty, the Rich (detail)

Painted limestone   JE 10065 = CG 20
H. 198 cm; W. 48 cm; L. 78 cm
Sakkara, mastaba of Ty (no. 60), discovered by Mariette in 1860
Old Kingdom, 5th dynasty, reign of Niuserre, about 2428–2398 B.C.

Ty, a high official of considerable wealth and one of the most influential personages of the court, was in charge of two 5th dynasty pyramids and several solar temples. His large mastaba at North Sakkara is renowned for its admirable painted bas-reliefs which depict the various activities carried on in his numerous domains and workshops, and the different kinds of offerings being brought from them to the master.

The statue of Ty was found standing in the *serdab* hidden behind the south wall of the offering chapel. Here it received

51   Ground floor, gallery 47

Meresankh and his two daughters

Painted limestone   JE 66617
H. 43.5 cm; W. 21 cm; L. 20.5 cm
Giza, mastaba of Meresankh excavated by Selim Hassan in
1929–30
Old Kingdom, end of the 5th dynasty, about 2325 B.C.

Here Meresankh is depicted with his two daughters, each of whom embraces him with one arm while placing the other hand on one of his arms. The elder is named Iymeret, the younger Hathor-wer. The father holds the title of Director of funerary priests. The proportions of the figures are awkward. The rather puffy faces are placed atop of thin bodies with very long legs and large feet. Nevertheless, the little family group has a touching charm, and the asymmetry created by the difference in height between the two girls gives it a certain originality.

Bibliography: PM III, 1, p. 270; S. Hassan, Excavations at Gîza I, p. 116 and pl. 74; Vandier, Manuel III, p. 78, pl. 26.

52   Ground floor, gallery 47

Figurine of a female brewer

Painted limestone   JE 66624
H. 28 cm; W. 10 cm; L. 16 cm
Giza, mastaba of Meresankh excavated by Selim Hassan in
1929–30
Old Kingdom, end of the 5th dynasty, about 2325 B.C.

Figures of servants at work reproduce in the round themes usually depicted in the reliefs. Funerary statuary is in this way enriched by the inclusion of figures belonging to the milieu of the master's household: brewers, millers, bakers, potters and butchers, who continue to contribute their daily services in the next world.
Although these figurines are generally mediocre in style, they are nevertheless lively and expressive, accurately depicting the activities of each craft. The

earliest limestone models known to us date to the 4th dynasty, but the majority belong to the 5th dynasty.

Here we have a robust female brewer with a heavy, rather uncouth face, who is energetically kneading the dough made of moistened bread in a strainer placed over a large jar with a short spout. The beer was produced by fermenting the barley bread in water, perhaps sprinkled with a little date liquor. Our brewer is nude from the waist upwards, wearing a half-length skirt and a roughly painted bead collar around her neck. Her head is raised as if she were in conversation with someone.

Bibliography: PM III, 1, p. 270; S. Hassan, Excavations at Gîza I, p. 115 and pl. 71; Lange/Hirmer, pl. VII; Leclant, Les Pharaons I, fig. 198; Nofret – Die Schöne, no. 40.

53   Ground floor, gallery 47

Man coating a jar with clay

Painted limestone   CG 112
H. 13 cm; W. 18 cm; L. 28 cm
Sakkara, mastaba of Ptahshepses (no. 49), excavated by Mariette in 1860
Old Kingdom, 5th dynasty, about 2325 B.C.

The servant is seated on a block of wood or a low stone, his legs spread apart to leave room for the jar which he is holding with one hand while with the other he is coating the interior with clay for the better conservation of the beer with which it will be filled. In front of him three oval depressions cut into the base of the statue mark the place where three more jars, now disappeared, were lying.

The man's close cropped hair is painted black. He wears a short kilt marked in light relief. His body is coarsely modeled but the face on the contrary is relatively carefully carved.

Bibliography: PM III, 2, p. 464; Borchardt, Statuen und Statuetten (CG) I, p. 87, pl. 25; H. Breasted Jr., Egyptian Servant Statues, Bollingen Series XIII, Washington 1948, p. 46.

53

54   Ground floor, gallery 47

Kaemheset

Painted limestone   JE 44174
H. 50 cm; W. 16.5 cm; L. 24 cm
Sakkara, tomb of Kaemheset, excavations of the Egyptian Antiquities Service directed by Quibell, 1912
Old Kingdom, 5th dynasty, about 2300 B.C.

Here is a particularly agreeable example of conventional private statuary which is notable for its good execution and excellent state of preservation.

The sprightly face is noticeably asymmetrical, the body strongly built and of good proportions. It is above all to its colours — red ochre for the skin, yellow ochre for the skirt, blue for the beads of the necklace and black for the wig, eyes and small moustache — that the statue owes its attractiveness. Kaemheset's name is painted in white on the black background of the base.

The statuette was found in the tomb of Kaemheset with a second, group statue, representing him with his wife and young son (on view in room 42). Kaemheset had the titles of royal architect and chief of sculptors, which explains the fine quality of his statue.

Bibliography: PM III, 2, p. 542; Quibell/Hayter, Teti Pyramid, North Side, Excavations at Saqqara, Cairo 1927, pl. 29 and pp. 18, 44.

55

Ground floor, room 32

The wife of Mitri ▷

Wood, stuccoed and painted   JE 51738
H. 150 cm; W. 35 cm; L. 20 cm
Sakkara, mastaba of Mitri; excavation of the Egyptian Antiquities
Service, 1925–26
Old Kingdom, end of the 5th dynasty – beginning of the 6th dynasty,
c. 2325 B.C.

Eleven wooden statues filled the serdab (funerary chapel) of
the mastaba of Mitri, which was discovered intact to the
southeast of Djoser's enclosure wall at Sakkara. Mitri was an
official of high rank whose titles include: administrator of the
nome, priest of the goddess Maat, great one of the Tens of
Upper Egypt, unique companion and overseer of scribes.
The majority of the statues from his serdab represent Mitri
and his wife. Five of the better preserved examples are on display in this Museum, five others are now in the Metropolitan
Museum of Art in New York, and the eleventh is on exhibit in
the Museum of Stockholm. In the same room one can see the
statue of Mitri as a scribe with inlaid eyes which never fail to
catch the visitor's attention. Among the group was also found
a statuette of a hunchback (on exhibit in gallery 47), perhaps
a servant of the household. Mitri's wife bore the title of priestess of Hathor. Her large figure here is carved from a single
block of wood. This fact undoubtedly accounts for the rigid
pose: the arms, though free of the body, hang close to the
sides, and the shoulders are cramped. Is it to adapt to the
width of the block that the face turns gently toward the left
shoulder, or does she glance in the direction of the statue of
her husband? Whatever the case may be, the interrupted symmetry does not lack originality, and the statue certainly gains
something in the way of presence.
The lady wears an elegant striated wig which falls in three sections over the shoulders and back. Its central part is carefully
concealed by a delicately tressed lock. A long narrow garment
hugs the body and stops at the shins. The large collar around
her neck is weighed down by a pectoral suspended from a
band of beads; two bracelets cover the wrists.
The face is perhaps severe but nonetheless impressive. The
body is exaggeratedly long, but a concern for elaborate modelling is readily apparent. This piece derives from a period
when statuary consciously diversified its expression, physiognomy and poses. By individualizing, it attempted to break out
of the rather hieratic canon and standardization of the previous dynasty.

*Bibliography: PM III, 2, p. 632; C. M. Firth, in: ASAE 26, 1926,
p. 101, and pl. 5; cf. the other statues on display in the Metropolitan
Museum of Art, New York: Hayes, Scepter I, p. 110, figs. 64–65; for
the Stockholm statue: B. Peterson, in: Medelhavsmuseet Bulletin 19,
Stockholm 1984. pp. 10–18.*

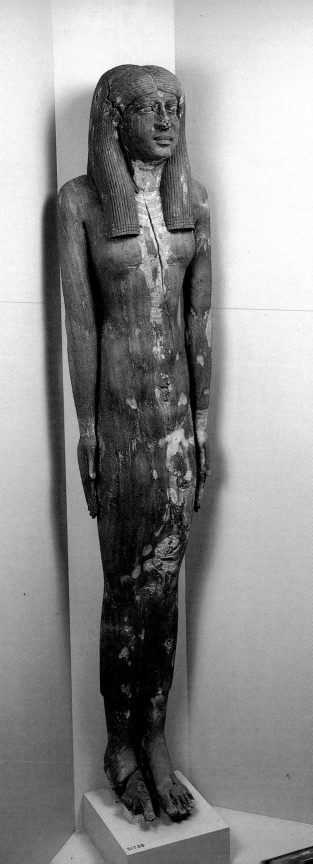

56   Ground floor, gallery 47

The Memphite family of Nefer-herenptah called Fifi

Painted limestone
Standing statue of Fifi H. 65 cm   JE 87804
Standing statue of Sat-meret H. 53 cm   JE 87806
Seated statue of Tesen H. 37 cm   JE 87805
Seated statue of Meretites H. 39 cm   JE 87807
Giza, mastaba of Nefer-herenptah, excavated by S. Hassan in 1936
Old Kingdom, end of the 5th dynasty − beginning of the 6th dynasty, c. 2325 B.C.

Nefer-herenptah called Fifi was a purification priest and prophet of the mortuary cults of Chephren and Mycerinus. Four *ka*-statues of the members of his family were discovered in the serdab of his tomb. The largest statue of Nefer-herenptah shows him standing, his body stiff and supported by a back pillar. He wears traditional costume: a wig with curls, bead necklace and plain short kilt. His imposing stature is marked by a stylized musculature, while the large face betrays a rather awkward attempt at genuine portraiture. The painted eyes, with blue irises, are surmounted by long eyebrows which follow the curve of the eyes. The nose is fleshy and a fine moustache is delineated above the lips.

The wife of Fifi, "the royal acquaintance" Sat-meret, stands with legs together and arms closely hugging the body. Her wig with long tressed locks and central part reveals her underlying natural hair in front. A full-length sleeveless garment hugs her body. Around her neck she wears a band, a broad collar of polychrome beads and an open-work rectangular pectoral. Her full face is treated similarly to that of her husband, but careful modelling of her body relieves the figure of conventional stiffness.

The son of Fifi, called Tesen (Itisen), butcher in the palace slaughterhouse sits erect on a backless cube seat in traditional pose wearing a round wig with little curls. The hasty and schematic rendering is further evidenced by the collar which was never painted. Nevertheless, care has been taken to display the wavy pleats of the kilt's overlapping fold, a fashionable style of dress at this period. The daughter Meretites, also seated on such a seat, wears a tressed wig and long garment similar to those of her mother. The loss of color exposes the formalism of this thoroughly conventional sculpture.

The statues were arranged in the serdab in the following order: son, daughter, father, mother (from left to right).

Bibliography: PM III, 1, p. 253; S. Hassan, Excavations at Gîza (V) 1933−34, Cairo 1944, pp. 279−87, figs. 143−50; P. Ghalioungui, in: BIFAO 62, 1964, pp. 63−64.

57 False door of Nikaure
Ground floor, room 42

Painted limestone
H. 227 cm; W. 235 cm
Sakkara; 1885
Old Kingdom, 5ᵗʰ dynasty, reign of Neferirkare, c. 2453 B.C.

CG 1414

False doors played an important part in the architecture of Old Kingdom tombs. Erected in the chapel of the funerary cult, they functioned magically as actual doors through which the deceased could communicate with the world of the living and receive offerings and prayers necessary for his survival in the next world.

This element started out as a simple niche, but eventually grew to resemble an actual door with a frame, a drum representing a rolled-up mat and even a window above the lintel. In front of this door was a table which contained the offerings deposited by the living.

In the event that the provision of offerings was neglected, the deceased could make do with the funerary formulae and offering lists inscribed in imperishable stone. Most important, however, was the perpetuation of his name and titles on the available surfaces, especially on the tablet which dominated the top of the door, showing, as if through an open window, the interior of the eternal dwelling. Seated before a table laden with loaves of bread, the deceased could partake forever of all the offerings represented, a motif borrowed from the earliest stelae from the Memphite region. In the form of rectangular stone slabs set into the niches or the ceiling of the chapel, they already portrayed at that early period the funerary repast.

This false door is a beautifully decorated piece from the tomb of the judge, overseer of envoys, and chief administrator of the palace, Nikaure. The chapel of his funerary cult contained two false doors, one intended primarily for Nikaure, the second, illustrated here, for his wife Ihat, who was a priestess of Hathor. It is her figure which appears in the niche, and her name and titles which are carved above her and on the drum of the door. Ihat is surrounded by her entire household, children and cult-servants included. On the jambs of the door, facing toward the niche appear Ihat on the left and her husband dressed as a priest on the right, accompanied by their two daughters. Below these approach their sons, each one represented naked, wearing the sidelock of youth and holding a bird by the wings. The exterior jambs show Ihat on the left embracing her mother, and on the right sniffing a lotus flower, while her eldest son extends his arm around her legs. At the bottom, a harpist plays along with a singer, and a priest and priestess serve the cult from outside the tomb.

Above, the couple is depicted seated facing each other over an offering table, flanked by their two children. Still further up, on the lintel, they appear again seated side by side before a long list of offerings.

Bibliography: PM III, 2, p. 697; L. Borchardt, Denkmäler des Alten Reiches (CG) I, pp. 80–84, pl. 19; Vandier, Manuel II, 1, p. 416, fig. 280. Cf. also: S. Wiebach, Die ägyptische Scheintür, Hamburger Ägyptologische Studien 1, 1981; LÄ V, 563–71.

False door of Ika

Acacia wood   JE 72201
H. 200 cm; W. 150 cm
Sakkara; excavations of the Egyptian Antiquities Service, 1939
Old Kingdom, 5th dynasty, before the time of Unas, 2475–2355 B.C.

Here is a rare wooden version of the false door common to tombs of the Old Kingdom (see no. 57). The different elements of the door have been assembled in this case by means of tenons, pegs and leather thongs. We can thus confirm that the drum over the entrance was in fact a roll fixed in the recess of the door.

The owner of this false door was Ika, royal *wab*-priest and chief of the Great House. His wife Iymeret was priestess of Hathor. In the tablet scene above, we see them seated face to face at a table laden with loaves of bread. Below, they appear again standing with their children in the niche and on the jambs. On the right hand jamb, Iymeret sniffs a lotus blossom and wears a long dress with shoulder-straps which leave her shoulders and breast exposed. The bold figure cut by Ika, is portrayed wearing a short kilt with a finely plaited zigzag pattern, and holding a staff and a scepter, both attributes of his rank.

Accompanying all the representations are the couple's names and titles carved in sunk relief. On the jambs and the two lintels, offering formulae are reserved for the husband. The upper lintel reads: "An offering which the king and Anubis, foremost of the divine booth, give that he [Ika] might be buried in the necropolis, the royal acquaintance, Ika." On the lower lintel is written: "An offering which the king gives, that there might be made for him offerings of bread and beer, oxen and fowl for the royal acquaintance, chief of the Great House, Ika." On the left jamb: "An offering which Anubis gives, that he [Ika] might proceed upon the beautiful paths upon which the revered ones proceed, under the great god." On the right: "An offering which the king gives, that invocation-offerings might be made for him [Ika] [consisting of] bread, beer and fowl, on the first of the year festival, the festival of Thoth, the first day of the year, the Wag festival, the festival of Sokar and every festival every day."

In front of the false door a stone libation basin provided the only other funerary equipment from this tomb, which was built of mud brick. Like many other tombs, it was later filled in, in the reign of Unas, who buried them under the causeway which connected his valley temple to his mortuary temple.

Bibliography: PM III, 2, p. 637; Zaki Saad, in: ASAE 40, 1940, pp. 675–80, pl. 73 and 74; Leclant, Les Pharaons I, fig. 109.

Reliefs from the mastaba of Kaemrehu

Painted limestone   CG 1534
H. 97 cm; W. 235 cm
Sakkara, mastaba D 2; excavations of Mariette
Old Kingdom, end of the 5th dynasty, c. 2325 B.C.

This fragment of relief sculpture comes from the funerary chapel wall of a mastaba whose decoration now rests for the most part in the Ny Carlsberg Glyptothek in Copenhagen. Kaemrehu, the mastaba's owner, held the title, among others, of priest of the pyramid of Niuserre at Abusir.

Conforming to the decorative program of mastabas of the Old Kingdom, the scenes here portray aspects of daily life caught in motion and intended to describe the origins, materials and manufacture of all objects and offerings expected in the next world. Through the magic of imagery the representations would perpetuate forever the existence all these products. We are thus granted the unique opportunity to observe scribes, artists and craftsmen all engaged in their daily routines.

The four registers preserved depict in descending order scenes of fieldwork, brewing, baking and various crafts. From the left to the right we see:

1) A threshing scene: donkeys watched over by two men trample the ears of grain deposited on the threshing-floor. Peasants working with pitchforks heap the chaff into piles, and winnowers proceed to separate the wheat.

2) The harvest is measured into bushels under the careful supervision of scribes and overseers. Further to the right, foremen forcefully introduce two individuals before the administrative authorities seated in front of the granary portico and taking notes on the report being made.

3) Jars of beer are refilled after their interiors have been coated with clay. Bread batter is being watered down. After baking (not shown), it is then brewed and kneaded through a sieve into a large vessel resting on a stand. Nearby, dough is kneaded and formed into loaves. A woman sifts out the grain which two men and another woman grind with a pestle in a tall mortar. The pile of crushed grains is next cleaned again by a woman who removes by hand the last impurities. Another woman presses the meal through a sifter while the miller facing her grinds the grain in a trough. The dough is then made to rise; it is placed in the oven, moulded into bell-shaped forms and heaped on the fire which a woman stokes while protecting her face from the flame.

4) Carpenters are at work. Two dwarfs work gold into moulds. A blacksmith beats the metal, which two others have just blown. The metal is weighed at the right under the

observance of a scribe. Two sculptors chisel away at a statue, which is then polished with hard stones. The stone vases, which the artisan to the right has just hollowed out with a drill, are also being polished.

Some of the scenes are provided with hieroglyphic texts which serve as legends to the activities, such as "filling the beer," "straining," "stirring," or "sorting the grain." They also express snatches of dialogue between individuals, not unlike the "bubble captions" of modern day comic strips. The assistant says, for example, to the miller: "Grind it well. I have finished with the flour." The miller responds: "Hey! I am grinding with all my strength."

Bibliography: PM III, 2, p. 486; Borchardt, Denkmäler des Alten
Reiches (CG) I, pp. 232–35, pl. 48; M. Mogensen, Le Mastaba Egyp-
tien de la Glyptothèque Ny Carlsberg, Paris 1921; Vandier, Manuel
IV, pp. 272–96; Corteggiani, no. 23. Cf. also: R. Drenkhahn, Die
Handwerker und ihre Tätigkeiten im Alten Ägypten, Ägyptologische
Abhandlungen 31, Wiesbaden 1976.

60
Sporting competition

Ground floor, room 32

Painted limestone
W. 145 cm
Sakkara, from an unknown tomb
Old Kingdom, 5th dynasty, c. 2400 B.C.

JE 30191
= CG 1535

Sports and games form part of the repertoire of scenes of daily life which developed in the decoration of private tombs, along with religious and biographical texts. Here we see a sportive combat between boatmen in a small stream or pond full of

water-lilies. Such nautical games were usually performed in the presence of the master and his family during an outing to visit his estates in the Delta marshes.

The men wrestle using long poles with forked ends to strike at their opponents. Each figure is slim and wears a short wig, with the exception of the two bald men in the skiff at right. Their clothing consists only of light aprons to allow them free movement.

The game is portrayed with realism and animation. One of the men has fallen into the water; another helps to drag him back on board. The others strike at their opponents with fiery spirit. Even their cries are registered in the inscription which labels the scene. One of them encourages his fellow by shouting "Hack his back," while a second says "Smash his noggin," and a third cries "How's that? You are falling into the field!" The skiffs are loaded with sacks of fruit. It is uncertain whether they represent the stakes involved in this challenge, or if victory belonged to the team which could keep its fruit "afloat" on board the longest.

Bibliography: Borchardt, Denkmäler des Alten Reiches (CG) I, p. 236, pl. 49; Terrace/Fischer, no. 11. Cf. also: Vandier, Manuel V, pp. 510–31; A. D. Touny/S. Wenig, Der Sport im Alten Ägypten, Leipzig 1969, pp. 63–64.

61

62

Bas-reliefs from the mastaba of Ipy (details)

Limestone   CG 1536 and 1537
H. 112 cm
South Sakkara
Old Kingdom, 6th dynasty, reign of Pepi I, c. 2281–2241 B.C.

We have seen the magic of images could eternally renew provisions indispensable to the deceased's survival by bringing wall reliefs and paintings symbolically to life.
Accompanied here by the members of his family, Ipy surveys the various activities of his estate. The scenes are divided into four registers (illustration above), which we will consider from the bottom upwards. The first register contains a butchery scene. Above this appears the cutting of the first flax of the year, a product necessary for the manufacture of clothing, sheets, and rope for nets used in fishing and fowling. The men uproot the flax by the stem, and the binders arrange them in regular sheaves before placing them on the ground. The harvest appears in the next register, depicting grains of either barley or emmer. While the harvesters busy themselves with cutting the stalks of grain, two men converse with each of the two superiors who frame the scene with staves in hand. In the topmost register, the sheaves are tied up and stacked. The farmers gather them in sacks before loading them onto donkeys whom they strive to calm with patting or a few stalks of grain.
Another scene shows the tomb-owner inspecting the port where his fleet of transport ships is visible. For this outing, Ipy has chosen the most comfortable means of travel; the sedan chair (illustration below). Cutting a dignified pose, Ipy surveys the scene from a large, high-backed and cushioned chair, his feet resting on a low footstool. He sports a wig with small curls, a large collar, a kilt with a well-starched triangular frontal tab and a panther skin attached at the left shoulder. In one hand he holds a small baton, in the other a fly whisk. He sits under an assembled canopy, and the two poles which support it are borne by two rows of seven men, directed by a foreman. The overlapping of each pair of bearers is skilfully rendered; this method of representation remained fundamental to Egyptian art at all periods. Flanking this procession are sunshade bearers advancing with hasty strides, while the entire household, even the family dog, takes part in the event.

Bibliography: PM III, 2, pp. 671–72; L. Borchardt, Denkmäler des Alten Reiches (CG) I, pp. 237–42, pl. 50; Corteggiani, no. 28. Cf. also: Vandier, Manuel IV, pp. 328–40.

61

Entertainment scene

Painted limestone   JE 28504
H. ca. 70 cm (detail); W. 111.5 cm   = CG 1533
Sakkara, tomb of Nenkhefetka (D. 47);
brought to the Museum in September, 1888
Old Kingdom, 5th dynasty, c. 2400 B.C.

Egyptian tombs usually reflect the wealth and social status of their owners. The scenes of daily life carved or painted upon tomb walls served to recall the deceased's life in this world. They formed a pleasant surrounding in which he could participate with his loved ones.
Here is the entertainment scene which generally accompanied the funeral repast. An orchestra of male musicians is seated in the upper register. They play the harp, double clarinet and flute, while others beat the time by snapping their fingers or slapping one hand upon their knee. The singer places one hand behind the ear and keeps time with the other, much as modern musicians do today.
In the lower register are female dancers with tall, slender figures and arms raised. They wear short hair and flared kilts supported by two crossed suspenders. Two women standing at the right enliven the dance by clapping their hands.

Bibliography: PM III, 2, pp. 580–81; Borchardt, Denkmäler des Alten Reiches (CG) I, pp. 231–32, pl. 47. Cf. also: Vandier, Manuel IV, pp. 364–417.

62 a

62 b

63

Pepi I (detail)

Copper   JE 33034
H. 177 cm
Hierakonpolis (Kom el-Ahmar). Found by Quibell in 1897–98
Old Kingdom, 6th dynasty, reign of Pepi I, about 2281–2241 B.C.

This life size statue of King Pepi I is an exceptionally well preserved example of copper statuary which, according to the
Palermo stone, was known as early as the 2nd dynasty. It was
discovered buried under the floor of a lateral chapel in the
temple of Hierakonpolis together with a statue of King Khasekhem (see no. 14) and a terra cotta figure of a lion. Inside this
statue, which is hollow, was found a smaller figure, also of
copper, representing Pepi I's son (?); the two statues originally
stood side by side on a single base before being dismantled
and buried.

As concerns the technique, it is thought that the metal was
hammered into shape over a wooden core to which it was
nailed. The kilt and the headdress were made separately, probably of plaster, and were perhaps gilded. This procedure re-
calls that used for wooden statues, which, moreover, often
repeat the same attitude: the left hand stretched out in front
holding a cane, the right hand hanging by his side.
The particularly elongated body is unfortunately much corroded. The relatively small head is treated realistically and
Pepi's expression strikes us as rather grave. The elongated eyes
are enlivened as usual by stone inlays (limestone and obsidian).

Bibliography: PM V, p. 193; Quibell/Green, Hierakonpolis II,
London 1902, pls. 50–54, pp. 27–28, 45–47; Vandier, Manuel III,
pp. 34–35; Lange/Hirmer, pl. 80; Leclant, Les Pharaons I, p. 203;
Smith, Art and Architecture, pp. 146–47; Corteggiani, no. 26.

64

Statuette of Merire-hashetef

Ebony
H. 73 cm; W. 12.5 cm; L. 38 cm
Sedment, tomb of Merire-hashetef, excavations of the British School
of Archaeology in Egypt, directed by Petrie in 1920–21
Old Kingdom, middle of the 6th dynasty, about 2230 B.C.

JE 46992

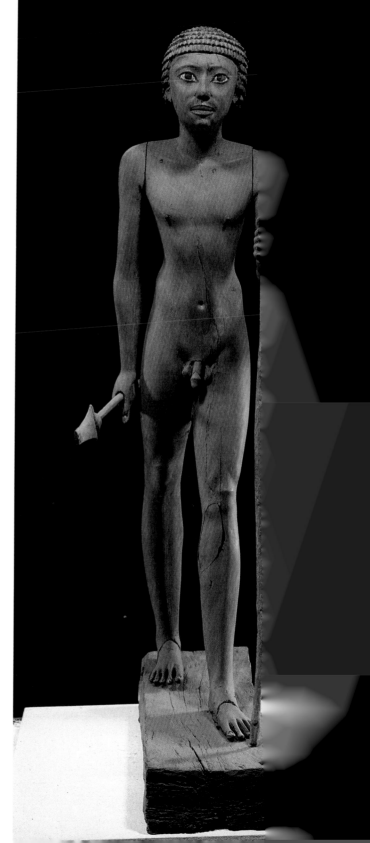

Provincial funerary art closely imitates that of the court, and
the less important cemeteries, with some variation, show the
same desire to construct an eternal world as is seen in the
great official necropoleis. Because of the configuration of the
local terrain, or perhaps in order to economize on building
stone, provincial tombs are often rock tombs cut into the
cliffs; possibly they were influenced by the tradition already to
be recognized at Giza during the 4th dynasty.

The tomb of Merire-hashetef in the necropolis of Sedment,
was cut at the foot of a hill. A courtyard gives access on the
one hand to a rock cut chamber in which were found three
coffins containing female skeletons, and on the other hand to
a deep pit which led to the underground burial chamber of
Merire-hashetef himself, likewise buried in a coffin.

Three quarters of the way up amidst the debris blocking the
pit was found a group of statues aligned according to decreas-
ing height: three statues of the deceased and a fourth statue of
a woman, were surrounded by three groups of servant figures
going about their occupations.

Here is one of three similar statues representing Merire-hashetef at various periods of his life. Next to the statue which
appears to depict him in early youth (now in the British
Museum) and to that which shows him in the prime of life
(now at the Glyptothek, Copenhagen), our statue, the largest,
depicts a young man with a tall, admirably modeled body. He
is nude, wearing only a short curled wig and holding a cane
and scepter of authority. His visage is expressive and realistic,
the eyes wide open, the cheeks well drawn, the chin strongly
marked. The lean body is elegantly sculptured, the collar-
bones, hips and knees treated with great care, the muscles har-
moniously indicated and the fingers and toes beautifully
worked. The male member is circumcised. As in most wooden
statues, the arms, made separately, are held in place at the
shoulders by tenons. The nipples are small inlaid pieces of
wood.

During the 6th dynasty, private statuary continues to follow
the realistic trend already observed since the 4th dynasty, without trying to idealize its model. A certain formalism which
had appeared at the end of the 5th dynasty was now avoided in
the better quality of individual portraits.

Bibliography: PM IV, p. 115; F. Petrie/G. Brunton, Sedment I,
London 1924, pp. 2–3, pls. 7 and 10; Vandier, Manuel III,
pp. 141–43, pl. 45; M. Gamal El-Din Mokhtar, Ihnâsya El-Medina
(Herakleopolis Magna) Bibliothèque d'Etude 40, Cairo 1983, pl. 14.

65

The porter of Niankh-pepi

Plastered and painted wood
H. 36.4 cm; W. 7.7 cm; L. 17.7 cm
Meir, tomb of Niankh-pepi, excavations of the
Egyptian Antiquities Service, 1894
Old Kingdom, end of the 6th dynasty, reign of Pepi II,
about 2235–2141 B.C.

JE 30810
= CG 241

Servant figures deposited near the statue of the dead were at this time made of wood. They are found in great numbers and reproduce, in the round, the various groups of artisans and other workmen included in the mural decoration of the earlier tombs.

The unique porter shown here is a small masterpiece of this kind of domestic statuary, which rarely exhibits such a high degree of elaboration. He is advancing with an attentive air and eyes on the lookout, carrying a bast-basket and a painted chest. He is one of a large collection of model wooden figurines grouped around the statue of the chief of Upper Egypt, Niankh-pepi, called Hepi the Black, in the pit belonging to one of the rooms of his tomb at Meir. These delightful model figurines represent the whole household of the tomb owner, including brewers, dough-kneaders, bakers, cooks, potters, farmers, sailors and musicians (on view in room 32 on the upper floor).

Bibliography: PM IV, p. 247; Borchardt, Statuen und Statuetten (CG) I, p. 157, pl. 51; Blackman, The Rock Tombs of Meir I, London 1914, p. 14; Vandier, Manuel III, p. 142.

66
Head of a falcon

Gold and obsidian   JE 32158
H. 37.5 cm; W. 7.5 cm;   = CG 14717 and CG 52701
weight (gold): 635 gr., (obsidian): 32 gr.
Hierakonpolis, discovered by Quibell in 1897–98
Old Kingdom, 6th dynasty, c. 2350 B.C.

This magnificent falcon's head in beaten gold was found in the
temple at Hierakonpolis. It belonged to a bronze statue of the
falcon Horus, patron deity of this city, which was the predynastic capital of Upper Egypt.
Like other ancient votive objects (see nos. 8, 14, and 63), the
statue of the falcon was buried during the restoration of the
temple in New Kingdom times. It was discovered in a pit carefully lined with bricks set into the floor of the reconstructed
temple's central chapel. It was certainly the cult statue of the
ancient temple, which was replaced during the New Kingdom.
In its cachette, the statue was set up on a base with a royal
statuette placed under its protection. The base was supported
by a hollow metal post fitted in a vase and inserted into the
center of a tall clay support.
The body of the falcon was formed of plaques of beaten
copper probably attached to a wooden body which has disappeared. The completely preserved head was connected to the
body by means of gold and bronze nails. Rounded and
polished ends of an obsidian rod form the eyes, crossing clear
from one side of the head over to the other. The eyelids and
the fleshy area above the curved beak are hammered in relief,
the details around the beak itself delicately worked with a
chisel.
A uraeus is fixed to the diadem, which supports two tall open-
work feathers, attached with bronze tenons. It is very likely
that this headdress was only added during Dynasty 18, as was
the royal statuette placed in front of the deity. The style and
technique of the falcon itself, however, relate to Dynasty 6
(see Pepi I, no. 63).

Bibliography: PM V, pp. 191–93; Quibell/Green, Hierakonpolis I,
pls. 41–43 and p. 11; Hierakonpolis II, p. 27; Quibell, Archaic
Objects (CG), pp. 315–16 and pl. 64; Vernier, Bijoux et Orfèvreries
(CG), pp. 233–35, pls. 58–61; U. Rössler-Köhler, in: MDAIK 34,
1978, pp. 117–25; M. Eaton-Krauss, in: Göttinger Miszellen 42,
1981, pp. 15–18; Corteggiani, no. 34. Cf. J. Weinstein, in: Journal of
the American Research Center in Egypt 9, 1971–72, pp. 133–35.

King Nebhepetre Mentuhotep II

Painted sandstone   JE 36195
H. 138 cm; W. 47 cm; L. 101 cm
Thebes, funerary temple of Mentuhotep at Deir el-Bahari.
Discovered by Carter, 1900
Middle Kingdom, 11th dynasty, reign of Mentuhotep II, 2061–2010 B.C.

The fall of the Old Kingdom came about towards the end of the almost hundred-year reign of Pepi II when political disruption and famine were troubling the capital and Upper Egypt. The central government at Memphis having gradually lost control of the more distant provinces, energetic local governors finally took over control as quasi-independent rulers. After a few decades of uncertainty, two parallel dominant powers succeeded in imposing their authority on the divided country. In the north a family of Heracleopolis held the Delta, the Memphite region including the former royal residence, and the Middle Egyptian nomes, maintaining there the artistic traditions of the end of the 6th dynasty. In the south, Upper Egypt was controlled by a Theban family using the names Antef and Mentuhotep under whose rule a provincial art style was evolved, popular in character and liberated from the strict conventions of the capital.

The two rival kingdoms co-existed for about a century in a permanent state of mutual hostility, each pretending to hegemony over the whole country. Finally, around 2025 B.C. the Theban armies were victorious over their northern neighbours under the energetic leadership of Mentuhotep II. In later tradition, this king was revered as another Menes, the second unifier of the Two Lands. During his 51-year reign Thebes became a city of first importance next to Memphis and Heliopolis. It was not only an artistic and political center but also emerged as a powerful religious capital with the rise of the god Amon, whose importance was continually on the increase. It was at Thebes that Mentuhotep built his funerary monument, in accordance with the Theban tradition, on the west bank deep in a desert valley. It consists of an elevated terrace, preceded by a portico and surmounted by a massive construction surrounded by a colonnade, which brings to mind the primaeval hillock. Behind this monument was the funerary temple proper which was linked to the tomb cut into the mountain, by a long passageway.

The statue of Mentuhotep had been ritually buried in a chamber situated under the terrace and which seems to have been the king's original tomb, before it was transformed into a cenotaph. The entrance to this chamber opened on to the first court of Mentuhotep's funerary monument. The statue was discovered accidentally one day when Carter's horse, trampling on the floor slab which covered the entrance to the chamber, caused it to give way, and horse and rider fell into the tomb. To this day the tomb is called 'Bab el-Hosan' (the tomb of the horse) on account of this accident.

The statue had been wrapped in a linen cloth and seems to have been painted black just before it was buried. It represents

67b

Mentuhotep seated, wearing the red crown and enveloped in the white jubilee mantle which barely reaches to the king's knees. His black skin and his beard curved at the end like the beards of the gods, as well as the position of his arms crossed on his chest, place him in relation to the god Osiris with whom the king was identified after his death. The strong face, heavy mouth and broad nose, are evidence of the provincial style, characterized in particular by the thick legs and massive feet. The strength which radiates from the whole statue emphasizes the force, stability and dignity attached to this powerful monarch.

Bibliography: PM II, pp. 382–83; H. Carter, in: ASAE 2, 1901, pp. 201–205, figs. 1, 2; E. Thomas, The Royal Necropoleis of Thebes, Princeton 1966, p. 17ff.; Leclant, Les Pharaons 1, fig. 204; Wildung, Sesostris und Amenemhet, fig. 39. For the temple, see D. Arnold, Der Tempel des Königs Mentuhotep von Deir-el-Bahari, Archäologische Veröffentlichungen 8, Mainz 1974.

Sarcophagi of Kawit and Ashait

Within the precinct of Mentuhotep's funerary temple at Deir el-Bahari, six tombs belonging to daughters and royal wives were prepared during an early phase of the building's construction. Originally associated with superstructural chapels, these tombs were later concealed by enlargements of the original temple. Here successive excavators were able, despite theft by ancient robbers, to discover remains of the funerary equipment, especially the sarcophagi of the princesses, all of whom were priestesses of Hathor. This title associates them with a chapel of the same goddess cut into the mountain a short distance away, and explains the presence of their tombs within Mentuhotep's enclosure.

Each sarcophagus was composed of six slabs held in place by metal braces which passed through holes perforated at the corners of each slab. The box thus formed served as an eternal resting-place.

The sarcophagi of the two royal wives Kawit and Ashait are among the most noteworthy examples of the art of bas-relief sculpture at a provincial court during Dynasty 11. The decorative scenes, carefully carved in sunk relief, remind us of similar specimens found in Old Kingdom mastabas. But added to the inherent subtlety and finesse of the Memphite artists, we find a new provincial Theban element which blends the more traditional vigor with a naive simplicity. The result is an original composition liberated from the constraints of register division. It makes its own contribution to the genre of scenes of daily life, and, by means of its own proportional canon, helps to engender a new ideal of beauty at this period.

Sarcophagus of Kawit (details)

Limestone   JE 47397
H. 119 cm; L. 262 cm; W. 119 cm
Thebes, Deir el-Bahari, temple of Mentuhotep II – Nebhepetre
Excavations of the Egyptian Exploration Fund, 1903–1907
Middle Kingdom, 11th dynasty; beginning of the reign of Mentuhotep II, c. 2050 B.C.

The cycle of representations in sunk relief around the sarcophagus of Kawit serves to perpetuate the activities of a princess of the palace. On the side to which the mummy's head would have turned appears a palace facade topped with a cavetto cornice. The central doors are decorated with Udjat eyes which permitted the deceased to view her surroundings. What she hoped to see was the continuation of her life in the

68a

68b

hereafter actually displayed on slabs of limestone. In the representation of her toilet, for example, Kawit is seated on a high-backed armchair, mirror in hand, adorned with simple but elegant jewellery. Her body is sheathed in a close-fitting robe and she sips with a graceful gesture from the milk offered by an attendant who says "For your Ka, O mistress". Behind Kawit is another servant who with dainty fingers lovingly arranges the locks of her lady's wig.

The milk in the scene most likely came from the cow at the left, whose calf remains bound to her foreleg. A tear flows from the cow's eye as it is milked, a touching detail from an age which believed that the cow suffered pain in losing milk destined for her calf.

On the other side a servant holding a feathered fan offers her mistress an unguent vessel. Kawit gracefully sniffs at the bou-

quet of a lotus blossom while wearing a round, finely curled wig and a long robe with two ribbed shoulder straps. A finely plaited shawl covers her shoulders and she wears necklaces, bracelets and anklets. Behind the no less carefully carved servant figure we see Kawit's jewellery arranged next to an unguent jar near a chest which apparently held all of the articles shown.

The bodies are elongated, the musculature visible but restrained, the facial features coarse but nevertheless enticing. From these clear and reserved representations we thus gain an impression of the ideal of feminine beauty in Thebes in the age of a belligerent monarch who was soon to reunite the Two Lands.

Bibliography: PM II, p. 113; E. Naville, The XIth Dynasty Temple at Deir el-Bahari I, London 1907, pp. 48–49, 53–56, pls. 19–20.

68 c

68 d

69a

69   Upper floor, hall 48

Sarcophagus of Ashait (details)

Painted limestone   JE 47267
H. 97 cm; L. 250 cm; W. 97 cm
Thebes, Deir el-Bahari, temple of Mentuhotep II – Nebhepetre
Excavations of the Metropolitan Museum of Art, New York, 1920
Middle Kingdom, 11ᵗʰ dynasty, beginning of the
reign of Mentuhotep II, c. 2050 B.C.

Upon discoverey of the tomb of Ashait, the interior wooden
coffin still contained the deceased's mummy. The body was
that of a fairly short, slightly plump woman of about twenty-
two years of age. Both coffin and mummy had already been
violated and left upon the large limestone sarcophagus.
The interior decoration of the sarcophagus is painted in vivid
colors and reproduces scenes of palace life nearly identical to

69b

those carved in sunk relief on the exterior. Despite rather coarse features and stout figure, Ashait still conveys a certain charm. She sniffs a lotus blossom, symbol of life, while an attendant fans her. A servant presents a choice duck from among the victuals piled high behind him.

Further to the right, below the scene of the inspection of a livestock procession, a delightful composition portrays the

bustling activity at a granary. In a columned hall, with lotus-shaped capitals, two servants mount the stairs leading to silos, four at a time, under the watchful gaze of both the administrator seated at right and an attentive recording scribe. Here they will proceed to empty their containers of grain.

Bibliography: PM II, p. 113; H. Winlock, Excavations at Deir el-Bahari, New York 1942, p. 37, pls. 6–10.

70

The Theban general Antef

Painted sandstone   JE 89858 (head)
H. 58 cm   JE 91169 (torso)
Thebes, Assassif, funerary chapel of the tomb of Antef
Excavations of the German Archaeological Institute, 1963–64
Middle Kingdom, 11th dynasty, reign of Mentuhotep II, c. 2050 B.C.

Private statuary from the reign of Mentuhotep at Thebes is attested by a mere handful of examples, of which Antef's statue is a good representative. The piece thoroughly imitates contemporary royal sculpture in style, proportions, attitude and even costume. The realistic style compares well with that of Mentuhotep II's portraits (see, for example no. 67), clearly exuding a sense of power. The torso is massive and squat; the general expression suggests a vigor devoid of any aesthetic idealism. The rather bland face is composed of narrow eyes, horizontal eyebrows, straight nose and a thick, almost brutal mouth. The short curled wig likewise derives from royal examples such as those often found in bas-reliefs. Even the short, pleated kilt with central tab follows an essentially royal form. Antef once rested on a cubical seat which, along with legs, has long since broken away.
Antef served as chancellor and overseer of His Majesty's troops. His large tomb, cut into the limestone bedrock (in significantly close proximity to Mentuhotep's own funerary temple), its massive pillared facade, and original painted wall scenes all point to Antef's privileged position at court towards the beginning of the reign.

Bibliography: D. Arnold/J. Settgast, in: MDAIK 20, 1965, p. 60, pl. 18; Götter Pharaonen, no. 14; Wildung, Sesostris und Amenemhet, fig. 188.

71

Sarcophagus of Dagi (detail)

Painted limestone
H. 110 cm; L. 291 cm; W. 127 cm
Thebes, tomb of Dagi at Deir el-Bahari
Middle Kingdom, 11th dynasty, middle of the reign of Mentuhotep II, c. 2030 B.C.

JE 25328
= CG 28024

Middle Kingdom private sarcophagi and coffins show a variety of forms and sizes. Depending on the social status of their owner or the "style" of a particular necropolis, they could range from a simple mask of stuccoed cloth to enormous boxes of cedar wood imported from Syria, and even to gigantic coffins of limestone.

Intended essentially to protect the mummy and insure the deceased's eternal life in the hereafter, the sarcophagus, or exterior case, served as a dwelling place. The coffin, on the other hand, often formed in the image of the deceased or the living, could take the place of the mummy which it enclosed, if for any reason the latter should be destroyed.

In this search for protection, eyes, doors, friezes of objects needed in the afterlife and funerary texts all began to enliven the walls of these eternal dwelling-places.

The present sarcophagus illustrates a Theban type. The exterior design of the body is restrained, containing only one band of carved hieroglyphs. The text reproduces an offering formula addressed to the gods Osiris on one side and Anubis on the other. On the side to which the mummy was turned, a carved pair of eyes allowed the deceased to peer outside. Corresponding to the eyes, a painted representation of a false door appears on the exterior, so that the spirit of the deceased could exit at will. Above on the interior walls, a band of colored hieroglyphs repeats the offering formula. On both one long side (illustrated) and one short side, the middle frieze depicts objects of everyday use: sandals, bows and quivers, vessels, bracelets, collars, linen, etc. The rest of the wall and even the bottom of the coffin are inscribed with the "Coffin Texts." These are spells and formulae deriving in part from the older Pyramid Texts – originally reserved for royalty – but now enriched with new texts resulting from popular beliefs.

Taken together, the number of these fairly heterogeneous texts, arranged in haphazard order, exceeded 1200. Through the magic of writing, they prevented or resolved the difficulties facing the deceased in the afterlife, assuring him pleasurable moments and beneficent metamorphoses.

Bibliography: PM I, 1, p. 217; P. Lacau, Les Sarcophages antérieurs au Nouvel Empire (CG) I, pp. 56–61; R. O. Faulkner, The Ancient Egyptian Coffin Texts, Warminster 1973–80, Spells 12–17, 63–74, 179, 180, 723. Cf. also: G. Jéquier, Frises d'Objets des Sarcophages du Moyen Empire, MIFAO 47, 1921.

72

72–73   Upper floor, room 37

72 Nubian archers

Painted wood   JE 30969
H. 5.5 cm; W. 72.3 cm; L. 190.2 cm   = CG 257

73 Egyptian pikemen

Painted wood   JE 30986
H. 59 cm; W. 62 cm; L. 169.8 cm   = CG 258

Assiut, tomb of Mesehti, discovered in 1894
Middle Kingdom, 11th dynasty, about 2000 B.C.

The use of wooden model figures retains its popularity; very
elaborate groups are sometimes reproduced depicting an entire

73

princely household with its domains, workshops and even its military personnel. For example, there exist already at the end of the Old Kingdom in the mural decoration of certain tombs, representations of soldiers besieging fortresses and this becomes a frequent theme during the First Intermediate Period and the Middle Kingdom. It is well known that during the period of disorders, the independent nome chiefs gave military training to their young men and recruited auxiliaries from abroad for their armies. Thus, the prince of Assiut was accompanied in his tomb by wooden soldiers reproducing in the round companies of archers and pikemen, elsewhere depicted on the walls of the tombs.

On the left are 40 Nubian archers grouped together on the same pedestal, advancing in rows of four, holding in one hand their bows and in the other bunches of arrows. Their red kilts with green designs, the white lines of the headbands holding their hair, the necklaces and above all the whites of the eyes give life to the black bodies of the archers which the sculptor has executed with great realism, varying the stature and the facial expression of the different soldiers.

The pikemen are natives of the nome. They march together with a disciplined step, carrying a shield covered with an animal skin in the left hand and in the right holding a lance vertically in front of them. Here again, monotony is avoided by the inclusion of varying individual traits.

Bibliography: PM IV, p. 265; Borchardt, Statuen und Statuetten (CG) I, pp. 164–65, pls. 55–56; G. Posener/S. Sauneron/J. Yoyotte, Dictionnaire de la civilisation égyptienne, p. 22, figs. see p. 20 and p. 21; M. Bietak, in: Mélanges Gamal Eddin Moukhtar I, Cairo 1985, pp. 87–97, pls. I–IV.

74–78   Upper floor, room 27
Meketre's Models
Painted wood

74) Offering bearer
H. 123 cm; W. 17 cm; L. (base) 47 cm   JE 46725

75) Fishing with nets
H. 31.5 cm; L. 90 cm; W. 62 cm   46715

76) Counting the cattle
H. 55.5 cm; W. 72 cm; L. 173 cm   46724

77) Weavers' workshop
H. 25 cm; W. 43 cm; L. 93 cm   46723

78) Carpentry
H. 26 cm; W. 52 cm; L. 66 cm   46722

Thebes, tomb of Meketre (no. 280), Excavations of the Metropolitan Museum of Art, New York, 1919–1920
Middle Kingdom, 11ᵗʰ dynasty, about 2000 B.C.

An extraordinary group of 25 models in wood peopled chancellor Meketre's serdab cut into the cliffs of the so-called Valley of Seankhkare Mentuhotep, south of Deir el-Bahari. Equally divided between the Metropolitan Museum of Art in New York and our Museum, these models depict with astonishing precision the entire household of Meketre, his gardens, workshops and storehouses, life on his domains and even his fleet of ships. It is a real miniature world which has preserved for us the fascinating spectacle of a whole community in action.
The offering bearer (no. 74) is in fact a personification of one of the dead man's domains, such as they are frequently represented in procession on the walls of mastabas during the Old Kingdom. She walks along carrying on her head a basket containing four stoppered wine jars, and in her hand holds a live duck by its wings. Her tall stature, the beauty of her tight-fitting robe, decorated with a net of vari-coloured beads and supported by straps, together with her jewels and her long wig give her an air which distinguishes her from the ordinary run of offering bearers, usually of much rougher workmanship.
Meketre's fishermen (no. 75) divided into two groups are busily at work on their two papyrus barks manipulated by squatting oarsmen. They are about to pull in the net stretched between the two boats. The net, with wooden floaters attached all around the rim, is full of fish and two of the lar-

gest have already been hauled up on to one of the barks. The pleasure boats in back of the fishermen's barks transport the master alone, or accompanied by his son, comfortably installed in the cabins.

The counting of the cattle (no. 76) is a scene of striking realism. In the courtyard of a country house, the farmers urge forward their troops of piebald cattle while the chief herdsman bows before the master of the house. The latter is seated under a portico upheld by four lotiform columns, with his son and four scribes who count the number of beasts. Guards armed with sticks silently survey the scene ready to apply the bastinado if the tally of beasts is not correct.

In the weavers' quarters, two horizontal looms are activated by weavers squatting on the floor, while a number of girls spinning thread keep them company (no. 77). As for the carpenters who occupy a well-equipped workshop, they are busy on woodworking of various kinds. One of the workmen is using a long saw to cut planks from a beam attached vertically to a pole. Others working with adzes, finish a board which yet another group is polishing. Finally a workman using a mallet and chisel cuts out the mortice holes, indispensable to the final assemblage of the planks. At the farther corner of the workshop a number of men crouching around a fire, reforge the metal blades of their tools. The tools held in reserve were carefully guarded in the big chest in which were found a stock of axes, adzes, reserve blades, chisels, drills and saws (no. 78).

Bibliography: PM I, 1, pp. 360–61; H. E. Winlock, Models of Daily Life in Ancient Egypt, Publications of the Metropolitan Museum of Art, Egyptian Expedition XVIII, Cambridge Mass. 1955, models C, H, J, K, U and V; J. H. Breasted Jr., Egyptian Servant Statues, pp. 9–10, 51, 54, 64, 78; pls. 6 (b), 46 (a), 48 (b), 58 (b), 68; Wildung, Sesostris und Amenemhet, pp. 110–20.

77

78

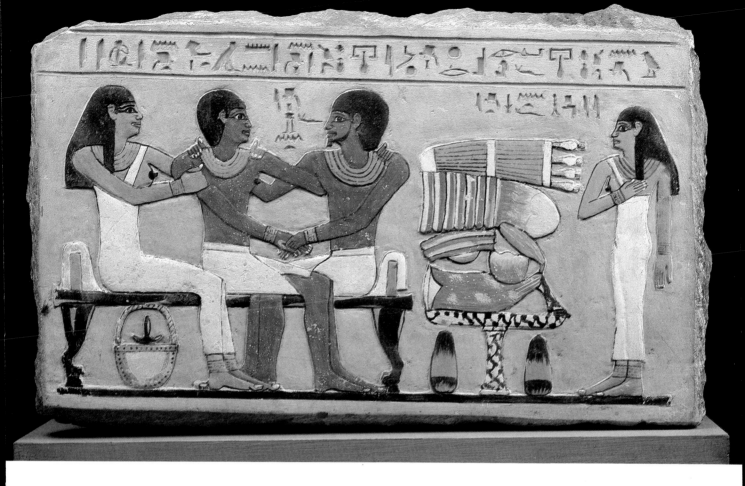

79

Funerary stela of Amenemhat

Painted Limestone   JE 45626
H. 30 cm; W. 50 cm
Thebes, Assassif, Tomb R4. Excavations of the Metropolitan Museum
of Art, New York, in 1915–16
Middle Kingdom, 11th dynasty, about 2000 B.C.

This rectangular stela is notable for the freshness of its colours
and the originality of its composition. Instead of the traditional scene of the funerary repast, we see here the two spouses
sitting on a bench face to face holding their son between them
in an embrace, while their daughter-in-law stands respectfully
on the farther side of the offering table.
Father and son, their legs crossing each other, are holding
each other by the hand and around the shoulder while the
mother embraces her son with both arms. The two men, their
skin painted a reddish-brown, wear short kilts, necklaces,
bracelets and short, rounded wigs. The father likewise sports a
short beard. The women, light-skinned, are sheated in strait-
falling robes supported by a single strap. They wear long tripartite wigs, necklaces, bracelets and anklets.
Under the bench is placed a basket from which the handle of a
mirror emerges; two loaves of bread are stowed away underneath the offering table, itself piled high with vegetables and
cuts of meat.
The line of hieroglyphic inscription in sunken relief is an
invocation for food offerings in favour of Amenemhat and his
wife Iyi. The son and daughter-in-law are accompanied by
their names: Antef and Hapy respectively.

*Bibliography: PM I, 2, p. 618; A. Lansing, in: BMMA May 1917,
p. 13, fig. 9; Posener/Sauneron/Yoyotte, Dictionnaire de la civilisation
égyptienne, p. 28; Götter Pharaonen, no. 17.*

80

81

80

Female figurine

Blue faience   JE 47710
H. 13 cm; W. 5 cm
Thebes, tomb of Neferhotep (no. 316) at Deir el-Bahari
Excavations of the Metropolitan Museum of Art,
New York, 1922–23
Middle Kingdom, 11th dynasty, end of the reign
of Mentuhotep II, c. 2010 B.C.

The corpus of smaller objects deposited in Middle Kingdom
private tombs included seductive female figurines colored brilliant blue, lacking feet and completely naked. Their only ornament consisted of tattoos, jewellery, and girdles of shells
strung together. Such figurines combine the qualities of the
puppet, the seductive attraction of the tattooed naked dancer,
the pelvis of fertility goddesses venerated since the prehistoric
age, and finally the blue color symbolic of eternal resurrection
and renewal. Thus they apparently fulfilled the feminine role
of entertaining and regenerating the tomb-owner, and are
often called "concubines of the deceased." However, such
figurines have also turned up in young girls' tombs, a fact
which throws some doubt on the above explanation.
Was it to prevent their flight that these statuettes were

deprived of their legs, or is this simply a reflection of the most
ancient female representations in which limbs are rarely fully
articulated? Whatever the answer may be, our figurine has lost
her arms as well, this time owing to an unfortunate fracture.

*Bibliography: PM I, 1, p. 390; H. Winlock, Excavations at Deir el-
Bahari, p. 72 and pl. 35; Nofret – Die Schöne, no. 65. Cf. also: Desroches-Noblecourt, in: BIFAO 53, 1953, pp. 7–47.*

81

Paddle doll

Painted wood, Nile mud   JE 56274
H. 23 cm; W. 5.8 cm
Thebes, private tomb in the Assassif (no. 816)
Excavations of the Metropolitan Museum of Art,
New York, 1929–30
Middle Kingdom, 11th dynasty, reign of a Mentuhotep,
c. 2050–1991 B.C.

Here is a wooden version of the female figurine intended to
rejuvenate the deceased. In this case the accent is upon the
playful aspect. One is almost tempted to explain it as a rattle

in the form of a puppet whose summarily treated figure serves as handle and whose abundant wig, formed of chaplets of unbaked mud beads, was to be shaken. One must also take into account, however, the female private parts explicitly painted both beneath the robe of this tattooed figurine and on the naked breast, which also displays a bead necklace. These elements clearly indicate the desire for a female presence in the tomb without which the deceased, equipped as he was with all manner of food offerings, would have remained unable to regenerate his reproductive abilities.

Bibliography: H. Winlock, Excavations at Deir el-Bahari, p. 203, pl. 38; Corteggiani, no. 31. Cf. also: P. Barguet, in: BIFAO 52, 1953, pp. 101-102.

82–83   Upper floor, hall 48
Hippopotami

82 Standing hippopotamus

Blue faience   JE 21365
H. 11.5 cm; L. 21.5 cm

83 Recumbent hippopotamus

Green faience   JE 21366
H. 7 cm; L. 18 cm

Thebes, excavations of Mariette at Drac Abu'l-Naga, 1860–63
Middle Kingdom or Second Intermediate Period, 11th to 13th dynasties, c. 2000–1650 B.C.

Every great collection of Egyptian antiquities includes at least one blue or green faience hippopotamus shown standing, lying peacefully, or even sitting with a growling, wide open mouth. Known in Egypt since prehistoric times, the hippo was feared for its enormous size and voracity. Its plump form, however,

also led to an association with fertility, such that the female hippo was eventually venerated as a goddess named Taweret (Taueris) the Great.

Very early on the hippo figure was sculpted in the round, either carved in stone or formed into a vase with rounded belly. It occurs in the Thinite period as a votive figurine deposited in the court of the earliest sanctuaries.

A favorite theme found on Old Kingdom mastaba walls is the hippopotamus hunt, an ancient ritual originally performed by the king himself. The hunt served to demonstrate the struggle against this most powerful animal of the marshlands.

In the Middle Kingdom the hippopotamus becomes a subject for a charming little faience sculpture, a miniature version of the great beast, as blue as the water which surrounded it and adorned with the aquatic plants among which it bathed: primarily lotus flowers, symbols of life and rebirth. The blue color was also chosen for concubine and dancer figurines (see no. 80) deposited along with the hippo statuettes in tombs as representatives of the feminine element through which the deceased hoped to be rejuvenated.

The hippo also appears once as the rather enigmatic subject of a dispute described in a New Kingdom literary papyrus: Apophis, king of the Hyksos and occupant of Avaris in the Delta, complains to the Upper Egyptian king, Sekenenre, of the unbearable din which the hippopotami east of Thebes are making. Sekenenre seems momentarily confused and can think of no suitable reply. The story's conclusion is lost, but we know that the Theban king eventually defeated and then ousted the Hyksos from Egypt. Equally enigmatically, the faience hippos disappear from the funerary repertoire with the close of the Seventeenth Dynasty.

Bibliography: PM I, 2, p. 605; Keimer, in: La Revue de L'Egypte Ancienne II, 1928, pp. 210–53, no. 2 and 3, pp. 29–33; H. W. Müller, Ägyptische Kunst, Frankfort 1970, no. 88. Cf. also: J. D. Cooney, in: The Brooklyn Museum Bulletin 12, Fall 1950, pp. 5–13; S. Aufrère, in: Egypte et Province, Musée Calvet, Avignon 1986, pp. 64–65.

82

83

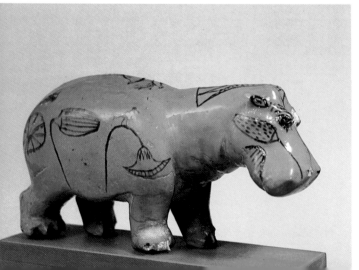

Stela of Nit-Ptah and his family

Painted limestone   JE 45625
H. 23 cm; W. 31 cm
Thebes, Assassif, Tomb R. 6. Excavations of the Metropolitan
Museum of Art, New York in 1915–16
Middle Kingdom, 12th or 13th dynasty, about 1780 B.C.

This stela, naive and conventional but attractive because of its
brilliant colours, was found like that of Amenemhat (no. 79)
in the Assassif, in one of the early tombs which were later covered up or destroyed by the causeways belonging to the 18th
dynasty temples at Deir el-Bahari and by the valley temple of
Hatshepsut.
Four persons, three of whom are advancing while the fourth is
simply standing, follow each other in the usual attitudes. The
contrast in skin colour between the men and the women,
which accords with artistic conventions originating already in
the Old Kingdom, breaks the monotony of the procession.
In front is the head of the family, Nit-Ptah, holding a cane and
a stick. He wears a round wig and a beard, a kilt with a
starched front panel, a wide bead collar and bracelets. He is
followed by his wife (?) Seni, daughter of Tai, who sniffs a
blue lotus flower and in her other hand holds a bud. Her very
attractive robe, held up by two straps, is covered with a net of
multicoloured beads. She wears a long tripartite wig and the
usual feminine ornaments: necklace, bracelets and anklets.
Her son Antef, behind her, differs from his father in wearing a
longer wig. The daughter Ded, at the end of the line, resem-

84   Upper floor, hall 48

Hedgehog

Blue faience   JE 30742
H. 5.3 cm; L. 7 cm; W. 3.8 cm
Thebes, Gourna; acquired in 1893
Middle Kingdom, 11th Dynasty, c. 2000 B.C.

Representations of hedgehogs occur at all periods in Egyptian
art. In the Old Kingdom, they are often found on the prows of
ships, or in desert scenes, leaving their burrows to catch a
grasshopper. Delightful little vases and faience statuettes in the
form of hedgehogs are also quite common. This bright blue
statuette is highlighted by dark spots along its back, while its
feet rest firmly on an oblong base. Its little pointed nose and
stubby legs are naturalistically rendered, while a more schematic system of incised grid lines delineates the spine. The
hedgehog's presence in the tomb with the deceased certainly
bore a magical, protective significance. Hedgehog fat or oil
was also reputed to cure baldness.

*Bibliography: V. v. Droste zu Hülshoff, Der Igel im alten Ägypten,
Hildesheimer Ägyptologische Beiträge 11, Hildesheim 1980, no. 101,
p. 135 and pl. 11. Cf. also: E. Riefstahl, Ancient Egyptian Glass and
Glazes in the Brooklyn Museum, no. 9.*

bles her mother in all respects except that her dress is of a single colour.

The dedicatory inscription engraved above this little family group places them under the protection of Ptah-Sokar in order that he may provide their *kas* with food offerings.

Bibliography: PM I, 2, p. 618; Nofret – Die Schöne, no. 19.

86
Ground floor, gallery 21

Pillar of Sesostris I

Limestone
JE 36809

H. 434 cm; W. 95 cm

Karnak, temple of Amon-Re. Excavations of the
Egyptian Antiquities Service, 1901

Middle Kingdom, 12th dynasty, reign of Sesostris I, 1971–1929 B.C.

In the year 1991 B.C. Amenemhat I founded the 12th dynasty and after a reign of thirty years fell victim to a conspiracy. His son Sesostris I, however, during a long reign of 44 years succeeded in stabilizing the authority of the monarchy. By his campaigns against Nubia, against the Libyans on the confines of the Oases in the western desert and along the shoreline, and even against the Bedouin of southern Palestine, he extended Egyptian domination beyond the natural frontiers of the country.

Throughout Egypt, the existing temples were refurbished and new ones constructed. It was also during the reign of this King that the first known monolithic obelisk was erected at Heliopolis in honour of the solar god Re.

With the beginning of the 12th dynasty and the reign of Sesostris I, the art of sculpture in low relief attained a precision, purity and delicacy whose perfection was rarely equalled in later times. Among other masterpieces of this reign, such as the reliefs from the temple of Koptos, or those of the White Chapel at Karnak, here is a pillar from a jubilee chapel which once also stood in the temple of Karnak. The pillar was found under the floor of one of the courts of the temple called the "cour de la cachette", where a large number of monuments had been buried (see nos. 105–106, 132–134 etc.).

Sesostris is depicted on all four faces of the pillar, each time in another costume and with a different headdress, accompanied by a god who embraces him. The latter are, respectively, Atum of Heliopolis wearing the double crown; Ptah of Memphis, mummiform as usual and wearing a small cap; the falcon-headed Horus of Edfu, and Amon of Karnak with his high feather crown. They represent the principal gods of the Egyptian pantheon, Amon having only recently attained to that rank (see no. 199).

On the side of the pillar here illustrated, Sesostris in the *nemes* headdress, is wearing the *shendjyt* kilt and is embraced by

Ptah inside his naos. The precise contours of this very low relief reveal in all their purity the perfectly proportioned forms of these two figures. The symmetry of the faces, the equilibrium and harmony of the attitudes, give to this rite in which the king is being received by the god, all the grandeur which imagination could conceive for it. The royal titulary as well as the name and epithets of the god are written in the large, very carefully sculptured hieroglyphs which form the glory of the official monumental script.

Bibliography: PM II, p. 133; Müller, Ägyptische Kunst, no. 61; Aldred, Middle Kingdom Art in Egypt, pl. 21; Corteggiani, no. 33.

Sesostris I

Limestone   JE 31139 bis = CG 414
H. 200 cm; W. 58.4 cm; L. 123 cm
(the ten statues: CG 411−420)
Lisht, funerary temple of Sesostris I. Excavation of the
Institut Français d'Archéologie Orientale, 1894
Middle Kingdom, 12th dynasty, reign of Sesostris I, 1971−1929 B.C.

The kings of the 12th dynasty abandoned Thebes and established their residence in the north between Memphis and the Fayum. Under the first two kings of the dynasty, the capital was located at Ittawy, the present-day Lisht. Not far distant in the desert lie the pyramids of these kings surrounded by funerary establishments modeled on those of the 6th dynasty at Sakkara. The funerary temple on the east side of the pyramid of Sesostris I was preceded by a porticoed court and a vestibule giving access to the ascending causeway. This vestibule was bordered by Osiride pillars − that is to say pillars against which were erected statues of the King represented in the guise of the god Osiris (exhibited in this room) − while our statues were found in a hiding place north-east of the temple.
Except for a few minor details, the ten statues are identical. The king is seated in the classical majestic pose, his right hand holding the folded cloth, the left placed outstretched on his knee. His headdress consists of the *nemes* with frontal uraeus; he wears the ceremonial beard and a short *shendjyt* kilt with central tab. The *nemes,* the beard and the kilt are striped on some of the statues, plain or only partly striped on others. On the upper face of the bases of three of these statues, the nine bows, symbols of the traditional enemies of Egypt, are depicted under the King's feet. On the same three statues the King's name is engraved on his belt buckle.
These highly idealized portraits in white unpainted limestone, only emphasized here and there by a touch of black around the eyes, give an impression of uniformity and total lack of expression. In reality, however, they all differ slightly from one another. The harmonious features are those of a young man with a serene countenance which would no doubt have gained in vitality if the execution of the sculpture had been less academic, as is evident in the schematic rendering of the musculature of the body and the legs.
One of the most remarkable things about these statues is the decoration on the sides of the thrones, again illustrating the theme of the *sematawy,* the union of the Two Lands. On five of the statues it is the androgynous Nile gods, symbols of fecundity and plenty, each a personification of the gifts of one half of the Egyptian soil, who knot around the hieroglyph for 'union' the heraldic plants of the Two Lands, the papyrus of the north and the lotus of the south. On the remaining five thrones, Horus and Seth replace the Nile gods in this activity. Here we have one of the rare cases in which the image of Seth was not destroyed through the superstition of later generations. For Seth who is here represented as the titulary god of Upper Egypt, came elsewhere to personify the desert, foreign lands and evil in general.
In all these reliefs the symbol for 'union' is surmounted by a royal cartouche; on one side of the throne it encloses the coronation name: Kheperkare, and on the other the personal name Senusret (Sesostris). The cartouches are accompanied by inscriptions giving the names of the deities depicted, with their epithets, and enumerate the offerings which they bring.
The statues are divided into two groups such that one would have been placed on the northern side, for Lower Egypt, and the other on the southern, for Upper Egypt. They were meant to stand in the court of offerings, or in the ten chapels at the back of the mortuary temple, but for some unknown reason they were left unfinished and carefully buried near the temple.

Bibliography: PM IV, pp. 82−83; J. E. Gautier/G. Jéquier, Fouilles de Licht, MIFAO 6, 1902, pp. 30−38, pls. 9−13; Borchardt, Statuen und Statuetten (CG) II, pp. 21−29, pl. 67; Vandier, Manuel III, p. 173; Centenaire de l'Institut Français d'Archéologie Orientale, 1981, no. 56.

88

Statuette of Sesostris I

Cedar wood   JE 44951
H. 56 cm; W. 11 cm; L. 26 cm
Lisht. Found in a private tomb near the pyramid of Sesostris I. Excavations of the Metropolitan Museum of Art, New York, 1915
Middle Kingdom, 12th dynasty, reign of Sesostris I, 1971–1929 B.C.

In addition to the large sized royal statues in stone, smaller wooden statuettes which were used in processions and festivals certainly existed in the funerary temple of Sesostris I. The two statuettes representing Sesostris I, made up of a number of pieces of wood joined together, probably come under this category. The one which is displayed in the Metropolitan Museum of Art in New York wears the red crown of Lower Egypt; the other, illustrated here, wears the Upper Egyptian white crown.

They were found in a room hidden in the enclosure wall of the tomb of the chancellor Imhotep which lies east of the royal funerary complex. With them were discovered a model boat and a naos of Anubis, both in wood.

The king is wearing a short kilt both overlaps of which are caught up in his belt; the kilt is covered with a coat of plaster and painted white with the details added in red ochre. The body is painted brown. Judging by the presence of a circular hole under the chin, the face was adorned with a ceremonial beard.

The king is holding a *heka*-sceptre, sign of royal authority, in his outstretched left hand while his right hand probably held the *sekhem*-scepter, symbol of power.

The admirable modeling of the face, with its large painted eyes, and the rendering of the slender body emphasize the royal dignity. This hieratic attitude is somewhat enlivened by the effect of movement stemming from the forward position of the left foot, in accordance with the usual convention for masculine statuary.

Bibliography: PM IV, p. 84; A. M. Lythgoe, in: BMMA, Feb. 1915, II, p. 16, figs. 13–14; Propyläen Kunstgeschichte 15, pl. 154; Smith, Art and Architecture, p. 178; Leclant, Les Pharaons I, fig. 207.

Three dancing dwarfs

Ivory   JE 63858
H. 7.8 cm; L. 15.8 cm; W. 4.5 cm
Lisht, excavations of the Metropolitan Museum of Art, New York, 1934
Middle Kingdom, 12th dynasty, c. 1900 B.C.

"Dwarfs of the god's dances" originating from "the Land of Spirits", these curious individuals represent the much coveted pygmies of southern Africa. The figures are executed with an astonishing realism. They form part of an ingenious toy: each dwarf stands on a base in the form of a pulley, pierced through transversally. They are embedded in a rectangular stand furnished with holes; a system of threads wrapped around the pulley and passing through the holes allows one to set the dwarfs to dancing. By tugging on the ends of the threads one makes them turn simultaneously to the left or right. This dance was no doubt overseen by a fourth figure, also mounted on a pulley, with hands together as if to set the rhythm. This piece is presently in the Metropolitan Museum of Art. The three dwarfs wear only thick shoulder straps; large, beaded necklaces adorn the two exterior figures.
The dwarfs' facial expression betray concentration and sustained effort. The treatment of the stout bodies, bulging buttocks and bowed legs all distinguish this group of figurines as a representative example of realistic Middle Kingdom art. The physiognomy has been both carefully observed and faithfully rendered.
The toy was discovered at the foot of a brick wall which sealed the burial chamber of a young girl named Hapi.

Head of a woman

Wood with gilding   JE 39390
H. 10.5 cm
Lisht, excavations of the Metropolitan Museum of Art, New York, around the pyramid of Amenemhat I, 1907
Middle Kingdom, early 12th dynasty, c. 1990 B.C.

This remarkable face with its delicately balanced features displays a softness quite different from the powerful, formal royal portraits of this period. The woman is clearly of high rank, a princess or perhaps even a queen of the early Twelfth Dynasty, whose (lost) uraeus no longer adorns her forehead. Composite statuettes such as this one, assembled from various materials, are rare indeed. Even the enveloping mass of hair, whose already dark wood has been painted black, is attached with tenons to the light-colored head. The body is lost; only the arms could be recovered by Winlock two years after the original excavation.
The eyes were once inlaid but have long since disappeared. This creates an expression of disquiet or even mystery, softened only by the beauty of the rest of the face. The coiffure with its tiny golden squares of overlay suggest a heavy wig adorned with gold jewellery.

Bibliography: PM IV, p. 81; Lythgoe, in: BMMA, Oct. 1907, p. 163, fig. 2; H. W. Müller, Ägyptische Kunst, no. 65.

Accompanying her were four faience female figurines, a statuette of the hippopotamus goddess Taueris, and a flail.
Dancing in ancient Egypt bore a cultic function, serving to entertain the god during his festival. Our dwarfs might therefore represent not merely a simple toy but a cult object deposited in the tomb.
This dance also entertained the living. One well-known story relates how Harkhuf, an official of Dynasty 6 en route home from his fourth expedition to Yam, reported to his eight year old sovereign, Pepi II, about his cargo of an "actual dancing dwarf." His Majesty was so overjoyed at the prospect of this gift that he despatched a letter to Harkhuf in order to thank him and above all command that he watch over the dwarf's health. Pepi II cautioned that strict attention be paid lest the dwarf fall into the Nile and die before reaching the palace!

Bibliography: Lansing, in: BMMA, Nov. 1934, II, pp. 30–36, figs. 30–31; H. W. Müller, Ägyptische Kunst, no. 89. See also: Hayes, The Scepter of Egypt I, pp. 222–23, fig. 139 (4ᵗʰ dwarf).

Stela of the chief goldsmith Nakht

Limestone   CG 20515
H. 95 cm; W. 53 cm
Abydos, 1881
Middle Kingdom, 12ᵗʰ dynasty, year 10 of the reign of Sesostris I, 1961 B.C.

During the Middle Kingdom there developed the practice of depositing ex-voto stelae in temples and other sanctuaries. The site of Abydos alone produced hundreds of stelae. During this period the cult of Osiris attained such a high degree of popularity that every individual aspired to approach the "terrace of the great god," if only by way of erecting a stela. The kings for their part constructed cenotaphs there.
These stelae give us a glimpse into the living conditions and beliefs of Egyptian officialdom, forming a rich source for the study of both language and artistic development. The present example contains all of these characteristics with the added advantage of being one of the best carved pieces. The sunk relief inscription begins with: "Year 10 under the Majesty of the King of Upper and Lower Egypt, Sesostris I, beloved of the foremost of the Westerners, living forever." The five following lines contain two formulae: one is a traditional offering formula which invokes Osiris, Khentamentiu, Wepwawet and the gods of the western desert to give provision to the stela's owner, the chief goldsmith, Nakht. The second formula is an appeal to the living, first developed on mastaba walls of the Old Kingdom, to recite offering spells: "O you living upon earth who will pass by this tomb, who love life and despise death, may you say a thousand of bread and beer, oxen and fowl, alabaster and linen, oblations, and every pure thing by which the god lives, for the revered one, the chief goldsmith, Nakht, born of Hetep."
Representations follow the inscription divided into three registers. The first one shows Nakht and his wife Iynebu seated before an offering table piled high with bread, a lettuce, a bundle of green onions, a duck and cuts of meat. These offerings are consecrated by their son Nakht, senior lector priest and painters' scribe in the residence at Lisht. He is clothed in a carefully plaited kilt with a large triangular tab and sports a long wig. Behind the couple stand the younger children, one of whom is a girl with long tresses. Due to lack of space, the newest arrivals were later on added hastily to the left hand margin.
The couple's elder sons and daughters appear in a defile in the second register. The third register is carved in sunk relief to indicate that the scene takes place outside; on either side of a false door, servants of the cult advance, bringing the offerings.

Bibliography: PM V, p. 57; Lange/Schäfer, Grab- und Denksteine des Mittleren Reiches (CG) II, pp. 105–108; IV, pl. 57; W. K. Simpson, The Terrace of the Great God at Abydos, The Offering Chapels of Dynasties 12 and 13, Publications of The Pennsylvania-Yale Expedition to Egypt 5, 1974, pl. 46; D. Franke, Ägyptische Verwandtschaftsbeziehungen im Mittleren Reich, Hamburger Ägyptologische Studien 3, 1983, pp. 54–55.

91

which, judging by what can still be seen, were formerly painted blue. The first line names various oils; the other four contain offering formulae addressed to Osiris, Wepwawet and all the gods of Abydos.

The lower part of the stela illustrates the complicated genealogy of Antef's family. Antef himself together with his wife are seated in the first register in the presence of Antef's deceased first wife, receiving the respects and offerings of their children. In the second register it is a certain Nakhti and his wife who are likewise venerated by their children, while the third register depicts a procession of three priestesses and two priests followed by three girls.

The silhouettes of the figures are all beautifully outlined against the background of green painted hieroglyphs. The women are dressed in white with long wigs and all except the priestesses are wearing green painted jewelry, some holding their husbands by the arm, others scenting a lotus blossom or holding a mirror or a folded cloth; of the men dressed in short white kilts set off by the red-brown of their skin, some are also wearing green painted bead collars; the cult servants are portrayed bringing the various offerings.

Bibliography: Mariette, Catalogue général des monuments d'Abydos, Paris 1880, no. 615; Lange/Schäfer, Grab- und Denksteine des Mittleren Reiches (CG) II, pp. 139–42; IV, pl. 39. Cf. also: D. O'Connor, in: Mélanges Gamal Eddin Moukhtar II, Cairo 1985, pp. 171–77.

92   Ground floor, room 22
Stela of Antef

Painted limestone   CG 20535
H. 68 cm; W. 46 cm
Abydos, north necropolis. Mariette's excavations in 1881
Middle Kingdom, 12th dynasty, about 1900 B.C.

This stela, contemporary with the preceding one, has the same provenance as the latter and is of an analogous type. The two stelae differ however in that this one mentions no official date or royal name; none of the numerous persons depicted has a distinctive title, and the epigraphy is of poorer quality. It nevertheless has the advantage of having retained some of its colour and the careful sculpturing of the figures in sunk relief makes of it an example worthy of representing the Abydene type stela of the Middle Kingdom.

The upper part of the stela is decorated with five lines of text,

93   Ground floor, gallery 26
Queen Nofret   ▷

Black granite   JE 37487
H. 165 cm; W. 51 cm; profile 98.5 cm   = CG 381
Tanis
Middle Kingdom, 12th dynasty, reign of Sesostris II, c. 1897–1878 B.C.

The soft and gentle quality found in some early Twelfth Dynasty statues (see nos. 88 and 89) and strongly influenced by Memphite art of the Old Kingdom proved to be shortlived. Official art rapidly came to develop a realistic tendency, as it revived the forceful modelling inherited from its Theban ancestors (see no. 67). Female royal statuary follows this new canon, whose primary emphasis is power.

This tendency is well illustrated by the portrait of Sesostris II's wife with her large face, enormous, almost detached ears, oversized limbs and powerful stature.

Changes in fashion usually accompanied changes in style, a feature reflected in statuary of all periods in Egypt. Thus Nofret's wigstyle was in fashion at court, and was automatically adopted and democratized throughout the land. Apparently the wig's feminine qualities were responsible for its ultimate association with the goddess Hathor. It was known thereafter as the "Hathor wig" par excellence. It consists of three separate tresses; a large one falls behind the head. Two other undulating tresses, drawn around in front and wrapped in

◁ 93

narrow bands, terminate over the breast in two spirals encircling disks. The uraeus at the brow is reduced to tiny size. The opening of the robe is very low, and large bands ornament the thick ankles. Incised upon the breast is an open-work pectoral of a type often worn by contemporary aristocratic women; tomb discoveries have revealed a number of magnificent examples (see nos. 109 and 110).

The inscription carved upon the jambs of the throne, better preserved on the second statue of Nofret, provides the queen's titles: "The noblewoman, favorite and greatly praised one . . . beloved of Khakheperre [Sesostris II]."

Bibliography: PM IV, pp. 18–19; L. Borchardt, Statuen und Statuetten (CG) II, pp. 1–2, pl. 60; Evers, Staat aus dem Stein I, pls. 74–5; H. W. Müller, Ägyptische Kunst, no. 68; H. Sourouzian, in: MDAIK 37, 1981, pp. 448–49, pl. 71b.

94

Upper floor, room 37

Sarcophagus of Senbi (detail)

Painted wood   JE 42948
H. 63 cm; L. 212 cm
Meir; excavated by A. Kamal in 1910
Middle Kingdom, 12th dynasty, c. 1900 B.C.

The sarcophagus was the deceased's final resting-place in the netherworld, hence its decoration with vibrant colors in imita-

tions of house exteriors, complete with wooden columns, painted matting and floral patterns. The door, with two leaves and double bolt, provided the deceased with the opportunity to magically leave his resting-place at will. Inside the sarcophagus, his body was turned to one side in order that he could also gaze out at the outside world through the large eyes painted on the exterior.

This rectangular wooden sarcophagus belonged to a man named Senbi. His tomb was located at Meir in Middle Egypt in one of the vast necropoleis of the western desert. Here were interred the high officials of the nome of Cusae from the end of the Old Kingdom to the Twelfth Dynasty. Their decorated tomb walls contain magnificent bas-reliefs; the chambers were packed with painted sarcophagi and a rich array of funerary equipment which survived undisturbed for millennia. It was only in the last century that they were discovered and left to the fellahin. Nevertheless, some remains from the tombs were saved, and many of the world's museums were allowed to enrich their collections with the legal purchase of sarcophagi, coffins and other objects. See also the canopic chest of Senbi on exhibit in this room (RT 19.11.27.9).

Bibliography: PM IV, p. 256; A. Kamal, in: ASAE 12, 1912, p. 121.

95

95

Upper floor, room 37

Sarcophagus of Sepi (detail)

Painted wood   JE 32868
H. 70 cm; L. 233 cm; W. 65 cm   = CG 28083
El-Bersheh, excavations of the Egyptian Antiquities Service, 1897
Middle Kingdom, 12th dynasty, c. 1900 B.C.

One of the most beautiful of the Middle Kingdom inscribed and painted sarcophagi is unquestionably that of the general Sepi. This great dignitary of the Fifteenth Upper Egyptian nome was buried at El-Bersheh. His anthropoid inner coffin is likewise in the Museum.

The coffin has been dismantled in order to facilitate the display of the richly painted interior sides. The exterior decoration, concealed today, consists of incised and painted offering formulae. As usual, two *udjat* eyes placed above a false door appear on the side to which the mask of the anthropoid coffin is turned.

The interior decoration, visible to the viewer, is entirely painted. It contains a series of spells in cursive hieroglyphs taken from the body of mortuary literature known as the Coffin Texts.

On the panel at the head of the coffin (illustrated here), we see a well-preserved composition in restrained colors. The oblong sky sign, filled with stars, surmounts a band of large, carefully painted hieroglyphs which reads: "Revered under Nepthys — at your head —, the general Sepi, justified." Below, resting on two low tables are vessels of stone, a linen bag, two folds of cloth, a lamp with a wick and two headrests. A tiny band of cursive hieroglyphs directly above lists all of the objects in this frieze.

In the lower half of the representation, a funerary text called the "Book of Two Ways" is accompanied by a map illustrating the netherworld. Here sits Osiris enthroned, wearing the Atef crown and holding the *was*-scepter and the sign of life. The signs for millions of years are inscribed on his throne.

At a period when the netherworld is in the west, and the lord of the dead is Osiris, and when the funerary texts aim above all at providing for the well-being of the deceased, here is an attempt at a topographical description of the realm of the hereafter. This anticipates the great "funerary books" of the New Kingdom which were to develop on the walls of the royal tombs in order to reveal the actual geography of the land of the dead.

Bibliography: PM IV, p. 183; Daressy, in: ASAE 1, 1900, p. 39; Lacau, Sarcophages antérieurs au Nouvel Empire (CG) I, pp. 170–99, pl. 25; Corteggiani, no. 40.

96

Funerary mask

Linen, stuccoed and painted   RT 24.4.26.1
H. 71 cm
Provenance unknown
Middle Kingdom, c. 2100–1800 B.C.

"May you revive, may you revive forever; you are hereby rejuvenated for all time." This is the formula recited at the end of the embalming ritual in order to revitalize the mummified body. A funerary mask, covering the head of a body deprived of its viscera and embalmed and wrapped in bandages, lends the figure a lifelike appearance and serves as both face and head. Such masks were in use from the end of the Old Kingdom onwards. They were formed from multiple layers of linen coated with stucco, then modelled and painted in the image of the deceased. Occasionally a painted breast-panel completed the mask.

This specimen clearly represents a young individual with large, spirited eyes, in a face fitted with beard and moustache. A large collar painted on the breast is partially covered by the lappets of a long wig with central part.

The body is missing and the provenance of the mask is unknown, but many similar examples represent officials of the Middle Kingdom, thus allowing us to date our example to the same era.

Bibliography: Cf.: Centenaire de l'Institut Français d'Archéologie Orientale, Cairo 1981, no. 8; Hayes, The Scepter of Egypt I, p. 304, fig. 196.

97

Canopic jars of Inpuhotep

Limestone and painted wood   JE 46774
H. 34 cm; Diam. 11cm
Sakkara, excavations of the Egyptian Antiquities Service, north of the pyramid of Teti, 1914
Middle Kingdom, 12th dynasty, c. 1900 B.C.

Canopic jars are urns of ceramic or stone which the Egyptians used from the Old Kingdom onwards to store the human viscera extracted during the process of mummification.

The term derives from the village named Canopus by the Greeks (present day Abukir, derived from Saint Car), once rich in vessels with Osiriform stoppers which the first antiquaries named canopics.

At first bulky stoppers served to seal these jars. Thereafter, one finds them crowned with human heads. Eventually they were placed under the protection of four genii who guaranteed the function of the viscera in the next world. These are the four sons of Horus: Amset, Hapi, Duamutef and Kebehsenuef, respective patrons of the liver, lungs, stomach and intestines. While Amset appeared beardless and light-skinned, the other three genii were given beards and dark-colored skin.

The stoppers next began to imitate the heads of the genii. Amset kept his human appearance while Hapi was shown with a baboon's head, Duamutef with that of a jackal and Kebehsenuef that of a falcon (see the numerous sets of canopics of this type on display both in this room and in corridor 24).

Our four canopics display the original feature of painted wood stoppers on top of limestone jars. They were discovered in a Middle Kingdom tomb sealed in a wooden chest with the name of Inpuhotep. The heads are executed in a style of modelling visible in numerous other pieces from this tomb. The work is somewhat hasty, the expression naive but touching.

This is art concerned with the immortalization of a particular idea or action. Seen from this point of view, even the coarsest modelling would have fulfilled its purpose.

Bibliography: Quibell/Hayter, Excavations at Saqqara, Teti Pyramid, North Side, Cairo 1927, p. 15, pl. 21 (4). Cf. also: Reisner, Canopics (CG); LÄ III, 316−19.

98
Sesostris III

Granite   RT 18.4.22.4
H. 150 cm; W. 58 cm; L. 54 cm
Thebes, Deir el-Bahari. Found in the front court of the temple of Mentuhotep II
Middle Kingdom, 12th dynasty, reign of Sesostris III, 1878−1842 B.C.

The serenity of the earliest royal portraits of the 12th dynasty gives way in favor of a certain brutality in the rendering of the hard, tormented and prematurely aged visages which reflect without mercy the complex images of the later sovereigns of this illustrious dynasty. Aggressive and belligerent conquerors, they pursued a policy of military expansion which led to the subjugation of neighbouring countries. In Egypt itself, they definitely suppressed the autonomy of the nomarchs and succeeded in controlling a centralized state with the aid of a widespread administrative organization. They reclaimed for agriculture certain marshy regions and in particular sponsored projects for utilizing the available water resources of the Fayum depression. These kings seem to have been conscious of their duties as administrators placed by the gods at the head of a human hierarchy in order to govern the state. The concept of royalty had thus undergone a considerable change, which is reflected in these surprising effigies. The king is now "the good shepherd", responsible to the gods in the difficult exercise of his royal function. He no longer, as in the Old Kingdom, appears as their absolute representative on earth (see Chephren, no. 31), but has learned to display himself in prayer before them.

This statue was found on the causeway in front of the temple of Mentuhotep at Deir el-Bahari which was used as a processional way during the "Beautiful feast of the valley". It represents Sesostris III in an attitude of prayer. He wears the pleated *nemes* headdress with attached uraeus and a starched kilt asymmetrically pleated on which his two hands rest in a pious pose. His extraordinary physiognomy reflects a synthesis of royal grandeur. His body, admirably sculptured to illustrate the strength and beauty of youth, is that of a conqueror. The dramatic expression of his face is almost cruel; the eyes with their heavy lids seem tired; the realistic, strongly marked wrinkles between the eyes, the bitter mouth, the protruding chin and enormous ears are all traits which, leading beyond individual portraiture, express the monarch's consciousness of his responsibilities as chief of a totalitarian state.

Bibliography: PM II, p. 385; Vandier, Manuel III, p. 186, pl. 63; Evers, Staat aus dem Stein I, pl. 83; Götter Pharaonen, no. 21; Wildung, Sesostris und Amenemhet, fig. 177.

99

The daughters of Djehutyhotep

Painted limestone   JE 30199
H. 80 cm; W. 70.5 cm
El-Bersheh, tomb of Djehutyhotep (no. 2); excavations of the Egypt Exploration Fund, 1892
Middle Kingdom, 12th dynasty, reign of Sesostris I – Sesostris II, c. 1900 B.C.

Three daughters of the nomarch Djehutyhotep are represented here in a procession. This painted relief is only a fragment from a wall of one of the most important rock-cut tombs of the Middle Kingdom. El Bersheh, like Meir, Beni Hassan or Aswan, was one of the provincial necropoleis which the powerful nomarchs now chose for their burials, near their own residences in their own domains, instead of clustered around the royal pyramid as in the Fourth Dynasty.
It was in the tomb of Djehutyhotep, governor of the Fifteenth Upper Egyptian nome, that travellers from the last century discovered and copied the famous scene of transporting a colossal statue. Mounted on a sledge, it is dragged along by four rows of forty-three men!

The nomarch's three daughters, great ladies of this provincial court, are shown gracefully sniffing lotus flowers. They are dressed in long garments of white linen with shoulder straps leaving the breast exposed. Their coiffure, with tresses rolled around a carnelian disk, reveals the contemporary fashion (see Nofret, no. 93). Each woman has a lotus diadem headband, made of blue lotus flowers for the first woman, and white lotus for the second. Openwork pectorals hang around their necks, and large bracelets and anklets complete their costume. The ideal of feminine beauty in the Middle Kingdom is well illustrated by these fairly stiff figures with very slim waist but ample breast, overlong arms, and accentuated hips marked by a slight change of plane in the relief. The elongated forms leave the wrists and ankles thick; the head seems disproportionately large, with its floral diadem of complementary colors weighed down by the sheer mass of flowers. The tiny ears contrast with the rather severe and heavy facial features.
The relief is, however, not without charm. The confidently executed modelling, harmony of color and beauty of the hieroglyphs naming the three ladies form a composition worthy of being termed a work of art.

Bibliography: PM IV, p. 180; Terrace/Fischer, no. 15.

100
Ground floor, room 22

Ukh-hotep and family

Grey granite JE 30965
H. 37 cm; W. 30 cm; thickness 14 cm = CG 459
Meir, tomb of Ukh-hotep
Middle Kingdom, 12ᵗʰ dynasty, reign of Sesostris III, 1878–1842 B.C.

The number of private statues increases toward the end of the Twelfth Dynasty. The once royal prerogative of placing a likeness in the tomb to insure the lifelike appearance of the deceased was extended at this time to the lower social classes as well. Furthermore, the high officials of the country, nomarchs or other dignitaries, acquired the right to deposit statues in the temples.

From the tomb of Ukh-hotep, one of the last nomarchs of the Middle Kingdom, comes this group statue representing him with his two wives and one of his daughters. Familial groups of this sort occur fairly frequently, and occasionally reproduce the genealogy all the way back to the deceased's aunt and maternal grandmother. Less common, however, are examples of polygamy. It may be explained in the case of this nomarch as a desire to imitate the practices of the royal court.

These four individuals, grouped asymmetrically, display the fashionable hairstyles and poses of the day. They bear the characteristically coarse features and large ears influenced by contemporary royal portraiture. The tall, tapering bodies create a cramped effect, aided by the exaggeratedly long limbs. The figures are attached to a sort of stela decorated with Udjat eyes and the heraldic plants of the north and south. Their titles and functions are inscribed upon their garments. The

101

hereditary prince and count Ukh-hotep was also overseer of priests of the goddess Hathor and beloved of his nome.

Bibliography: PM IV, p. 257; Borchardt, Statuen und Statuetten (CG) II, pp. 51–52, pl. 76; Vandier, Manuel III, p. 244, pl. 85,2; Terrace/ Fischer, no. 16. Cf. another group statue of Ukh-hotep in Boston: W. K. Simpson in: Boston Museum Bulletin 72, no. 368, 1974, pp. 100–104.

101
Upper floor, hall 48

Head of a female statuette

Painted wood JE 6366
H. 7 cm = CG 812
Sakkara, discovered in 1860
Middle Kingdom, 12ᵗʰ dynasty, c. 1900 B.C.

Despite severe gashes, especially around the nose, this arresting portrait still manages to retain its intense expression. The youthful face, with wide, staring eyes and herring-bone eyebrows, is framed by an undulating wig divided into three tresses. The two front tresses, lost today, would have fallen to the breast. The third came to rest upon the back (compare Nofret, no. 93). What remains of the intricately carved wig, as well as the subtle modelling of the face, displays great facility in wood sculpture on the part of the ancient artist.

Bibliography: PM III, 2, p. 725; Borchardt, Statuen und Statuetten (CG) III, p. 107, pl. 150; Wildung, Sesostris und Amenemhet, fig. 81.

102
Sphinx of Amenemhat III

Ground floor, gallery 16

Grey granite
H. 150 cm; L. 236 cm; W. 75 cm

JE 15210
= CG 394

Tanis (San el-Hagar). Discovered by Mariette in 1863
Middle Kingdom, 12th dynasty, reign of Amenemhat III, 1842–1798 B.C.

The word 'sphinx' used by the Greeks derives perhaps from Egyptian Shesepankh "living statue". It designates a type of statue joining a human head to the body of a lion and symbolizes sovereignty combining the strength of the lion with a human intelligence.

In addition to this classical type of sphinx, best represented by the great Sphinx of Giza, there are other varieties such as the criosphinx of Amon, with ram's head attached to a lion's body, and our Tanis sphinxes having a human face with a lion's mane and body. There exist likewise female sphinxes with a queen's head like those of Hatshepsut (gallery 11, ground floor).

This sphinx belonged to a group which were perhaps originally located in the temple of the cat goddess Bastet at Bubas-tis. First usurped by one of the Hyksos kings, they were subsequently transferred to the Ramesside capital in the eastern Delta. Later still, during the reign of King Psusennes I of the 21st dynasty, they were again removed, this time to Tanis, the new capital. The sphinxes still display evidence of these successive usurpations: that of the King Nehesy, of Ramses II, Merenptah and Psusennes.

The vigorous countenance of this sphinx is a portrait of Amenemhat III. Its sovereign gravity indicates, as in the portrait of his father Sesostris III (no. 98), the strength, grandeur and wisdom of the monarch, who continued his ancestors' policy of conquest and was enabled to bring to a successful conclusion the ambitious irrigation projects which were to make of the Fayum a fertile agricultural oasis. The grandeur of the features is amplified by the lion's mane which here exceptionally replaces the royal *nemes*. It adapts itself perfectly to the contours of the visage and reinforces the impression of the irresistible power of the supreme authority.

Bibliography: PM IV, p. 16; Borchardt, Statuen und Statuetten (CG) II, p. 12, pl. 64; Evers, Staat aus dem Stein I, pls. 121–23; Habachi, in: Studien zur Altägyptischen Kultur 6, 1978, pp. 80–90, pl. 25.

Amenemhat III in priestly costume

Black granite   JE 20001
H. 100 cm; W. 99 cm   = CG 395
Fayum, Mit Farēs. Found in 1862
Middle Kingdom, 12th dynasty, reign of Amenemhat III, 1842–1798
B.C.

This colossal bust found on the site of the ancient capital of
the Fayum, Shedet (the Crocodilopolis of the Greeks), was for
long considered to be a monument of the Hyksos period. In
fact it represents Amenemhat III recognizable by his characteristic facial features. The impressive visage with its high cheek-
bones, wrinkled cheeks and prominently marked muscles
around the bitter mouth is a masterpiece of realistic sculpture.
The magnificent head is framed in an enormous archaic-type
wig whose heavy plaits rest on the shoulders and the back of
the neck. The body of the uraeus, whose head is missing, is
stretched out across the top of the wig. The false beard, now
broken off, is attached to the chin by a naturalistic band of
wavy locks. The king is dressed in a panther skin whose head
and paws lie on his shoulders. It is supported by a double
band across his chest passing under the *menat* collar which
adorns his neck. The extremities of two scepters terminating
in falcon heads, which he was holding against his body, are
visible on each side of the wig.
Amenemhat III thus presents himself as the primordial sovereign in his sacerdotal function which theoretically he alone is
empowered to fulfill. This is another manifestation of the
extraordinary devotion shown by this king who constructed
near his pyramid in the Fayum a funerary temple of gigantic
proportions, regrouping in a maze of sanctuaries the innumerable cult chapels of the gods, a complex which was later
admired by the Greeks under the name of the Labyrinth.

*Bibliography: PM IV, p. 99; Borchardt, Statuen und Statuetten (CG)
II, p. 13, pl. 64; Evers, Staat aus dem Stein I, pls. 127–28; Vandier,
Manuel III, p. 210; Terrace/Fischer, no. 17; Yoyotte, Treasures of the
Pharaohs, pp. 50, 53; Corteggiani, no. 42; Wildung, Sesostris und
Amenemhet, fig. 148.*

Double statue of Amenemhat III as a Nile god or "The offering bearers of Tanis"

Grey granite   JE 18221
H. 160 cm; W. 100 cm; thickness 80 cm   = CG 392
Tanis, found in 1861
Middle Kingdom, 12th dynasty, reign of Amenemhat III, 1842–1798
B.C.

Two identical masculine figures are carrying in front of them
trays of fish from which depend strands of lotus flowers, fish
and geese. This double statue is so unusual in both its type
and attributes that for a long time it was considered to be the
effigy of one of the Hyksos kings, formerly called the "Shepherd kings". In fact, it depicts Amenemhat III whose characteristic style leaves no doubt as to the date to be assigned to it.
Although the headdress and beard are archaic, not having
been in use since the predynastic period, this type of statue is
not unique. It is recognized by analogy with other more or less
well preserved monuments that these statues represent the
King himself in the guise of the Nile god who comes forth
from the bowels of the earth in order to provide his land with
all the nourishment indispensable to life.
As for the redoubling of the royal personage, a theme occurring since the time of the 5th dynasty, it was particularly in
favour during the Middle Kingdom. Both royal dyads and
twin sphinxes are known (see the dyad and one of the twin
sphinxes preserved on a double base, from Bubastis, on view

104a △

104b

◁ 104c

in this room). This phenomenon can be explained by the supposition that the two figures represent the King as ruler of Upper and Lower Egypt respectively, or by taking the two figures as illustrating a cycle of regeneration where one is the reigning King and the other his deified counterpart.

On examining the statue from all sides we discover the marvelous modeling of the figures, which are wearing short, finely pleated kilts and wigs with long locks. We can likewise admire the excellent quality of the sculpture in high relief on each side of the dyad where groups of geese are suspended from the arms of the two figures, mingled with the hanging lotus flowers.

The composition is well balanced and the symmetry of the various parts is so carefully observed that it results in a contradiction of one of the established canons of Egyptian art, namely that masculine persons are always depicted with the left foot forward. Here the outer foot of each figure is extended in front of him with the result that the figure on the spectator's left advances his right foot.

The inscriptions were added by King Psusennes of the 21st dynasty when this group was removed, like many other monuments, to Tanis.

Bibliography: PM IV, p. 17; Borchardt, Statuen und Statuetten (CG) II, pp. 9–11, pl. 63; Vandier, Manuel III, pp. 208–209; Propyläen Kunstgeschichte 15, fig. 166; Wildung, Sesostris und Amenemhet, fig. 185–86.

105
Amenemhat III

Black granite   JE 37400
H. 73.5 cm; W. 31 cm; profile 26 cm   = CG 42015
Karnak, court of the cachette, cleared by Legrain in 1904
Middle Kingdom, 12th dynasty, reign of Amenemhat III, 1842–1798
B.C.

Amenemhat III dedicated several granite statues in the temple
of Amen at Karnak which were discovered in the "court of the
cachette." The most beautiful example has returned to Thebes
for permanent exhibition in the Luxor Museum after a stay of
eighty years in Cairo.
The so-called cachette court is located in front of the seventh
pylon at Karnak. The excavation of its floor from 1901–5
provided one of the most fabulous discoveries ever made in
Egypt. In addition to architectural elements and some shrines,
the floor of this court concealed more than two thousand statues of kings, deities and private individuals dating from
Dynasty 11 to as late as the Ptolemaic period. Deposited over
generations in the temple, these statues eventually began to
choke up the courts and passages. Hence they were buried and
hidden in the cachette for they were not to be destroyed.
Amenemhat III is shown here in the attitude of prayer already
observed in the case of his predecessor (no. 98). One notes
once again that during this period of political, literary and
artistic magnificence, this king (two of whose statues once
dominated the bank of the Fayum lake at Biahmou) represented himself no longer in a divine pose but in prayer before
his god, despite his greatly exalted power.
If the *nemes* headdress, starched projecting triangular kilt and
bead necklace render this statue more conventional in appearance than the preceding pieces (nos. 102–104), the extreme
realism of the face on the other hand ranks with their portraits. The severity and force are perhaps slightly muted, but
the undeceived, even sad expression, the anxiety and fatigue
are clearly visible. Despite the aging visage, however, the body
remains youthful and vigorous. The treatment of the physiognomy is worthy of the best works of the period.

*Bibliography: PM II, p. 137; Legrain, Statues et Statuettes (CG) I,
p. 11, pl. 9.*

officials of this dynasty. Under his chin is an unusually long, striped beard.

In imitation of his sovereign, undoubtedly one of the last kings of the 12th dynasty, the vizier is shown with very large ears (see nos. 98–105); the compact body and thick legs are derivative of the "Theban style" characteristic of the preceding 11th dynasty (see no. 67). During the 22nd dynasty this statue was usurped by a certain Djed-Djehuty-iuf-ankh who added his own inscriptions on the statue; the name of the original owner is consequently unknown to us.

Bibliography: PM II, p. 148; Legrain, Statues et Statuettes (CG) III, pp. 17–20, pl. 14; Götter Pharaonen, no. 22.

107   Upper floor, room 3
Jewellery of the princess Khnumit   ▷

Gold, carnelian, lapis lazuli, turquoise   JE 31113–6
Max. L. 35 cm; max. W. 3 cm   = CG 52920–21/26–27/29–30,
                      35–36/55–56/58/59–74 and 53018
Dahshur, funerary complex of Amenemhat II, tomb of Khnumit. Excavations of De Morgan, 1894
Middle Kingdom, 12th dynasty, reign of Amenemhat II, 1929–1897 B.C.

The sarcophagus, mummy and funerary equipment of the daughter of Amenemhat II were discovered intact in a tomb prepared to the west of the royal pyramid. Three other tombs in the same area likewise shared in this good fortune.

These pieces represent some of the more beautiful bracelets and necklaces chosen from the rich collection of jewellery found during excavation.

The bracelets are composed of simple little chains of gold beads and clasps with slide-bars in gold cloisonné inlaid with semi-precious stones. In addition to their ornamental beauty, the clasps are shaped into the hieroglyphic signs for such concepts as "Joy", "Birth", and "All protection and life behind her."

The blue-colored necklace contains threaded beads of gold, turquoise and lapis lazuli, as well as a row of tear-drop pendants worked in gold cloisonné set with turquoise and lapis lazuli.

The second, more open necklace takes the form of the broad Wesekh-collar, and was discovered in scattered pieces upon the breast of the mummy. Its elements consist of gold cloisonné set with stones, and two magnificent falcon heads serving as clasps. Instead of beads, the central area contains pairs of amulets arranged on either side of a central *ankh* sign. They stand for Life, the Two Ladies, Unification, Stability, Power, Protection, etc. A row of tri-colored pendants hangs below the amulets, which in turn are fastened to chains of little gold beads.

Bibliography: PM III, 2, p. 886; J. de Morgan, Fouilles à Dahchour en 1894–1895, Vienna 1903, p. 55, pls. 5 and 7; Vernier, Bijoux et Orfèvreries (CG), pp. 306–17 and 336, pls. 71–72 and 75; Aldred, Jewels, pls. 30–31.

106   Ground floor, room 22
Statue of a vizier

Grey granite   JE 36931
H. 113 cm; W. 35 cm; L. 67.5 cm   = CG 42207
Karnak, court of the cachette. Excavated by Legrain in 1904
Middle Kingdom, end of the 12th dynasty, about 1800 B.C.

At this period, important officials of non-royal rank had acquired the privilege before reserved for the King and his family, of placing their statues in the temples of the gods. This unnamed vizier took advantage of the situation to perpetuate his memory in the temple of Amon-Re at Karnak. Seated on a cubical seat with a low back, his hands resting on his knees, the right hand holding a folded cloth, the vizier wears the costume characteristic of his position; a comparatively long skirt knotted over the chest and supported by two straps. The wide wig which leaves the ears uncovered is also typical of high

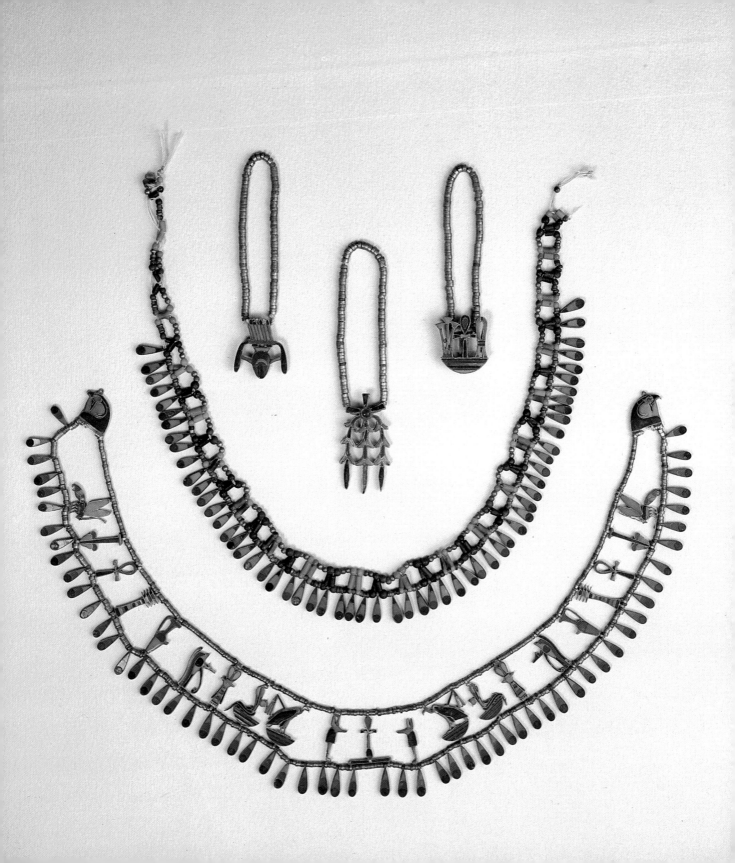

108

Uraeus of Sesostris II

Gold, lapis lazuli, carnelian, feldspar   JE 46694
H. 6.7 cm; W. 3 cm   = CG 52702
Lahun, pyramid of Sesostris II; excavations of the British School of Archaeology by F. Petrie, 1920
Middle Kingdom, 12th dynasty, reign of Sesostris II, 1897–1878 B.C.

This golden serpent, with its arresting, noble posture, vibrant colors and gleaming eyes, is the uraeus, or royal insignia affixed to the front of the royal headdress in order to protect the king against evil. Its name derives from the Latinized form of the Greek "ouraios," which in turn comes from the Egyptian Iaret, "the cobra," that is, the female cobra tense with rage. By spitting fire, she could annihilate all foes.

The origins of the uraeus are lost in the distant past, and it is uncertain whether it represents a Lower Egyptian tradition handed down from Buto, the northern capital which worshipped the cobra form of the goddess Wadjet, or the influence of the foreign frontal lock once worn by Libyans. Whatever the case, the uraeus become royal insignia was attached to the *nemes* headdress and to royal diadems in the Old Kingdom. Later, from the Middle Kingdom onwards, numerous royal crowns are also furnished with a frontal uraeus.

The example chosen here was quite likely once part of a crown or headdress of Sesostris II. It was discovered among the debris of the room adjoining the royal sarcophagus chamber. The serpent's body is solid gold worked with a hammer, onto which the details have been soldered; the stones are set into cloisons.

The head is fashioned of lapis lazuli and the eyes of garnet set in gold rims. The decoration on the neck contains pieces of feldspar, lapis lazuli and carnelian. The tail, hollowed out from the bottom, takes two looping turns, then terminates in an undulating point. Two ringlets, soldered to the back of the hollowed body, apparently allowed the uraeus to be attached to the cloth or leather headdress.

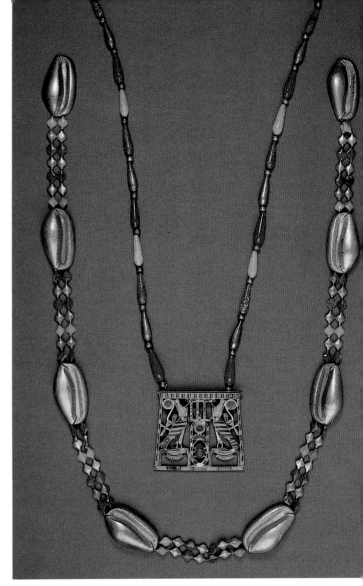

109

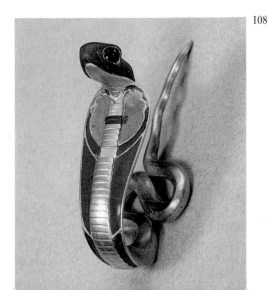

108

Bibliography: PM IV, p. 109; F. Petrie/G. Brunton/M. A. Murray, Lahun II, London 1923, pl. 25, pp. 12–13; Vernier, Bijoux et Orfèvreries (CG), p. 235, pl. 47; Aldred, Jewels, pl. 43.

109

Jewellery of Sat-Hathor

Gold, lapis lazuli, feldspar and carnelian
Pectoral   JE 30857
H. 4.9 cm; W. 5.6 cm   = CG 52001
Belt   JE 30858
L. 70 cm   = CG 53123 and 53136
Dahshur, mortuary complex of Sesostris III, tomb of Sat-Hathor; excavated by De Morgan in 1894
Middle Kingdom, 12th dynasty, reign of Sesostris III, 1887–1842 B.C.

Two princesses buried next to the pyramid of Sesostris III were both owners of dazzling funerary treasures. The first, Sat-Hathor, was a daughter of Sesostris II, sister and perhaps wife of Sesostris III. After disentangling her rich collection of scarabs, golden shells, recumbent lion cubs, buckles for clasps, and countless beads, the restorers were able to reconstruct fabulous collars, bracelets, belts and rings.

The openwork pectoral, hung from a chain of stone and gold beads, consists of gold cloisonné work and precious stones. Its frame takes a form inspired by architecture, crowned with a cavetto cornice. On either side of the centered praenomen of Sesostris II, two striped falcons perched upon the sign for gold portray the god Horus. The king is also an incarnation of this god, hence the two birds wear the Double Crown and are flanked by the sun-disk with uraeus holding an *ankh*.

The reverse of this pendant is in gold leaf. Its similar decoration was embossed and chased before the front was worked with cloisons.

The girdle alternates between gold cowrie shells and a double row of little "acacia seed" stone beads. The length of the belt is noticeably reduced due to the loss of some of the cowries; the piece has been reconstructed based on the elements still preserved. The cowrie shells are identical on both sides. Only the two exterior ones, serving to attach and close the belt, have a flat reverse. As they are joined one to the other, by means of a groove, they form together an entire cowrie which fastens this magnificent girdle.

Bibliography: PM III, 2, p. 883; de Morgan, Fouilles à Dahchour 1894, p. 60, pls. XV–XVII, XXI; Vernier, Bijoux et Orfèvreries, pp. 1–4 and 373, pl. 1; Aldred, Jewels, pl. 33.

110

110

Pectorals of Mereret

Gold, carnelian, turquoise, lapis lazuli, amethyst   JE 30875
H. 6.1 and 7.9 cm; W. 8.6 and 10.5 cm   = CG 52002 and 52003
Dahshur, mortuary complex of Sesostris III, tomb of Mereret; excavated by De Morgan in 1894
Middle Kingdom, 12th dynasty, reigns of Sesostris III and Amenemhat III, 1878–1798 B.C.

The second treasure discovered near the pyramid of Sesostris III was that of the princess Mereret. Daughter of Sesostris III and sister of his successor, Amenemhat III, this princess' life spanned both reigns.

Her two marvelous openwork pectorals are set within a framework whose form borrows from architecture. Inside this "chapel", the vulture-goddess with outstretched wings hovers protectively over scenes of the victorious king despatching his enemies.

The first pectoral contains the name of the father, Sesostris III. Between elegant lotus flowers, the king appears in the form of a griffin subjugating and trampling his foes. The griffin combines here the power of the falcon with the strength of the lion.

The second, larger pectoral is inscribed with the name of the successor, Amenemhat III. In this case, the king brandishes his mace, about to smite the chieftains of foreign lands. This warlike theme once adorned the breast of a lady! The pectorals were nevertheless royal gifts dating to one of Egypt's most militarily successful periods. Most noteworthy, however, is the detailed workmanship on even the smallest cloisons, and the precision of the joins.

Bibliography: PM III, 2, p. 884; de Morgan, Fouilles à Dahchour 1894, p. 64, pls. XIX–XXI; Vernier, Bijoux et Orfèvreries (CG), pp. 4–5, pls. 1–2; Aldred, Jewels, pls. 41 and 42.

Upper floor, room 3

Jewellery of Mereret

Gold, amethyst

Belt	JE 30879 and 30923
L. 60 cm	= CG 53075
Anklet chain	JE 30884 a and 30923
L. 34 cm	= CG 53169−53170

Dahshur, mortuary complex of Sesostris III, tomb of Mereret;
excavated by De Morgan, 1894
Middle Kingdom, 12th dynasty, reigns of Sesostris III
and Amenemhat III, 1878−1798 B.C.

Coquetry enhanced with a prophylactic symbolism adorned
women's hips and ankles with delicate chains, formed of amethyst beads connecting to leopard heads or claws. It displays a
remarkable combination of color, creative taste in ornament
and competence in repoussé work. Beautiful jewellery, amuletic protection of the individual and technical precision are all
united in successful harmony.

Bibliography: De Morgan, Fouilles à Dahchour 1894, p. 65, pl. 22;
Vernier, Bijoux et Orfèvreries (CG), pp. 352−53, 384, pls. 79, 81;
Leclant, Les Pharaons I, p. 246, fig. 240. Cf. Aldred, Jewels, pl. 36
(similar jewellery of the same epoch from Lahun).

Diadem of Sat-Hathor-Yunet

Gold, lapis lazuli, carnelian, green faience
H. ca. 44 cm; W. 19.2 cm
Lahun, mortuary complex of Sesostris II, tomb of Sat-Hathor-Yunet.
Excavated by Petrie for the British School of Archaeology in Egypt, 1914
Middle Kingdom, 12ᵗʰ dynasty, reign of Amenemhat III, 1842–1798 B.C.

JE 44919
= CG 52641

The diadem takes the form of a large flat band of solid gold, ornamented with the uraeus and rosettes. Additional gold decoration consists of two tall feathers and three loose double streamers attached with rivets. The entire piece would have been set on a wig with long braids, each one of which was clasped tightly in numerous little gold rings. The effect has been reconstructed and exhibited in the Metropolitan Museum in New York.

Both the gold cloisonné rosettes and the uraeus are ornamented with lapis lazuli, carnelian and green faience, the latter replacing the feldspar or turquoise preferred on earlier examples. The uraeus' head is of lapis lazuli, while its eyes are of garnet set in gold rims.

The owner of this magnificent diadem was Sat-Hathor-Yunet, one of the daughters of Sesostris II. Having outlived her brother, Sesostris III, this princess died in the reign of her nephew Amenemhat III. She was then buried in a tomb long since prepared for her next to the pyramid of her father. Among her other jewellery, a pectoral with the name of Sesostris II, now in New York, and a second with that of Amenemhat III, on view in this room attest to Sat-Hathor-Yunet's long lifespan.

Bibliography: PM IV, p. 109; Brunton, Lahun I, The Treasure, London 1920, pp. 26–27, pl. V; Vernier, Bijoux et Orfèvreries (CG), pp. 201–202, pl. 38; Aldred, Jewels, pl. 39.

113

Mirror of Sat-Hathor-Yunet

Silver, gold, obsidian, stone, faience, and electrum
H. 28 cm; W. 15 cm
Lahun, mortuary complex of Sesostris II, tomb of Sat-Hathor-Yunet.
Excavated by Petrie for the British School of Archaeology in Egypt, 1914
Middle Kingdom, 12ᵗʰ dynasty, reign of Amenemhat III, 1842–1798 B.C.

JE 44920
= CG 52663

The toilet articles of these princesses are as elaborate as their jewellery. This beautiful mirror, discovered among elegant black unguent vessels with gold veneered rims, is actually a masterpiece of the goldsmith's craft.

The thick silver disk is attached by a small tongue in the obsidian handle in the shape of an open papyrus. Under the umbel covered with electrum leaf, the head of the goddess Hathor with cow's ears is connected by means of a socket in the stem of the papyrus. The head is double-faced, and both of the identical sides are made of gold with eyes of lapis lazuli. The four cloison rings at the neck, as well as the pointed cloison corolla at the base, are inlaid with carnelian, stone and faience. Along the shaft are fine, granulated bands which form the four edges of the mirror's handle.

This utilitarian object, transformed via creative fancy into a work of art, symbolically lends its owner the protection of the goddess Hathor, who ensures youth, beauty and pleasure.

Bibliography: PM IV, p. 109; Brunton, Lahun I, p. 36, pl. 11; Vernier, Bijoux et Orfèvreries (CG), pp. 213–14, pl. 47.

114

The marvelous Wesekh ("broad") collar adorned the breast of Neferuptah. It is a network of tubular beads of feldspar and carnelian arranged vertically in six rows alternating with files of little gold beads all joined together. Teardrop-shaped pieces inlaid with feldspar and carnelian border the lowest row of gold beads. The remarkable falcon heads which fasten the collar are of hammered gold leaf worked in repoussé. A counterpoise hangs over the neck of the wearer to balance the falcons and the rest of the collar. Attached by two chains of small beads, this counterpoise is well matched to the design of the collar. The third falcon head reproduces a miniature version of the two larger clasps and tops a flaring series of carnelian beads alternating with rigid bars of gold in imitation of rows of beads.

The Wesekh collar was a favorite ornament of gods, kings and private individuals alike. Worn by the living, or deposited on the breast of the deceased, this extremely elegant collar also possessed a prophylactic significance.

Bibliography: N. Farag/Z. Iskander, The Discovery of Neferuptah, Cairo 1971, pp. 66–69, pls. 40 and 49.

114

Collar of Neferuptah

Gold, carnelian, feldspar   JE 90199
L. 36.5 cm; W. 10 cm
Hawara, pyramid of Neferuptah; excavations of the Egyptian Antiquities Service, 1956
Middle Kingdom, 12th dynasty, end of the reign of Amenemhat III, c. 1800 B.C.

The discovery and excavation of the unviolated tomb under a ruined brick pyramid two kilometers southwest of the pyramid of Amenemhat III produced the granite sarcophagus and funerary equipment of the princess Neferuptah, possibly a daughter of Amenemhat III.

The mummy and wooden coffins had decomposed in the mud of millennia during the course of periodical infiltration of ground water. What remained at the bottom of the large sarcophagus revealed, after conscientious restoration, the usual toilet articles such as unguent vessels, as well as staves, scepters, a club, the breast-panel from the mummy and a collection of jewellery consisting of collars, bracelets, kilts and a beaded apron.

115

Bracelets and anklets of Neferuptah

Gold, carnelian, feldspar   JE 90197/98
L. 14 and 16.6 cm; W. 4 cm
Hawara, pyramid of Neferuptah; excavations of the Egyptian Antiquities Service, 1956
Middle Kingdom, 12th dynasty, end of the reign of Amenemhat III, c. 1800 B.C.

These two pairs of ornaments once adorned the wrists and ankles of the princess Neferuptah. Well preserved and admirably restored, they form matching accessories to the broad Wesekh collar (no. 114).

Ten rows of threaded beads, held at the edges by two gold clasps, are kept in place by means of rigid cross-pieces in the form of columns of gold beads. These in turn are interspersed between every three rows of stone beads. The bracelets alternate in feldspar, carnelian and gold, while the anklets keep to a simpler combination of carnelian and gold.

Bibliography: N. Farag/Z. Iskander, The Discovery of Neferuptah, pp. 70–71, pls. 41 and 51.

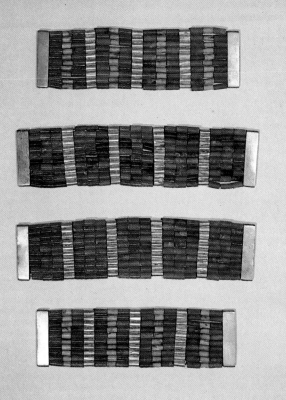

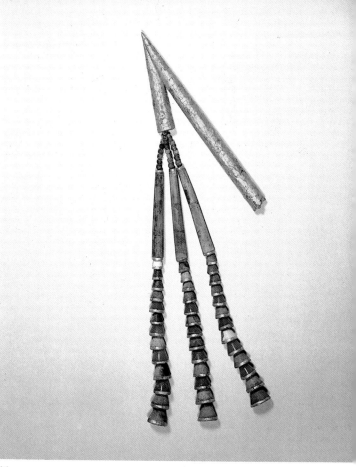

115

116

116
Flail of Neferuptah

Faience, carnelian, gold leaf, wood (modern)   JE 90200
Present-day L. 36.5 cm
Hawara, pyramid of Neferuptah; excavations of the Egyptian Antiquities Service, 1956
Middle Kingdom, 12th dynasty, end of the reign of Amenemhat III, c. 1800 B.C.

The princess' flail was partially restored from preserved pieces and slim fragments of gold leaf spread about after the disintegration of the original wood. Half of the handle is missing, as are three sections which originally lengthened the three strands of the whip. Each of the three strands is composed of seven spherical beads of brownish faience, a long cylindrical section gilded at both ends, and thirteen little "bells" of faience and carnelian, likewise gilded at the edge.
The flail, also known as the *flagellum*, functioned since the beginning of Egyptian history as a symbol of royalty (cf. Narmer, no. 8; Cheops, no. 28). Together with the crook, it was also part of the insignia of Osiris. Both emblems, held by this god of the dead, were acquired in the Middle Kingdom by private individuals, who, after their death, became Osiris, just as the king (alone) used to do earlier. Thus one finds the two objects included in paintings on sarcophagi, or placed in the tomb with other emblems of authority. They also recur in the New Kingdom in the hands of the king's mummy, as well as in royal iconography ritual ceremonies, as in the Old Kingdom.
If the flail differs from the fly-whisk normally seen in the hands of private individuals since the Old Kingdom (cf. Ipy, no. 62), and which has a more flexible shape, then the original function of this object called a "flail" is lost in prehistory and remains unknown to us.

Bibliography: N. Farag/Z. Iskander, The Discovery of Neferwptah, pp. 83–85, pl. 52. Cf. Hayes, Scepter of Egypt I, fig. 188, p. 286.

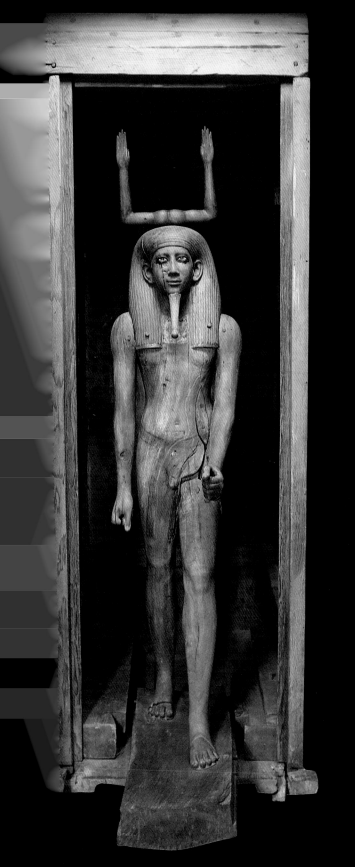

Ka-statue of King Auib-rê Hor

Wood   JE 30948
Statue: H. 170 cm; W. 27 cm; L. 77 cm   = CG 259
Naos: H. 207 cm; W. 70 cm; L. 105 cm
Dahshur, mortuary complex of Amenemhat III;
excavations of De Morgan, 1884
Middle Kingdom, 13th dynasty 13, c. 1700 B.C.

Man's personality in ancient Egypt was composed of several elements such as the "Ba": spirit, "Khat": the body, "Shoot": the shadow, "Ib": the heart, "Ren": the name, "Akh": the beneficent spirit and "Ka": the double or vital force. This last aspect is considered an independent entity which resides within the being and provides him with protection, health and purity. The *Ka* remains with the being even after his death; this is why it was important to preserve the body so that the *Ka* could occupy it when it desired and continue its life in the next world. The *Ka*-statue received oblations presented on an offering table at the foot of the false door.

This magnificent and well-preserved statue of the *Ka* of King Auib-rê Hor is clearly marked by the hieroglyphic sign for *Ka* (two upraised arms) which crowns the head. At the time of discovery, the statue was covered with a fine layer of painted stucco which disintegrated to powder upon exposure to the air.

The king strides forth with left foot advanced and appears to be completely naked, but traces of a belt and the beginning of a kilt are still visible on the body. He wears a striated tripartite wig with lappets reaching to the chest but leaving the ears free. A long, tressed and curved divine beard is attached under the chin. The inlaid eyes lend a lifelike appearance to his expressive face. The rims of the eyes are of bronze, the pupils of rock crystal and the whites of quartz.

The statue once clutched a scepter horizontally in the right hand and held a staff vertically in the left. The arms, the left leg and the edges of the feet are attached to the rest of the body with pegs. Traces of gilding observed on the statue reveal that the attributes and certain parts of the face were once covered in gold leaf. The statue was discovered within its accompanying naos in a tomb situated to the north of the pyramid of Amenemhat III at Dahshur.

Bibliography: PM III, 2, p. 888; de Morgan, Fouilles à Dahchour, Mars-Juin 1894, pls. 33–35; Borchardt, Statuen und Statuetten (CG) I, p. 166, pl. 56; Smith, Art and Architecture, p. 179, ill. 170; Corteggiani, no. 44.

118
Stela of King Ahmose

Limestone   JE 36335
H. 225 cm; W. 106.5 cm   = CG 34002
Abydos. Discovered in the mortuary monument
dedicated by Ahmose to the Queen Tetisheri.
Excavations of the Egypt Exploration Fund, 1903
New Kingdom, beginning of the 18th dynasty,
reign of Ahmose, 1554—1529 B.C.

The Middle Kingdom was followed by an obscure period in which Egypt, governed by a series of ineffective monarchs, was divided into separate regions and finally weakened by a foreign invasion from Asia. The invaders, whom Manetho names the Hyksos, settled at Avaris in the Delta. The Theban princes led a long and determined struggle against the Hyksos, and eventually succeeded in liberating the country.

It was under Ahmose that the expulsion of the Hyksos and the establishment of the new regime took place. The new dynasty, the Eighteenth, proved to be one of Egypt's most glorious periods.

Ahmose began the dynasty's long series of territorial conquests. In Egypt, he restored the temples and dedicated new sanctuaries. He also began to venerate his ancestors, as is shown on this stela dedicated to his grandmother, Queen Tetisheri.

The stela's decoration displays a remarkable clarity. In the lunette, the figures seem lightly etched with a chisel, a technique well known from the Middle Kingdom in which relief sculpture remains very low. The hieroglyphs of the main text are in sunk relief, carved with a flat base and extremely clean lines.

Underneath the winged sun disk, from which hang two uraei, a tableau divided into two symmetrical scenes shows King Ahmose presenting offerings to Queen Tetisheri. He stands in the traditional offering pose, and wears the blue crown in the left hand scene, and the double crown on the right. He wears a kilt with a sporran and an animal tail, and grasps a tall staff and a ritual mace in his hand. Seated upon her throne, Tetisheri wears a long garment and a wig which is covered with a vulture's body surmounted by two tall feathers. She holds the floral scepter, a characteristic attribute of queens.

The text inscribed beneath the tableau records a conversation between Ahmose and his sister and wife, Ahmose-Nefertari. Seated in the audience hall of the palace, they consider how to best pay homage to their dead and provide their offerings on festival days. After his wife asks how the idea came to him, Ahmose replies that he was thinking especially of "the mother of his mother, and mother of his father, the Great Royal Wife and King's Mother, Tetisheri." Even though she already possesses a tomb at Thebes and a mortuary chapel at Abydos, he wishes to construct an additional mortuary monument in the sacred necropolis of Abydos. The edifice consists of a pyramid and a chapel to be endowed with a lake and plantations. It should be furnished with offerings, equipped with personnel, with land and livestock, and finally with priests who will guarantee the mortuary cult. Never, according to Ahmose, did any previous king do the like for his mother.

Bibliography: PM V, p. 92; Ayrton/Currelly/Weigall, Abydos III, London 1904, pl. 50, 52, pp. 43—45; Lacau, Stèles du Nouvel Empire (CG), pp. 5—7, pls. 2, 3; Corteggiani, no. 47. Texts: K. Sethe, Urkunden IV, 26—9 (7), Berlin 1984 (reprint).

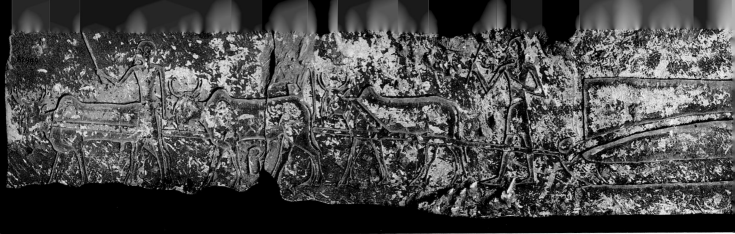

119

Transporting scene

Limestone
H. 31.5 cm; W. 117 cm   JE 62949
Quarries of Maasara; purchased from a collector in 1934
New Kingdom, beginning of the 18th dynasty, year 22 of Ahmose I,
ca. 1530 B.C.

This sunk relief scene represents the transport of a large block
upon a sled drawn by three pairs of oxen and driven by three
overseers. The quarries at Maasara, whence the scene originates, extend those of Tura, and supplied the Egyptians at all
periods with beautiful white limestone. This was used for the
casing of pyramids and mastabas, the construction of temples,
and for statues.
During the Hyksos domination, work in the quarries was
interrupted. Their formal reopening in year 22 of King
Ahmose I was commemorated by two stelae carved at the
quarries' entrance. At the bottom of one of the stelae appeared
this scene, which was unfortunately quarried away in modern
times. Without the vigilance of J. Capart, who bought it for
the Museum, we would today have only the copies made by
early explorers.
The relief demonstrates that fairly heavy weights were pulled
along flattened roads by oxen. For more important loads, use
was made of special teams of men; the most famous example,
from a Middle Kingdom tomb (see no. 99), shows the transport of a colossal statue.
In our scene three foremen, equipped with batons, supervise
the operation. They are clearly of foreign extraction, as is evident from their pointed goatees. The first figure is an Asiatic,
and the third a Libyan wearing the characteristic sidelock.
Neither is the type of hunchbacked oxen indigenous to Egypt;
these beasts represent spoils of war seized in conquered foreign lands.
We know that in the Old Kingdom, the kings recruited their
manpower from among their own subjects; it is only by means
of this extraordinary organization, directed by Pharaoh, that
Egyptians could build the pyramids stone by stone. Later,
when the sovereigns had prisoners of war at their disposal,
they utilized them for large construction projects. But the Her-
culean task of organizing the labor remained in Egyptian
hands. Pharaoh gave the order for dispatching expeditions;
the army provided the direction while the administration
assigned the technicians, raised the corvée labor, and organized the logistics and communications. A formidable division
of laborers in teams, further split into phyles and subdivided
again into sections, efficiently carried out their tasks in shifts,
from initial quarrying up to the final touches of construction.
An inscription from the end of the New Kingdom at Wadi
Hammamat informs us that such an expedition, organized
under Ramses IV, mobilized more than 8000 men, of whom
130 were quarry masons and stone transporters.

*Bibliography: PM IV, p. 74; Vyse, Operations carried on at the Pyra-
mids of Gizeh in 1837, III, London 1842, p. 99, no. 6; G. Daressy,
in: ASAE 11, 1911, pp. 263–64. Cf. also: Erman/Ranke, Aegypten
und aegyptisches Leben im Altertum, pp. 639–42; L. Christophe, in:
BIFAO 48, 1949, pp. 1–48.*

120

Order of Valor

Gold   JE 4694
L. (chain) 59 cm; (fly) 0.9 cm; weight 249 g   = CG 52671
Thebes, tomb of Queen Ahhotep at Drac Abu'l-Naga, discovered by
agents of Mariette in 1859
New Kingdom, beginning of the 18th dynasty, reign of Ahmose,
1554–1529 B.C.

The tomb of Queen Ahhotep was discovered in an isolated
area of Drac Abu'l-Naga in the winter of 1859 by Mariette's
agents. It contained the gilded wooden sarcophagus (on exhibit in hall 47) with the queen's mummy richly ornamented with
marvelous jewellery and weapons. These objects were given to
the queen by her sons Kamose and Ahmose, who led the

struggle for liberation against the Hyksos at the end of the Seventeenth Dynasty.

Among the rich collection is this exceptional necklace with three pendants in the form of flies. This type of gold jewellery corresponds to a military decoration bestowed upon troop leaders for their courage or their valor on the battlefield. Always in the form of jewellery, the gold of valor is particularly well attested at this period. The presence of this necklace and gold rings of similar value among the funerary furniture of a queen is unique; it is explained by the important political role played by Ahhotep during the wars of liberation. She actively supported her husband Seqenenrê, who died on the battlefield, and later her two sons, assuming the role of regent during the campaigns of Ahmose.

These marvelous stylized flies are formed of plaques of gold summarily decorated. At the end of the long, flat wings two bulging eyes and an openwork body admirably reproduce the appearance of the insect. Little ringlets on the flies connect them to the chain, which is furnished with a simple hook-and-eye fastener.

Bibliography: PM I, 2, p. 600; Von Bissing, Ein thebanischer Grabfund aus dem Anfang des Neuen Reiches, Berlin 1900, pl. 6; Vernier, Bijoux et Orfèvreries (CG), pp. 220−21, pl. 51; Aldred, Jewels, pl. 53, p. 201; Corteggiani, no. 46. Cf. C. Vandersleyen, Les Guerres d'Amosis, 1971, pp. 41−48, 135 and 190−91.

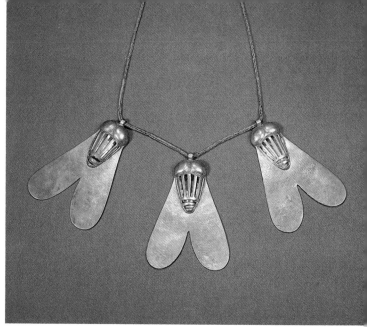

120

121a

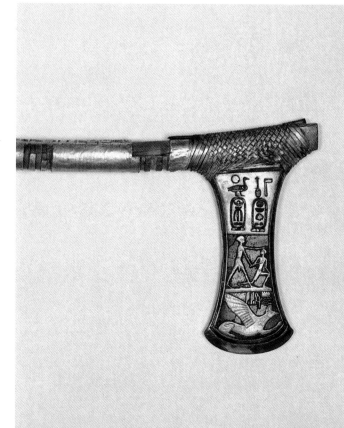

121

Upper floor, room 3

Ceremonial axe of King Ahmose I

Gold, electrum, copper, precious stones and wood   JE 4673
L. 47,5 cm; L. (axe only) 16.3 cm; W. 6.7 cm   = CG 52645
Thebes, tomb of Queen Ahhotep at Draᶜ Abu'l-Naga, discovered in 1859 by Mariette's agents
New Kingdom, beginning of the 18th dynasty, reign of Ahmose I, 1554−1529 B.C.

This axe belonging to King Ahmose I is decorated with scenes celebrating the liberation of Egypt from the yoke of the Hyksos.

The copper axe together with its cedarwood handle is entirely covered with gold and ornamented with precious stones; the two parts are held together with gold bands.

The inlaid decoration of the axe is divided on each side into three compartments. At the top, on one side, are placed the two royal cartouches: "The good god Nebpehtetre, son of Re Ahmosis". In the center the king is depicted killing an Asiatic enemy, and at the bottom, a griffin symbolizing the king is designated as "beloved of Montu". On the other side, the king appears in the form of a sphinx with human arms holding aloft the head of an enemy; in the center are represented the

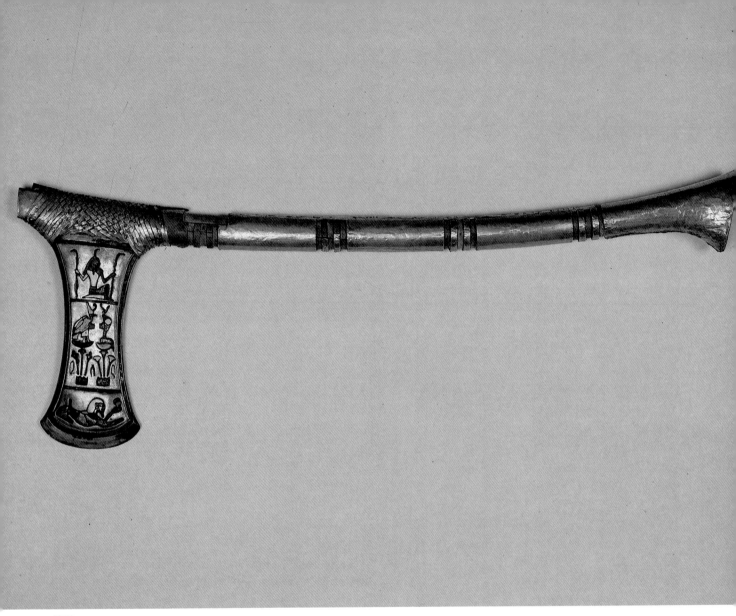

121 b

Two Ladies of Upper and Lower Egypt, the vulture and cobra goddesses wearing their respective crowns and placed on the heraldic plants of the south and the north. Finally Heh, the god of eternity, holds in each hand the budding plant stems signifying millions of years.

The handle, originally inlaid with rings of precious stones, is decorated at its base in cloisonné figuring the symbolic plants of Upper and Lower Egypt. On the back an inscription, cut in open work in a gold band ornamented with stones, gives the complete titulature of the king.

All these motifs are in fact allusions to the expulsion of the Hyksos and the reunification of the country by Ahmose. The king attacks an enemy, appears as a fighting griffin under the protection of the god of war Montu after having cut off the enemy's head; he wards off all danger of invasion from his country which he reunites under the auspices of the Two Ladies, and receives from the god of eternity millions of years of reign in the titles which he has assumed as King of Upper and Lower Egypt.

Bibliography: PM I, 2, p. 601; Von Bissing, Ein Thebanischer Grabfund, pl. 1; Vernier, Bijoux et Orfèvreries (CG), pp. 205–207, pls. 42, 43; Kühnert-Eggebrecht, Die Axt als Waffe und Werkzeug im Alten Ägypten, Münchener Ägyptologische Studien 15, 1969, pp. 92–95, 135, no. P53, pls. 30–31; Götter Pharaonen, no. 24.

122

Ceremonial dagger of King Ahmose

Gold, electrum, enamel and semi-precious stones JE 4666
L. 28.5 cm; W. (scabbard) 3.4 cm; = CG 52658
weight 134 g and 52659
Thebes, tomb of Queen Ahhotep at Dra' Abu'l-Naga, discovered by
agents of Mariette in 1859
New Kingdom, beginning of the 18ᵗʰ dynasty, reign of Ahmose,
1554–1529 B.C.

This dagger is also a royal gift from Ahmose to his mother
Ahhotep. The name and epithets of the king are inscribed on
the two faces of the gold blade. These inscriptions terminate
in very fine decorative motifs: on one side a lion pursues a calf
in a rocky landscape, followed by a row of four grasshoppers
and the head of an animal. On the other side (illustrated) is a
floral design crowned with a jackal's head shown frontally.
This decoration in gold thread, like the hieroglyphs, is backed
by a band of niello, i.e. black enamel obtained from a metallic
sulphide. This is a technique found later in Mycenaean objects
but already known at Byblos during the period of the Egyptian Twelfth Dynasty.
The wooden handle covered with gold leaf is ornamented on
each side with a bull's head in relief. It continues toward the
pommel with little triangles of elctrum, carnelian and lapis
lazuli, forming halves of arranged squares in twelve bands.
The pommel is ornamented with four female heads aligned
with the axes of the blade. Stones have been set into wood at
the top of the pommel.
The scabbard consists of two welded gold plaques bordered
by four rows of very fine chains. A sliding golden ring around
the upper part is provided with a welded loop allowing the
weapon to be attached to articles of clothing.

*Bibliography: PM I, 2, p. 601; Von Bissing, Ein Thebanischer Grab-
fund, pl. 2; Vernier, Bijoux et Orfèvreries (CG), pp. 209–11, pl. 45;
Smith, Art and Architecture, pp. 220–22, fig. 215.*

122

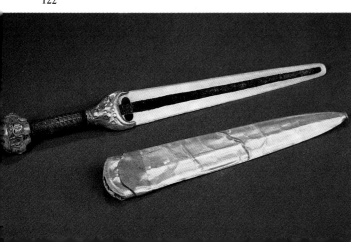

123

123

Barque upon a chariot

Barque: JE 4681
Gold and silver = CG 52666
L. 43.3 cm; W. 6.5 cm; weight 375 g
Chariot: JE 4669
Wood and bronze = CG 52668
L. 20 cm; W. 16 cm
Thebes, tomb of Queen Ahhotep at Dra' Abu'l-Naga, discovered by
agents of Mariette in 1859
New Kingdom, beginning of the 18ᵗʰ dynasty, reign of Ahmose, c.
1554–1529 B.C.

The barque was always the most common mode of transport
in Egypt. In fact, no representations of wheeled vehicles
appear before the Second Intermediate Period. The first example known is a chariot which transports a mummy, represented on the wall of a Thirteenth Dynasty tomb at El-Kab. It
is doubtless as a result of the influence of the recently introduced chariot (generally ascribed to the Hyksos domination)
that one of the barque models of Queen Ahhotep was placed
upon such a vehicle.
The beaten gold hull of the barque takes a graceful form.
Curved at both prow and stern, it terminates in papyrus
umbels. The three principal figures on board are worked in
gold. One stands at the prow upon a little bridge between two
gold cloisons which form a shelter. With one finger pointing
towards his mouth, he faces the stern. The cloisons are decorated with incised motifs called Isis knots, symbols of protec-

tion. The second figure is the helmsman who mans the steering oar at the stern. Behind him is a sort of gold armchair, the sides of which bear incised decoration showing a lion and the cartouches of Kamose, brother and predecessor of King Ahmose. The third person is seated in the middle of the barque, apparently holding the baton of authority in his right hand, and an axe in the left. This figure is removable.

All three individuals are on a much larger scale than the silver team of twelve seated rowers. Each figure is attached to his bench by means of a little tenon welded into the square "cushion" on which he sits. Only one oar is missing from each of the two rows. Four gold rings are attached to the hull of the barque.

The chariot consists of a piece of wood fixed onto a chassis with bronze wheels. At the time of discovery, the chariot held the silver barque (on exhibit to one side).

Bibliography: PM I, 2, p. 602; Von Bissing, Ein Thebanischer Grabfund, pl. 10; Vernier, Bijoux et Orfèvreries (CG), pp. 216–19, pl. 49; Smith, Art and Architecture, p. 219, and fig. 214; Propyläen Kunstgeschichte 15, pl. 378a.

124

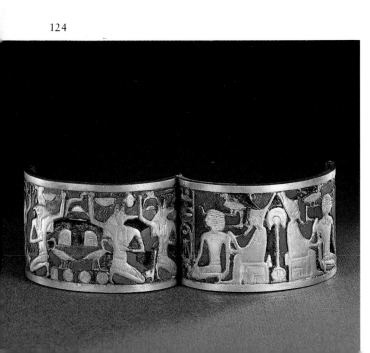

124

124

Upper floor, room 3

Bracelet of Queen Ahhotep

Gold and lapis lazuli   JE 4684
Diam. 5.5 cm; H. 3.4 cm; weight 96 g   = CG 52069
Thebes, tomb of Queen Ahhotep at Draᶜ Abu'l-Naga, discovered by Mariette in 1859
New Kingdom, beginning of the 18th dynasty, reign of Ahmose, 1554–1529 B.C.

From the treasure of Queen Ahhotep comes this rigid gold bracelet with lapis lazuli inlays. It consists of two half-cylinders, bordered by a rim and jointed by two hinges, one of which has a retractable clasp-pin which allows the bracelet to open.

Scenes and hieroglyphs cut into the gold and delicately worked with a chisel make up the decoration. Two representations fill the right half: on either side of a fan set into a *shen* ring (duration), the god Geb sits enthroned wrapped in a short garment and wearing the Red Crown on the left and the Double Crown on the right. The god protects the kneeling figure of Ahmose who wears a curled wig with frontal uraeus and a short kilt. Geb thus supports the king as he prepares to don the crown. Between the two figures is the god's name and, to the side of both scenes, the names of the king.

On the other half of the bracelet are the souls of Pe and Nekhen, ancestors of the kings of Upper and Lower Egypt respectively, prior to the unification of the Two Kingdoms. With heads of both falcons and jackals, they lift their arms signifying *henu*, jubilation, conferring upon the king respectively "all joy," and "all life and sovereignty." The crowned king is thus recognized as the legitimate descendant of divine pharaohs.

Bibliography: PM I, 2, p. 601; Von Bissing, Ein Thebanischer Grabfund, pl. 5; Vernier, Bijoux et Orfèvreries (CG), pp. 34–35, pl. 9; Aldred, Jewels, pl. 57, p. 203.

125

Upper floor, room 3

Bead bracelets of Queen Ahhotep

Gold and semi-precious stone
H. 4.3 cm; Diam. 4.7 cm; weight 61.5 g   JE 4685 = CG 52070
H. 3.6 cm; Diam. 5.4 cm; weight 51 g   JE 4687 = CG 52072
Thebes, tomb of Queen Ahhotep at Draᶜ Abu'l-Naga, discovered by the agents of Mariette in 1859
New Kingdom, beginning of the 18th dynasty, reign of Ahmose, 1554–1529 B.C.

125

Pendant of Ahhotep

Gold and lapis lazuli   JE 4695
L. 202 cm; scarab: 3 cm; weight 378 g   = CG 52670
Thebes, tomb of Queen Ahhotep at Draᶜ Abu'l-Naga, discovered by
agents of Mariette in 1859
New Kingdom, beginning of the 18th dynasty, reign of Ahmose,
1554–1529 B.C.

This beautiful scarab suspended from a chain is considered to
be one of the finest examples of early Eighteenth Dynasty
jewellery. It is composed of two heavy gold plates. The upper
plate which forms the insect's back, is decorated in cloisonné
with pieces of lapis lazuli. The separately worked legs are
welded to the plate which formed the abdomen, lending it a
naturalistic appearance. The front legs hold a ring through

The bracelet at left consists of eighteen rows of beads strung
together with gold thread and forming alternating bands of
gold, lapis lazuli, carnelian and turquoise. The seven gold
bands are rigid and comprise rows of beads welded one to the
other, through which the gold threads pass. An eighth band,
likewise rigid, takes the form of a box which the threads pass
through; it is decorated with hieroglyphs of polished gold set
into a base of lapis lazuli. The text reads: "The good God
Nebpehtetrê, given life." The bracelet closes by means of a
gold plate in two pieces which are connected by a peg. To
enlarge the bracelet, an additional gold plate provided with
hinges and a second peg was attached between the two halves
of the clasp. However, the inscription "The perfect God, lord
of the Two Lands Ahmose, given life forever," which is
engraved on the clasp is split in two when the additional plate
is added.

The second bracelet was one of an identical pair. In this case,
thirty rows of threaded beads follow the same procedure, but
in a different design. The cylindrical beads of gold, carnelian,
lapis lazuli and turquoise, form square motifs divided into two
triangles of which one is always gold. The rows of beads pass
through the holes pierced in the side panels of oblong clasps,
which hold the rows firmly in place. The bracelet is closed by
two bands provided with interlocking loops to form a hinge
and attached by a removable peg.

When the two halves are joined, one sees the complete inscription engraved with a chisel on the plate of the clasp: "The
good God Nebpehtetrê, beloved of Amon" ("Son of Rê,
Ahmose, beloved of Rê" appears on the other bracelet of this
pair).

*Bibliography: PM I, 2, p. 601; Von Bissing, Ein Thebanischer Grab-
fund, pl. 5; Vernier, Bijoux et Orfèvreries (CG), pp. 35–38, pl. 9;
Aldred, Jewels, pl. 49, pp. 199–200.*

126

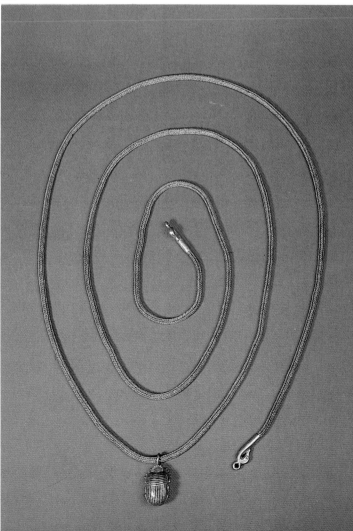

which the chain passes; another ring, welded between the hind legs, is attached to the first by a gold thread which forms a buckle. It seems this buckle served to hold the chain which, due to its length, must have wrapped around the queen's neck more than once. The buckle would also have related the two rings of the edges of the chain to the scarab, hiding them behind the insect.

These rings are welded to the back of two curved goose-heads which terminate the chain's sextuple-loop pattern. The neck of each goose is inscribed with one of the cartouches of Ahmose, the son of Ahhotep.

Bibliography: PM I, 2, p. 600; Von Bissing, Ein Thebanischer Grabfund, pls. 6 and 7; Vernier, Bijoux et Orfèvreries (CG), pp. 219–20, pl. 50; Aldred, Jewels, pl. 56, p. 203.

127

127   Upper floor, hall 46
Anthropoid coffin of Ahmose Merit-Amon

Cedar   JE 53140
L. 313.5 cm; W. 87 cm
Thebes, tomb no. 358 at Deir el-Bahari; excavations of the Egyptian Antiquities Service and of the Metropolitan Museum of Art, New York, 1929
New Kingdom, beginning of the 18th dynasty, c. 1550 B.C.

The tomb of Queen Ahmose Merit-Amon, sister and wife of Amenophis I, was sunk into the northern slope of the natural cove of Deir el-Bahari at Thebes. At the beginning of Dynasty 18, queens were buried in huge anthropoid coffins, entirely decorated with patterned feathers. This type of coffin, called rîshi after the Arabic word for feathers, had already achieved a high popularity under the kings of Dynasty 17. Royal examples were covered in gold leaf, which was nevertheless very quickly stripped away by robbers in antiquity. The priests of Dynasty 21 subsequently took great pains to restore these violated coffins, and replaced the lost gold with yellow paint.

The coffin of Merit-Amon still makes an imposing impression despite the loss of the precious materials inlaid into the gold. Both the lid and the base, which fit together perfectly, are formed of numerous boards of cedar. The admirably sculpted face is imbued with a lifelike expression. The eyes and eyebrows, later restored in glass paste, were once inlaid with lapis lazuli and obsidian. The queen holds in her hands two papyriform scepters symbolizing youth and life.

The decorative feather pattern lends the piece a birdlike quality reminiscent of the Ba, the roving spirit outside the body which fly about at will through the netherworld. The interior coffin, of smaller dimensions, contained the queen's mummy. It too was inlaid in precious materials which failed to escape the tomb robbers.

Bibliography: PM I, 1, p. 421; H. Winlock, The Tomb of Queen Meryet-Amun at Thebes, New York 1932; Leclant, Les Pharaons II, fig. 211. Cf. LÄ V, 267–69.

Stela of Nebnakhtu and family

Painted limestone   JE 46993
H. 109 cm; W. 52.9 cm; thickness 14 cm
Sedment el-Gebel, excavated by F. Petrie for the British School of
Archaeology in Egypt, 1921
New Kingdom, beginning of the 18ᵗʰ dynasty, c. 1550 B.C.

Sedment el Gebel is a mound which served as necropolis for
the town of Heracleopolis, ancient Neninisut, located on the
west bank of the Nile at the entrance to the Fayum. The
cemetery was in use during the Old Kingdom (see the wooden
statuette, no. 64) and once again in the New Kingdom.

Beside the tombs, there is also a funerary chapel here intended
for the cult of a family of priests of Harsaphes, the god worshipped in the form of a ram at Heracleopolis. It was at the
back of a little chamber in this chapel that this polychrome
stela was erected. Its owner is a priest of Harsaphes by the
name Nebnakhtu, who was also priest of Sekhmet, royal
scribe and overseer of cattle. Before the stela stood a table of
offerings (likewise exhibited here) with the name of Amenmose, the father of Nebnakhtu. A few paces in front of these,
the stelophorous statue of a certain scribe named Minmose
faced the entrance to the chamber.

The round-topped stela is crowned by the Udjat eyes which
flank the ring of protection known as *shen*. The three registers
below depict offering scenes. In the topmost register, the priest
Nebnakhtu, accompanied by his wife Sheritre, pays homage to
his stepfather Sennefer. The latter, a high official whose titles
include that of high priest of Heliopolis, high priest and chief
of artisans (at Memphis), is seated before a table of offerings.
At the foot of his chair stands his favorite pet monkey. The
high priest is clothed in a leopard skin, and sports a wig and
an elaborate collar.

In the middle register, the same Nebnakhtu, followed by his
wife, offers incense and pours a libation over a Clotus in front
of his own parents: Amenmose (priest of Harsaphes and son
of the priest Ahmose) and the lady Iuty.

Below, the son of Nebnakhtu, Amenhotep, likewise a priest of
Harsaphes, is clothed in a leopard skin and accompanied by
his mother Sheritre while he pours a libation over his father
and paternal grandmother Iuty.

The three lines of inscription at the bottom of the stela recite
an offering formula to Harsaphes, Osiris and the Great
Ennead, for the *ka* of the high priest Sennefer and of the priest
Amenmose, made by the latter's son, Nebnakhtu.

*Bibliography: Petrie/Brunton, Sedment II, London 1924, pls. 49, 50
and pp. 23–24; M. Gamal El-Din Mokhtar, Ihnâsya El-Medina
(Herakleopolis Magna) Cairo 1983, p. 101–102, note 3.*

130a

129

Ground floor, room 11

Queen Hatshepsut

Painted limestone   JE 56259 A and 56262
H. 61 cm; W. 55 cm
Deir el-Bahari, mortuary temple of Hatshepsut; excavations of the
Metropolitan Museum of Art, 1926–27
New Kingdom, 18th dynasty, reign of Hatshepsut, 1490–1470 B.C.

Upon the death of her father, Tuthmosis I, Hatshepsut became
sole legitimate heir. Tradition demanded, however, that only a
male heir could ascend the throne. Hatshepsut married her
half-brother Tuthmosis II, who died prematurely, leaving the
queen with only one daughter. Once again it was a stepson,
Tuthmosis III, born of a concubine, who was crowned. Serving first as regent for the young king, Hatshepsut seized the
royal titulary in the second year of this reign and, as "King of
Upper and Lower Egypt," ruled the country for two prosperous and relatively peaceful decades.
This wonderful head of Hatshepsut derives from one of the
Osirian statues which once adorned the pillared facade of the
portico of the uppermost terrace of the queen's temple at Deir
el-Bahari. Additional statues on a smaller scale occupied the
niches at the back of the terrace. The Red Crown, of which
one can just make out the beginning, suggests that our statue
corresponds to a pillar on the terrace's nothern side, where all
statues had the Double Crown. On the southern side, they
wear the White Crown.
The portrait of the queen as Osiris, idealized as it is, bears
nevertheless distinctive feminine features, such as the gently
curving eyebrows, wide eyes extended by cosmetic lines, delicate aquiline nose, full cheeks and gracious mouth. A certain
intelligence emanates from this face, whose luckily well-preserved colors enhance the expression and enliven the faintly
alluring smile.
One should compare the statues and sphinxes of the queen, in
red granite from the same mortuary temple, exhibited in gallery 7.

*Bibliography: PM II, p. 372; H. Winlock, Excavations at Deir el
Bahari, 1942, p. 141, pl. 55; Smith, Art and Architecture, p. 223,
fig. 227; Müller, Ägyptische Kunst, no. 93; R. Tefnin, La statuaire
d'Hatshepsout, Monumenta Aegyptiaca 4, 1979, p. 45, pl. 12.*

130

Ground floor, room 12

Expedition to the land of Punt

Painted limestone   JE 14276, JE 89661
Max. H. of one block 49.3 cm; max. W. 45 cm
Thebes, temple of Hatshepsut at Deir el-Bahari
New Kingdom, 18th dynasty, reign of Hatshepsut, 1490–1470 B.C.

These five fragments of relief form a part of an extraordinary
cycle of scenes in the southern portico of the middle terrace of
the temple of Hatshepsut at Deir el-Bahari. The scenes depict
in great detail the maritime expedition which the queen sent
via the Red Sea to Punt (somewhere on the Somali coast), just
before her ninth regnal year, ca. 1482 B.C. The expedition,
directed by a high official named Panehsy, lasted three years.
Its mission was to exchange Egyptian merchandise for the
products of Punt, such as incense and myrrh, ivory, ebony,
malachite, gold and electrum. This is the first pictorial docu-
mentation of an expedition to Punt, otherwise attested since
the Old Kingdom in written sources.
On one of the fragments appears the chief of Punt Parehu
along with his wife Ati, represented with their characteristic
ethnic features. The sovereign cuts a slender figure with
pointed beard, necklace and a short kilt with two tassels, held
in place by a belt from which hangs a dagger. His rather
deformed wife has been treated with realism and humor. She
clearly suffers from obesity; one can recognize Decrum's dis-
ease manifested by the steatopygia, excessive curvature of the
vertebral column, and the folds of fat protruding over relatively slim wrists and ankles.
The retinue of the chief of Punt follows behind bringing gifts
to the representatives of the queen of Egypt. Care has even
been taken to depict and identify "the donkey which bears his
wife," i.e. Ati's mount.

*Bibliography: PM II, p. 344; P. Ghalioungui/Z. El Dawakhly, Health
and Healing in Ancient Egypt, 1965, fig. 33; Terrace/Fischer, no. 21;
E. Brunner-Traut, in: Mitteilungen aus der Ägyptischen Sammlung,
Berlin 1974, pp. 71–83, pl. 3b–6; Leclant, Les Pharaons II, fig. 55.*

130b △

130c ▽

Sarcophagus of Queen Hatshepsut (detail)

Red sandstone   JE 37678 and JE 52459
H. 100 cm (without lid: 86.5 cm); W. 87.5 cm; L. 245 cm
Thebes, Valley of the Kings, tomb of Hatshepsut (no. 20); excavations
of Th. M. Davis, directed by H. Carter, 1905
New Kingdom, 18th dynasty, reign of Hatshepsut, 1490–1470 B.C.

The reign of Hatshepsut was a period of both architectural
and aesthetic grandeur. The form, decoration and conception
of the sarcophagus was enriched at this time with new elements, eventually to be adopted wholesale or selectively by the
rest of her New Kingdom successors.

The palace facade decoration is now finally abandoned in
favor of sides and end-panels set off by columns of hieroglyphs, a feature introduced earlier with the wooden sarcophagi of the Middle Kingdom. The decoration is completed by
sunk relief figures of deities and of genii mentioned since the
Old Kingdom as protectors of the deceased's body.

The form itself is no longer rectangular. The small side at the
head of the sarcophagus is now rounded, while the lid is
framed by the outline of a cartouche. The concept of a dwelling place is thus replaced by that of a solid receptacle with a
monumental cartouche capable of holding up to three wooden
anthropoid sarcophagi, and acting as the bier which supports
them. The coffins of Hatshepsut are lost but Tutankhamon's
tomb has provided illustrative examples (see no. 175). The
goddess Mut appears on the lid and on the bottom of the sarcophagus, protecting with outstretched arms the body which
lay within.

The sarcophagus has been manufactured with such precision
that each side is perfectly smooth, perfectly equal and parallel
to the opposite side to within a millimeter's discrepancy. The
whole piece is enhanced with a reddish coating, as well as
some other colors which have since disappeared. It once rested
on an alabaster base, fragments of which are gathered here.

The side facing the viewer corresponds to the feet of the
mummy. Isis crouches upon the sign for gold and holds the
shen-ring of protection; Nephthys appears in a similar image on
the opposite end of the sarcophagus. Each goddess displays
her own particular emblem upon her head above the *khat*-
headdress with frontal uraeus. Their beautiful faces reproduce
the features of the queen. The same goddesses appear once
again on the interior on the corresponding sides.

In the titulary carved around these panels, Maakare Hatshepsut is called *King* of Upper and Lower Egypt and *daughter* of
Re. The words spoken by Isis read: "Geb, your arms are
around the king Maakare, justified. You have illuminated *her*
face and opened *her* eyes."

Of the two long sides, the left one contains the two Udjat eyes.
The genii appearing on both sides are the four anthropomor-

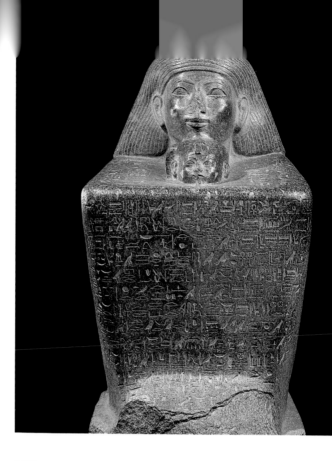

131

phic sons of Horus and two forms of the jackal-headed Anubis. To the left we see Hapi, Anubis-Imiut, and Kebehsenuef, and on the right, Mesti, Anubis Khenty-seh-netjer and Duamutef. The formulae recited by these genii concern the protection and preservation of the body of the deceased.

Exhibited beside this sarcophagus is the queen's canopic chest which likewise formed part of her burial equipment. A second sarcophagus, similar but rectangular, was also found in the tomb. It was originally inscribed with the name of Hatshepsut, but the queen subsequently replaced it with the name of her father, Tuthmosis I, whom she wished to be buried beside her. (This sarcophagus is now in the Boston Museum.)

All three of these monuments date to the queen's period of sole rule. Reigning as a king, she accordingly possessed a tomb in the Valley of the Kings. Earlier, however, when she was still chief wife of Tuthmosis II, a tomb was begun for her in the necropolis of royal Wives and children, beyond the Valley of Queens. Subsequently abandoned, the tomb still contained Hatshepsut's first sarcophagus, much smaller, still rectangular and decorated solely with formulae recited by the genii, who this time were not represented (on display to one side; JE 47032).

*Bibliography: PM I, p. 547; Th. Davis/E. Naville/H. Carter, The Tomb of Hatshopsitu pp. 93–100; W. C. Hayes, Royal Sarcophagi of the XVIII*th *Dynasty, Princeton 1935, sarcophagus D, pp. 17–20, 44–50, 161–63, pl. V, VI.*

132   Ground floor, room 12

Senmut and Neferure

Grey granite   JE 37438 bis
H. 130 cm   = CG 42114
Karnak, court of the cachette. Found by Legrain in 1904
New Kingdom, 18th dynasty, reign of Hatshepsut, 1490–1470 B.C.

Senmut, the most favoured person of the reign of Hatshepsut, was also the most influential. Of modest background, he was promoted to the highest official positions and counted among his more than eighty titles that of steward of the estates of Amon, overseer of the Queen's household and chancellor of the King of Lower Egypt. Senmut was likewise tutor to the princess Neferure, the only child of Hatshepsut and Tuthmosis II, who seems to have died about the 11th year of the Queen's reign. It was as the Queen's chief architect in charge of the construction of her great temple at Deir el-Bahari that he became particularly famous; he was also responsible for works undertaken at Karnak, Luxor and Armant. He was rewarded by the Queen with two tombs at Thebes (nos. 71 and 353), a perquisite of only the most eminent persons. The end of his career is veiled in uncertainty. He seems to have fallen into disgrace or to have died around the 16th year of the Queen's reign; his name was erased on certain of his monuments and his tomb (no. 71) ruined.

More than 20 statues of Senmut are known, of which eight, dispersed among the Museums of Egypt, Europe and America represent him together with Princess Neferure. Our statue is of the type called a block statue, that is to say a statue sculptured in a compact mass of stone, representing schematically the form of a squatting man, with his arms crossed under his chin and his hands on his knees, the whole figure hidden in a long mantel. This type of statue first made its appearance during the Middle Kingdom although squatting figures were known from the time of the first dynasties. It is the introduction of the child's head emerging from its tutor's mantel which represents an innovation of the 18th dynasty. This combination displays in a touching manner the exclusivity of the tutor's charge.

Senmut appears here with the features of a young man: full cheeks in a smooth, round face, wide-open eyes with long lashes represented in relief, rather large ears and a small straight, full mouth. The chubby child wears her hair in the plaited tress characteristic of royal children, ornamented with the uraeus, sign that she was the heir to the throne. Her name, inscribed in a cartouche next to her head, is preceded by the title: "god's wife".

The sides of the statue were ideal for placing a long inscription enumerating Senmut's numerous titles and functions in connection with the place and with the cult of Amon.

On the upper part of the statue, near Senmut's shoulder, two groups of hieroglyphs represent the Queen's two names: "Maakare" and "Hatshepsut" in cryptographic form. In the inscription which accompanies them Senmut proudly boasts of having invented these cryptograms himself.

A second statue of Senmut shows him seated, with the princess on his lap (on view in this room, CG 42116).

Bibliography: PM II, p. 134; Legrain, Statues et Statuettes (CG) I, pp. 62–64, pl. 66; Vandier, Manuel III, p. 475; Aldred, New Kingdom Art, p. 30; Drioton, in: ASAE 38, 1938, pp. 231–38; S. Ratié, Hatschepsut. Die Frau auf dem Thron der Pharaonen, Wiesbaden 1974, pp. 156–67; Ch. Meyer, Senenmut. Eine prosopographische Untersuchung, Hamburger Ägyptologische Studien 2, 1982.

133

133

Ground floor, room 12

Tuthmosis III (detail)

Greywacke   JE 38234 bis
H. 200 cm   = CG 42053
Karnak, court of the cachette; cleared by Legrain in 1904–5
New Kingdom, 18th dynasty, reign of Tuthmosis III, 1490–1439 B.C.

Some twenty statues deriving from Karnak, Deir el-Bahari or elsewhere, have preserved for us the physiognomy of this illustrious sovereign, considered the greatest conqueror in all of Egyptian history.

Kept waiting in the wings for twenty-two years by Queen Hatshepsut, Tuthmosis III embarked after the death of his aunt upon a vast building program and an aggressive foreign policy of conquest which was to result in Egyptian supremacy over the Near East. In the course of seventeen campaigns, all recorded in Tuthmosis' annals at Karnak, and thirty years of independent rule, the Egyptian frontiers were extended from Gebel Barkal in the south, downstream from the Fourth Cataract, all the way to the Euphrates in the north.

Nevertheless, the statues of this king hardly take the form of imposing colossi imbued expressly with the spirit of domination. Such a characteristic is present here only in the traditional symbol of the Nine Bows (or enemies) under the feet of His Majesty. Owing much to characteristics developed already under Hatshepsut, statuary of Tuthmosis III now perfectly expressed the concept of sovereignty. In this new idiom, idealism and realism, inherited from earlier periods, were now combined in an elegance never before achieved. Aesthetic qualities go hand in hand with technical precision.

The statue repays observation from all angles, even from the back. Furnished with the traditional royal attributes, the body is elegant, the face radiant under the white crown and surmounted by the uraeus. The aquiline nose, almost feline eyes, and slightly smiling mouth all lend to the piece an undeniable sense of nobility.

Bibliography: PM II, p. 137; Legrain, Statues et Statuettes (CG) I, p. 32, pls. 29, 30; Desroches-Noblecourt, L'Art Egyptien, Paris 1962, pp. 119–20, pl. 22; Lange/Hirmer, pl. 140–41; Propyläen Kunstgeschichte 15, pl. 175; Leclant, Les Pharaons II, fig. 134.

King. Sanctuaries were erected for the principal divinities of the country and more particularly for Amon-Re at Karnak, in the Theban nome and in Nubia.

One can easily recognize in this sphinx the remarkable features of the monarch which have been preserved for us in numerous portraits: the feline eyes, the arched nose, the full cheeks and the delicate mouth with the slightly incurved lower lip.

The King is wearing a striped *nemes* headcloth protected by an uraeus; the false beard is attached to his chin by two bands which rejoin the headdress.

The hybrid alliance between man and lion is artistically achiveded and the well known elegance of Tuthmosis III's statues transpires even through the lion's body, whose prominent musculature and stylized ribs are represented with great dexterity.

On the sphinx's chest an inscription in sunk relief gives the coronation name of Tuthmosis III: "The good god, Lord of the Two Lands, Menkheperre, beloved of Amon forever."

Bibliography: PM II, p. 138; Legrain, Statues et Statuettes (CG) I, pp. 40–41, pl. 41; Leclant, Les Pharaons II, fig. 132.

134

Sphinx of Tuthmosis III

Grey granite   JE 37981
H. 32 cm; W. 21 cm; L. 61 cm   = CG 42069
Karnak, court of the cachette; found by Legrain in 1905
New Kingdom, 18th dynasty, reign of Tuthmosis III, 1490–1439 B.C.

Tuthmosis III saved Egypt from the menace of Asiatic tribes such as the Hurrites of Asia Minor who had partially invaded Syria-Palestine. Tuthmosis III defeated them at Megiddo in Palestine where peace was established. Later, he advanced as far as Carchemish on the upper Euphrates and managed, after 14 campaigns, to subdue and pacify his north-eastern neighbours. To the south, Egypt's frontier was established at the 4th Cataract. The booty and tribute brought back to Egypt contributed in large part to the construction activities of the

135

Tuthmosis III offering *Nu*-jars

Marble   JE 43507 A
H. 26.5 cm; W. 9 cm; profile 14.5 cm
Deir el-Medina; excavated by J. Baraize in 1912
New Kingdom, 18th dynasty, reign of Tuthmosis III, 1490−1439 B.C.

Kneeling on a base, bearing two spherical vessels and wearing a *shendjyt* kilt and *nemes* headdress with uraeus, Tuthmosis III piously offers *Nu*-jars, most likely filled with wine or milk. The inscription on the back pillar gives his titulary and informs us that it is Amon to whom he offers, calling himself beloved of the god.
The image of the king, full of youth, gentleness and grace, is a miniature replica of his many larger statues, once again incorporating technical competence with an aesthetic concern.
The statue was doubtless offered as an ex-voto in one of the Theban temples, whence it was probably stolen and subsequently hidden at Deir el-Medina behind the west wall of the enclosure of Hathor. The area later became buried in debris from the mountain.

Bibliography: J. Baraize, in: ASAE 13, 1914, p. 37, pl. 10; Lange/ Hirmer, pl. 144; Corteggiani, no. 49.

136

Offering table of Tuthmosis III

Pink granite   JE 88803
H. 22.5 cm; W. 44 cm; L. 71.5 cm
Karnak, temple of Amon-Re, "court of the Middle Kingdom;" excavated by H. Chevrier in 1949
New Kingdom, 18th dynasty, reign of Tuthmosis III, 1490−1439 B.C.

Whether in the shape of circular plaques or rectangular slabs, offering tables are almost always decorated with the *hetep*-sign for offerings, representing a loaf of bread resting on a tray. This motif eventually dictates the form of the entire table, and the loaf of bread projecting out in front of the slab often served to pour libations.
This form continued through the centuries. Royal altars deposited in temples are larger and more elaborate, and were fashioned from more durable materials. When they are decorated, they depict representations similar to those of private offering tables, consisting of food offerings in raised relief, libation vessels or basins in sunk relief, the Niles of Upper and Lower Egypt, and personified nomes or domains in procession, a theme attested since the Middle Kingdom. In the New Kingdom, the king appears on the front of the altar presenting offerings.
An original feature of this table of Tuthmosis III is the replacement of offerings with numerous round cavities intended to hold vessels and loaves of bread. These vessels and loaves are actually shown in the double scene on the front of the table: before the kneeling figure of the king bearing offering jars, they are laid out on a low table in rows of three, matching exactly the holes on top of the altar. Altogether, forty cavities recall the forty holes of an altar from Dynasty 13 (on display in the central atrium).
The sides are decorated with djed-pillars and Isis knots − stability and protection − a pattern also found on the openwork sides of chairs. The text on the projecting loaf in front gives Tuthmosis III's titulary, while dedicatory inscriptions run around all four sides of the table. The piece is dedicated to the god Amon-Re of Karnak.
We have several altars and offering tables of Tuthmosis III from Karnak; this king enlarged the temple and rearranged the sanctuary. In a representation in the sixth court, to the south of the bark sanctuary, we see him "consecrating numerous offering tables to Amon-Re, Lord of the Thrones of the Two Lands in Karnak."

Bibliography: PM II, p. 108; H. Chevrier, in: ASAE 49, 1949, pp. 257−58; J. Leclant, in: Orientalia 19, 1950, pl. 39, fig. 12 and p. 364 ff.

136

137

Isis, mother of Tuthmosis III

Black granite   JE 37417
H. 98.5 cm; W. 25 cm; L. 52.5 cm   = CG 42072
Karnak, court of the cachette; cleared by Legrain in 1904
New Kingdom, 18th dynasty, reign of Tuthmosis III, 1490–1439 B.C.

This attractive statue of the queen mother Isis was dedicated
by her son, Tuthmosis III, to the temple of Amon-Re at Karnak. The queen sits in classical pose, the hands resting on the
thighs. A floral scepter hangs from her left hand. She wears a
tripartite wig with long, equally sized tresses. On top of the
wig rests a cylindrical base which once held two tall feathers,
while frontal uraei wear the crowns of Upper and Lower
Egypt. The queen's jewellery consists of a large collar and two
bracelets.

The facial features and modelling of the figures are well
balanced, the pose though stiff, is not without charm. The
queen's feet rest on a base incorporated into her seat, the
jambs of which bear the dedicatory inscription: "The perfect
god, Lord of the Two Lands, Menkheperre (Tuthmosis III),
beloved of Amon-Re, Lord of the Thrones of the Two Lands.
He made (it) as his monument for his mother, the king's
mother Isis, justified."

Like most royal statues, this one once displayed portions covered in gold leaf, such as the base for the feather headdress.
Surviving traces indicate that the queen's jewellery was once
likewise gilded.

*Bibliography: PM II, p. 144; Statues et Statuettes (CG) I, pp. 41–42,
pl. 42; Propyläen Kunstgeschichte 15, pl. 178.*

Chapel with the Hathor cow

Painted sandstone   JE 38574−5
H. 225 cm; W. 157 cm; L. 404 cm
Deir el-Bahari, temple of Tuthmosis III; excavations of the Egypt
Exploration Fund 1906
New Kingdom, 18th dynasty, end of the reign of Tuthmosis III, begin-
ning of the reign of Amenophis II, c. 1440 B.C.

Hathor appears here in the form of a cow surrounded by
papyrus. She comes out of the necropolis mountain supplying
the fertility wished for in arid regions. With speckled body
and frontal uraeus, she is crowned with the sun disk and tall
feathers enclosed by her two horns.
Both the statue and the chapel which houses it derive from
Deir el-Bahari, where they were hidden under stone debris
between the temples of Mentuhotep and Hatshepsut. During
the clearance of the area, Naville recommended to his foreman
that work be ceased for fear of causing an avalanche. The avalanche subsequently did occur, and once the dust had dissi-
pated, the excavator found himself facing the opening which
housed the Sacred Cow. Both statue and chapel were in an
excellent state of preservation, as can be seen by the extremely
fresh colors.
The sanctuary was dedicated by Tuthmosis III, who is shown
upon the walls. To the left he is accompanied by his wife
Meritre and consecrates the offering piled high before the
starred naos of the divine cow, who simultaneously protects
the royal figure and suckles the infant king. We also see the
king before Hathor, this time in the form of a woman with her
characteristic coiffure. To the right, the same scenes repeat,
although the king is followed by two princesses in place of his
wife Meritre. At the back of the shrine, Tuthmosis III pours a
libation and makes a burnt offering to Amon-Re, seated at
right. The scene is crowned by a frieze of stars, while a
khekher frieze (originally a plant motif) crowns the side walls.
The dark blue vaulted ceiling imitates the star-studded heavens.
The statue of the sacred cow itself bears the name of Tuthmosis' successor, Amenophis II whose cartouche is inscribed on
the neck. The piece reproduces in three dimensions a common
mural scene: the cow protecting the sovereign who stands
against her breast, while she suckles the infant king shown
crouching to the left.
The cult of the celestial cow in the arid mountain is an ancient
one. It was associated with Hathor very early on, for she was
the goddess of the Theban necropolis, and was worshipped in
a rock sanctuary. One might recall that in the reign of Mentuhotep the princesses buried near the royal temple at Deir el-
Bahari were priestesses of Hathor (see nos. 68 and 69). In the
New Kingdom, Hatshepsut dedicated a sanctuary to the goddess incorporated into the enclosure of her mortuary temple.
This served as the destination for the procession of the Sacred
Bark, which came from Karnak during the Beautiful Festival
of the Valley. Later, Tuthmosis III closed this temple, de-

stroyed all trace of the queen, and constructed a new temple to receive the procession of Amon, along with this chapel to the Hathor cow beside it. The director of this project was the famous vizier Rekhmire. According to the graffiti of the area, the cult of Hathor was maintained up to the Ramesside period, when earthquakes destroyed the temple and buried the entrance to the chapel of the Sacred Cow.

Bibliography: PM II, pp. 380–81; E. Naville, The VIth Dynasty Temple at Deir el-Bahari I, London 1907, pp. 63–67, pls. 27–31 and frontispiece; J. Lipinska, The Temple of Thutmosis III, Deir el-Bahari II, Warsaw 1977, pp. 38–45; LÄ I, 1022–23.

139

Ground floor, room 12

Amenophis II

Schist (greywacke) JE 36680
H. 68 cm = CG 42077
Karnak, court of the cachette; cleared by Legrain in 1904
New Kingdom, 18th dynasty, reign of Amenophis II, 1439–1414 B.C.

The elegance, charm and sense of proportion which characterized the first half of the Eighteenth Dynasty was even able to idealize the image of a monarch as belligerent and aggressive as Amenophis II.

The king stands clothed in a pleated *shendjyt* kilt, holding rolled napkins in either hand. He wears the *khat* headdress, similar to the *nemes* but baggier, hanging down in a large section over the back.

Amenophis II is known from less amiable portraits which better characterize his personality: extremely strong and energetic, enamored of the hunt and demonstrations of force. He boasted of being the only man in Egypt or Syria able to bend his bow. He followed his father's policy of conquest, and quelled revolts in Asia fairly quickly. Endowed with a certain cruelty, Amenophis brought back defeated princes of Takhsy in order to hang them on the gates of Thebes.

The end of his reign, however, was quite peaceful, and Egypt came to enjoy one of the most prosperous periods in her history.

Bibliography: PM II, p. 139; Legrain, Statues et Statuettes (CG) I, pp. 44–45, pl. 47; Vandier, Manuel III, pp. 306–7, pl. 101,2; Terrace/Fischer, no. 23; Leclant, Les Pharaons II, fig. 140.

Thebes (TT no. 96), with its interesting scenes of the afterlife and its beautiful painted grape-arbor ceiling, still reflect the legacy of this high official. As a functionary of distinguished rank who was highly praised by the king, Sennefer was granted the right to deposit this double statue in the temple of Karnak, in the same manner as contemporary royal representations (see the double statue of Tuthmosis IV and his mother Tia on exhibit in this room). Sennefer was thus able to receive the offerings and the prayers of visitors. He was also proud of being a "royal favorite", to whom the king presented the massive gold necklace of honor as well as the heart-shaped amulets, insignia of his office, which he wears both on this statue and in the painted scenes in his tomb.

Sennefer and his wife Senay are seated on a high-backed chair, their arms interlaced. The husband wears a heavy wig the echeloned curls of which reach to his shoulders, leaving the ears exposed. His features are those of a middle-aged man with a serene expression. The sagging breast and rolls of fat on his torso express his well-being and prosperity, a fashion introduced into Egyptian art during the Middle Kingdom, and still popular in the Eighteenth Dynasty (see Amenhotep son of Hapu, no. 148–149).

Senay, whose titles name her as royal nurse, wears a tripartite wig with tresses covering her ears, a broad collar and a long dress with two shoulder-straps. Her face is also given a light smile.

One of Sennefer's daughters, Mut-nofret, stands on a small base between the legs of her parents. Her wig terminates in tresses spread over her shoulders. The same Mut-nofret appears carved on the right side of the seat, on her knees before a table of offerings, sniffing a lotus flower and accompanied by an offering formula. On the left side, a similar representation depicts her sister, Nefertari.

Sennefer's right shoulder is stamped with the two cartouches of the name of Amenophis II. Upon the couple's clothing are offering formulae invoking "a million of bread and beer, wine, oxen, fowl and everything good and pure" for the Ka of both individuals.

It is noteworthy that this sculpture is one of the very few Egyptian works of art ever to be signed. The artists Amenmes and Djed-Khonsu have placed their names in the vertical inscription on the left side of the seat.

Bibliography: PM II, pp. 283–84; Legrain, Statues et Statuettes (CG) I, pp. 76–78, pl. 75; Vandier, Manuel III, pp. 511–12; Terrace/ Fischer, no. 24; Nofret – Die Schöne, no. 6.

140

Ground floor, room 12

Sennefer and Senay

Grey granite   JE 36574
H. 120 cm   = CG 42126
Karnak; discovered to the north of the great hypostyle hall by the Egyptian Antiquities Service in 1903.
New Kingdom, 18th dynasty, reigns of Amenophis II – Tuthmosis IV, 1439–1403 B.C.

Sennefer was mayor of the southern city (Thebes) during the reign of Amenophis II. The burial chamber of his tomb at

New Kingdom. The members of this community were buried in tombs which they excavated and decorated themselves in the slope of the Theban cliff, next to their village.

Among the tombs of the Eighteenth Dynasty, that of Satnem still contained all of its funerary equipment. Two statuettes of sycamore wood represent the deceased and his wife. They were placed, enveloped in linen, facing the entrance to the tomb. The statue of Satnem, which had been set upon a chair, is currently in the Louvre.

The statuette of his wife Ibentina, illustrated here, stood on the ground inside a naos furnished with a grooved sliding lid. The base of the statuette is fitted within a small pedestal which slides into an opening carved out of the bottom of the naos. Ibentina cuts an exquisite figure, with elongated arms and legs. She wears a tripartite wig with twisted locks held together by hairbands. A long, close-fitting dress covers her figure, and bracelets are painted around her wrists. Her chain of blue faience beads tied around her left forearm goes well with the natural color of the wood. The statuette was once entirely covered with stucco and painted.

The inscription on the base contains an offering formula addressed to Osiris, lord of Busiris and lord of Abydos, that he might grant the deceased all manner of food offerings and every pure thing which comes forth upon the altar of the lord of eternity.

Bibliography: PM I, 2, p. 701; B. Bruyère, Rapports sur les fouilles de Deir el Medineh, 1934–35, Fouilles de l'Institut Français d'Archéologie Orientale 15, 1937, pp. 124–30 and figs. 70–71; Centenaire de l'Institut Français d'Archéologie Orientale, Cairo 1981, no. 21. Cf. also: Un siècle de fouilles françaises en Égypte 1880–1980, Paris 1981, no. 227.

142a

141
Ground floor, room 12

The lady Ibentina

Painted wood   JE 63646 A/B
Naos: H. 62 cm; W. 26.5 cm; profile 26 cm
Statuette: H. 31.8 cm
Deir el-Medina, tomb of Satnem (no. 1379); excavations of the Institut Français d'Archéologie Orientale, 1933–34
New Kingdom, 18th dynasty, reign of Hatshepsut and Tuthmosis III, 1490–1470 B.C.

Deir el-Medina was the village of craftsmen who were responsible for preparing the royal tombs at Thebes during the

142b △

142c ▽

Book of the Dead of Maiherperi

Papyrus   CG 24095
L. 117.5 cm; H. 35 cm
Thebes, Valley of the Kings, tomb no. 36; discovered by Loret in 1899
New Kingdom, 18th dynasty, c. 1450 B.C.

Exhibited today in five separate pieces, this beautiful papyrus was once rolled up complete among the funerary equipment of a certain Maiherperi. Perhaps of Nubian descent, and granted the extraordinary privilege of a tomb in the royal necropolis, he held the titles "Fan-bearer on the right of the King," and "Child of the nursery," that is, page in the court of pharaoh. He was most likely a foster brother or son of an early Eighteenth Dynasty king and possibly a Nubian concubine, hence his dark complexion.

The text of the papyrus, written in a beautiful cursive hieroglyphic hand, contains the Book of the Dead, or "Book of going forth by day" to use the Egyptian term, whose mere presence inside the tomb was enough to insure the survival of the deceased in the netherworld. Any and all difficulties there were overcome with the aid of spells illustrated by vignettes, three of which are shown here. The simplicity of their form and freshness of their colors are both noteworthy.

The first vignette represents the funeral procession (chapter 1). With the aid of a sledge drawn by oxen, the deceased's mummy is transported to the tomb; it lies on a bed surrounded by a naos placed within a bark. The goddesses Isis and Nepthys, one on each side of the naos, protect the body. The second vignette depicts the weighing of the heart of Maiherperi before Osiris and under the careful observance of Thoth, god of wisdom, represented here as a baboon. The spell consists of "preventing the heart of the deceased from bearing witness against him in the land of the dead" (chapter 30B). To the right, the spirit of the deceased, in the form of a human-headed bird, flies unhindered out of the tomb having acquired the "use of its legs" (chapter 92).

The vignette with the seven cows and one bull being adored by the deceased illustrates the "spell for provisioning the blessed in the necropolis" (chapter 148), which simultaneously serves to remove all sorts of harmful obstacles. The seven cows always lend their assistance, and the virile bull insures the continuity of the species. The four steering oars, symbolic of the four corners of heaven, provide for the needs of the deceased, whom they protect. The latter is presented with brown skin and kinky hairstyle. He wears a transparent tunic, beneath which is a short kilt.

Bibliography: Daressy, Fouilles de la Vallée des Rois, 1898–1899 (CG), pp. 38–57, pls. 13–15; Corteggiani, no. 53. Cf. also: E. Thomas, The Royal Necropoleis of Thebes, Princeton 1966, pp. 157–58; E. Hornung, Tal der Könige, 1985, pp. 55 and 149; M. Saleh, Das Totenbuch in den thebanischen Beamtengräbern des Neuen Reiches, Mainz 1984.

Stela of Amenophis III (details)

Painted limestone   JE 31409
H. 206.5 cm; W. 110 cm   = CG 34026
Thebes; discovered reused in the mortuary
temple of Merenptah, by Petrie, 1896
New Kingdom, 18th dynasty, reign of Amenophis III,
c. 1403−1365 B.C.

This stela was originally erected in the court of the mortuary
temple of Amenophis III at Thebes; one of the largest temples
of the region, constructed in beautiful white limestone, it was
completely dismantled very early on to provide material for
other Theban buildings from the Nineteenth Dynasty and
later. Merenptah removed much of the stone for his own mortuary temple, including this particular stela.
Temple courts were once filled with statues and stelae, both
royal and private. This stela illustrates pharaoh's victory over
his enemies. The first register is conventional: under the
winged sun-disk two symmetrical scenes show the king in
ceremonial costume offering Maat − Truth − (on the left) and
two wine jars (on the right) to Amon. The very fine facial features and almond-shaped eyes are typical of this king. The
Amon figures were destroyed during the reign of Akhenaten
but later restored under Seti I, who added the incised inscription.
The second register is of greater interest. In the two parallel
scenes the king stands in his horse-drawn chariot. Above him
the vulture-goddess Nekhbet spreads her wings in a gesture of
protection and offers Amenophis the signs for life, stability
and dominion. Pharaoh wears the blue Khepresh crown with
uraeus and a plaited kilt with hanging tab. In his hands he

holds the reins, a bow and a whip. A quiver of arrows hangs
over his back while another larger one is attached to the open-
work body of the chariot. The elaborately harnessed horses
dash along at a gallop, crowned with ostrich feathers and covered with red saddle blankets. In the scene to the right they
bear on their backs four Nubian captives with hands bound
behind them, while a fifth is tied by the feet to the shaft of the
chariot, and the head of a sixth protrudes from the bottom of
the chassis. The left hand scene shows the horses in the process of trampling Asiatic foes. It is an extraordinary composition in which the artist's imagination has admirably rendered
this chaotic world which pharaoh has conquered. The con-
torted bodies of enemies overlap everywhere; one even hangs
from His Majesty's chariot. The expressive faces are in some
cases even shown frontally, contrary to Egyptian convention.
This world of captives is truly "vile" from the Egyptian perspective, and serves to contrast sharply with the sense of pharaonic order, while also offering the artist a brief opportunity
to liberate himself from rigid, official convention.
At the bottom of the stela is a frieze of Rekhyt birds, lapwings
with human arms who symbolize all peoples represented in
endless adoration of pharaoh. The text which concludes the
stela describes the illustrations: "All countries, all states, all
peoples, Mesopotamia, the vile land of Kush (Ethiopia), Upper
and Lower Retenu (Syria-Palestine) are under the feet of this
perfect god, like Re forever."

Bibliography: PM II, p. 448; Petrie, Six Temples at Thebes, London
1897, pp. 10, 23, pl. 10; P. Lacau, Stèles du Nouvel Empire (CG),
pl. 20−21, pp. 59−61.

144
Queen Tiye

Green steatite   JE 38257
H. 7.2 cm
Sinai, temple of Hathor at Serabit el-Khadim;
discovered by F. Petrie in 1904
New Kingdom, 18th dynasty, reign of Amenophis III, c. 1403–1365
B.C.

Queen Tiye was the wife of Amenophis III and the mother of
Akhenaten. This excellent portrait, carved in a beautiful green
steatite, belonged to a statuette dedicated to the temple of
Hathor in the Sinai. The goddess was venerated there since the
Middle Kingdom as the Mistress of the Turquoise. She protected the productive mines of the Sinai worked since the Old
Kingdom at Maghara (see no. 24) and since the Middle Kingdom at Serabit el-Khadim, where a temple was constructed for
her.
Queen Tiye wears a long wig with little curls carved in an
echelon pattern. On top of her wig, a circular base, which
once supported two tall feathers, is decorated with two uraei
with outstretched wings and undulating bodies. They protectively flank the queen's cartouche. The same serpent deities
appear again on the queen's brow wearing the crowns of
Upper and Lower Egypt.
The oval face with high cheek-bones, narrow almond-shaped

eyes and full, almost disillusioned mouth, is that of a determined and serious woman with noble spirit, despite her apparent youth. Stylistically, this portrait belongs to the end of the
reign of Amenophis III and introduces an artistic tradition
which was to be embraced by the Amarna Period.

Bibliography: PM VII, pp. 361–62; F. Petrie, Researches in Sinai,
London 1906, p. 126, pl. 133; Vandier, Manuel III, pp. 329–31;
pl. 107; Corteggiani, no. 55; Leclant, Les Pharaons II, pl. 150; Nofret
– Die Schöne, no. 31.

145 Mummy mask of Thuya

Gilded cartonnage, semi-precious stones, glass   JE 95254
H. 40 cm; W. 28 cm   = CG 51009
Thebes, Valley of the Kings, tomb of Yuya and Thuya (no. 46);
discovered and excavated by the Antiquities Service for T. Davis in
1905
New Kingdom, 18th dynasty, reign of Amenophis III, 1403–1365
B.C.

Spell 151b of the Book of the Dead describes the funerary
mask as an indispensable element for the protection of the
head of the deceased and identifies its different parts with
those of the principal deities of Egypt.
The mummy mask has a forerunner in the stone "reserve
heads" of Dynasty 4. These were intended to act either as substitute for the head or entire body of the deceased, so that the
spirit (Ba) could recognize it, or alternatively, as we have seen
(no. 32), as a cast for the mask.
We have masks in plaster from the end of the Old Kingdom
moulded upon the face of the deceased to preserve his features. From the First Intermediate Period on, a cartonnage
mask (layers of linen reinforced by plaster) modelled in the
image of the deceased's head covered it entirely (see no. 96).
Usually painted, or occasionally gilded or ornamented with
semi-precious stones, these masks animated the features of the
well-to-do. Royal masks were generally of beaten gold
adorned with inlays of stone or glass paste.
This mask in gilded plaster once covered the head of the
mummy of Thuya, mother of Queen Tiye, wife of Amenophis
III. It was sealed within a series of wooden coffins (on display
on the floor of this gallery along with those of her husband
Yuya), and was discovered broken in two pieces which were
carefully restored in 1982. At the time, the restorers partially
removed the linen gauze, originally glued to the mask, and
exposed the marvellous face of this lady with her exquisite
smile, enlivened by the inlaid eyes of blue glass and quartz,
with touches of red.
Her coiffure consists of a long striated wig passing behind the
ears and tied with a floral band. A broad collar of several
rows of carefully inlaid, polychrome glass, bordered by a row
of gilded beads imitating petals, entirely covers the breast.
Part of the gauze, now blackened with time, remains attached
to the mask; the back bears traces of a black resin.

Bibliography: PM I, 2, p. 563; Quibell, The Tomb of Yuaa and Thuiu
(CG), p. 28, pl. 13.

these inscriptions is composed of a repeated group of signs wishing "all life and prosperity" to the owner of the casket. The funerary furniture of this tomb included a chariot, several beautiful chairs, numerous small coffers, shawabti figures and jewels (all on display in this hall).

Bibliography: PM I, 2, p. 564; Quibell, The Tomb of Yuaa and Thuiu (CG), pp. 56–57, pls. 46, 47.

147   Ground floor, room 12
Fragments of Palace decoration

Plaster painted in distemper	RT 3.5.27.4
H. 80 cm; W. 120 and 149 cm	and 3.5.27.6

Thebes, Malgata, palace of Amenophis III
New Kingdom, 18th dynasty, reign of Amenophis III, 1403–1365 B.C.

Egyptian palaces built mainly of brick and wood disappeared very quickly and only rare remains have come down to us as witnesses of the grandeur of these enormous constructions whose innumerable rooms were completely covered with paintings, pillars, floors and ceilings included, and sparkled with inlaid faience (see Ramesside palace no. 226).

146   Upper floor, hall 13
Jewel Casket of Thuya

Gilded wood, faience, ivory and ebony	JE 95248
H. 43 cm; W. 26.8 cm; L. 38.5 cm	= CG 51118

Thebes, Valley of the Kings, Tomb of Yuya and Thuya (no. 46).
Discovered and excavated by the Egyptian Antiquities Service for T. Davis in 1905
New Kingdom, 18th dynasty, reign of Amenophis III, 1403–1365 B.C.

This is one of the most beautiful objects belonging to Thuya's funerary equipment: a jewel casket in the form of a naos with a cornice, standing on raised feet and closed with a vaulted lid. The inlaid decoration includes elements made of ebony, rose-tinted ivory and blue faience. The lid, divided in its length into two symmetrical parts, is decorated in gold on a blue faience background. In the upper register are placed the cartouches of Amenophis III surmounted by the feathers and sundisk; in the lower register, facing each other, are two figures of the god Heh kneeling on the hieroglyph for "gold", and holding in each hand the plant stem signifying millions of years.
Around the outside of the casket, two inscriptions in gold hieroglyphs on a background of faience, give the titulature of Amenophis III. Starting on either side of the knob which serves to bind the lid to the casket, the two symmetrical inscriptions cover the small side and the two long sides of the casket. The opposite small side is occupied by the name of the royal wife Tiye. The frieze of gold hieroglyphs underneath

The first example known to us of such decoration comes from the palace of Amenophis III at Thebes, a vast building which stretched out beyond where the temple of Medinet Habu now stands into the western desert.

These two fragments come from this palace; they were originally in a room with aquatic decoration like that of one of the better known audience halls, whose painted floor depicted a pool filled with fish and framed with a frieze of aquatic plants and marsh fowl (fragments of this floor are now dispersed among various museums).

Our two panels, bordered with a frieze of rosettes, represent luxuriously growing tufts of papyrus and plants with long leaves, dotted with blue flowers, among which wild geese are flying.

The painting is freely executed without previously drawn guide lines, and is applied on a dry surface, not like fresko on a humid base. The combination of colours used, although simple and limited in number, give a bright and many-shaded effect. In fact, the colours employed by the painter are restricted to: chalk white, carbon black, red and yellow ochre, and frit (ground silicious glass) for the blues and green.

Bibliography: PM I, 2, pp. 778—79; Desroches-Noblecourt, Toutankhamon et son temps, Tutankhamon exhibition catalog in Paris, no. 10. Cf. also: Robb de P. Tytus, A preliminary report on the re-excavation of the Palace of Amenhotep III, New York, 1903; Daressy, in: ASAE 3, 1903, pp. 165—70; Winlock, in: BMMA VII, 1912, pp. 184—89; H. W. Müller, Alt-Ägyptische Malerei, München, pl. 25; Smith, Art and Architecture, pp. 283—95; Hayes, The Scepter of Egypt II, pp. 244—47.

148—149   Ground floor, room 12
Amenhotep son of Hapu

This remarkable individual hailed from an unimportant family in the Delta town of Athribis (modern Benha). He began his career as a scribe of recruits in the court of King Amenophis III at Thebes. His administrative talents and energies resulted in numerous promotions until he reached some of the highest offices in the country. His building activities in Karnak, Luxor and the Theban necropolis bear witness to his genius and great responsibilities as "director of all royal works." His reputation as a sage continued in ancient Egypt for many generations after his death. He was eventually even worshipped, along with Imhotep, as a god of healing. In the Ptolemaic era, a chapel was dedicated to both of them at the back of the third terrace of the temple of Hatshepsut at Deir el-Bahari. During his life time, Amenhotep was permitted through royal favor to display his statues in the great temple of Amon at Karnak. It is here that our two statues were found. He also enjoyed the unprecedented privilege of building his own funerary temple in the area reserved for royal temples, as well as excavating a vast tomb in the Theban necropolis.

148

148
Amenhotep son of Hapu as a young man

Grey granite   JE 44861
H. 128 cm; W. 81 cm; L. 72 cm
Karnak, Tenth pylon; discovered by Legrain in 1913
New Kingdom, 18th dynasty, reign of Amenophis III, 1403—1365 B.C.

The statue of the youthful Amenhotep son of Hapu and two statues of the vizier Pa-Ramessu, were found at the foot of the staircase east of the gate of the Tenth pylon at Karnak. It shows him seated as a scribe with legs crossed. This is a statue type intended to represent a great man of letters, and not necessarily a mere scribe.

The sculptor has succeeded in reflecting both the youth and well-being of this individual in the serene visage and vigorously modelled torso, with its folds of fat conventionally rendered. The wig displays wavy locks terminating in curls, covering Amenhotep's forehead and stopping above the thick eyebrows. It flares toward the shoulders and hides the upper part of the ears.

Amenhotep's head gently inclines toward the unrolled papyrus on his lap on order to read the text which is oriented towards him. A palette with two inkwells, one for red and one for black, hangs over his left shoulder, while a second, circular one rests on his left knee. The inscription on the body contains the birth and coronation names of Amenophis III. The text inscribed on the papyrus gives the name and titles of Amenhotep son of Hapu and mentions the large royal statues which he erected in the west – a probable allusion to the mortuary temple of Amenophis III where the colossi of Memnon stand today. In the socle inscription Amenhotep declares himself able to intercede before Amon-Rê in order to forward their prayers.

Bibliography: PM II, p. 188; Legrain, in ASAE 14, 1914, pp. 17–20, pl. 3; Vandier, Manuel III, p. 515; Lange/Hirmer, Ägypten, pl. 91; Terrace/Fischer, no. 25; Desroches-Noblecourt, Toutankhamon et son temps, no. 2. Compare the identical statue in the Luxor Museum: The Luxor Museum of Ancient Egyptian Art, 1979, no. 117.

149

149
Amenhotep son of Hapu as an aged man

Grey granite   JE 38368
H. 117 cm; W. 70 cm; L. 78 cm   = CG 42127
Karnak, discovered to the north of the Seventh pylon (court of the cachette) by Legrain in 1901
New Kingdom, 18th dynasty, reign of Amenophis III, 1403–1365 B.C.

The second statue depicts Amenhotep son of Hapu in his old age, a sage full of experience. This time he wears a long wavy wig held behind the ears and framing an emaciated face with a meditative expression. The folds of fat have now disappeared from the body, which is wrapped in a long kilt tied unter the breast. His hands rest flat upon the knees in the attitude of prayer. This sculpture is an extremely realistic piece which bespeaks an individual portrait.

The long inscription informs us, after the biographical phrases praising the merits of this great dignitary, that Amenhotep had reached the age of eighty when this sculpture was produced and that he hopes yet to attain the wise old age of 110.

Bibliography: PM II, p. 169; Legrain, Statues et Statuettes I (CG), pp. 78–80, pl. 76; A. Varille, Inscription concernant l'architecte Amenhotep fils de Hapou, Cairo 1968, p. 4ff.; Helck, Urkunden der 18. Dynastie, Übersetzung zu den Heften 17–22, Berlin 1984, pp. 274–75; LÄ I, 219–20.

150   Upper floor, hall 48
Shawabti of Ptahmose

Polychrome faience   CG 48406
H. 20 cm; W. 6 cm
Abydos; excavations of Mariette, 1881
New Kingdom, 18th dynasty, reign of Amenophis III, 1403–1365 B.C.

Of remarkably fine workmanship, this mummiform statuette from the necropolis north of Abydos represents the vizier, mayor and high priest of Amon at Thebes, Ptahmose. The tomb of this important man was doubtless at Thebes, but the

150

god of the dead Osiris, with whom the deceased became identified, traditionally received some sort of dedicatory monument at Abydos. In this case it takes the form of a standing statuette of Osiris, with body enveloped in a close fitting garment, and arms crossed over the breast, which is in turn protected by a vulture with outspread wings. A large collar adorns his neck, and his coiffure is striated yellow and violet. The carefully executed central column of hieroglyphs lists the name and titles of the statuette's owner, while the horizontal lines surrounding the body are taken from chapter 6 of the Book of the Dead, an appeal to the *shawabti*. *Shawabtis* were figurines equipped with the name and features of the deceased and intended to take care of the domestic work in the realm of the dead. Each time he was called upon to cultivate the fields, irrigate the banks, or transport fertile earth, the shawabti deposited in the tomb was to reply "Here I am!"

The word *shawabti*, of obscure etymology, came to be reinterpreted by the Egyptians themselves and confused with the word *ushabti*, "he who answers."

Bibliography: PM V, pp. 60–61; Newberry, Funerary Statuettes and Model Sarcophagi (CG) II, pp. 343–45; III, pl. 27; Legrain, La statuette funéraire de Ptahmos, in: Recueil de Travaux 26, 1904, p. 81; H. D. Schneider, Shabtis I, Leyden 1977, p. 200.

151

Upper floor, hall 48

Shawabti and model sarcophagus of Amenhotep called Huy

Faience   JE 88902
H. (sarcophagus) 18 cm; L. 8 cm
H. (shawabti) 13.8 cm
Abydos. Acquired in 1950
New Kingdom, 18th dynasty, c. 1380 B.C.

Shawabtis placed in miniature sarcophagi became fashionable at the end of Dynasty 17. For the most part they are made of wood. The Eighteenth Dynasty saw them also manufactured of clay which was carefully enamelled, such as the beautiful specimen illustrated here.

The bearded mummiform shawabti figure, wearing a long wig with little locks and holding the amulets *sa* (protection) and *djed* (stability), is inscribed with the traditional shawabti text. It rests within a likewise mummiform coffin whose lid, modelled with the image of the deceased-become-Osiris, attaches to its base by means of mortise and tenon joints. The deceased was a certain royal scribe Amenhotep called Huy, perhaps identical with an official of the same name, known from other sources as great steward of Amenophis III.

Bibliography: 5000 ans d'art égyptien, Brussels 1960, no. 91. Cf. also: H. D. Schneider, Shabtis I, Leyden 1977; W. Helck, Zur Verwaltung des Mittleren und Neuen Reiches, Leyden/Cologne 1958, pp. 483–85; LÄ I, 222.

151

152

Upper floor, hall 48

Khaemwas and Manana

Steatite, with limestone base   JE 87911
H. 27.3 cm; L. 13.5 cm; W. 10.8 cm
Zagazig; discovered in 1946
New Kingdom, 18th dynasty, reign on Amenophis III, ca. 1403–1365
B.C.

The art of sculpture under Amenophis III reached a perfection and finesse visible even in small private statuary. Exquisite detail enhances elaborate wigs and clothing with multiple plaits; faces display gentle and attractive features.

This statuette of a couple is chosen here for the high quality of its workmanship, the beauty of the lady's face and the minute details of the costumes. The man wears a long wig with undulating locks set off in front against an echelon pattern of curls. His clothing consists of a tunic with short sleeves, tied at the neck, and a loose skirt held at the waist by a long plaited sash, whose fringed edge hangs down in front. The cartouches of the reigning king Amenophis III are carved on his breast and arm.

The woman's graceful figure is adorned with an extravagant wig of chevroned curls, tied by a lotus diadem and large band. A Wesekh collar with several rows of beads ornaments her breast, which is also decorated with two rosettes. A large bracelet covers each wrist. She wears a long, tight-fitting gown; a great pleated shawl hangs about her shoulders. In her left hand she holds the *menat* collar, symbol of Hathor.

On the base and back pillars are inscribed the names and titles of the couple, and an offering formula runs around the limestone base. The little pair statue was discovered during the foundations of a hospital at Zagazig.

Bibliography: Leclant, Les Pharaons II, ill. 316, p. 289.

153

Ground floor, room 12

The Stablemaster Tjay

Ebony   JE 33255
H. 58 cm; L. 33.8 cm; W. 10.2 cm
Sakkara; discovered by V. Loret in 1899
New Kingdom, 18th dynasty, reign of Amenophis III, ca. 1380 B.C.

Of all the statuettes of officials of Dynasty 18, a period rich in masterpieces, this one is without doubt the most alluring. Carved with such finesse and perfection, this sculpture seems to reproduce in three dimensions the magnificent reliefs found in the contemporary tombs at Thebes (Ramose, Kheruef, Khaemhat, etc.).

The youthful and graceful facial features display exquisite beauty and delicate modelling. The slightly inclined almond-shaped eyes are surmounted by arching eyelids and elongated on either side by a cosmetic line. The nose hardly protrudes, the mouth is fleshy but sensitive, the cheeks full.

The fine chevron curls of the wig, which terminate in little

153

154   Upper floor, hall 48
Statuette of the young Tama

Painted wood, gold, faience   JE 35057
H. 14.2 cm; L. 7.2 cm; W. 3.6 cm
Fayum, tomb at Hawaret Gurob; discovered by Daninos Pacha in 1900, excavations of the Egyptian Antiquities Service
New Kingdom, 18th dynasty, reign of Amenophis III, ca. 1380 B.C.

The tomb of this young lady named Tama contained two mummified bodies and the usual funerary equipment, including vessels, a headrest and a beautiful collection of toilet articles such as a mirror, kohl jars with the names of Amenophis III and Tiye, little glass and stone vessels, combs and pins. The statuette was placed among these objects as a symbol of eternal beauty. Surviving colors enhance the juvenile features: red for the lips and black for the cosmetic lines on the eyes and for the wig adorned with the sidelock of youth. She still wears her jewellery: a necklace of faience beads, a twisted gold collar and one earring (the latter is not on exhibit). A single group of hieroglyphs on the top of the base preserves the name of Tama.

Bibliography: Quibell, in: ASAE 2, 1901, pp. 141–43, pls. 1 and 2.

locks, are a tour de force in minutely detailed sculpture. The collar, composed of four rows of compact 'gold' ringlets is of the type awarded by the king to his officials as a mark of distinction.

Tjay wears a tunic with plaited sleeves, and a skirt with a plaited frontal section attached to the waist by means of a plaited sash wrapped around twice. One end of the sash hangs down in front, the other is tied at the stomach.

The traditional offering formula accompanied by Tjay's name and titles is inscribed on the frontal section of the skirt and on the top of the base. This graceful individual was royal scribe and chief of the stables of Pharaoh.

The statuette was found wrapped in linen gauze coated with stucco, which gave it the appearance of a limestone sculpture. It was cleaned in 1935. A piece of gauze remains attached to the left arm, which is partially broken away.

Bibliography: PM III, 2, p. 553; V. Loret, in: Bulletin de l'Institut Egyptien, Série III, no. 10, 1899, pp. 99–100; Smith, Art and Architecture, fig. 273; Corteggiani, no. 61.

Upper floor, hall 48

◁ The lady Henut-Nakhtu

Wood, originally gilded and painted   JE 6056
H. 22.2 cm; L. 12.1 cm; W. 5.4 cm   = CG 804
Sakkara, 1859
New Kingdom, end of the 18th dynasty, ca. 1300 B.C.

Numerous beautiful wooden statuettes of women in New
Kingdom tombs now grace the collections of the world's
museums. They represent, in miniature sculpture in the round,
the seductive figures carved and painted on tomb walls.
The fashion displayed here reflects elegance and luxury. An
enormous wig held by a lotus diadem surrounds the delicate
face. A long, transparent fringed and pleated linen robe is tied
below the breast. It covers one shoulder, exposes the other,
and envelops the rest of the body without hiding the attractive
figure. The asymmetrical pose gives the impression of a graceful stride.
Henut-Nakhtu clutches a tiered bouquet. The object once
inserted in her left hand has disappeared, as has the cone of
scented fat which originally crowned her wig. The inscription
carved on the base of the statuette wishes for the provision of
offerings for the *ka* of the deceased lady Henut-Nakhtu.

*Bibliography: PM III, 2, p. 726; Borchardt, Statuen und Statuetten
(CG) III, pp. 101–2; pl. 148; Nofret – Die Schöne, no. 71.*

156

Bowl with aquatic scene

Blue faience   JE 63672
Diam. 17 cm; H. 5.7 cm
Deir el Medina, tomb 1382, discovered by Bruyère in 1934
New Kingdom, 18th dynasty, c. 1300 B.C.

Numerous examples of bowls and dishes in faience of an
intense blue color are preserved. Their floral decoration symbolizes on the one hand the regenerative forces of nature, and
on the other the liquid contents which the vessels once held.
Sure and flowing brushstrokes have sketched out a symmetrical design: two lates fish swim about in the water of a basin
represented at the bottom of the bowl. In their mouths they
hold lotus buds. Two fleurs-de-lis flank the basin while all
four corners sway with flowers and blue lotus buds. The lotus,
which opens at sunrise and closes with the setting sun, is a
symbol of rebirth, while the fish, *tilapia nilotica,* as a mouth
hatcher, by its peculiar mode of fertility and generative reproduction is reminiscent of myths of primeval creation.
The bowl's exterior takes the form of a corolla surrounded by
a crown of sepals, which is indicated with fine brushstrokes.
The piece was discovered together with a ring-base deposited
in a basket in the tomb of a craftsman.

*Bibliography: Bruyère, in: Fouilles de l'Institut Français d'Archéologie
Orientale 15, 1934–35, p. 87; E.-Ch. Strauß, Die Nunschale, eine
Gefäßgruppe des Neuen Reiches, Münchener Ägyptologische Studien
30, 1974; Corteggiani, no. 31; Desroches-Noblecourt, Le grand Pharaon Ramsès II et son temps, no. 41.*

Cosmetic spoon

Painted wood   JE 28737
L. 30.5 cm; W. 5 cm; H. 6.2 cm   = CG 45117
Fayum, Gurob; 1889
New Kingdom, 18th dynasty, ca. 1350 B.C.

This period of luxury and opulence saw a profusion of toilet
articles in all manner of forms, bearing witness to the ingenu-
ity with which coquetry was displayed. Included among both
private and royal tomb equipment were unguent vessels, cas-
kets, kohl containers, combs, mirrors, and a variety of cosmetic spoons. The most original form of the latter, illustrated
here, is often called "swimming-girl spoons".
The handle consists of a naked girl in swimming pose. She
holds onto a spoon in the form of a little basin or duckling
with hollowed body. In this example, the duckling's head has
been added separately, as have the pivoting wings which cover
the spoon. The stylized plumage is inlaid in blue paste. The
swimmer's pretty face is enhanced with color: her fringed wig
is painted black and her collar is inlaid, again in blue paste.

*Bibliography: G. Bénédite, Objets de Toilette (CG) II, pl. 29; I. Wal-
lert, Der verzierte Löffel, Ägyptologische Abhandlungen 16, Wiesbaden 1967, p. 95, K 13; Nofret – Die Schöne, no. 50.*

157

158

from Syria. Terra cotta examples have been discovered in New Kingdom tombs. The cover attaches to the handle by means of a string sealed with clay. A system of knobs or buttons connected by a tie served to fasten the vessel shut. The neck is decorated with geometric and floral patterns, and the belly by a nature scene in which three calves frolic about under trees. On the cover is an inlaid ivory figure of a calf.

This new taste for refinement and luxury was introduced in Egypt as a result of her Asiatic campaigns. The simple and pure forms of cosmetic vessels of the past now give way to all manner of unexpected shapes and designs. The owners were no longer exclusively royal. The lady Siamon bore only one title, that of mistress of the house, generally given to women of high society but also found among the middle classes. Her coffin was placed in the unfinished and undecorated tomb of a granary official of the temple of Aton, beside two other coffins of women of no distinctive rank. And yet the cosmetic articles placed in a bronze vessel (JE 31389, gallery 49 s) under the neck of this lady are among the most creative of the minor arts of this period.

Bibliography: PM I, 2, p. 672; Daressy, in: ASAE 2, 1901, p. 9, fig. 9; Le Règne du Soleil, Brussels 1975, no. 68; Nofretete Echnaton, no. 35; Corteggiani, no. 60.

158   Upper floor, room 34
Unguent vessel

Painted wood, inlaid ivory   JE 31382
H. 14 cm
Thebes, Sheikh Abd el Gourna, tomb of Hatiay; excavations of Daressy, 1896
New Kingdom, 18th dynasty, reign of Amenophis III or beginning of the reign of Amenophis IV, ca. 1360 B.C.

Intended to contain the unguents necessary for her toilet, this little cosmetic jar was included in the lady Siamon's coffin. Its exquisite form portrays a vessel borne upon the shoulders of a servant. His head is shaven and he wears a short pleated kilt; the pudgy face is an exact reproduction of those found on men who are bustling about their tasks in bas-reliefs and mural paintings in tombs and temples at the end of Dynasty 18.
The load which he carries is a miniature version of the amphorae with handles which the Egyptians customarily imported

159   Ground floor, room 3
Bust of Amenophis IV   ▷

Sandstone   RT 29.5.49.1
H. 153 cm
Karnak, temple of Aten; excavated by the Egyptian Antiquities Service under H. Chevrier, 1926
New Kingdom, 18th dynasty, beginning of the reign of Amenophis IV (Akhenaten), ca. 1365–1360 B.C.

There are statues which touch us with their grandeur, seduce us with their beauty, or overwhelm us with their power. Less common are the statues which fascinate us with harsh exteriors as intense as the inner characters they represent. The portraits of Amenophis IV belong to this second, exceptional category. They introduce a new art style which breaks with iconographic tradition to express an entirely new concept of divine royalty.
Early on in his reign, before moving the capital to Amarna,

Amenophis IV, the future Akhenaten, whose two decades of religious reforms would overthrow millennia of traditional religious and civil life, erected at Karnak a temple to the sun god, now the only deity, worshipped solely in his form of the sun's disk. Located outside the enclosure wall to the east of the great temple of Amon, the Aten temple contained a peristyle court whose twenty-eight pillars supported colossal statues of the king. Four of these statues are to be found in this museum, two others in the Luxor Museum, one in the Louvre, one in Munich and the others in the museum depots at Karnak.

Differing from traditional Osiride statues, this series of colossi retains merely the pose of the deified dead king, and the royal insignia crossed over the breast. However, the king is no longer mummiform but appears either in the costume of the living, or even without costume, the body naked, androgynous and asexual. The headdresses alternate between *nemes* and *khat*, sometimes combined with the Double Crown, or imitate a composite form of *nemes* with hanging curls. All of the statues show the royal beard, frontal uraeus, and all bear the double cartouche of the Aten carved on various parts of the body.

If this original iconography poses certain problems, both the style, clearly reflecting the king's personality, and the motives behind the style are even more controversial. Obese or beautiful, realistic or mannerist, caricature or expressionism, degenerate or inspired, diseased or mystical; these are the sort of questions one asks as one gazes up at the five-meter height attained by these colossi. Akhenaten's characteristic features include long, tapering half-closed eyes with heavy eyelids, lengthy delicate nose, immense protruding mouth, exaggerated chin, harsh musculature, long ears with pierced lobes, and two outlined wrinkle lines on the neck.

The break is quite deep from the prevailing artistic tradition which had attained − before the accession of Amenophis IV − the purest and most perfect form of idealization. The development was perhaps to be expected, but it was provoked by a revolution in religious thinking. In order to translate this revolution into sculpture, a new canon and a certain mannerism was created. This style derives certainly from the king's own features, but these are deliberately exaggerated. This is clear because even the beautiful queen Nefertiti, whose undeniably pure visage is well-known from the busts in Cairo (see nos. 161 and 162) and Berlin, was to be represented at both Thebes and later at Amarna in this new style (see nos. 164−167).

These Karnak statues of Amenophis IV are the first to translate the new conception of this king, who was a man with an intense personal side, but also an absolute monarch and fervent priest serving as the unique and indispensable intermediary between God and men. This unique god encompassed all the divine qualities in existence, while the king was at once his spiritual and physical representative on earth. Hence the diversity of these statues within a cycle which contains death, regeneration, rebirth and invigorating radiance. These notions were formerly represented by specific deities: the asexual Osiris who resurrects the dead, the androgynous and fertile Hapi, and Re, propelling forces of life and cosmic order.

Bibliography: PM II, p. 253; Chevrier, in: ASAE 26, 1926, p. 125, pl. II; Vandier, Manuel III, pp. 332−33; Ch. Desroches-Noblecourt, in: La Revue du Louvre, nos. 4/5, 1972, pp. 1−12; eadem, in: Monuments et Mémoires, Fondation Eugène Piot 59, Paris 1974, pp. 1−44; The Luxor Museum of Ancient Art, 1979, nos. 156 and 161; Aldred, Akhenaten and Nefertiti, pp. 28−31, fig. 12; Le Règne du Soleil, Brussels 1975, no. 11; Nofretete Echnaton, no. 9.

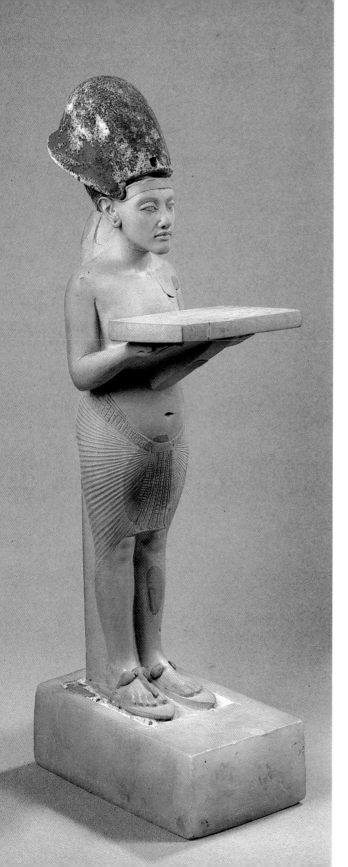

160

Akhenaten presenting an offering tablet

Limestone   JE 43580
H. 35 cm
Discovered by the Deutsche Orient-Gesellschaft in 1911 in a house at
Tell el-Amarna
New Kingdom, 18th dynasty, time of Akhenaten, ca. 1365–1349 B.C.

Akhenaten, originally named Amenophis IV, ruled Egypt for
about seventeen years. He was probably raised and educated
at Iunu (Heliopolis), the centre of the sun-cult, where he was
influenced by the instructions of its priesthood. Like his father
and grandfather before him, Akhenaten recognized the power
of the priests of Amon-Re at Thebes. Upon his coronation, he
changed the state cult of Amon-Re to that of Aten, the unique
god, and moved the capital of Egypt from Thebes to his new
residence at Akhetaten ("Horizon of Aten") in Middle Egypt
(Tell el-Amarna).
Akhenaten stands holding a tablet of offerings for the sun-god
Aten, in a pose similar to that of the king represented as Nile-
god (see no. 104). The tablet is carved with representations of
food and lotus flowers. This particular portrait displays facial
features and a physiognomy much less deformed or exaggerated than those found on other monuments of Akhenaten.
Nevertheless, one can still recognize the characteristic features
of this king: the elongated face, large pelvis and heavy thighs.
Unlike his other portraits, his face here shows a serene and
contented expression. He wears the blue crown (Khepresh)
which in this case is made of a separate piece of stone, a common convention in the Amarna Period. A short pleated skirt
and sandals complete his costume. Standing male statuary
normally places the left foot forward, but Akhenaten here
strikes an unusual pose with both feet together. Two other
innovations of this period are the pierced ears and the lines on
the neck, details which do not appear previously in official
statuary.

Bibliography: Vandier, Manuel III, pp. 336–38 and p. 351; Aldred,
Akhenaten and Nefertiti, pl. 42; Desroches-Noblecourt, in: Monu-
ments et Mémoires, Fondation Eugène Piot 59, 1974, fig. 27, p. 39.

made of a different material must have fitted on the rough-hewn upper part of the head on which the construction lines are still clearly discernible.

Although unfinished, the portrait is a masterpiece of purity and equilibrium. It demonstrates that, parallel to the revolutionary art of Akhenaten in which Nefertiti, like the rest of the family, is represented with the deformations of that particular style, (see no. 164), the research for pure beauty was never abandoned, there exists hardly another piece of sculpture in which it has been rendered in so striking a manner.

The oval face reproduces the sensibility and grace of a woman of great spirit. The eyebrows naturally elongated towards the temples, the projecting superciliary arches and cheek-bones, the eyes half dimmed by the slightly downcast eyelids, and the mysterious mouth, are all rendered with harmonious proportions.

This head is without doubt the most beautiful of all the portraits we possess of the queen. Most likely due to the absence of paint on the eyes, which lends them a distant and mysterious quality, and also to the natural color of the quartzite, this piece is marked with a subtle charm which makes it every bit as arresting as the celebrated bust of Nefertiti in the Berlin Museum, whose radiance is incontestable.

Bibliography: J.D.S. Pendlebury, in: JEA 19, 1933, p. 117, pl. 12, 18; Vandier, Manuel III, p. 341; Aldred, Akhenaten and Nefertiti, fig. 36; Lange/Hirmer, pl. 188; Corteggiani, no. 63.

162

161 Ground floor, room 3
Unfinished Head of Nefertiti

Brown quartzite   JE 59286
H. 35.5 cm
Tell el-Amarna. Found in the sculptor's atelier in 1932. Excavations of the Egypt Exploration Society.
New Kingdom, 18th dynasty, reign of Akhenaten, 1365–1349 B.C.

Not much is known about the antecedents of Nefertiti, the beautiful wife of King Akhenaten and the mother of the six Amarnian princesses who make their appearance little by little in the reliefs. Many suppositions have been put forward but at the present time it is generally agreed that she was descended from an Egyptian family of importance. We know that she acquiesced in the religious reform sponsored by her husband and that she upheld and practiced the new doctrine with him. She appears constantly at his side in all the official representations of the period.

This extremely beautiful head of the queen formed part of a composite statue made of several elements each sculptured separately and assembled after they were finished, a practice particularly in vogue in Akhenaten's workshops. A crown

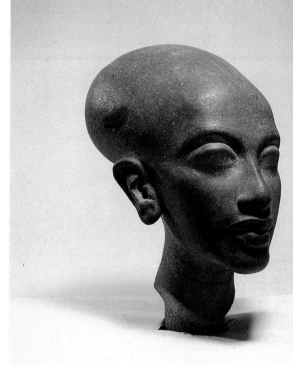

162
Nefertiti

Ground floor, room 3

Quartzite
H. 18 cm
Memphis; excavated by the University of Pennsylvania in 1915
New Kingdom, 18th dynasty, reign of Akhenaten, 1365–1349 B.C.

JE 45547

The expressionist and revolutionary art eventually came to acquire a harmony and elegance of its own. An impression of serenity gradually replaced the rather tormented forms of the earlier portraits.
Perhaps influenced by the always pure and perfectionist Memphite style, this Memphite portrait of Nefertiti marks precisely the period of transition, and is a masterpiece of the new interpretation. The mannerism which tended to emphasize particular physical features is now softened into visible grace and irresistible beauty.
One of the loveliest representations of the queen, this quartzite head once belonged to a composite statue assembled from several separately carved pieces (see no. 161). To the warm reddish color of the quartzite would doubtless have been added a blue material for the crown and inlays for the eyes.
This technique of composite assemblage, practiced since the Old Kingdom in wooden statuary, was utilized by Akhenaten for stone. Particularly favored was quartzite in warm tones, whose color recalled the warmth of the sun. Composite stone statues are rarely preserved (see no. 201), but they may well have been quite numerous, for Diodorus has recorded a description of the process of manufacture.

Bibliography: PM III, p. 223; C. S. Fischer, in: The Museum Journal University of Pennsylvania 8, 1977, p. 228; Aldred, Akhenaten and Nefertiti, fig. 37; Nofretete Echnaton, no. 54.

163
Head of a Princess

Ground floor, room 3

Brown quartzite
H. 21 cm
Tell el-Amarna. Found in the workshop of the chief sculptor Tuthmosis by the expedition of the Deutsche Orient-Gesellschaft in 1912
New Kingdom, 18th dynasty, reign of Akhenaten, 1365–1349 B.C.

JE 44869

Between the first "Amarna" style with its extreme deformations and the rather conventional reaction to it, there exists at Amarna an intermediate stage which by modifying the first and reanimating the second, manages to achieve a skilful synthesis which perfectly reproduces the spirit of the reform.
This princess's head alone would suffice to illustrate the trend. The portrait represents a happy blending of the mode introduced by Amenophis IV – elongated cranium and long, rather harsh visage – with the measured traits of the portrait of Nefertiti. The result is a work of the highest artistic quality whose softened expression has not lost any of its spiritual radiance.
The statue perhaps represents Meritaten, the eldest daughter of Akhenaten. Here again we are dealing with a composite statue, witness the tenon underneath the neck by which the head was to be attached to a separately sculptured torso.

Bibliography: Aldred, Akhenaten and Nefertiti, fig. 26; Le Règne du Soleil, no. 17; Nofretete Echnaton, no. 36.

Ground floor, room 3

Akhenaten and his family offering to the Aten

Alabaster   RT 30.10.26.12
H. 102 cm; W. 51 cm
Tell el-Amarna; discovered by F. Petrie in the royal palace in 1891
New Kingdom, 18th dynasty, reign of Akhenaten, 1365–1349 B.C.

The temple of the sun-god Aten was conceived, both in plan and in structure, quite differently from the classical Egyptian temple. In contrast to the temple of Amon-Rê, for example, which was closed, concealing sombre chambers, that of the Aten was entirely open to the sky, without any roofing whatsoever. Thus this god who illuminated even the most remote corners, was seen by all the whole day long, in conformity with the new doctrine.

No longer were there any anthropoid or hybrid divine forms; the sun god appears solely in the form of the sun's disk, whose rays terminate in human hands (the last anthropomorphic vestiges), spreading the goodness which the sun lavished on mankind. These rays brought life, joy, and prosperity, revealing beauty and reaching to the very depths of the oceans.

On this carved slab we see Akhenaten and his family officiating personally and directly under the rays of the Aten. The royal couple offers a libation to the god, while the eldest daughter Meritaten plays a sistrum (instrument used in cultic ritual, see no. 264).

The bodies seem deformed: long face, narrow neck, rounded breast, delicate, high waist, enormous buttocks, and bulging thighs. The king wears the White Crown of Upper Egypt, ornamented with the uraeus, a long pleated kilt extending down to the calves, and sandals. The queen sports the *khat* headdress starched in the form of a bag which gathers her hair. Her long plaited robe, tied under the breast, shows a transparency which reveals the body underneath; open in front, it tumbles down to the sandals. Meritaten shows a princess' coiffure with side-lock and also wears a transparent robe. This slab is a fragment of the parapet of the ramp which led to the central chamber of the palace of Akhenaten.

Bibliography: PM IV, p. 198; Aldred, Akhenaten and Nefertiti, fig. 33; Le Règne du Soleil, 1975, no. 16; Nofretete Echnaton, no. 46; Corteggiani, no. 65.

As the traces of color show, this altar was once entirely painted. It has recently been restored and partially reconstructed.

Bibliography: PM IV, p. 201; H. Frankfort, in: JEA 13, 1927, pls. 45, 47, p. 212; Aldred, Akhenaten and Nefertiti, fig. 52.

166

Akhenaten and family

Painted limestone
H. 53 cm; W. 48 cm; thickness 8 cm
Tell el-Amarna; discovered by the Egyptian Antiquities Service in a chamber of the royal tomb in 1891
New Kingdom, 18th dynasty, reign of Akhenaten, 1365–1349 B.C.

RT 10.11.26.4

This rectangular slab decorated with an offering scene was found abandoned among the debris of the royal tomb. The king and queen offer lotus bouquets to the Aten, while still more flowers are piled onto tall stands. Aten sends his rays provided with human hands to present them with the signs for

165

Facade of a shrine

Painted limestone
H. 98 cm; W. 118 (after restoration)
Tell el-Amarna; discovered in the house of Panehsy during the excavations of the Egypt Exploration Society in 1926–27
New Kingdom, 18th dynasty, reign of Akhenaten, 1365–1349 B.C.

JE 65041

The Amarna period introduces the practice of placing shrines in the form of temple facades (pylons) in private houses to serve as altars for the cult of the royal family and, through the latter, to the Aten. Thus the god and the family of Akhenaten were simultaneously present in the temple and in the private house, and could receive offerings in one just as in the other. Below the cavetto cornice are inscribed the cartouches of the Aten, followed by the wish that it "live forever and ever". The two symmetrical scenes executed in sunk relief of the two wings of the pylon show the royal family presenting offerings under the Aten's disk.
Akhenaten wears the typical blue crown with streamer floating at the back, and a pleated kilt. A broad collar adorns his breast. To the left he offers a libation; to the right he consecrates offerings. Nefertiti wears her characteristic high blue crown and a long transparent robe open in the front. She presents a libation vase at the left, and the *kherep* scepter at the right. She holds hands with the princess Meritaten, provided with the princely side-lock and holding a sistrum. Above, the Aten projects his rays with human hands to dispense life to the nostrils of the couple.

life (*ankh*) and prosperity (*was*). One hand even embraces the king below his right arm. Behind the couple, the eldest daughter Meritaten rattles a sistrum, followed by her little sister Meketaten, whom she holds by the hand.

Nefertiti wears a long wig tied with a diadem of uraei surmounted by the disk headdress with two feathers inserted between two horns. Her daughters are dressed similarly in long transparent robes which expose the body, and they wear wigs with sidelocks. A prayer addressed to Aten, as well as the titulary of each member of the family crowns the scene.

Once again the figures are deformed, almost caricatured. They show receding front, protruding chin, bulging lips, overlong ears, drawn out eyes, and projecting cheek bones, slender torsos and deformed buttocks. This type of representation is so contrary to tradition, that one might ask if we are dealing with a case of actual deformity, which has simply been stylized to excess.

The relief was once painted. Traces of grid lines in red ochre suggest that this slab could have served as a model for the sculptors responsible for the decoration of the royal tomb.

Bibliography: Aldred, Akhenaten and Nefertiti, fig. 34. On the Amarna period, see: LÄ I, 173–81, 210–19, 526–40; LÄ VI, 310–19.

167

167   Ground floor, room 3

The Royal Family as "Holy Family"

Painted limestone   JE 44865
H. 44 cm; W. 39 cm
Tell el-Amarna; excavations of the Deutsche Orient-Gesellschaft under Borchardt, in 1912
New Kingdom, 18th dynasty, reign of Akhenaten, 1365–1349 B.C.

A totally new form of personal piety arose at Amarna. The royal family united in a scene of private intimacy is represented on a stela as a "holy family". This sort of icon was kept in the private chapels of Amarna houses. It was protected by shutters of wood whose hinges were set into pivots which are still visible on the base of the stela.

At the top, the solar disk illuminates the scene with its rays terminating in human hands which hold the signs *ankh* and *was* (life and prosperity) to the nostrils of the royal couple. The life thus presented will be transferred through the king as intermediary to others. Akhenaten and Nefertiti are comfortably seated on stools complete with cushions. Between them stands their eldest daughter Meritaten, while the younger sisters Meketaten and Ankhsenpaaten (the future wife of Tutankhamon) appear on the lap of their mother. Akhenaten holds out an earring with strands to Meritaten; a similar earring and two necklaces are placed on his lap. Meketaten stands on the queen's knees seeking her attention by reaching for her chin, while dangling an earring under the eyes of her little sister, who plays with its strands.

The king wears the blue crown and a plaited kilt which falls to the shins. The queen's costume consists of the well-known high blue crown, and the traditional long robe held in place with a belt. A collar covers the breast and shoulders.

This scene captures an intimate moment with the royal family where the central themes are harmony, love and affection. This moment, exclusive to Amarna art, marks the range of the reform in both religion and royal iconography.

Bibliography: PM IV, p. 204; Desroches-Noblecourt, Toutankhamon et son temps, Tutankhamon exhibition catalog in Paris, no. 4; Terrace/Fischer, no. 28; Aldred, Akhenaten and Nefertiti, fig. 2; Le Règne du Soleil, 1975, no. 15; Nofretete Echnaton, no. 47.

168   Ground floor, room 3

Akhenaten kissing his daughter

Limestone   JE 44866
H. 39.5 cm; W. 16 cm; L. 21.5 cm
Found by the Deutsche Orient-Gesellschaft in a sculptor's studio at Tell el-Amarna in 1912
New Kingdom, 18th dynasty, reign of Akhenaten, 1365–1349 B.C.

168

Princess eating a duck

Limestone   JE 48035
H. 23.5 cm; W. 22.3 cm
Tell el-Amarna; discovered by the Egypt Exploration Society in 1924
New Kingdom, 18th dynasty, reign of Akhenaten, 1365–1349 B.C.

We have only brief glimpses of dining customs in ancient Egypt from conventional representations on stelae, tomb and temple walls, and always in a funerary or otherwise religious context. The person seated at table is always shown merely with one hand outstretched toward the food which he/she plans to eat.

This symbolic representation of the repast is broken at Amarna, beginning with the royal family. On this limestone plaque which is a sculptor's study, we see a very unusual scene of a princess actually eating a duck – just as we see Nefertiti lift a roast duck to her mouth (in the tomb of Huya at Tell el-Amarna), or a priest break bread in the corner of a temple at Karnak (wall on display in the Luxor Museum).

Nestled on a cushion with one hand on the food heaped upon a stand, the princess holds an entire duck to her mouth. She is naked, her head adorned with a thick shock of hair which covers the ear. Her petite figure displays all the characteristics of Amarna style: elongated head and pudgy belly, yet delicate legs and arms.

Besides the innovation of this genre, the sketch shows us the

Akhenaten holds his daughter, probably Meritaten upon his lap and kisses her in a touching gesture of affection and fatherhood. He sits on a cushioned throne and wears the blue crown as well as a long tunic with short sleeves. The princess turns her face towards that of her father to receive a kiss, while gently touching his arm. Her wig lacks the usual sidelock of youth, and her feet rest on a tall pedestal.

Despite the statue's unfinished state, the intimate relationship between Akhenaten and his daughter is successfully captured in this harmonious composition. Such affectionate royal representations were shown in works of art only in the Amarna Period. In this case, the artist was permitted to observe and reflect the life of the royal family in the palace.

Some believe that the female figure could also represent the queen Kiya (a less well-known wife of Akhenaten) because of the wig believed to be typical of her.

Bibliography: PM IV, p. 204; Aldred, Akhenaten and Nefertiti, fig. 54; Nofret – Die Schöne, no. 36; M. Eaton-Krauss, in: Chronique d'Egypte 56, 1981, Fasc. 112, pp. 257–58. For Kiya see: W. Helck, in: MDAIK 40, 1984, pp. 159–67.

grace and liberty of Egyptian drawing, which generally disappears underneath the sculpture. The artist who had begun to carve the sketch, has for some reason left it unfinished. This plaque was found broken in two, but is restored once again today.

Bibliography: Desroches-Noblecourt, Toutankhamon et son temps, Tutankhamon exhibition catalog in Paris, no. 8; Terrace/Fischer, no. 27; W. H. Peck/J. Ross, Drawings from Ancient Egypt, London 1978, fig. 12.

170   Ground floor, room 3

Ducks in papyrus marsh

Painted plaster   JE 33030/1
H. 101 cm; W. 160 cm
Tell el-Amarna, the southern palace (Maru-Aten)
Discovered 1896 by A. Barsanti
New Kingdom, 18ᵗʰ dynasty, reign of Akhenaten, 1365–1349 B.C.

Several fragments of painted floor from the southern palace at Tell el-Amarna bring before our eyes one of those marsh scenes with wild ducks flying overhead, which were a favorite subject for the decoration of a palace.
The tufts of reeds (cyperus) and of papyrus which intermingle with the floating leaves of a flowering plant are here rendered with an even greater ease and liberty than in the palace of Amenophis III (no. 147).
Those who trod on this painted floor discovered nature as it was created by the Aten, that nature which the god illuminated each day with his beneficent rays.

Bibliography: PM IV, p. 208; W. v. Bissing, Der Fußboden aus dem Palast des Königs Amenophis IV. zu El Hawata im Museum zu Kairo, Munich 1941, pl. VI, p. 21. Cf. also: Le Règne du Soleil, no. 33.

171   Ground floor, room 3

Amarna canopic jar

Alabaster (calcite)   JE 39637
H. 38.3 cm
Thebes, Valley of the Kings, tomb no. 55. Excavation of T. Davis, directed by E. Ayrton, in 1907
New Kingdom, 18ᵗʰ dynasty, reign of Akhenaten, 1365–1349 B.C.

This canopic jar was discovered along with its three mates in an unfinished tomb in the Valley of the Kings. The tomb, which the excavators attributed to Queen Tiye, contained in fact a gilded shrine belonging to Tiye and diverse Amarna funerary objects brought together for the burial of a member of the royal family after the abandonment of Tell el-Amarna. One of the four canopic jars is now in the Metropolitan Museum in New York.
Since the inscriptions decorating the belly of these jars have been thoroughly erased, the name of their original owner is lost. They are generally ascribed to Meritaten, the eldest daughter of Akhenaten and wife of his successor Smenkhkare. At the end of Dynasty 18 royal canopic jars have stoppers, all four of which represent the head of their owner (see also the example from the Middle Kingdom no. 97, and Tutankhamon no. 176).
The female royal head which forms the stopper of each of our four canopics is a masterpiece of Amarna art. It is an elegant portrait, full of feminine grace, which marks the culmination of this artistic style now stripped of the deformed caricatures of its early phase.
An elaborate wig with staged curls delicately frames the oval face. On the front was once the head of a uraeus whose body is carved upon the top of the wig. The eyes and eyebrows are inlaid in blue glass paste, quartz and obsidian. A broad floral collar covers the queen's shoulders.
These canopic jars, initially prepared for Meritaten, but attributed by some scholars to Kiya and more recently even to Akhenaten, have been apparently used for the burial of Akhenaten's successor, Smenkhkare, who died prematurely; for the woman's coffin of royal type, which was found in the same tomb, contained the body of a young man (on exhibit in this room).

Bibliography: PM I, 2, p. 566; Th. Davis et al., The Tomb of Queen Tîyi, London 1910, pls. 7–8; Yoyotte, Treasures of the Pharaohs, p. 118; Hanke, in: Studien zur Altägyptischen Kultur 2, 1975, p. 90; Le Règne du Soleil, 1975, no. 19; Nofretete Echnaton, no. 51; G. Martin, in: Mélanges Gamal Eddin Moukhtar, Cairo 1985, pp. 111–24, pls. 1–3.

171

hands crossed over the breast, clasping a hoe and a plough while a basket of grain hangs over the left shoulder.

The nine lines of hieroglyphic inscription contain an offering formula to the "living Aten, who illuminates every land with his beauty, that he might give the sweet breath of the north wind, a long life in the beautiful West, cool waters, wine and milk upon the altar of his (Hat's) tomb, for the Ka of the Adjutant Hat, may he repeat life."

Hat was probably an "adjutant" of the chariot force, and may well have owned a tomb in the region of Amarna. Illicit digging here seems to account for the discovery of our *shawabti*, which was found in the great necropolis of Tuna, on the west bank of the Nile across from Tell el-Amarna. It fortunately came to rest in the Museum's collections in 1908.

Bibliography: Maspero, Le Musée Egyptien III, pp. 27–28; pl. 23; Fechheimer, Kleinplastik, 1922, pl. 88; II. D. Schneider, Shabtis I, Leyden 1977, pp. 289–90; Corteggiani, no. 67. G. T. Martin, MDAIK 42, 1986, p. 111, pl. 8.

172

172
Upper floor, hall 48
Shawabti of the adjutant Hat

Painted limestone
H. 20.2 cm
Tuna(?), purchased in 1908
New Kingdom, 18th dynasty, c. 1350 B.C.

JE 39590

This fine yellow limestone *shawabti* is a masterpiece of small-scale sculpture in the round. A variety of colors still enliven the piece: the lips are red, traces of blue adorn the striated wig, broad collar and hieroglyphs, and black outlines are visible on the eyes, eyebrows, and at the corners of the mouth. The ears are pierced. The facial features typify the style of the late Amarna Period.

Of excellent manufacture and in nearly perfect condition, this example displays the classical form of the ushabti figure:

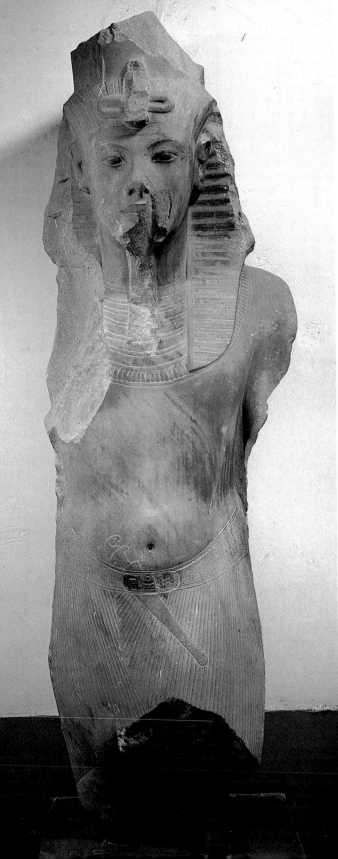

◁ Colossal statue of Tutankhamon

Painted quartzite   JE 59869 and 60134
H. 285 cm; W. 73 cm; thickness 87 cm
Thebes, funerary temple of Ay and Horemheb; excavations of the
Oriental Institute, University of Chicago, 1931
New Kingdom, 18th dynasty, reign of Tutankhamon, 1347–1337
B.C.

This statue most likely represents Tutankhamon; the facial
features, softened and enhanced with color, have preserved a
youthful and serene expression, despite the mutilation. Standing in the classic Egyptian pose, the king wears the double
crown, of which only the bottom remains, along with part of
a striped *nemes* headdress painted yellow and blue and
adorned with the uraeus. The rest of his costume includes a
ceremonial beard, broad collar and the traditional pleated
shendjyt-kilt. A dagger with a falcon-headed handle is slipped
under his belt, which in turn is ornamented with a pattern of
broken lines. On the belt buckle, Tutankhamon's name has
been replaced by that of Horemheb.
The statue, with its base now exhibited separately in this gallery, was originally located in Tutankhamon's mortuary temple at Thebes, and has a counterpart now in the Oriental Institute Museum in Chicago. Upon the death of Tutankhamon,
his successor Ay removed both statues to his own mortuary ·
temple, altered their facial features and added his own name.
His temple was in turn taken over and completed by Horemheb, who succeeded Ay very soon after the latter's accession.
Thus it is Horemheb's name that we find on the statues today,
and it was in his temple, destroyed after the New Kingdom by
a flood, that they came to light lying at the entrance to a
hypostyle hall.

*Bibliography: PM II, p. 458; U. Hölscher/R. Anthes, The Excavations
of Medinet Habu II, Oriental Institute Publications XLI, Chicago
1939, p. 102, pls. 44, 45b; Tutankhamon exhibition catalog in Paris,
no. 45.*

The gold mask of Tutankhamon

Gold, lapis lazuli, carnelian, quartz, obsidian, turquoise and coloured
glass   JE 60672
H. 54 cm; W. 39.3 cm; weight 11 kg
Thebes, Valley of the Kings, tomb of Tutankhamon (no. 62). Excava-
tions of Carter and Carnarvon in 1922–23
New Kingdom, 18th dynasty, reign of Tutankhamon, 1347–1337
B.C.

This marvellous, life-size mask, of excellent workmanship,
protected the head of the mummy of Tutankhamon. Further
protection was assured by a magic formula engraved on the

shoulders and the back of the mask. This formula, first introduced in Chapter 151b of the Book of the Dead during the
New Kingdom, identifies the different parts of the body of the
deceased with the corresponding members of various divinities
and the latter are invoked individually in order to protect that
particular limb.

The usual *nemes* headdress knotted back at the nape of the
neck, is striped blue-green imitating lapis lazuli. The uraeus
and vulture head in gold inlaid with semi-precious stones and
coloured glass ornament the brow. The mask's eyes are made
of obsidian and quartz with a touch of red at the corners; the
cosmetic lines and the lids are of inlaid blue glass. The divine
beard, plaited and turned up at the end is of cloisonné work,
coloured glass held in a framework of gold. Both earlobes are
pierced for the wearing of earrings. The wide necklace collar is
formed of rows of lapis lazuli, quartz, amazonite and coloured
glass beads attached at each shoulder to a gold falcon's head
ornamented with obsidian.

This mask presents us with a beautiful albeit idealized portrait
of the young king.

*Bibliography: PM I, 2, p. 573; Carter, Tut-ankh-Amen II, pp. 82–6,
pls. 27, 73; Desroches-Noblecourt, Tutankhamen, pl. 26; Edwards,
Tutankhamun, pp. 132–35; Tutankhamon exhibition catalogues:
Japan, no. 45; Paris, no. 43; London, no. 50; USA/Canada, no. 25;
Germany, no. 53.*

174 △

175a ▽

175   Upper floor, room 4

The gold coffin of Tutankhamon

Gold, semi-precious stones and glass   JE 60671
L. 187.5 cm; weight 110.4 kg
Thebes, Valley of the Kings, tomb of Tutankhamon (no. 62). Excava-
tions of Carter and Carnarvon in 1922–23
New Kingdom, 18th dynasty, reign of Tutankhamon, 1347–1337
B.C.

The kings and queens of the New Kingdom, as well as the
members of their families and certain non-royal personages of
high rank, were buried in several coffins one fitted into the
other, and all enclosed in a stone sarcophagus. The coffins are
generally mummiform, of gilded wood or cartonnage,
although some are in stone (granite or alabaster); occasionally
a king possessed a coffin of solid gold.

The mummy of Tutankhamon, who died at the early age of
about 19 years, was found in this gold coffin, placed inside
two larger wooden coffins richly gilded and ornamented with
semi-precious stones and glass. The three coffins were placed
in a rectangular quartzite sarcophagus with a red granite lid.
Over and around the sarcophagus, again placed one inside the
other were four gilded wooden chapels which almost completely filled the sarcophagus chamber.

The two inner coffins are those which are on view in the
Museum; the smallest one of gold and the other of gilded

wood covered with precious stones. The third outermost coffin was left in the tomb containing the King's mummy.

The hammered gold coffin is covered with incised decoration inside and out. Its shape is that of a mummiform Osiris figure, arms crossed on the chest, holding the sacred insignia: the hooked *heka* scepter and the flail *nekhakha*. Under the influence of the sun cult, the dead king is simultaneously identified with the god Rê whose flesh is of gold and his hair of lapis lazuli. The royal insignia, uraeus and vulture, are attached to the striped *nemes* headdress and under the chin the divine beard is of gold inlaid with blue glass in imitation of lapis lazuli. The lids and cosmetic lines are likewise of blue glass. The inlaid eyes are missing. The breast is covered with a wide collar richly adorned with precious stones and with a necklace made up of a double row of gold and faience lozenges. On the crossed wrists, wide bracelets are also inlaid with jewels.

The two protecting goddesses of Upper and Lower Egypt, Nekhbet the vulture and Wadjet the cobra with a bird's body, both holding in their claws the symbol *shen*, embrace the king's torso with their extended wings whose feathers are represented in cloisonné inlaid with multicoloured stones. Below them are engraved the goddesses Isis and Nepthys whose crossed wings protect the lower part of the King's body. The protective formulae which they recite are inscribed in the double column of hieroglyphs running down the middle of the coffin. A further inscription encircles it. Isis is again reproduced kneeling with her wings outspread, beneath the King's feet. The whole body of the coffin is adorned with a network of admirably engraved bird's feathers.

Bibliography: PM I, 2, p. 572; Carter, Tut-ankh-Amen II, pp. 76–79, pls. 24, 25, 70–72; Desroches-Noblecourt, Tutankhamen, pl. 56; Edwards, Tutankhamun, pp. 130–31.

Lid of a canopic jar

Alabaster (calcite)   JE 60687
H. 24 cm; W. 19 cm
Thebes, Valley of the Kings, tomb of Tutankhamon (no. 62), excavated by Carter and Carnarvon in 1922–23
New Kingdom, 18th dynasty, reign of Tutankhamon, 1347–1337 B.C.

The four canopic jar lids with the king's image were carved in a beautiful white alabaster which derives from the quarries of Hatnub, as does the chest in which these lids sealed the four receptacles with the royal viscera. Each portrait wears the *nemes* headdress with the uraeus and vulture fixed upon the brow. The details are enhanced with red or black paint in a rather hasty fashion.

After the four miniature sarcophagi containing the king's mummified viscera were placed in the cavities carved out of the canopic chest, the four heads, turned face to face in two pairs, sealed the openings, and a round, shrine-shaped lid covered the entire group.

The names of the four guardian genii of the viscera are inscribed on the chest which was drawn on a sled, while the four corresponding protective goddesses are carved in relief upon the four corners. Thus Imset and Isis protect the liver, Hapi and Nepthys the lungs, Duamutef and Neith the stomach, and Kebehsenuef and Selket the intestines.

The chest itself was in turn set within an immense shrine of gilded wood, decorated with reliefs and placed upon a sled beneath a large baldachin. The graceful figures of the four protective goddesses delicately keep vigil over the walls of this

175b

176

Selket was originally a water-scorpion goddess who could heal stings and bites. Even after assuming the form of a woman, she retained her original appearance as an identifying emblem, just as the seat remained the emblem of Isis, the house that of Nephtys and the two arrows that of Neith.

The four goddesses are responsible for guarding the mortal remains of the king. They are dressed like queens in contemporary costume, a feature which adds to their charm and elegance. The *khat*-headdress adorns the head and tumbles down over the back; a large collar covers the shoulders. The pleated shawl is tied at the waist, partially covering the elegant, long pleated robe tied with hanging sashes. Selket turns her head slightly to one side as if to ward off some danger; thus is broken the long tradition of frontality observed by official statuary of all periods. The Amarnan influence is clearly visible in the charming modelling of the body and the features of the face.

The figures of all four goddesses are of gilded wood; the eyes

177

gilded chest (see no. 177). The entire group was found in the so-called Treasury of the tomb.

Bibliography: Carter, Tut-ankh-Amen III, pls. 9—10, 53, p. 47; Desroches-Noblecourt, Tutankhamen, pl. 33; Catalogues of Tutankhamon exhibition: Paris, no. 30; USA, no. 24; Japan, no. 15; London, no. 8; USSR, no. 13; USA/Canada, no. 44; Germany, no. 38.

177   Upper floor, gallery 9

The goddess Selket
(from the canopic shrine)

Gilded and painted wood   JE 60686
H. 90 cm
Thebes, Valley of the Kings, tomb of Tutankhamon (no. 62), excavated by Carter and Carnarvon in 1922—23
New Kingdom, 18th dynasty, reign of Tutankhamon, 1347—1337 B.C.

This is one of four goddesses who with gracefully outstretched arms protect the gilded wooden shrine set within a baldachin, which in turn housed the alabaster chest containing the royal viscera (see no. 176).

178

and eyebrows are painted black. The goddesses reappear on the walls of the shrine which they protect, each one facing the genii associated with her, in order to insure the preservation of the viscera (see no. 176).

The shrine is crowned by a cavetto cornice and an attractive frieze of uraei with sun-disks, similar to that of the baldachin in which it is housed. These essentially architectural forms recur in bark shrines or in the sacred naoi enclosed within a dais; they are frequently represented on temple walls from the New Kingdom to the Late Period.

Bibliography: PM I, 2, pp. 573–74; Carter, Tut-ankh-Amen III, pls. 5, 7, 8, p. 47; Desroches-Noblecourt, Tutankhamen, pl. 31; Edwards, Tutankhamun, pp. 158–61; Catalogues of Tutankhamon exhibition: USA/Canada, no. 43; Germany, no. 1.

178

Upper floor, gallery 35

Golden shrine

Wood, covered with gold leaf (shrine) and silver leaf (sled)

JE 61481

H. 50.5 cm; W. 30.7 cm; thickness 48 cm
Thebes, Valley of the Kings, tomb of Tutankhamon (no. 62); excavated by Carter and Carnarvon in 1922–23
New Kingdom, 18th dynasty, reign of Tutankhamon, 1347–1337 B.C.

This appealing naos from the tomb's antechamber is entirely veneered with gold. Constructed in the form of a divine sanctuary, it rests upon a sled which is covered with silver. The walls are capped by a cavetto cornice; the roof is rounded towards the front in imitation of the primitive shrines of Upper Egypt. Each leaf of the double door is furnished with an ivory bolt which slides into a ring on the opposite side, and two additional rings between them allow the shrine to be sealed.

The (most likely golden) statue which once resided within the naos has been stolen by tomb robbers. There remained a gilded wooden base with "foot prints" and a back pillar inscribed with the name of Tutankhamon. The excavators also found a golden pendant representing a serpent goddess with a woman's head nursing the boy-king (on exhibit in room 4). This pendant was attached to a beaded chain and bears an inscription declaring Tutankhamon to be "beloved of the goddess Weret-hekau," the "One great of magic". This phrase recurs in all of the texts on the naos which reproduce the royal titulary.

The decoration of the naos is worked in repoussé; the details incised in gold leaf adhere to the wooden walls with the aid of a fine layer of stucco. On the roof, the vulture-goddesses spread their wings over the alternating cartouches of the king and queen. Two serpent goddesses shown on the sides of the lid hold the *shen* rings of protection. Both the exterior walls and leaves of the door depict Tutankhamon and his wife Ankhsenamon (Akhenaten's third daughter, originally named Ankhsenpaaten) in charming settings. The royal couple appear in a cycle of intimate scenes and in various types of hunting excursions. They are outfitted differently in each tableau with sumptuous jewellery, various wigs and hairstyles, and royal crowns. Contemporary fashion is reflected in the elaborate kilts, transparent pleated robes and fluttering streamers, and enveloping shawls which leave the torso free or the shoulder exposed. The couple sometimes hold hands, sometimes stand one before the other. Most often the king rests on a seat ranging from a simple stool up to the throne of Horus, while his wife stands or crouches at his feet. She accompanies him on a hunt in an elaborately decorated papyrus skiff, or offers him a new arrow as he draws his bow and takes aim at wild ducks in the marsh. She hands him flowers, a sistrum or menat necklace, or ties his collar around his neck. She adjusts his cone of scented fat, or takes perfume from him which he pours into her palm as she sits on a cushion. She anoints him, and even presents him with the staves of millions of years adorned with the symbols for jubilees, life and power.

On the interior of the door leaves, the symmetrical decoration depicts one scene arranged between the royal cartouches in which the queen again offers sistrum and bouquets to her husband. At the very bottom, two *rekhyt*-birds over the Neb sign ("all") cryptographically symbolize the adoration of all the people.

Alluring in their finesse and grace, these scenes are primarily intended to cause athletic prowess and intimate moments of the young king to endure in the next world. They form part of a ritual of permanent regeneration, not only of life but of royal power. Each element of the decoration possesses a symbolic importance: the profusion of lotus bouquets, mandrake fruits, sistra and menat collars are doubtless all symbols of life, love and rebirth. But the throne of Horus, staves of years, jubilees and *rekhyt* birds all help to transport royal power from this world to the next. The hunting scenes represent the triumph of order over chaos, but also evoke the image of the young Horus (i. e. the king) hidden in the marsh to protect him against his enemy (Seth).

We have seen the significance of the female aspects of rebirth in Egyptian art and thought. The representations of the queen here fill this role. Sometimes she is the priestess who pays homage to the king and carries out his duties for him. At other times she plays the role of a goddess who receives and introduces him into the company of the gods, saying "May you be received by the One Great of Magic". Thus the king is reborn as a god, nursed by the goddess, and finally enthroned as a god. He is then able to live for millions of years.

Bibliography: PM I, 2, p. 584 (pendant p. 583); Carter, Tut-ankh-Amen I, pls. 29 and 68; pp. 119−20; and II, pl. 1, pp. 14−15; Desroches-Noblecourt, Tutankhamen, pls. 7−9; Edwards, Tutankhamun, pp. 52−7; Catalogues of Tutankhamon exhibition: London, no. 5; USSR, no. 25; USA/Canada, no. 13; Germany, no. 13; M. Eaton-Krauss/E. Graefe, The small golden shrine from the Tomb of Tutankhamun, Oxford 1985.

179

Throne of Tutankhamon

H. 102 cm; W. 54 cm; thickness 60 cm   JE 62028
Thebes, Valley of the Kings, tomb of Tutankhamon (no. 62); excavations of Carter/Carnarvon in 1922−23
New Kingdom, 18th dynasty, reign of Tutankhamon, 1347−1337 B.C.

The throne of Tutankhamon is an accomplished example of the Egyptian craftsman's trade in the New Kingdom. It is constructed of wood, covered with gold leaf and ornamented with multicolored glass paste and semi-precious stones.

The arms of the throne take the form of two winged serpents wearing the Double Crown, who guard the cartouches of Tutankhamon. Two protective lion's heads top the front pair of legs; all four legs terminate in lion's paws. An openwork decoration symbolizing the union of the Two Lands once connected the legs together.

The back bears an exquisite composition in which Tutankhamon and his wife Ankhsenamon affectionately face each other. The king is seated casually on a comfortably cushioned throne; he wears an elaborate wig surmounted by a composite crown, a broad collar and a long plaited kilt with open-work central tab and sash falling to his side. His feet rest on the soft cushion of a footstool. The queen stands placing one hand upon the king's shoulder, while in the other she holds a jar of unguent. Her headdress consists of a uraeus diadem which is surmounted by the disk, two feathers and two horns. Around her neck is a broad collar which covers the shoulders and part of her long pleated robe.

The inlaid elements include blue glass for the wigs, and reddish brown for the bodies. The costumes are of silver and the ornaments of semi-precious stones.

The rays of the sun disk Aten dispense life to the nostrils of the royal couple, as they did during the period of the Amarna heresy. In addition, the back of the throne reveals the unchanged forms of the original names: Tutankhaten and Ankhsenpaaten.

Bibliography: PM I, 2, pp. 576−77; Carter/Mace, Tut-ankh-Amen I, pp. 2, 42−44; Desroches-Noblecourt, Tutankhamen, pl. 10; Lange/Hirmer, pls. 190−91; Edwards, Tutankhamun, pp. 38−41.

the costume and attributes are plastered and gilded. The statues were originally wrapped in sheets of linen, which had disintegrated over the centuries.

The king stands with left foot forward in a striding pose. He grasps in his right fist the handle of a pear-shaped mace, ornamented with scales. In his left hand he holds a tall staff with a papyrus umbel just below the handle. He wears the *khat* headdress – on the second statue he wears the *nemes* – which completely covers the hair but leaves the ears free. A gilded bronze uraeus is attached to his brow.

The eyes are inlaid into the black, beardless face. Both the outlines of the eyes and the eyebrows are of gilded bronze. On the breast hangs a gilded pectoral and broad collar; armlets and bracelets adorn the arms. The bronze sandals are gilded, as is the rest of the king's costume.

The pleated kilt is enhanced by a starched tab which projects in front and is held in place by side gussets with converging folds. The belt buckle contains the coronation name of the king, Nebkheperure; this name also occurs behind, on the widened part of the belt. The tab of the kilt is adorned with a vertical inscription: "The perfect god worthy of vaunting, a sovereign to be boasted of, the royal *ka* of Horakhty, the Osiris, King and Lord of the Two Lands, Nebkheperure, justified." The complimentary inscription on the statue with the *nemes* headdress introduces, in the second part of the text, the king's birth name, "Tutankhamon, living forever like Rê every day," and mentions neither the *ka* nor Osiris.

The two statues bear traces of Amarna influence, such as their bulging abdomens, relatively slim legs and pierced ears. As for the black color of the flesh, it is intended not to frighten intruders, but to evoke the Osirian quality of rebirth, resurrection and life.

Bibliography: PM I, 2, p. 570; Carter/Mace, Tut-ankh-Amen, I, pl. 16, 41, 45, p. 99, 112; Desroches-Noblecourt, Tutankhamen, fig. 32 and pl. 53; Edwards, Tutankhamun, p. 78–83; catalogue of Tutankhamon exhibition: Paris, no. 28.

180	Upper floor, gallery 50

Ka statue of Tutankhamon

Wood coated with bitumen and gilded, bronze   JE 60708
H. 192 cm; W. 53.5 cm; L. 98 cm
Thebes, Valley of the Kings, tomb of Tutankhamon (no. 62). Excavations of Carter/Carnarvon, 1922–23
New Kingdom, 18th dynasty, reign of Tutankhamon, 1347–1337 B.C.

The burial chamber of Tutankhamon was originally separated by a wall of stone coated with mud, whose blocked doorway was broken after burial by tomb-robbers, and later resealed by the necropolis administration, which then attached its official seal.

Two magnificent royal statues stood before this doorway as "guardians" of the burial chamber. Almost identical, they differ only in the respective types of wigs they wear. They are constructed of wood coated with bitumen for the flesh, while

---

181	Upper floor, room 25

Ceremonial chair

Ebony, ivory, gold, stone and faience   JE 62030
H. 102 cm; W. 70 cm; L. 44 cm
Thebes, Valley of the Kings, tomb of Tutankhamon (no. 62). Excavations of Carter/Carnarvon, 1922–23
New Kingdom, 18th dynasty, reign of Tutankhamon, 1347–1337 B.C.

By virtue of its marvelous inlays, this chair may be counted among the finest examples of cabinet-work, even if the unusual structure, that of a folding stool transformed into a backed chair, is not completely successful.

The back is decorated entirely in inlays of ebony and ivory, semi-precious stone and faience, all on a base of gold leaf. The frieze of uraei with disks which crowns the back is interrupted in the center by the solar disk Aten, a vestige of Amarna, which hovers over the two divine cartouches. Below this

Bibliography: PM I, 2, p. 577; Carter, Tut-ankh-Amen III, p. 111−13, pl. 33; Desroches-Noblecourt, Tutankhamen, pl. 12; Edwards, Tutankhamun, p. 224−25.

182

Upper floor, gallery 35

Shawabti of Tutankhamon

Wood, gold leaf, bronze   JE 60830
H. 48 cm
Thebes, Valley of the Kings, tomb of Tutankhamon (no. 62). Excavations of Carter and Carnarvon in 1922−23
New Kingdom, 18th dynasty, reign of Tutankhamon, 1347−1337 B.C.

From the New Kingdom on, the number of funerary figurines, called shawabtis (see nos. 150, 151 and 172), placed in a tomb attained a total of 401 including 365 workmen, one for each day of the year, carrying hoes and baskets in readiness for the work assigned to them, plus 36 overseers, one for each decade (week of ten days) to direct the work.

The tomb of Tutankhamon, however, contained 413 shawabtis: 365 workmen, 36 overseers and 12 supplementary foremen, one for each month. They are fashioned of diverse materials and vary considerably in quality.

Our shawabti of gilded wood is, like all the other figurines, an image of the King. Young and graceful, Tutankhamon is mummiform, crowned with the Khepresh crown and uraeus, adorned with a broad collar cut in gold leaf and holding in his crossed hands the insignia of Osiris. An abridged version of chapter 6 of the Book of the Dead is inscribed in two vertical columns on the front of the figurine: "Words spoken by the Osiris, King Nebkheperure. May this shawabti be glorified if he is named or invoked. If the Osiris Tutankhamon is called upon in the domain of the god to cultivate the fields, irrigate the river banks or transport sand from the East to the West", the shawabti must declare itself ready to do the work for him.

An inscription engraved under the feet of this shawabti informs us that it was a certain General Min-nakht who presented it to the dead king in order to be useful to him in the other world.

Bibliography: Carter, Tut-ankh-Amen III, pp. 82−84; Tutankhamon exhibition catalogues: USA, no. 42; Germany, no. 17.

frieze, the vulture goddess spreads her wings, and holds in each claw a fan and a shen-ring. She is flanked by two cartouches with the royal names Nebkheperure and Tutankhaten. The lower field is divided into vertical bands in which inscriptions bearing the names Nebkheperure and Tutankhaten appear respectively in the ebony and ivory. Tutankhaten is the earlier form of the king's name; the later form, Tutankhamon, occurs in the texts inscribed on the two horizontal pieces of ebony which enclose the decoration.

The seat is curved to receive a cushion, and is constructed of ebony with inlays of ivory imitating the skin of a spotted animal. The ebony feet, adorned with pieces of ivory and gold leaf, terminate in elegant ducks' heads, which attach in pairs to two cross-bars. Between the ducks' heads in front, and also the feet of the rear supporting slats, a latticework pattern symbolizing the unification of the Two Lands has been partially destroyed by tomb-robbers. Behind the back, reinforcing braces are inscribed with the name of Tutankhaten.

The rectangular stool placed at the foot of the chair, intended as the king's footrest, is ornamented with figures of bound captives from foreign lands, imprisoned "under the sandals" of His Majesty for all eternity.

This chair is often called Tutankhamon's "ecclesiastical throne," by analogy with the episcopal seats of the Middle Ages in Europe. It was discovered in the annex of the antechamber, among a jumble of furniture, boxes and objects of alabaster.

Upper floor, hall 10

Couch in the image of the primordial cow

Wood, stuccoed, gilded and painted   JE 62013
H. 188 cm; W. 128 cm; L. 208 cm
Thebes, Valley of the Kings, tomb of Tutankhamon (no. 62); excavated by Carter and Carnarvon in 1922–23
New Kingdom, 18th dynasty, reign of Tutankhamon, 1347–1337 B.C.

Three tall couches in the form of sacred animals facing the burial chamber were placed smallest to largest along the wall of the antechamber, opposite the entrance to the tomb.
The first couch is leonine, the second bovine, and the third takes a hybrid form with the head of a hippopotamus, and body of a leopard ornamented with crocodile scales around its neck. Three goddesses are thereby represented; the first is the lioness Mehet, an incarnation of Hathor, Sekhmet and Isis. She is the goddess who must be appeased in order to cause the Nile flood upon which the country depended. The second is Mehet Weret, "the Great Flood". This is the primordial cow who surfaces from the waters of the primordial sea (Nun), bearing Re the sun to the horizon of heaven. The third goddess is Ammut, the one "who devours the dead." She usually

stands near the heart during the judgment of Osiris. She may also appear as Nut, the sky and, in the form of a sow swallow the dead-become-stars in order to beget them once again.
The dead king could rest at will on any of the couches in the hope of obtaining revivifying force and survive as Re. He could then rise up in Nun, master of the great flood, traverse the heavens (see no. 216) and be received by Nut, whom he would then bear once again.
Each couch is constructed of four collapsible wooden pieces carefully fitted together. The bed or mattress inserts by means of pegs and rings between the two upright side pieces which form the animal's body. Their paws make up the four legs of the couch and are solidly implanted into a rectangular frame serving as a base.
The attractive cows' heads, especially the lyre-shaped horns surrounding the sun-disks, mark the head of the couch. At the foot, curved tails flank the foot-supports decorated with motifs of stability and protection. The entire couch is made of stuccoed and gilded wood. The eyes are inlaid with glass paste in the form of the Udjat eye. Trilobate ocelli are inlaid all over the body in a dark blue color, while the base is painted black. The mattress consists of woven fibres stuccoed and gilded.
Striking for their form and rich symbolism, these couches are strictly funerary. Others were found in the tomb of Horemheb with heads of cows and hippopotami. A representation of three similar beds in the tomb of Ramses III indicates that they formed part of the typical repertoire of royal funerary equipment in the New Kingdom.
The four other beds found in Tutankhamon's tomb take a more conventional shape, but do not lack originality either. Particularly noteworthy is the folding bed, which could be considered the ancestor of our collapsible cot.

Bibliography: Carter/Mace, Tut-ankh-Amen, I, pl. 18, pp. 98–99, 112–115; Desroches-Noblecourt, Tutankhamen, pl. 29; Tutankhamon exhibition catalogues: Paris, no. 27; London, no. 13.

Upper floor, gallery 9

Headrest of Tutankhamon

Ivory   JE 62023
H. 19.2 cm; L. 26 cm; thickness 10.5 cm
Thebes, Valley of the Kings, tomb of Tutankhamon (no. 62). Excavations of Carter/Carnarvon, 1922–23
New Kingdom, 18th dynasty, reign of Tutankhamon, 1347–1337 B.C.

The headrest, known in Egypt since the Old Kingdom, is still used today in certain African countries. A headrest is normally composed of a flat rectangular base, a central shaft and a curved neck-support. Provided with a cushion and placed at the head of the bed, the headrest apparently served first and foremost to protect the hair of the sleeper.
In funerary practices, the preservation of the head, the driving force of life, was indispensable. The headrest, in the form of an amulet accompanied by appropriate magical formulae, could both preserve and support the head. This supporting

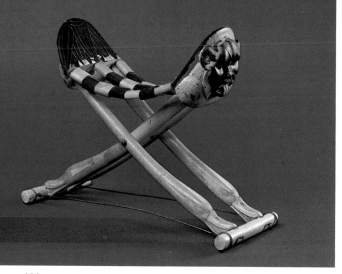

184

The statue is carved of wood which was then stuccoed and coated with a black resin. The interior of the ears, the scarf and the collar are gilded; the eyes are of gold, calcite and obsidian, the claws of silver. The body was originally covered with a linen shirt dated to year seven of Akhenaten; around the neck was tied a finer cloth, as well as a scarf and a floral collar composed of lotus and cornflowers.

Anubis is attached to the sliding lid of the gilded wooden chest. Crowned with a cavetto cornice and surrounded by a battered torus moulding, the chest is decorated with *djed*-pillars and *tit* (or Isis) knots. While serving as a base for the statue, the chest also contained amulets of blue faience, eight openwork pectorals, and two calcite cups, one of which held a resinous substance, while the other served as a lid. These objects, initially arranged in compartments, had been rifled through by the tomb-robbers.

Anubis is essentially a funerary god, venerated before Osiris as the lord of the necropolis. He guides the dead in the next world, watches over them, and is considered the inventor of mummification. He is the one who introduces the deceased into the tribunal of judges for the weighing of the heart. This statue, which represents him crouching on a shrine, was in all probability borne in the funeral procession, and was later deposited at the entrance to the chamber which held the canopic chest. Thus it fulfills the guardian role of this god. The inscriptions which adorn the chest give the two forms of Anubis, *Imiut* and *Khenti-sehnetjer*, in the formulae for protection.

Bibliography: PM I, 2, p. 574; Carter, Tut-ankh-Amen III, p. 33, 41–42, pl. 2 and 6; Desroches-Noblecourt, Tutankhamen, pl. 52; Edwards, Tutankhamun, p. 152–53; Corteggiani, no. 72.

185

function came to symbolize the rising of the sun. Chapter 166 of the Book of the Dead contains a spell for the headrest, reassuring the deceased with the following words: "Your head will not be carried away from you; your head will never be carried away from you." Figures of genii and beneficent spirits often decorate the headrest, so as to remove the demons which could attack the sleeper.

Under the neck of Tutankhamon's mummy was placed a model headrest, while several actual headrests were deposited among the king's funerary furniture. Some were of faience; one made of ivory shows a neck-support held up by a figure of the god Shu. Our example takes the form of a small folding stool with articulated legs.

The neck support is made of three bands composed of ivory pieces. They terminate at each end in fasteners whose upper surface is incised with a lotus flower design, and whose lower surface reveals the face of the god Bes in high relief. The lotus symbolizes the rebirth of the king, over whose sleep Bes, the protective genius faithfully watches. He dispels malevolent attacks, and insures the peaceful rest of the sleeper. The crossed legs terminate in ducks' heads, with beaks fitting into two cylindrical pieces of ivory.

Bibliography: PM I, p. 576; Carter, Tut-ankh-Amen III, pl. 36A, p. 117; Propyläen Kunstgeschichte 15, pl. 371.

185 Anubis

Upper floor, gallery 45

Wood, stuccoed, varnished and gilded, gold, silver, stone   JE 61444
Total H. 118 cm; L. 270 cm; W. 52 cm
Thebes, Valley of the Kings, tomb of Tutankhamon (no. 62). Excavations of Carter/Carnarvon, 1922–23
New Kingdom, 18th dynasty, reign of Tutankhamon, 1347–1337 B.C.

This statue of Anubis in the form of a black jackal was found in the entrance to the chamber known as the "treasury", and was turned to face the burial chamber. It rested upon a chest in the shape of a temple or shrine, mounted upon a portable sledge with four carrying poles.

The two short sides each depict a double scene in which the triumphant king appears in the form of a sphinx who tramples his enemies, one Syrian and one Nubian in each scene. The two enemies, shown in most un-Egyptian poses, find themselves subjected to the majestic authority of Pharaoh.

Another variation on the theme of triumph over chaos is the desert hunt. On the cover of the casket two superbly painted scenes represent the king and his troops of cavalry, archers and lance-bearers descending with terrifying speed upon desert game dispersed in a dizzy flight. On one side appear antelopes, gazelles, hyenas, wild donkeys and ostriches, all skilfully represented together and fleeing the arrows of His Majesty. In the parallel scene, powerful lions and lionesses, pierced by arrows, fall victim to the king's irresistible attack.

After having solved the conservation problems associated with the paint, which was in danger in falling off with the stucco, Carter needed three weeks to empty the contents of this chest. Piled inside was a mixture of all manner of objects, which Carter had to carefully disentangle: one pair of papyrus sandals, three other pairs richly worked in gold, a gilded headrest, embroidered ritual robes adorned with gold, of which one was studded with 3,000 golden rosettes, numerous necklaces, belts, scarves and labels.

Bibliography: PM I, 2, pp. 577–78; Carter/Mace, Tut-ankh-Amen I, pl. 21, pp. 50–54, 110–11, 164–65; II, pl. 2, pp. 17–18; Davies/Gardiner, Tut-ankh-amun's Painted Box, Oxford 1962; Desroches-Noblecourt, Tutankhamen, pls. 16–17; Edwards, Tutankhamun, pp. 76–77.

186
Upper floor, gallery 40
Painted casket

Wood, stuccoed and painted   JE 61467
H. 44 cm; L. 61 cm; W. 43 cm
Thebes, Valley of the Kings, tomb of Tutankhamon (no. 62), excavated by Carter and Carnarvon in 1922–23
New Kingdom, 18th dynasty, reign of Tutankhamon, 1347–1337 B.C.

This magnificent casket is both a masterpiece of painting and a miracle of preservation. Even the dust of millennia failed to dampen the excavators' amazement at the beauty of its decoration. It was discovered in the antechamber of the tomb.

Both the rounded cover and the box mounted on stubby legs are furnished with the usual knobs for tying the chest shut. The decoration is devoted to the official theme of triumph over the forces of chaos.

The tableaus are bordered by a frame of geometric and floral patterns, and come in pairs. Two battle scenes symmetrically ornament the long sides of the chest. Under the protection of the sun's disk and the vulture-goddess, the king fires an arrow from his chariot drawn by two horses charging at full gallop. Followed by his fan-bearers and his army, he attacks on one side the Syrians, Egypt's northern enemy, and on the other, the Nubians, her southern enemy. One will note immediately that everything about the Egyptian army is shown in the strictest pharaonic order: division into registers, disciplined ranks, and well-kempt soldier and horses. At the other side of the scene, however, chaos reigns supreme: warriors, horses and wounded individuals are all jumbled together in a disorganized heap. Some fall, others are trampled, and a few are even attacked by Pharaoh's hounds.

187
Upper floor, gallery 30
Cane with two prisoners (detail)

Wood, ivory, ebony and glass   JE 61732
Total H. 104 cm
Thebes, Valley of the Kings, tomb of Tutankhamon (no. 62), excavated by Carter and Carnarvon in 1922–23
New Kingdom, 18th dynasty, reign of Tutankhamon, 1347–1337 B.C.

Official texts always refer to vanquished "vile enemies." We see them represented bound on temple walls, around the bases of statues, or even stretched out on the stool upon which the king rested his feet. They appear before the gods, counted off like so much booty, or symbolically slaughtered as offerings. Here they are shown as the handle of a cane in the hand of His Majesty.

The fertile imagination of the royal atelier has jumbled them together; yet even bound, these vile prisoners have become true works of art through the skill of the Egyptian artist. The hirsute Syrian, wearing a costume ornamented with ribbons and circular and floral motifs, has hands, face and feet of ivory. The Nubian prisoner, on the other hand, is given a face and limbs of ebony, with kinky hair and a plaited garment with multicolored streamers.

When the king grasped this cane, the prisoners were turned upside down and rendered harmless; any threat they might have posed was averted. At the other end of the cane, a papyrus umbel inlaid with sepals bears the king's cartouche.

The oblong box which contained this cane, several others, and bows and arrows, was placed in the antechamber of the tomb, at the foot of the lion-headed couch.

Bibliography: PM I, 2, p. 581; Carter/Mace, Tut-ankh-Amen, I, pl. 70B, p. 115; Desroches-Noblecourt, Tutankhamen, pl. 18; Edwards, Tutankhamun, pp. 48—49.

188

188

Upper floor, gallery 40

Ornamented chest

Wood, painted ivory, ebony, bronze   JE 61477
H. 48.5 cm; L. 72 cm; W. 53 cm
Thebes, Valley of the Kings, tomb of Tutankhamon (no. 62), excavated by Carter and Carnarvon in 1922—23
New Kingdom, 18th dynasty, reign of Tutankhamon, 1347—1337 B.C.

This chest had already been searched by tomb robbers who subsequently stuffed it with everything which lay nearby, leaving the cover thrown into a corner. Despite this mistreatment the workmanship of the wood veneered with ivory remains remarkably well preserved.

The chest derives its form from architectural elements consisting of a cavetto cornice, torus moulding and hunchbacked or shrine-shaped lid. It rests upon tall legs which continue all the way up the sides. As is typical of such boxes, two knobs, around which string would have been wound, serve to close and "lock" the chest.

The exterior is composed of large pieces of ivory. The painted panels, bordered by a geometric frame, depict a lush floral landscape in which appears either the royal couple, or a frieze of animals.

The focal point of this dreamy landscape is of course the decoration on the cover (see illustration). One cannot but be touched by this tender scene consecrated to eternity. The great royal wife Ankhesenamon stands like a seductive spirit, dressed in elegant finery: a cone of scented fat flanked by uraei surmounts her wig, from which falls a heavy bundle of tresses ornamented with jewellery. Two uraei with sun-disks, large earrings and a broad collar complete her costume. Her transparent pleated robe, which falls to her sandals, reveals her beautifully modelled figure. She offers enormous bouquets composed of mandrake fruit, lotus and papyrus blossoms to the no less seductively modelled figure of Tutankhamon. The king wears a delightful wig with tiered layers of curls, floating streamers behind his back, and a very large collar which extends out to the shoulders. A pleated kilt covers his loins with a frontal tab and streamers which reach down toward

Senet, which means "passing," was an extremely popular game from the earliest times onward in Egypt. Two players would each try to advance their own pieces, while blocking or eliminating those of their opponent, as determined by the roll of the little sticks or astragal dice which were thrown prior to each move. The gaming board consisted of thirty spaces divided into three rows of ten, which could be placed on a low table, box, simple rectangular board or even on blocks of stone. *Senet* was played everywhere and at all social levels. The official Hesire had a *senet* game among the other games represented on a wall of his old Kingdom tomb at Sakkara; and prince Rahotep mentions *senet* in his list of funerary objects. Some pyramid construction workers take time out at work to play on a *senet* board hastily scratched on a block of stone. There is also a wooden model of a military vessel in which the two officers are seated playing *senet* while on watch. Later, at Medinet Habu, Ramses III is shown upon the walls of his palace playing *senet* with his daughters.

This favorite pastime also came to double as a religious ritual which verged on superstition. *Senet* began to symbolize the passage of the deceased through the netherworld, hence the profusion of New Kingdom scenes of play at senet found upon tomb walls and in the Book of the Dead (see no. 216). The deceased is represented seated before an often invisible adver-

the calves. Cornflowers, mandrakes, pomegranates and poppies form a border of flowering plants all around the couple. On the front of the box we find a hunting scene. Tutankhamon is seated comfortably on a cushioned stool and his wife crouches at his feet. Wearing the blue crown, he draws a bow which, following the conventions of Egyptian art, passes behind his neck. His arrow has hit one of the aquatic birds flying over a lake or marsh filled with large fish. A servant returns to the king with a bird and a fish pierced by his arrows.

On the other panels painted with floral motifs we see antelopes, calves and speckled bulls in combat with dogs, leopards or lions.

Bibliography: PM I, 2, p. 578; Carter, Tut-ankh-Amen III, frontispiece and pp. 118–19; Desroches-Noblecourt, Tutankhamen, pl. 5; Catalogues of Tutankhamon exhibition: Paris, no. 24; London, no. 21; USSR, no. 48; USA/Canada, no. 51; Germany, no. 35.

189   Upper floor, gallery 40
Gameboard of Tutankhamon

Gilded ebony, veneered with ivory   JE 62058
H. 20.2 cm; W. 16 cm; L. 55 cm
Thebes, Valley of the Kings, tomb of Tutankhamon (no. 62), excavated by Carter and Carnarvon in 1922–23
New Kingdom, 18th dynasty, reign of Tutankhamon, 1347–1337 B.C.

sary, striving to "pass" through the next world without mishap.

Tutankhamon owned four *senet* games, which were placed in the annex to the antechamber of his tomb. The largest one (shown here) is a deluxe model mounted upon carved lion's legs set in a wooden frame which imitates a sledge. The detachable box is elaborately decorated with the royal titulary. The gaming board on the top shows thirty squares for *senet*; on the bottom is a second board with twenty squares. The drawer which held the playing pieces and the dice was found empty and thrown aside. Manufactured of precious materials, these little objects were most likely stolen by thieves. The pieces we see here actually derive from the king's other game boxes. Likewise "reversible," the smaller, quite portable version served as a pocket *senet* game.

Bibliography: PM I, 2, p. 583; Carter, Tut-ankh-Amen III, pl. 75 B, pp. 130–32; Catalogues of Tutankhamon exhibition: London, no. 18; USSR and USA/Canada, no. 46; Germany, no. 44; W. J. Tait, Game-Boxes and accessories from the Tomb of Tutᶜankhamun, Tutᶜankhamun's Tomb Series VII, Oxford 1982, pp. 6–15 and pls. 1–5. Cf. also T. Kendall, in: Egypt's Golden Age, Boston 1982, pp. 263–64; E. B. Pusch, Das Senet-Brettspiel im Alten Ägypten I, Münchener Ägyptologische Studien 38, 1978; Vandier, Manuel IV, pp. 493–508.

◁190 Upper floor, gallery 20

Perfume vessel symbolizing the unification of the Two Lands

Alabaster, ivory, oil   JE 62114
H. 70.5 cm; W. 36 cm; L. 18.5 cm
Thebes, Valley of the Kings, tomb of Tutankhamon (no. 62), excavated by Carter and Carnarvon in 1922–23
New Kingdom, 18ᵗʰ dynasty, reign of Tutankhamon, 1347–1337 B.C.

This perfume vase was placed between the doors of the first and second of the four naoi positioned around the sarcophagi and mummy of Tutankhamon. It forms a translation into three dimensions of the symbol for the unification of the Two Lands.

The two Nile gods, whom we have frequently seen carved in relief and shown in profile in accordance with the conventions of Egyptian art, appear exceptionally in this case face front. Around the vessel itself, which reproduces the sign for Union, they tie the heraldic plants of Upper and Lower Egypt.

These extraordinary androgynous and fertile creatures are marvelously sculpted with sagging breasts and swollen bellies, under which two sashes hang from the waist. They display attractive faces, outfitted with beards and striped wigs which support their respective emblems: the papyrus for the Nile of Lower Egypt and the lily for that of Upper Egypt. These two lands are once again symbolized by vertical stems of papyrus and lily upon which two goddesses appear: serpents wearing respectively the crowns of the North and the South.

The mouth of the vase was carefully sealed with tie-strings. However, the most likely valuable stopper was never found. (The first naos had already been opened in antiquity by tomb robbers.) Perhaps it represented a figure of the king enthroned which would have been protected by the vulture-goddess with outstretched wings around the vessel's flattened rim.

The vessel is inscribed with the names of Tutankhamon and Queen Ankhesenamon. It rests upon a base in the form of an openwork table whose front and rear sides depict the same motif: two solar falcons surrounding one of the king's cartouches (*praenomen* at the front and *nomen* at the rear).

The entire object is constructed of four pieces of sculpted alabaster which all fit together perfectly. Details are accented by veneered gold leaf and pieces of painted ivory.

Bibliography: PM I, 2, p. 580; Carter, Tut-ankh-Amen II, pls. 48, 49, p. 34 and 229; Propyläen Kunstgeschichte 15, pl. 371; Edwards, Tutankhamun, pls. 94, 98–99.

191   Upper floor, gallery 9

Corselet of Tutankhamon   ▷

Gold, glass paste, ivory, carnelian   JE 62627
H. 40 cm; L. 85 cm
Thebes, Valley of the Kings, tomb of Tutankhamon (no. 62). Excavations of Carter/Carnarvon, 1922–23
New Kingdom, 18ᵗʰ dynasty, reign of Tutankhamon, 1347–1337 B.C.

A veritable piece of jewelry, this corselet is actually an element of both royal and divine state costume, and is known to us from representations in relief and sculpture in the round. It derives perhaps from the archaic corselet with one shoulder strap which Narmer wears on his famous palette (no. 8). From the Middle Kingdom the pillar of Sesostris I (no. 86) depicts the king and the god both wearing such a corselet, although that of the king shows only one shoulder strap, while the god's has two. In the New Kingdom, this element appears especially in divine representations, decorated with feather patterns and always accompanied by the short, close-fitting kilt.

The corselet found among the funerary furniture of Tutankhamon is an elaborate example which has recently been restored. It consists of an assemblage of numerous pieces, all individually worked. The body is made up of two rectangular patterns of stylized feathers composed of beads of glass which fit together. Divided in rows of alternating blue turquoise and lapis lazuli, they are ornamented with golden chevrons and triangles of red glass. Threads pierce these beads by passing through the point of one and the body of the next. Their edges are attached to small, rigid bars of gold equipped with loops to form a clasp, and close the corselet around the wearer's waist with the aid of pins. The uppermost row aligns half bead-feathers inlaid into gold worked in cloisonné, and is provided above with tiny rings which attach to the upper border

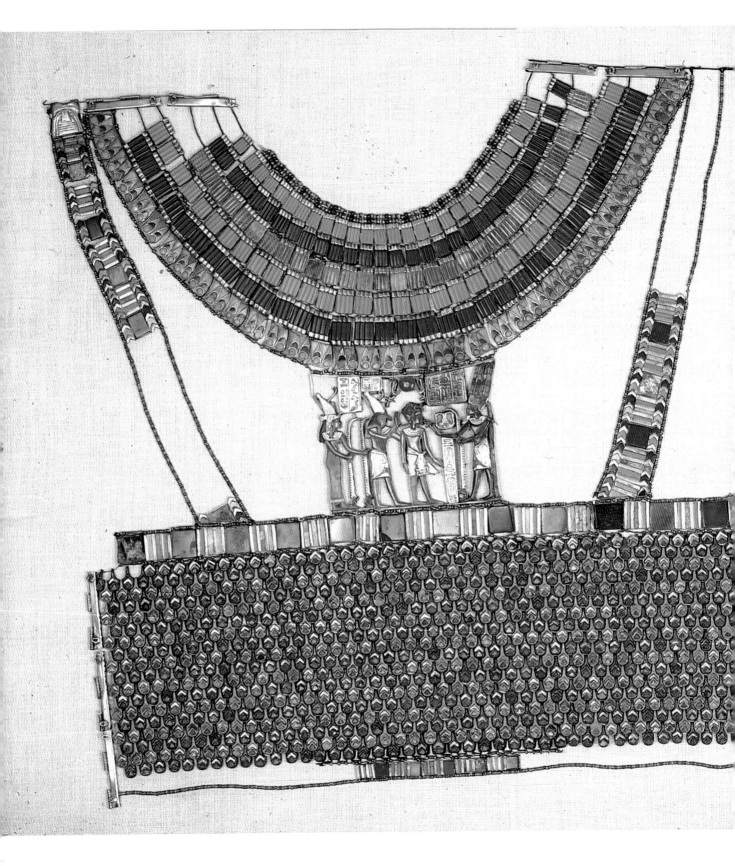

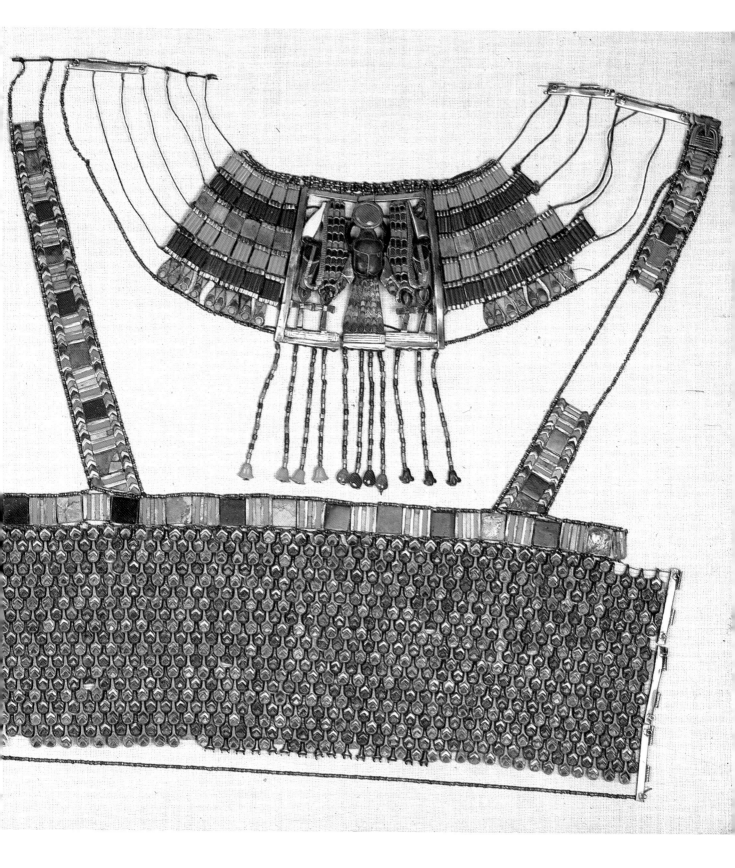

192

The collar is divided into two connecting halves which attach to each other with pin clasps. It is formed of five rows of rectangular gold panels filled with glass which imitate rows of tubular beads placed in a vertical arrangement. Between them are rows of gold beads. The collar is bordered above by two rows of small beads of various colors, and below by a band of articulated elements, worked in cloisonné, whose inlaid decoration imitates a series of floral pendants.

Over the breast an open-work pectoral has been placed between the collar and the corselet. It is made up of gold worked in cloisonné with glass inlays, ivory, and plaques of gold worked with a burin. At right, Amon-Rê of Karnak receives Tutankhamon in order to extend to him the staff of years, the sign of the jubilee and the *ankh*. The king stands underneath the solar disk with two uraei, each bearing *ankh* signs, and is introduced by the falcon-headed Atum, lord of Heliopolis, who wears the double crown. He is followed in turn by his companion Iusaas, whose head is covered with the vulture headdress capped by the double crown. She extends staves of years to the king.

Serving as a counterpoise, a similar pendant, set into the rear half of the collar, falls upon the back of the wearer. Enclosed within a trapezoidal frame of gold, the solar scarab with wings and tail of a falcon raises the sun disk. It is flanked on each side by two uraei wearing respectively the crowns of the north and south. Both beneath the uraei and within the claws of the scarab are the signs for life. Below this decoration hang tassels of tiny polychrome beads which terminate in pendants in the shape of papyrus umbels of blue turquoise, poppy flowers of carnelian, and fleurs-de-lis of blue lapis lazuli.

Bibliography: PM I, 2, p. 582; Carter/Mace, Tut-ankh-Amen I, pls. 37, 38, 66, pp. 136, 173−4; E. Riefstahl, Patterned Textiles in Pharaonic Egypt, fig. 41, p. 37.

of the corselet. By the same system, the last row of beads, which are merely upper halves of the feathers in gold, attach to the lower border of the corselet. These borders are composed of oblong gold cloisonné panels inlaid with glass paste and gold. Each panel contains one little square plaque of lapis lazuli or carnelian-colored glass, and one striated square of gold sticks and colored glass. These elements are bordered in turn by small soldered rings, such that a thread attaches them to the rings of the beaded pattern. By virtue of the little intercalated beads between the various rings, this system of attachment gives the appearance of a continuous row of beads.

The corselet has two shoulder-straps made of a series of articulated elements, assembled with the same system of rings and beads. Each of these gold cloisonné elements contains in the center a small rectangular plaque of striations alternating in blue or red glass, bordered by chevrons of colored glass alternating with gold. Two fasteners in chased gold in the form of a buckle, one of which is lost, close the shoulder straps over the wearer's shoulders with the aid of a clasp and pins. Here the fasteners connect by a system of loops to the collar which hangs around the wearer's neck.

192   Upper floor, gallery 35
Tutankhamon with harpoon

Wood, stuccoed and gilded, bronze   JE 60709
H. 69.5 cm; W. 18.5 cm; L. 70.5 cm
Thebes, Valley of the Kings, tomb of Tutankhamon (no. 62), excavated by Carter and Carnarvon in 1922−23
New Kingdom, 18th dynasty, reign of Tutankhamon, 1347−1337 B.C.

Thirty-two statuettes, seven of them royal, were placed within several black naoi, sealed and deposited in that chamber of the tomb known as the Treasury. The figures were wrapped in bolts of linen whose inscribed date of manufacture read year three of Akhenaton; only the faces were left uncovered. Some of the divine statues wore fillets of real flowers around their necks. With the exception of three figures colored black with bitumen, all of these wooden statues are stuccoed and gilded.

They resemble a divine pantheon, personifying various myths and legends, all grouped together, from the ennead of major deities to the sons of Horus. Most important of all, however, is the incarnation of Horus himself: the king.

The most moving of all the statues are the two showing Tutankhamon with a harpoon standing on a papyrus skiff. Wearing the red crown with uraeus at his brow, a *wesekh* collar, short pleated kilt with ornamented frontal tab and sandals, Tutankhamon is frozen in action just as he is about to hurl his harpoon into the flesh of an invisible enemy. Once pierced by the lance, this foe will be tied by the cord which the king holds in his left hand. The lifelike impression is created by the striding pose, with torso slightly inclined. It is an exceptional occurrence in the history of a royal statuary which has never been anything but static.

The hunt in the marshes is a theme known from reliefs or paintings in private tombs and royal temples. This theme concerns the triumph over evil, personified in this case by the hippopotamus in the swamp. The victorious king defeats the forces of chaos and preserves the universal order which it is his duty to insure. The development of this theme in the Late Period leads Horus to grapple with his enemy Seth in a series of episodes. In the end Seth, transformed into a hippopotamus, is finally vanquished.

Bibliography: Carter, Tut-ankh-Amen III, pls. 13, 60, pp. 54–55; Desroches-Noblecourt, Tutankhamen, pl. 45; Catalogues of Tutankhamon exhibition: London, no. 27; USSR, no. 8; USA/Canada, no. 35; Germany, no. 32.

193

193
Pectoral of Tutankhamon

Upper floor, room 4

Gold, silver, semi-precious stones, glass   JE 61884
H. 14.9 cm; W. 14.5 cm
Thebes, Valley of the Kings, tomb of Tutankhamon (no. 62). Excavations of Carter/Carnarvon, 1922–23
New Kingdom, 18th dynasty, reign of Tutankhamon, 1347–1337 B.C.

Within the gold coffin alone, one hundred and forty-three objects of value buried within the linen wrappings were discovered on the mummy of Tutankhamon. Among the finds were necklaces in flat gold or cloisonné adorned with polychrome stones, elaborate pectorals and theriomorphic pendants, intricately worked bracelets in a multitude of forms, sophisticated rings rich with symbolism, a heart scarab and a dagger. Almost all the jeweler's techniques are represented, from the simple incised gold plaque, to the mosaics of cloisonné, from settings of cabochon to filigree frames, not to mention the rings, scarabs or amulets, carved merely in stone with vibrant colors.

There were also other objects of jewelry among the funerary equipment, for example, in the chest serving as the base for the statue of Anubis (no. 185), but the richest harvest was reaped in the chamber called the "treasury." Here were found chests filled with diverse pieces of jewelry, which even after being looted by robbers, yielded an exceptional sample of necklaces, collars, pendants, earrings, bracelets and mirrors, as well as a box containing a fan of ostrich feathers. By way of example, here is a piece of jewelry which, although perhaps a little too elaborate, illustrates nevertheless intricate detail work, a taste for gold and polychromy, and above all, rich symbolism hidden behind each element of this luxurious specimen of the goldsmith's trade. It is a pectoral upon which several motifs have been arranged. In the center is a scarab, carved out of translucent chalcedony, and provided with a falcon's tail and wings, worked in cloisonné, as well as with a pair of gold claws which clutch *shen*-rings, symbols of duration and universal force. The left claw holds a fleur-de-lis, the right a lotus bouquet, each the respective insignia of Lower and Upper Egypt.

The hybrid scarab, which evokes the sun, is enclosed by two uraei with disks. Below it is an ornamental band of alternating red and blue disks, from which hangs a garland of pendants in the shape of lotus, poppy, composite buttons and papyrus, separated from one another by circular fleurons.

Raised up above by the legs of the scarab is a celestial barque bearing the *udjat*, left eye of Horus, that is to say, the moon. On the sides, the eye is accompanied by two uraei, viewed head on. The eye is surmounted by the emblem of the moon consisting of a lunar crescent of gold and a disk of silver, upon which three golden figures participate in a coronation scene. The king stands in the center wearing the *Khepresh* crown capped by the moon. At the left, the lunar deity Thoth bears

◁ 194

On the bank, a military file advances at a hasty pace; standard-bearers lead the way, followed by soldiers carrying lances, shields and sickles. A band of hieroglyphs in painted relief preserves the words they utter: "O Sovereign. You are like Montu, you are like Montu among your army, the gods being the protection of your limbs, since you have repulsed him who has arisen in the vile land of Kush."

Most interesting about this painted relief is its style, which demonstrates the influence of Amarna art during the reign of Tutankhamon. One will note that the subjects of the king use the word "sovereign"; this term has been carved inside the cartouche, taking the place of the royal name. The mention of a victory over the Nubians proves how much even young and militarily untested pharaohs were supposed to combat the vile enemy. This important block contributes much to the study of Tutankhamon's monuments at Karnak before the rearrangements which took place under his successors.

Bibliography: PM II, p. 40. Cf. Legrain, Les Temples de Karnak, Brussels 1929, fig. 87.

the lunar symbol on top of his ibis-head. At the right, the solar falcon-headed deity Rê-Horakhty wears the solar disk.

All the themes which illustrate an eternal cycle are thus represented on this piece of jewelry: the lunar and solar emblems; Upper and Lower Egypt, the king's ascent to heaven and his rule in the next world.

Bibliography: Carter, Tut-ankh-Amen III, pl. 19B, p. 76; Desroches-Noblecourt, Tutankhamen, pl. 36; Edwards, Tutankhamun, p. 171; catalogues of Tutankhamon exhibition: London, no. 30; USSR, no. 35; USA/Canada, no. 26; Germany, no. 42.

194

Ground floor, room 12

Military parade

Painted sandstone   RT 8.6.24.4
H. 65 cm; L. 142 cm
Karnak, temple of Amon-Re; discovered in the 2nd pylon
during the excavations of the Egyptian Antiquities Service
New Kingdom, 18th dynasty, reign of Tutankhamon, 1347–1337 B.C.

This block was found reused inside the second pylon of the temple of Amon-Re at Karnak. It clearly derives from a chapel or temple wall decorated in the reign of Tutankhamon. Based on a number of similar blocks found at Karnak, the scene represented here consists of a procession which sets in motion the royal bark escorted by boats with rowers and accompanied on land by an entire defile of soldiers, standard-bearers and officers. At the front of all this commotion, the king, leaving the bark and being acclaimed by a crowd of musicians, dancers and acrobats, came to offer bound prisoners to his god Amon-Re. It seems, then, that the entire composition illustrates the return from a successful military campaign, or at least a military parade.

It is one of the smaller escort craft that appears toward the top of our fragment. One can still distinguish the plaited kilts of the rowers who, with a regular rhythm, thrust their oars parallel into the blue waters of the river, represented by undulating lines.

195

Ground floor, gallery 15

The generalissimo Nakhtmin

Crystalline limestone   JE 31630
H. 34 cm; W. 34 cm; thickness 31 cm   = CG 779A
Provenance unknown; purchase c. 1897
New Kingdom, end of the 18th dynasty, reign of Ay(?), ca. 1337 B.C.

Nakhtmin and his wife (on view in the same case, see no. 196) formed together a pair statue which was connected by a dorsal slab with a rounded top. The unfortunate mutilation of the face has taken nothing away from the sober beauty of this head. Framed by one of the very popular New Kingdom wigs with undulating locks, the youthful face contains a perfectly polished surface and almond-shaped eyes. It is the face of an official of high rank. The fan which he holds is still visible on the right hand side of the wig.

The pierced ears and two incised neck lines date this admirable work of art to the post-Amarna period. An inscription preserved on the back of the statue, behind his wife, informs us that Nakhtmin was prince, royal scribe, and generalissimo. A final title, only partially preserved, begins with "King's son of...," which could be the title of viceroy of Ethiopia, called in Egyptian "King's son of Kush." However, no such viceroys by the name of Nakhtmin are attested elsewhere. On the other hand, the epithet "King's son, of his body" is extremely common among royal offspring, and it is more likely that our prince was a member of the royal family. From another group statue of Nakhtmin and his family we learn that his mother, Iuwy, was songstress of Isis and votaress of Min. The name of the prince himself is composed with that of Min, patron god of Akhmim, and it is therefore reasonable to assume that he was a member of the family of Ay, who originated from that city.

Bibliography: PM I, 2, pp. 784–85; Borchardt, Statuen und Statuetten (CG) III, pp. 87–89; Vandier, Manuel III, p. 520, pl. 145; Smith, Art and Architecture, p. 269, fig. 264.

196

196
Ground floor, gallery 15

The wife of Nakhtmin

Crystalline limestone   JE 31629
H. 85 cm; W. 44 cm   = CG 779B
Provenance unknown; purchased in 1897
New Kingdom, end of the 18th dynasty, reign of Ay(?), ca. 1337 B.C.

Sumptuously dressed, the wife of Nakhtmin once placed a hand on the shoulder of her husband. Even though she remains anonymous, the lady's chaste features, pensive expression, dignity and elegance distinguish her as one of the most beautiful women of antiquity.

Her perfectly oval face, revealed under her massive, enveloping wig, harmonizes well with her narrow, almond-shaped eyes. These in turn are enhanced by both cosmetic and incised lines marking the beginning of the eyelids. The mouth is serious, almost earnest; the lips retain traces of red color and the corners of the mouth are marked in black.

The artist has displayed a delicately fine taste in sculpting this masterpiece of beauty and elegance. The wig, in itself a work of art, consists of long twisted locks which terminate in tightly curled strands. It is encircled by a lotus diadem with a frontal bouquet. A band below gathers the mass of hair together, leaving one lock to fall freely on either side of the face.

Along with a *wesekh* collar around her neck and a *menat* necklace in her hand, the wife of Nakhtmin wears a seductive robe of fine, pleated linen, which is tied under the breast. This transparent garment follows the rounded forms of her delicate figure.

Bibliography: PM I, 2, pp. 784–85; Borchardt, Statuen und Statuetten (CG) III, pp. 87–89; Yoyotte, Treasures of the Pharaohs, pp. 136–37; Terrace/Fischer, no. 31; Götter Pharaonen, no. 50.

197
Ground floor, gallery 7

Stela of Amoneminet   ▷

Limestone   SR 11732
H. 148 cm; W. 109 cm
Sakkara, tomb of Amoneminet; acquired by the Museum in 1924
New Kingdom, end of the 18th dynasty, ca. 1310 B.C.

For each of the great ages in Egyptian history, the necropolis of Sakkara has revealed accomplished examples of the art of

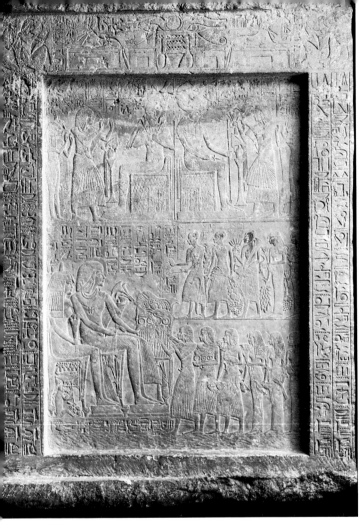

197

couple march eleven individuals from the household, divided into two registers. The first three men above, in priestly garb with shaven heads, are the sons of the couple. The whole group brings fresh water, incense, bouquets of flowers, bunches of assorted fruit, bread and cakes, geese, ducks, and even a fawn daintily curled up in the arms of the bearer. The elaborate wigs are meticulously crafted masterpieces, as are also the exquisite transparent garments of pleated linen.

Around the stela runs a projecting frame which is decorated above with a double adoration scene. Amoneminet and his wife kneel with hands raised before two representations of Anubis in the form of a jackal. The two sides are inscribed with funerary offering formulae for the *ka* of Amoneminet.

Bibliography: PM III, 2, p. 552; E. Otto/M. Hirmer, Osiris und Amun, Munich 1966, pl. 6.

198   Upper floor, hall 48

Polychrome glass vases

1) Three-handled vase   JE 47778
H. 9.5 cm
Sakkara; discovered in 1923

2) Vase without handles   RT 12.3.26.2
H. 8 cm
Provenance unknown

New Kingdom, 18th dynasty, c. 1450 B.C.

relief sculpture. From the end of the Eighteenth Dynasty, here is a stela from the tomb of Amoneminet, overseer of the king's craftsmen, who was buried near the pyramid of Teti in the northern part of the necropolis.

The stela is dedicated to him by his sons Ptahmose and Amonemheb. It takes its place stylistically in the post-Amarna period, when traditional earlier themes were revived, but without completely abandoning recent Amarnan artistic innovations. The latter is particularly successful in its representations of spontaneity and expressive grace.

The finely carved low relief sculpture presents two scenes of adoration in the first register. Amoneminet and his wife, Tahesy, dressed in elaborate wigs and robes, pay homage to Osiris seated on the left, and to Re-Horakhty-Atum on the right. In the more developed lower register, the couple is seated with bouquets in their hands, before a large offering table. Under the wife's chair, a crouching monkey next to a loaded basket devours scattered pieces of fruit. Towards the

These elegant glass vases, with tall base, bulging belly, large high neck and flattened rim illustrate a technique of manufacture which first appears during Dynasty 18. Glass with such decorative patterns was not blown but moulded hollow around a clay mandrel which was removed once the glass had cooled. In order to obtain the garland and chevron motifs, one applied little glass rods of yellow, white and blue to the smooth, reheated surface of the vessel. The colors fused together as they melted. At this point one could either elongate the base and the neck, or add them separately, as has been done with the handles.

Bibliography: Cf. Desroches-Noblecourt, L'Art Egyptien, Paris 1962, pp. 140—41; E. Riefstahl, Ancient Egyptian Glass and Glazes in the Brooklyn Museum, nos. 12 and 18; Propyläen Kunstgeschichte 15, pl. 369; Nofret — Die Schöne, no. 60.

199

Ground floor, room 12

Statuette of the god Amon

JE 38049

Greywacke (schist)
H. 58 cm; W. 14.5 cm; thickness 26 cm
Karnak, court of the "cachette", excavated by Legrain in 1905
New Kingdom, end of the 18th dynasty, about 1320 B.C.

Two animals, the goose and the ram, were sacred to the god Amon, "the Hidden One"; but from the time of his promotion to the position of Imperial god, the innumerable representations of him in his principal temple at Karnak, from the depth of the sanctuary up to the doors of the temple, depict him almost invariably in his human aspect. Exceptionally, he is represented in front of the temple in the form of a criosphinx. This delightful statue which dates from the period after the Amarna heresy when the cult of Amon was restored at Thebes, was found in the court of the "cachette" at Karnak together with the thousands of other statues which had been buried there. Partly restored, the statue represents Amon in his usual human form, wearing the high feather crown (the feathers have disappeared), a plaited divine beard, a corselet and pleated kilt attached by a belt whose buckle is decorated with an Isis knot, bracelets and a wide collar.

Amon incarnates the aerial element: air, wind, breath, which accounts for his close association with the high feather crown and for the blue colour generally assigned to his flesh. Initially the local god of a district of Thebes, his name is also included among the Ogdoad of Hermopolis. When he rose to be tutelary god of the empire, the possibilities for associating him with the older supreme gods became much greater, witness the combinations: Amon-Re, in which name he took on the attributes of a solar god; Amon-Re-Montu, god of war; Amon-Min, god of fertility, and so on until in Roman times he became Jupiter-Amon. As father in the Theban triad, his wife was Mut the local goddess associated with him, and their child was the lunar god Khonsu-in-Thebes. From an obscure local divinity, he became the Demiurge who created himself as

199

well as the universe. Amon is patron of life, of war and particularly of the King who puts himself entirely under his protection.

From the 12th dynasty on, numerous are the Kings whose names incorporate in their composition the name of Amon, and the New Kingdom Kings never failed to add to their titles the epithet "beloved of Amon". His political influence spread even into Asia, and at the end of the New Kingdom it is his High Priest who takes over the royal power. Even before the Amarna period, many hymns praise the beneficence of Amon-Re, the sun. "You are beautiful, you are beautiful, O Amon-Re! the eldest of the sky and of the earth, who came into existence, appearing in the air".

Amon is everywhere; it is he who on the walls of the Theban temples receives the booty of war and who presents to the King the scimitar of victory. The epic poems of the Ramesside period extol the preeminence of this god. "What then is a father who forgets his son? Have I ever accomplished anything without you?" cries Ramses II when face to face with the Hittite army at Kadesh. "Have I not erected a great number of monuments for you so that I could fill your temples with my booty? ..... I have never ceased to enrich your sanctuaries with offerings..... I pray to you, O my father Amon. I am in the midst of innumerable foreign peoples whom I do not know. I am all alone... And yet my voice has reached Hermonthis". The god hears him and speeds to his assistance. Ramses is victorious.

One of the King's greatest desires is to follow Amon not only in victory on earth but in his nocturnal voyages through the 12 hours of the night in the subterranean regions. He hopes to be born at daybreak with the god who reappears rejuvenated on the eastern horizon. Thus Amon, in his form of Amon-Re, is the most universal god conceived by the Egyptians. He is a solar god, but as the nocturnal sun he becomes Osiris and this transformation is what religious texts call: "the greatest secret".

Bibliography: Götter Pharaonen, no. 49; Corteggiani, no. 77. See also: LÄ I, 237–48; J. Assmann, Ägyptische Hymnen und Gebete, Zurich/Munich 1975.

200

Ground floor, gallery 20

Coffin of Ramessu

Grey granite
JE 72203
L. 192 cm; W. 51 cm
Thebes; discovered in a pit outside the enclosure wall of Medinet Habu in 1939
New Kingdom, 18th dynasty, reign of Horemheb, 1332–1305 B.C.

This coffin may have belonged to the founder of the Nineteenth Dynasty, Ramses I, while he was still merely vizier under King Horemheb. He was known then as Ramessu or Paramessu, as attested by two statues at Karnak, and by another, even larger granite coffin (on exhibit in gallery 9). Both coffins represent the image of their owner on the lid. On our coffin, Ramessu wears a striated tripartite wig, short beard, and the costume of the vizier, consisting of a long kilt enveloping the body and suspended from the shoulders by two straps. A scarab pectoral adorns his breast which is in turn covered by a crouching figure of Isis with outstretched wings. The decoration on the rest of the sarcophagus is typical of most New Kingdom examples. The four sons of Horus and four Ibis-headed genii alternate with bands of hieroglyphic texts listing the name and titles of the deceased, who is placed under divine protection.

The face is of primary interest, for it presents a well preserved and skilfully carved example of sculpture from the period of transition between Dynasties 18–19. Thus the features recall those of Tutankhamon, yet the face is more oval, the ears straighter and larger, the eyebrows more rounded, and the lips less fleshy, but well delineated and clearly framed with an outline.

The features of the second coffin repeat those described above. Onto both coffins, which nest perfectly one within the other, was later added a series of new inscriptions with the name of Ramessu − now designated heir apparent and "son" adopted by Horemheb. The interior coffin, under discussion here, was buried without a mummy at Thebes, while the other one was found in the Fayum, containing the mummy of a thirty year old hunchback. The Fayum necropolis was associated with the royal residence at Gurob, a favorite abode of queens and royal widows of the Eighteenth and Nineteenth Dynasties.

This mystery remains to be solved. However, Ramessu would no longer have needed either of these coffins, since he would have been provided with royal sarcophagi. His titles here indicate that this individual, called prince and count, fan-bearer on the right of the king, had accumulated administrative positions (overseer of the city, controller of the entire land, vizier), military functions (chief of bowmen, overseer of the cavalry), and sacerdotal responsibilities (judge and priest of Maat). But the highest promotion which he obtained came when Horem-

heb designated him as his successor, whereupon he mounted the Egyptian throne as Ramses I.

Bibliography: PM I, 2, p. 777; G. Brunton, in: ASAE 43, 1943, pp. 133–48, pls. 7–10; D. Polz, in: MDAIK 42, 1986. Cf. also: A. P. Thomas, Gurob: A New Kingdom Town, Vol. 1, Warminster 1981, pp. 17–18; LÄ V, 100–105.

◁ 201   Ground floor, room 14

Statue of Seti I

Alabaster   JE 36692
H. ca. 238 cm; W. 73 cm   = CG 42139
Karnak, court of the cachette; cleared by Legrain in 1904
New Kingdom, 19th dynasty, reign of Seti I, 1305–1290 B.C.

This impressive statue is composed of several elements individually sculpted and assembled. It was originally dedicated to the temple of Karnak by one of the pious sovereigns who returned to the cult of Amon after the fall of Amarna. During the Late Period, when the all too numerous statues at Karnak were buried to make room in the temple, this piece was dismembered and deprived of its more valuable materials. Thus it was later discovered lying in six pieces under the debris of the Karnak cachette.

The head attaches to the body by means of a hole cut in the top of the torso, into which the neck fits. The hands join the wrists using straps which pass through perforations. The legs hold the thighs by a similar method; the holes are visible partway up the thighs.

These various elements provide an idea of the original appearance of the ensemble. We should imagine the statue set up in the temple glittering with gold and other precious materials. The *nemes*, the only headdress possible given the cuts at the nape and the front, was composed of gold leaf and covered the head entirely, falling onto the shoulders over a large collar. The latter served to conceal the junction marks at the neck. A gold beard was attached under the chin, where a deep hole is still visible. The eyes and eyebrows were inlaid with gold and precious stones. Large armlets and bracelets adorned the king's arms while hiding the attachment of the hands. Two rolls of some precious substance were inserted in the fists.

The garment, poorly restored at the beginning of this century,

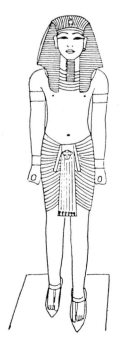

was in fact not the classical *shendjyt* but rather a pleated kilt, tied under the waist. A central section flanked by ribbons, traces of which survive below the navel, protruded in front, ornamented no doubt with a leopard's head and a border of uraei and sun-disks. Golden sandals once adorned the feet, as attested by a hole pierced between the first two toes of the left foot. The soles of the feet were not attached to the base but remained free. The entire weight of the statue was supported by a back pillar installed behind the legs and touching the base. Although empty today, the pillar was once filled with a compact and heavy substance. The top of the base bore the decoration of nine bows, symbolic of Egypt's hostile foreign lands. Two bows are still visible, preceded by the beginning of the king's titulary.

Both the back pillar and the plinth joining the two legs are covered with inscriptions preserving the name of the king. He is Seti I, and claims to have provided the temple, which he restored, with a statue of pure alabaster, that his name might endure in the temple of his father Amon.

Seti I's reign is characterized by great piety towards the gods and extraordinary building activity throughout the land. Cults abandoned during the reign of Akhenaten were reinstated everywhere by Seti. It is to this sovereign that we owe the major portion of construction on the great hypostyle hall at Karnak, as well as the restoration of Theban temples.

Bibliography: PM II, p. 140; G. Legrain, Statues et Statuettes (CG) II, pp. 1–4, pl. 1; Vandier, Manuel III, p. 391; Corteggiani, no. 81.

202

Bust of Ramses II

Grey granite   CG 616
H. 80 cm; W. 70 cm
Tanis (San el-Hagar)
New Kingdom, 19th dynasty, reign of Ramses II, 1290–1224 B.C.

The most celebrated of all the Pharaohs, Ramses II, is well known to everyone because of the length of his reign, the numerous temples which he built in Egypt and in Nubia, and his omnipresent colossi which have perpetuated his cult even up to the present day. The royal residence of the Ramesside period in the eastern Delta, mentioned in the Bible, is named after him. His military campaigns recorded on the walls of his temples glorify his name. Who has not read of the battle of Kadesh where Ramses II, still a young man in the 5th year of his reign faced the army of Muwattali, King of the Hittites, whose expanding empire in Asia Minor menaced the supremacy of Egypt in Syria? The two armies having proved to be of approximately equal strength, an armistice was agreed upon. A lasting peace was finally brought about in the 21st year of Ramses' reign by the signing of the first official peace treaty known to history.

This bust from a seated statue of Ramses II is a portrait of the young king in which grace and grandeur are intermixed. The sensitive face is framed by a sumptuous round wig covered with small regular curls, and encircled by a band, to which the uraeus is attached. The narrow slits of the eyes, partly veiled by the lowered lids, are surmounted by protruding eyebrows which follow the curve of the eyes. The mouth is full with slightly upturned corners.

A broad collar of several rows of beads covers the King's chest. He is wearing a delicately pleated costume with wide sleeves, underneath which can be distinguished the fine modeling of the torso. A bracelet decorated with the sacred *Udjat* eye, symbol of protection, adorns his wrist and in his right hand he holds the *heka* sceptre, emblem of sovereignty.

The position of his body, slightly bent forward in sign of reverence towards the gods, is inherited from the time of Seti I, a mark of humility which Ramses II quickly abandoned in his later representations.

Bibliography: Terrace/Fischer, no. 32; Ramsès le Grand, no. 16; Götter Pharaonen, no. 53; Le grand pharaon Ramsès II, no. 67.

203   Ground floor, gallery 10

Ramses II as a child with the god Hurun

Grey granite and limestone (face of the falcon)   JE 64735
H. 231 cm; L. 133 cm; W. 64.5 cm
Tanis. Excavations of Montet in 1934
New Kingdom, 19th dynasty, reign of Ramses II, 1290−1223 B.C.

This colossal statue associates Ramses II as a child with the Canaanite god Hurun in the form of a falcon.

The squatting child is conventionally depicted, nude, with his finger to his mouth. A tight-fitting cap covers his head surmounted by a sun-disk and adorned with the princely sidelock. He holds in his left hand the plant *sw*. This image of the royal infant is simultaneously a monumental transposition of the hieroglyphic group which goes to form the name of Ramses II: *Ra* (the sun disk) + *mes* (the child) + *sw* (the plant) = *Ramessu*, Ramses.

The child is leaning against the breast of the immense falcon which protects him with its folded wings whose feathers are carefully crossed at the back, and with its powerful talons covered with marvellously stylized scales. This protection is confirmed by the inscription on the base of the statue which names "The good god Usermaatre Setepenre, the son of Re Ramses Meryamon, beloved of the Hurun of Ramses Meryamon."

The falcon's face, separately sculptured in a block of limestone, was found in a room adjacent to that in which the colossal granite figure was found. The latter had apparently been deposited temporarily in one of the brick workshops next to the enclosure wall of the great temple at Tanis. The face which was perhaps destined to be covered with gold leaf, seems to have been only just finished. Possibly it was made to replace the original face of the granite falcon, destroyed during the transport of the statue to Tanis. For, as we have already seen, the monuments at Tanis all come from other Delta sites or even from as far away as the Memphite region (see nos. 102, 104).

The cult of the god Hurun is limited almost exclusively to the environs of Giza where during the New Kingdom colonies of Asiatics were installed near the great Sphinx, whose Egyptian name Harmachis they confused with that of a similarly named deity of their own: Hurun, and whom they adopted as a god of the dead. But according to New Kingdom tradition the Sphinx was the god who designated the crown prince: therefore Ramses places himself as a child under the protection of the god Hurun who confers on him the succession to the throne.

Bibliography: Montet, in: Kêmi 5, 1935, pp. 11−14, pls. 10−11; Ramsès le Grand, no. 1; Le grand pharaon Ramsès II, no. 4; R. Stadelmann, in: Festschrift G. Fecht, Bamberg 1987.

204–205

Two naoi of Ramses II

Red quartzite
204 H. 156 cm; W. 190 cm; L. 271 cm   JE 37475
= CG 70003

205 H. 157 cm; W. 215 cm; L. 267 cm   JE 37476
= CG 70004

Tanis; discovered by F. Petrie in 1904
New Kingdom, 19th dynasty, reign of Ramses II, 1290–1224 B.C.

Like many Ramesside monuments found at Tanis, these two
naoi were originally located at Pi-Ramesse in the capital
founded in the eastern Delta by the kings of the Nineteenth
Dynasty. They were subsequently removed to Tanis for the
great temple of Amon-Re, itself constructed entirely of materials taken from the Ramesside city. Petrie discovered them
facing each other on either side of the main axis of the temple.
They are carved both inside and out in sunk relief with scenes
of Ramses II offering to the gods of Heliopolis. On the exterior, these are three forms of the sun: Re-Horakhty crowned
with the sun disk, Atum with the Double Crown, and Khepri
with another sun disk (see illustration). The back side shows
the sky god Geb and the air god Shu, both receiving offerings.
The roof is decorated with a series of vultures with outstretched wings.
The interior of each naos is conceived as a rock-cut chapel
whose rear wall contains the figures of three seated deities, cut
almost free-standing from the wall. Atum appears on the left,
Amon-Re in the center and Khepri on the right.
Rock-cut chapels are numerous in Upper Egypt and particularly in Nubia. Our two naoi perhaps serve to "provide" rock
monuments in the Delta, where no cliffs or mountains are
present.
Both of these two pseudo-speos functioned as cult places in
front of the temple. Visitors not admitted to the temple's holy
of holies were free to approach the naos and worship the
deities there.

Bibliography: Petrie, Tanis I, London 1885, p. 15, pl. 16 (6); Tanis
II, 1888, p. 9, pl. 1 (68); G. Roeder, Naos (CG), pp. 11–22, pls. 4, 5,
54, 74, 83–87. Cf. K. Myśliwiec, in: BIFAO 78, 1978, pp. 172–95;
H. Sourouzian, in: MDAIK 39, 1983, pp. 222–23.

206

Ramses II smiting enemies ▷

Painted limestone   JE 46189
H. 99.5 cm; W. 89 cm; L. 50 cm
Mit Rahina (Memphis); acquired by the Museum in 1917
New Kingdom, 19th dynasty, reign of Ramses II, 1290–1224 B.C.

This block originally belonged to a structure of Ramses II at
Memphis. It was discovered, however, reused in a building of
King Merenptah.
Ramses II stands in the heroic pose, with ornate costume, blue
crown and sandals. He holds an axe in his left hand and with
his right he grasps the tufts of hair of three prisoners. Each is
recognizable by his characteristic facial features and costume:
a Nubian, a Libyan and a Syrian. The last two each raise an
arm by way of begging for mercy, displaying the only artistic
liberty allowed by this rather strict iconography. The king's
cartouches are partially visible above the prisoners, and
behind Ramses himself appears the phrase normally accompanying all royal representations: "Protection behind him, like
Re."
The image of the king subjugating or slaughtering bound prisoners is a favorite theme in official Egyptian art. Repulsing the
dangers posed by a chaotic and hostile world signified par
excellence the maintenance of peace and order in the land of
Egypt. Hence we find all public areas of the temple, especially
the facade, and all palaces abundantly decorated with such
scenes.

Bibliography: PM III, 2, p. 862.

206

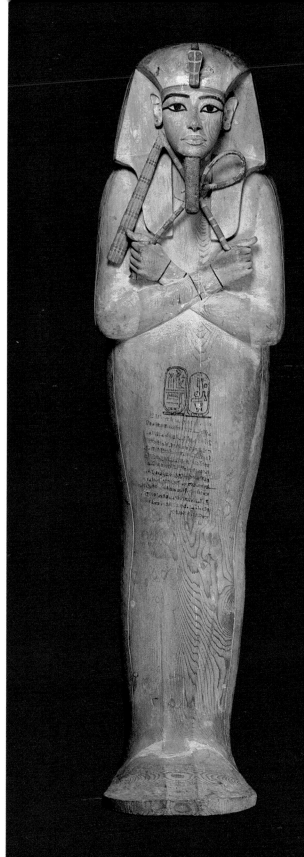

207

Upper floor, gallery 31

Coffin of Ramses II (lid)

Painted wood
L. 206 cm; W. 54.5 cm; H. 36.5 cm
Thebes, cache of Deir el-Bahari; discovered in 1875; cleared in 1881
by the Egyptian Antiquities Service under Maspero
New Kingdom, 19th dynasty, reign of Ramses II, 1290–1224 B.C.

JE 26214
= CG 61020

Toward the end of the New Kingdom the royal tombs fell
prey to robbers searching for gold and other treasures. In
Dynasty 21 the high priests of Amon succeeded in rescuing the
pillaged royal mummies, which they then rewrapped and
buried in two special caches. One lies to the south of Deir el-
Bahari and was originally prepared for Queen Inhapi, wife of
Ahmose I; the other was in the Valley of the Kings in the tomb
of Amenophis II. Thus it was here that the mummies finally
came to rest. Both caches were, however, discovered at the
end of the last century. The Deir el-Bahari cache was found by
three villagers from Sheikh Abd el Gourna who agreed to keep
the news of their discovery to themselves. Eventually legal
action initiated by the Antiquities Department provoked sufficient familial discord for one of the members to divulge the
secret to the authorities. In 1881, Maspero cleared the only
recently revealed cache and transported the mummies by boat

to the Museum. Between Thebes and Cairo crowds lined both river banks to view and cheer the royal cortege. The other cache was discovered by V. Loret in 1898.

It was in the first, or "royal cache", that Ramses II lay in the company of his father, his grandfather and other great monarchs of the New Kingdom. His body had been placed in this anthropoid coffin of painted wood. The gold which covered the coffin, the precious stones and colors are lost forever. We see on the lid a somewhat deprived simplicity in the youthful image of the king in Osirian pose, holding the crook and flail. He wears a *nemes* headdress with uraeus and a tressed beard is attached under his chin. His facial features resemble those of Tutankhamon, and one wonders if the coffin might actually represent a king of the end of Dynasty 18 – many coffins were, after all, mixed up in the haste of transporting the caches. On the other hand, Ramses ascended the throne at an early age, and it is equally likely that a coffin doubtless begun during the first years of his reign would reflect his youthful features.

The coffin is constructed of several pieces of wood assembled with pegs and tenons. This in itself might speak against Ramses II as the original owner, for one might expect this great monarch to be buried in a coffin of solid gold. The problem remains to be solved.

We are, at least, informed about the various salvage operations carried out on the mummy, as recorded by three statements written on the front and on the top of the head of the lid. We read that the mummy was removed originally to the tomb of Seti I before being deposited in the cache of Deir el-Bahari.

Bibliography: PM I, 2, p. 661; Maspero, Les Momies Royales de Deir el-Bahari, in: Mémoires publiés par les membres de la Mission Archéologique Française au Caire J. 1889, pp. 556–60; G. Daressy, Cercueils des cachettes royales (CG), pp. 32–34, pls. 20–22; Ramsès le Grand, no. 72; Le grand pharaon Ramsès II, no. 66.

208

208   Ground floor, gallery 15

The queen Merit-Amon

Painted limestone   JE 31413
H. 75 cm; W. 44 cm; profile 44 cm   CG 600
Thebes, chapel of the queen, north-west of the Ramesseum; excavated by F. Petrie in 1896
New Kingdom, 19th dynasty, reign of Ramses II, after year 21, ca. 1271–1224 B.C.

This statue was often called "the white queen," "the queen with the Menat", or, for lack of a personal name, "a wife of Ramses II," until a foundation trench sunk near a road at Akhmim happened to reveal an identical statue – but ten times the size – of the same queen. There she flanked a colossal statue of Ramses II, bearing the same titles as on our statue, the same accoutrements, and in addition revealing her name. She is Merit-Amon, one of the daughters of Ramses II, who was promoted to the position of great royal wife on the death of her mother, Nefertari, the distinguished chief wife of the king.

Youthful grace, a gentle smile and well-preserved color all mark this statue as one of the most beautiful of the Ramesside period. The tripartite wig, composed of blue-painted locks in an echelon arrangement, is held in place by a double band which supports the two royal serpents wearing the crowns of Upper and Lower Egypt.

Upon Merit-Amon's head a circular base, surrounded by a frieze of uraei with sun-disks, would once have supported the large disk and double feathers that are typical of queenly headdresses. The queen's jewellery includes two round earrings, a large collar with several rows of yellow beads imitating gold and a double bracelet. Rosettes ornament her breast. The object which she grasps in her left hand is the Menat-necklace, composed of many rows of beads with a counterpoise fashioned in the form of the goddess Hathor. The queen was therefore a priestess associated with the cult of the goddess, as is also indicated by her titles: "Player of the sistrum of Mut and the Menat of Hathor."

Bibliography: PM II, p. 431; Petrie, Six Temples, London 1897, pp. 6–7, pl. 23; Borchardt, Statuen und Statuetten (CG) II, p. 152, pl. 108; Ramsès le Grand, no. 14; Le grand pharaon Ramsès II, no: 28. Cf. the Merit-Amon from Akhmim: Yahia S. Al-Masri, in: ASAE 9, 1983, pls. 1–3, pp. 7–10; A. Eggebrecht, Das Alte Ägypten, fig. p. 448.

209

209

Ground floor, room 14

Prince Khaemwas

Yellow sandstone   JE 36720
H. 77 cm; W. 21 cm; profile 42 cm   = CG 42147
Karnak, court of the cachette; cleared by Legrain in 1904
New Kingdom, 19th dynasty, reign of Ramses II, 1290–1224 B.C.

Prince Khaemwas was a son of Ramses II and of the great royal wife Isetnofret. During the first half of Ramses II's reign, when the heir apparent was Amonherkepeshef, born of Queen Nefertari, Khaemwas, the fourth prince in line, pursued a career in the clergy and became high priest of Ptah at Memphis. Khaemwas became an important individual in a number of duties and activities. He carried out reconstructions on the temple of Ptah at Memphis, announced the first five royal jubilees throughout the land, erected several monuments in various Egyptian temples and, concerned about monuments fallen into ruin in the Memphite necropoleis, he became the first actual restorer in Egyptian history. At Sakkara he worked for the extension of the Serapeum and directed the entombment of the Apis bull, sacred to the god Ptah who was worshipped at Memphis. When he died in year 55 of Ramses II, his mummy was doubtless buried at Sakkara.

The prince dedicated this statue to the temple of Amon-Re at Karnak. It represents him kneeling and holding before him a naos of Ptah-Tatenen, god of generative power worshipped in the Memphite and Heliopolitan regions. The deity appears within the naos mummiform and bearded, with a striated wig topped by two feathers set into two horns.

Khaemwas himself is clothed in a *shendjyt*, or royal pleated kilt, and wears a round wig with little curls. A short beard at the chin and a lock of hair terminating in a spiral on the left shoulder (the traditional lock worn by high priests of Ptah) are the attributes of his position. The face is round with somewhat mellow features conforming to the style of official statuary towards the middle of the reign of Ramses II, particularly visible in standard-bearing statues.

The base was set into a pedestal which is lost today. The inscriptions carved on the sides of the naos, the base and the back pillar contain offering formulae to the gods Ptah of Memphis and Ptah-Tatenen, while naming the prince and high priest Khaemwas.

Naophorous statues, deposited in temples since the New Kingdom, placed the donator under the protection of the god represented in the naos. He also hoped to participate in the offerings brought into the temple for the god each day or during festivals.

Bibliography: Legrain, Statues et Statuettes (CG) II, p. 12, pls. 9–10; F. Gomaa, Chaemwese, Sohn Ramses' II. und Hoherpriester von Memphis, Ägyptologische Abhandlungen 27, Wiesbaden 1973, p. 86, no. 61.

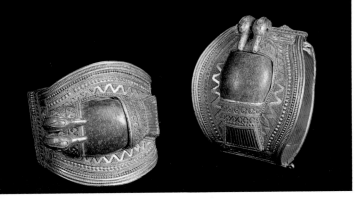

210

Upper floor, room 3

Bracelets of Ramses II

Gold, lapis lazuli   JE 39873
W. 6 cm; max. Diam. 7.2 cm; weight 101 gr   = CG 52575
                                    and 52576
Tell Basta (Bubastis), treasure discovered in 1906 near Zagazig; cleared by the Egyptian Antiquities Service
New Kingdom, 19th dynasty, reign of Ramses II, 1290–1224 B.C.

This magnificent pair of bracelets was accidentally uncovered at Tell Basta during the construction of a railway embankment. It was found together with gold and silver objects, mainly vessels, apparently hidden in a deposit of the temple of Bubastis, now known as the treasure of Zagazig. The objects are divided between the Cairo Museum (see no. 222), the Metropolitan Museum of Art in New York and the Berlin Museum. Some months earlier, a first hoard discovered by the workmen had revealed the beautiful silver vessel (same case) whose handle forms a standing goat.

The solid gold bracelets are articulated. On the upper half, a large piece of lapis lazuli forms the body of a goose whose two heads and large tail are worked in gold and admirably ornamented with filigree and granules. Around the central body are marvelous decorative motifs of plain, beaded or twisted wires. The lower half shows a more restrained design with simply parallel or striated wires.

Between the hinge and the head of the birds is the king's cartouche, worked in repoussé. Beautiful pieces of jewelry, these bracelets were most likely royal gifts.

Bibliography: PM IV, pp. 34–35; Edgar, in: Maspero, Le Musée Egyptien II, p. 106, pl. 54; Vernier, Bijoux et Orfèvreries (CG), p. 388, pl. 83; Aldred, Jewels, pl. 129; Ramsès le Grand, nos. 64–65; Le grand pharaon Ramsès II, no. 23.

211

Ground floor, gallery 9

King Merenptah

Grey granite   JE 31414
H. 91 cm; W. 58 cm   = CG 607
Thebes, mortuary temple of Merenptah; discovered by F. Petrie in 1896
New Kingdom, 19th dynasty, reign of Merenptah, 1224–1214 B.C.

The thirteenth son of Ramses II, Merenptah was already middle-aged when he succeeded his father and ruled for about ten years. Residing like Ramses II at Pi-Ramesse, Merenptah had to dwell temporarily in Memphis to organize the struggle against the invasion of Libyans and Sea Peoples, foes whom he successfully repelled (see no. 212).

This bust derives from a colossal seated statue of Merenptah located in the second court of his mortuary temple at Thebes. Clear traces of polychromy survive on the headdress, the face and the collar. The king wears the *nemes* headdress, whose two lappets fall over the collar ornamenting his neck. On his brow is the protective royal uraeus; at the chin, the false beard, broken today, is held in place by two straps.

This is an idealized portrait which shows the sovereign at a much younger age. It tends to emphasize the personality and power rather than the actual features of the king, who was then probably over fifty years old. The narrow eyes are surmounted by a broad and long cosmetic line, the nose is slim, the mouth firm and straight.

On the shoulders of the statue are carved the king's cartouches: "Lord of the Two Lands Ba-en-rê Mery-Amon" on the right shoulder (coronation name), and "Lord of Diadems Merenptah Hotep-her Maat" on the left (birth name). The back pillar begins the titulary: "King of Upper and Lower Egypt, ruler . . ."

Bibliography: PM II, pp. 448–49; Petrie, Six Temples at Thebes, London 1897, p. 13, pl. 6; Borchardt, Statuen und Statuetten (CG) II, pp. 156–57, pl. 110; Ramsès le Grand, no. 55.

212

Ground floor, room 13

Victory stela of Merenptah, also called "the Israel stela"

Grey granite   JE 31408
H. 318 cm; W. 163 cm; thickness 31 cm   = CG 34025
Thebes, funerary temple of Merenptah; excavated by F. Petrie in 1896
New Kingdom, 19th dynasty, reign of Merenptah, 1224–1214 B.C.

This commemorative monument was erected in the first court of Merenptah's funerary temple at Thebes in order to celebrate his victory in year five against the Libyan coalition which had come to invade Egypt along with the aid of the Sea Peoples. The list of defeated place-names includes at the end of the text the only occurrence of the name Israel known today from Egyptian sources, hence the name Israel stela.

211

The account concludes with a list of vanquished place-names: "Their chiefs prostrate themselves and beg for peace, none among the Nine Bows raises his head any longer. Libya is destroyed, the Hittite empire is at peace, Canaan is devastated, Ashkalon is vanquished, Gezer is taken, Yenoam annihilated, Israel is laid waste, its seed exists no more, Syria is made a widow for Egypt, and all lands have been pacified."

Since no military campaign in Asia is attested under Merenptah, the listing of Palestinian names serves as a reminder that, because Egypt has repulsed the Libyan invasion, it need no longer fear the menace of her neighbors to the east. As for the name of Israel, it is now clear that the reference is not to a country, but to a tribe of the same name; this is indicated by the determinative of men and women grouped behind the name Israel, instead of the sign of the city which traditionally serves to determine place-names. Unless the similarity of the name is pure coincidence, this would be the tribe of Israelites which had already settled in Palestine prior to the reign of Merenptah. Thus Merenptah is no longer considered the pharaoh of the Exodus, first of all because he lived on for at least five years after this victory, and secondly for the simple reason that his well-preserved mummy cannot be that of a king lost in the waters of the Sea. Before being inscribed under the reign of Merenptah, our stela was originally placed in the mortuary temple of Amenophis III at Thebes, from which Merenptah

212

In the lunette, under the winged sun-disk, two scenes appear side by side carved in sunk relief: the king, dressed in ceremonial costume, is received by Amon-Re of Karnak, who offers him the sickle of victory and the scepters of royalty. Behind the king stand, on the left, the goddess Mut, and on the right, the god Khonsu. They each provide the king with the staff of millions of years and the symbol for jubilees. This scene, frequently represented on the walls of the temples at Thebes, serves to place the king under the protection of the triad of Theban deities. The figures and inscriptions are painted yellow, while the jewellery, necklaces, bracelets and anklets, are colored blue.

The twenty-eight lines of inscription which follow below are a metered poetical composition conceived as a hymn to the king in order to glorify his acts of heroism. This epic genre was quite popular in the Ramesside era, the account of the Battle of Kadesh under Ramses II being the most celebrated example. The text of our stela begins with the date of year 5, 3rd day of the 3rd month of summer, under the Majesty of King Merenptah. There follows the proclamation of victory and the eulogy to the king as liberator, who has avenged Memphis, opened its gates, caused its god Tatenen to rejoice in his subjects and the temples to receive their offerings.

During this time, disaster has struck the Libyans. Their vile chieftain, who has fled under cover of the night, alone, without a feather on his head, barefoot, deprived of food and water, is accursed by his own people. His wives and children are captured, the camps of his generals burned. Meanwhile Egypt is celebrating its liberation, and no one fears any more, for the peril has been averted.

213a   213b

removed almost all of the material used in the construction of his own mortuary temple. One the other side of the stela (i. e. the actual recto), one can still see the original decoration in which Amenophis III offers to Amon-Re and describes in a long inscription the splendors of his buildings.

Bibliography: PM II, p. 448; Petrie, Six Temples at Thebes, London 1897, p. 13; Lacau, Stèles du Nouvel Empire (CG), pp. 47–59, pls. 15–19; W. Helck, Die Beziehungen zu Vorderasien im 3. und 2. Jahrtausend vor Christus. Ägyptologische Abhandlungen 5, Wiesbaden 1962, pp. 240–47; Corteggiani, no. 87; H. Sourouzian, in: Le Monde de la Bible 41, Paris, Nov.–Dec. 1985, pp. 35–38, fig. 38.

213   Ground floor, atrium, section 33

Sarcophagus of Merenptah usurped by Psusennes at Tanis (lid)

Pink granite   JE 87297 B
H. 66 cm (lid); 89 cm (coffin); L. 240 cm; W. 120 cm
Tanis, tomb of Psusennes; excavated by P. Montet in 1939–40
New Kingdom, 19th dynasty, reign of Merenptah, 1224–1214 B.C.;
reused during the 21st dynasty, reign of Psusennes, 1054–1004 B.C.

The lid of this sarcophagus (but less likely the body) belonged to King Merenptah. It was usurped by the Tanite king Psusennes, whose tomb in the royal necropolis at Tanis was discovered intact by Montet (see nos. 240–242).
The king's mummiform figure is sculpted in the round on the lid. With hands crossed in the attitude of Osiris and holding crook and flail, he wears a long striated wig and the braided beard of the same god. He lies between two small pillars, one of which serves as a back support for the little figure of a goddess who protects him. Figures of Isis and Nepthys are carved upon the exterior sides of the pillars.
On the buckle of the royal belt one can still read the cartouche of Merenptah; this is the only case where his name was not replaced by that of Psusennes. On the lid's interior, an elegant figure in high raised relief of the sky goddess Nut, with stars covering her entire outstretched body, forms the celestial vault over the mummy. She is accompanied by astral divinities as well as the bark of the Second Hour of the Night.
The body of the sarcophagus (on display to one side) curiously reproduces the archaizing motif of the palace facade with its niches and doorways. The texts are taken from funerary compositions of the New Kingdom, such as the Book of Gates and the Book of the Dead. On the floor are found the objects typically represented in friezes on Middle Kingdom sarcophagi: crowns, ornaments, linen, staves, scepters and weapons are divided into twelve registers. Perhaps we see here an unexpected return to older traditions, or, on the other hand, the body of this sarcophagus may date to the Middle Kingdom – it is well known that most of the monuments at Tanis were reused from earlier sites (see nos. 103–104 and 204–205). The sarcophagus of Takelot II, for example, found in this same necropolis, was likewise decorated with niches, and is certainly a reused piece from the Middle Kingdom. Be that as it may, our sarcophagus, inscribed with the name of Psusennes, contained within it a grey granite anthropoid coffin and a silver mummiform coffin (exhibited in galleries 11 and 16), which housed the mummy. It was lying between a long sheet of gold and a plate of silver. A gold mask and sumptuous jewellery (see no. 249) covered the head and limbs.
At Thebes, however, two centuries earlier in the tomb of Merenptah, the same lid would have formed part of a group of granite sarcophagi placed one within the other; two lids remain in place, as do fragments of an enormous coffin. Our usurped lid would have enclosed the alabaster mummiform coffin, of which only one fragment remains, preserved today in the British Museum.

Bibliography: P. Montet, Psousennès, La Nécropole Royale de Tanis II, Paris 1951, pls. 75–89, pp. 111–18; Lange/Hirmer, pl. 255.

214

214

Funerary procession

Limestone
H. 51 cm; L. 105 cm
Sakkara; found reused in the Serapeum in 1859
New Kingdom, 19th dynasty, ca. 1300–1200 B.C.

JE 4872

This beautifully carved tableau certainly derives from a Ramesside tomb at Sakkara. We have seen that representations of rapid movement and rhythm were the legacy of the Amarna Period, and that they achieved widespread popularity during the following era. At Sakkara an entire region of the necropolis has already revealed several sculpted reliefs in this expressive and animated post-Amarna style.

Here we see a rhythmic dance, as a group of women, accompanied by tambourines, shake their heads and wigs in time with their feet. Beside them two little girls, hair flapping in the breeze, dance frenetically to the noise of their clappers. Together they welcome the cortège which advances with great strides (a similar cortège accompanies the funeral procession in the New Kingdom tombs of Userhet and Ramose at Thebes, of Paheri at El-Kab). One man in front, holding a baton and wearing a short kilt, directs the march along with his companion beside him. Behind these two follow clean-shaven men with long plaited kilts, and at the back of the procession come dignitaries in ostentatious costume. All rejoice with arms upraised. The artist has cleverly and successfully superimposed the forearms of both the central and final groups of men.

Bibliography: PM III, 2, p. 754; Vandier, Manuel IV, p. 444; Terrace/Fischer, no. 33; Ramsès le Grand, no. 25; Nofret – Die Schöne, no. 46.

The door to the tomb of Sennedjem shows hinges still preserved. It is formed of several pieces of wood held together with pegs. It was sealed to protect the chamber in which the members of the family rested: twenty bodies were found, nine of them still enclosed in their coffins.

Funerary scenes adorn the door. The interior side depicts Sennedjem and his wife Iyneferti seated within a pavilion upon lion-footed chairs, with a gaming table before them. A large astragal appears at the foot of the table, while offerings are piled high upon a stand to the right, flanked by vases and lettuces.

Sennedjem and his wife play at *senet*, the game of "passing" through the nether world (see no. 189). Winning this passage was apparently crucial to the survival of the player, as confirmed by a text from the Book of the Dead, divided into eleven columns under the scene.

The exterior side of the door shows two scenes. In the upper scene, Sennedjem, his wife and daughter Irunefer adore Osiris and Maat. In the lower scene, seven sons of Sennedjem pay homage to Ptah-Sokar-Osiris, god of the dead, and to Isis. Between the gods and their worshippers are represented bouquets of flowers and libation vases resting upon little stands. The composition has been executed in a sure and spontaneous fashion. One can note the hand of a master painter especially in the bold rendering of the curled wigs and the fringed garments.

Bibliography: PM I, 1, p. 4; Bruyère, La Tombe No. 1 de Sennedjem, in: MIFAO 88, 1959, pp. 21–23, 52–53, pls. 16–17; Ramsès le Grand, no. 44; Le grand pharaon Ramsès II, no. 45. See also: D. Valbelle, Les Ouvriers de la Tombe, Deir el-Médineh à l'époque Ramesside, Cairo 1985, pp. 287–98.

215

Door to the tomb of Sennedjem (detail)

Stuccoed and painted wood
H. 135 cm; W. 78 cm
Deir el-Medina, tomb of Sennedjem (no. 1); cleared by Maspero in 1886
New Kingdom, 19th dynasty, reign of Ramses II, 1290–1224 B.C.

JE 27303

The tombs of the artisans responsible for excavating and decorating the royal tombs were cut in the Theban mountain, at the foot of which lay their village, today called Deir el-Medina. The tombs were provided with superstructures in the form of a pyramidal chapel, occasionally preceded by a pylon, and substructures with chambers housing the mummy and funerary equipment of the deceased.

Most of these chambers are decorated with paintings in vibrant colors. Anyone who has visited the tomb of Sennedjem cannot easily forget the extraordinary freshness of the colors preserved intact on the walls for more than three millennia.

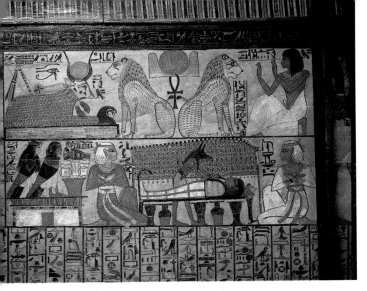

Funeral sledge of Khonsu

Wood, stuccoed, painted and varnished   JE 27302
H. 125 cm; L. 262 cm; W. 98 cm
Deir el-Medina, tomb of Sennedjem (no. 1); cleared by Maspero in 1886
New Kingdom, 19th dynasty, reign of Ramses II, 1290–1224 B.C.

Among the mummies found in the tomb of Sennedjem were those of his son Khonsu and his daughter-in-law Tamaket. Like his father, Khonsu was "servant in the Place of Truth," a title borne by the inhabitants of Deir el-Medina.

The two anthropoid coffins which preserved, one within the other, the body of Khonsu are now in the Metropolitan Museum of Art, New York. The sarcophagus shown here, furnished with a curved lid, imitates the roof of a naos with cavetto cornice. Mounted on a sledge which allowed it to be dragged along, the sarcophagus served to transport the body during the funeral. After reaching the tomb, it was dismantled and placed in a corner in similar fashion to the sarcophagus of Sennedjem.

The sarcophagus is one of the best decorated of its kind; paintings of rare beauty accompany the texts of exquisitely multicolored hieroglyphs. On the long sides, the texts and representations are taken from the Book of the Dead and concern all that the deceased had to know to become one of the blessed in the next world. Ibis-headed deities alternating with the four sons of Horus frame the text of Chapter 17 of this Book. On the small sides, elegant goddesses, arranged two by two, protect the deceased's head (Selket and Neith) and feet (Isis and Nepthys).

The vignette of Chapter 17 is the most beautiful of the lot. In the upper register, two lions with bushy manes support the sun disk nestled in the horizon, from which hangs the sign for life. The scene symbolizes the passage from "yesterday" to "tomorrow." It is placed in the middle of an adoration scene: to the right of the sun disk Khonsu kneels, with upraised arms, worshipping Re-Horakhty, who appears to the left in the form of a falcon. The god exits out of the primordial waters born by the celestial cow Mehet-weret, "the great flood." In the lower register the god Anubis embalms Khonsu's body, which lies on a leonine couch under a dais with multicolored hangings. On either side, Isis dressed in red, and Nepthys dressed in white keep watch over the body (illustrated).

Standing upon the roof of their tomb, to the left, the *Bas* (spirits) of Khonsu and Tamaket, with human heads and feet attached to bird's bodies, enjoy the offerings of flowers and bread placed before them.

The colors are extremely fresh, the design simple but expressive. The touching beauty of the profiles with large, serene eyes, the elegant costumes and finery, and the harmonious mixture of men, gods and spirits render this panel an admirable work of art.

Additional vignettes from Chapter 17 continue on the opposite side. In the upper register, two crouching genii and two Nile gods make allusion to the annual inundation of the river, the one by placing his hands over two basins filled with water, and the other by holding the staff of millions of years and the eye of the falcon. The lower register (illustrated) shows on one side the adoration of the celestial cow by Khonsu, and on the other, the famous game of "Senet." While the deceased plays out his survival in the nether world, his wife observes his success, the rich bouquets behind her symbolic of vital and regenerative forces.

Bibliography: PM I, 1, p. 5; Ramsès le Grand, no. 45; Le grand pharaon Ramsès II, no. 48.

217
Upper floor, room 17
Shawabti box of Khonsu

Wood, stuccoed and painted   JE 27299
H. 35.6 cm; L. 20 cm; W. 12.5 cm
Deir el-Medina, tomb of Sennedjem (no. 1); cleared by Maspero in 1886
New Kingdom, 19th dynasty, reign of Ramses II, 1290–1224 B.C.

The shawabti box takes the form of a Lower Egyptian double shrine, in which the barrel-vaults rise between high lateral walls. It was once mounted on a sledge like the other boxes from this tomb. A system of knobs served to hold the string which tied the box shut.

On one of the walls, Khonsu and his wife are depicted seated side by side dressed in contemporary costume, adorned with long wigs. They seem to take part in a repast. The other wall (illustrated) shows the purification ritual of Khonsu's mummy, carefully wrapped and covered with a funerary mask surmounted by an unguent cone. The priest officiant is his son, Nakht-Mut, dressed in elegant costume.

The mummy of Khonsu appears again on the lateral sides of the box, accompanied by his names and title: "servitor in the Place of Truth."

Bibliography: PM I, 1, p. 5; cf. Hayes, The Scepter of Egypt II, figs. 273–74.

218
Upper floor, room 17
Lid of the coffin of Isis

Wood, stuccoed and painted
       JE 27309
L. 193.5 cm; W. 47 cm; H. 31.8 cm
Deir el-Medina, tomb of Sennedjem (no. 1); cleared by Maspero in 1886
New Kingdom, 19th dynasty, reign of Ramses II, ca. 1290–1224 B.C.

The lady Isis was perhaps one of the wives of a son of Sennedjem, Khabekhnet, who was the owner of tomb no. 2 at Deir el-Medina. Nevertheless, Isis was buried in Sennedjem's tomb (cf. no. 215). Enclosed within this graceful painted coffin, where it was held by means of a wooden framework, the mummified body of this lady was wrapped in a mat of reeds. Her head was surrounded by a mask with a breast panel which in turn contained a second, flatter mask.

The coffin is an assemblage of wooden planks covered with cloth coated with stucco. Over this the painting was applied. The lid of the coffin fit into its body by means of tenons. The lid reproduces the image of its owner, prepared for eternity in the pose of the living. She is a beautiful, slender figure, displaying youthful freshness and rich jewellery. She coquettishly holds a clump of liana which gracefully fall down along her body. Her long pleated tunic is bordered by a fringe and tied under the breast. A heavy wig with fine tresses is tied with a large diadem, whose front is decorated with a lotus blossom. Rings and buttons are affixed to the tresses which cover the ears. A magnificent *wesekh* collar masks the

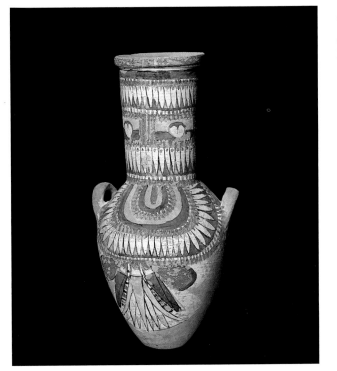

219

219

Jar with painted decoration

Painted terra cotta
H. 33.2 cm
Deir el Medina, tomb of Sennedjem (no. 1); cleared by Maspero in 1886
New Kingdom, 19th dynasty, reign of Ramses II, ca. 1290–1224 B.C.

JE 27216

Painted pottery enjoyed a wide popularity during the Nineteenth Dynasty. This oviform example with very tall neck, two handles, protruding lip and rounded bottom is decorated only on one side. The painting imitates, for funerary uses, the floral arrangements with which such vessels were ornamented during festivals. A veritable floral collar thus hangs over the "breast" of this jar alternating in garlands of petals and leaves. A large lotus flower flanked by buds and poppies hangs below the collar. On the neck between the rows of flower petals, mandrakes are shown.
The painted design, in red ochre, dark green, light green and white, has been added hastily onto a layer of pale slip. The effect is vibrant and spontaneous, and the variegated bands enliven the decoration.

Bibliography: Propyläen Kunstgeschichte 15, pl. XLVIIb; Le grand pharaon Ramsès II, no. 42. Cf. M. Bell, in: Bulletin de Liaison du groupe international d'étude de la céramique égyptienne X, Cairo 1985, pp. 50–55.

220

Ostracon with the beginning of the story of Sinuhe

Limestone, inscribed with red and black ink
H. 21 cm; L. 106.5 cm
Deir el-Medina, tomb of Sennedjem (no. 1), 1886
New Kingdom, 19th dynasty, reign of Ramses II, 1290–1224 B.C.

JE 27419
= CG 25216

From the Old Kingdom onward, those who could not afford costly papyrus made use of pottery sherds and limestone flakes, known as ostraca, for all manner of designs and

entire breast; the bosom, shaped in relief, is decorated with rosettes. Charming bracelets, chains, rings and bands ornament all the limbs of this graceful lady.

Bibliography: PM I, 1, p. 5; Ramsès le Grand, no. 37; Götter Pharaonen, no. 59; Le grand pharaon Ramsès II, no. 35.

220

inscriptions. In the Theban necropolis alone, particularly in the workmen's village of Deir el-Medina, ostraca turn up by the thousands, dating to the New Kingdom. They contain sketches, free drawings in which the artist could experiment outside of the official canon, or inscriptions in cursive Egyptian (hieratic) concerning daily life and business, letters, accounts, lists of workmen, accusations, but also copies of literary works. The majority of the latter are scribal students' exercises.

One of the literary pieces most preferred and most often copied was the tale of the adventures of Sinuhe. This is a work which was originally penned in the Middle Kingdom, towards the end of the reign of Sesostris I, and which is preserved for us in numerous papyri and ostraca of the New Kingdom. In the form of a historical autobiography, it recounts the story of an Egyptian official who accidentally learns of the death (which is quite likely an assassination) of his sovereign Amenemhat I, while the crown prince (Sesostris I) is on campaign in Libya. Seized with fear and considering himself threatened by the knowledge of such a state secret, Sinuhe flees, crosses the Delta, clears the eastern border and reaches the desert. He is first assailed, but later helped by Bedouin. "City gave unto city," and Sinuhe was received with kindness in Asia by a prince of Upper Retenu, before whom he praises the new king of Egypt. He marries the prince's eldest daughter, is promoted to chief of a tribe, and enjoys long and prosperous years in the lands which have been granted him. A champion from Syria then comes to provoke our hero into single combat. Sinuhe returns the challenge and the duel commences, culminating in the defeat of the Syrian.

Successful but nostalgic with age, Sinuhe hopes to return to Egypt. In response to his appeal to the Egyptian king, a royal messenger comes to announce that all is forgiven and Sinuhe might return home.

There follows the return to his country. His arrival at the palace is spectacular: Sinuhe is received by the princes in front of a portal lined with sphinxes. He traverses a court with a portico and reaches the golden hall in which the king awaits him. Awestruck by all the splendor, Sinuhe falls to the ground and loses consciousness. The king addresses him kindly, and the queen and her children welcome him. He is then brought to one of the princes' houses. In the bath, he is shaved, clothed in fine linen and anointed with precious oils. Finally, Sinuhe receives a beautiful dwelling, and the king grants him a tomb of stone, for nothing was as despicable for an Egyptian as being buried far from one's own country.

It is the beginning of this fabulous tale, rich in stylistic variation, which is written in beautiful hieratic script on this ostracon (one of the largest known). Sennedjem took it with him to his tomb, much as one takes along a favorite story for a long voyage.

Bibliography: Daressy, Ostraca (CG), pp. 46−47, pl. 41. Cf. also: LÄ V, 950−55. Translations (a selection): G. Lefèbvre, Romans et contes Egyptiens de l'époque pharaonique, 1949; E. Hornung, Meisterwerke Altägyptischer Dichtung, 1978, pp. 23−38; W. K. Simpson, The Literature of Ancient Egypt, New Haven/London 1972.

221   Ground floor, gallery 15

Small stela with ears

Painted limestone   JE 43566
H. 24.5 cm; W. 14 cm
Deir el-Medina. Found by Baraize in the temenos of the temple of Hathor in 1912
New Kingdom, Ramesside period, 19th−20th dynasties, about 1200 B.C.

This round-topped stela whose decoration is both sculptured and painted is dedicated to the "Good Ram" of Amon by Baï, an inhabitant of the ancient village of Deir el Medina called "The Place of Truth".

In the upper part of the stela the god is twice depicted in the form of a ram wearing the high feathers of Amon. The two animals are standing facing each other on either side of a low stand, on which is placed a ewer. Above them are two symmetrical inscriptions identifying them as "Amon-Re, the Good Ram".

The register below is divided into two parts by a vertical line. On one side are three pairs of ears painted dark blue, light yellow and green respectively. On the opposite side the dedicator, Baï, in a pleated kilt, a curled wig and a wide collar is kneeling. The inscription above his figure pronounces "The adoration of Amon-Re by his servant in the Place of Truth, Baï". Stelae "with ears" belong to a category of votive objects which private persons dedicated to a particular form of the divinity worshipped namely "He who listens to prayer". During the New Kingdom personal devotion having brought the individual and his gods closer together, the former manages to attract the attention of the latter in a number of ways of which that making use of the device of the "hearing ear" is one of the most original and ingenious. "The god who listens comes to him who calls, splendid of mien, rich in ears", chants one hymn. He is invoked through the medium of an ear, a pair of ears, or more frequently of several pairs of ears; there exist stelae on which are depicted several hundred.

Stelae with ears appear in all those places where the popular religion has recognized a "god who listens to prayers". Thus at Memphis "Ptah who listens to prayers" is a god of the common people as is "Amon who listens to supplications" at the doors of the temple of Karnak. Ptah received innumerable "ear" stelae and in the Theban necropolis Amon, Horus, Queen Ahmose Nefertari and the deified Ramses II are called upon in the same way.

By whispering directly into his ear, the suppliant, according to his needs could implore the god for grace, ask him for a favour or thank him for a prayer granted.

Bibliography: PM I, 2, pp. 698–99; Bruyère, in: ASAE 25, 1925, pp. 82–83, pl. II, 1. Cf. also: LÄ IV, 562–66.

222

Vase   Upper floor, room 3

Gold   JE 38706 and JE 39870
H. 11.2 cm; max. Diam. 8.3 cm; weight 209 gr   = CG 53261
Tell Basta (Bubastis); treasure discovered in 1906 near Zagazig
New Kingdom, end of the 19ᵗʰ dynasty, ca. 1200 B.C.

This vase is one of the best pieces of the Zagazig treasure (see also no. 210), discovered under a heap of debris near the temple of ancient Bubastis. Along with a similar vase in gold and another in silver, whose handle forms a standing goat, this object may be termed a luxury vessel. The rounded body displays a hammered decoration consisting of grains arranged in regular rows which imitate those of an ear of corn. The cylindrical neck with rounded lip is decorated with incised floral motifs, laid out in four rows each separated by two lines; they represent (from top to bottom): a series of lanceolate leaves, a frieze of flaring lotus blossoms hanging between clusters and dotted rosettes, a row of rosettes and finally a garland of umbels turned upside down.

The handle is a movable ring whose upper part is wound with wires extending from the ring's two ends. The ring passes through the body of a recumbent calf upon a small bar which is riveted under the rim of the vessel. The edges of the bar flare out in the form of palmettes.

Bibliography: PM IV, p. 34–35; Edgar, in: Maspero, Le Musée Egyptien II, pl. 45; p. 100–01; Vernier, Bijoux et Orfèvreries, p. 415–16, pl. 104; I. Woldering, Ägypten (Kunst der Welt), Baden-Baden 1964, p. 187.

223   Earrings of Seti II   Upper floor, room 3

Gold   JE 39675
H. 13.5 cm   = CG 52397 and CG 52398
Thebes, Valley of the Kings, cachette of objects found by Davis in 1908
New Kingdom, 19ᵗʰ dynasty, reign of Seti II, about 1210–1204 B.C.

Earrings, rarely attested before the New Kingdom, make their appearance during the 18th dynasty. Men, women, young girls and children of both sexes wear such ornaments in the form of rings, disks, studs or multiple pendants. They are made of glass, faience or the less precious metals, stone or

shell. Kings and queens naturally possessed very elaborate specimens.

Earrings were worn both by the living and the dead; they are found on mummies or among the jewels included in the funerary equipment. The mummy of Tuthmosis IV is the earliest known to have pierced ears; several pairs of earrings were found among Tutankhamon's possessions.

We have already seen the statuette of Tama (no. 154) wearing an earring, the Amarna princesses adorned with such jewels and trifling with pendants (no. 167). Akhenaten himself is responsible for introducing the pierced ear in royal statuary thus suggesting the widespread use of these ornaments (nos. 159 and 163). Queen Nefertari's magnificent earrings painted in her tomb at Thebes are in the form of erect serpents; the "Queen with the *menat*" has convex studs (no. 208) and Seti II owned this impressive pair of gold pendants.

They were found with other precious objects marked with the name of Seti II and of his wife Tauseret in an anonymous tomb which had probably served as a hiding place for the thieves who pillaged the tombs of the royal couple. The two pendants are identical, each formed of three articulated parts. From the flat trapezoidal center piece on which are engraved the names of Seti II hang seven pendants in the form of cornflowers with long stems attached to the trapezoid by means of small rings. The main part of the earring from which this pendant hangs on two thick rings, is formed of a concave corolla with eight petals and a stud connected by two hollow tubes which screw together to hold the earring in place in the pierced earlobe. The name of Seti II is repeated on each of these two parts.

Bibliography: PM I, 2, p. 567; Vernier, Bijoux et Orfèvreries (CG), pp. 137−38, p. 28; Aldred, Jewels, pl. 130; Ramsès le Grand, no. 66; Götter Pharaonen, no. 60; Le grand pharaon Ramsès II, no. 24. Cf. also LÄ IV, 566−67.

224

224
Upper floor, gallery 49
Queen Tauseret's foundation deposit

Faience, copper, wood   JE 31431
Max. L. 10 cm   CG 16004 to 16121 (passim)
Thebes, funerary temple of Tauseret. Excavations of Petrie in 1896
New Kingdom, 19th dynasty, reign of Tauseret, about 1200 B.C.

A foundation deposit is a group of objects taken from the material of daily life or especially made as miniature models, which were placed in or under the foundations of a religious or funerary construction before work began on the superstructure. Specially dug pits were made to hold the deposits at the four corners of the edifice, under the doorways, etc.

Foundation deposits are known from as early as the 1st dynasty and the custom continued to be in use until the Late Period. Late temples display on the walls of their court or hypostyle hall relief scenes illustrating the ceremonies accompanying the foundation of a temple among which we see the King bringing a table laden with specimens of stone which are to be deposited under the foundations. Besides real bricks with impressed inscriptions in the name of the founder, we discover in these deposits: miniature bricks of gold, stone or faience inscribed with the royal name, food and floral offerings, specimens of tools such as axes, saws, adzes, chisels and borers; scepters, lengths of material (usually linen) and an abundance of pottery for libations and censing are also present.

These objects, chosen from among those found by Petrie scattered under the foundations of Queen Tauseret's destroyed funerary temple, together with a sandstone block bearing her name, a stamped brick, pottery and animal offerings, illustrate the kind of material contained in such deposits. We note the model legs of beef, floral amulets, heads of bulls and calves, a plaque of blue faience bearing Tauseret's name and another of white faience, a scarab, a white plaque on which are depicted three trussed fowl, bound headless oxen, a fish and various copper implements, among them one with a wooden handle. A foundation deposit thus includes offerings, tools and construction materials. Theoretically they are always royal offerings and serve either to mark the building as the property of the founder (in the case of a royal monument) or as a dedication (consecration of a temple to a divinity). It is also supposed that they may have had a prophylactic function.

Bibliography: PM II, p. 447; Petrie, Six Temples at Thebes, London 1897, pp. 14−15, pls. 16−17. Cf. also Ramsès le Grand, no. 8; LÄ II, 906−912; J. M. Weinstein, Foundation Deposits in Ancient Egypt, Pennsylvania 1973; S. Abd el-Azim el Adly, Das Gründungs- und Weiheritual des Ägyptischen Tempels von der frühgeschichtlichen Zeit bis zum Ende des Neuen Reiches, Tübingen 1981, pp. 285−87; M. Azim, in: Cahiers de Karnak VII, Paris 1982, pp. 93−117. CG unpublished.

Ramses III as a standard-bearer of Amon

Grey granite   JE 38682
H. 140 cm   = CG 42150
Karnak, court of the cachette; cleared by Legrain in 1905
New Kingdom, 20th dynasty, reign of Ramses III, c. 1193–1162 B.C.

Ramses III was the son of Setnakht, founder of the Twentieth Dynasty. Nevertheless, it was Ramses II whom he considered as his spiritual father, and whom he strove to imitate. He claimed the same coronation name for his own, resided at Pi-Ramesse, gave important donations to the temples and institutions of the country, and personally dedicated several temples, of which the most impressive is his mortuary temple at Thebes. His most important political accomplishment lay in his victory against the Sea Peoples, whom he repulsed at the Egyptian border. But contrary to his illustrious predecessor, Ramses II, he fell victim to a palace conspiracy.

The statue which he dedicated to the temple of Amon-Re at Karnak represents him in the traditional striding pose, the standard of Amon topped with a ram's head held against his side. The king is beardless and wears a wig with twisted locks. The ceremonial kilt is of the type frequently worn by New Kingdom pharaohs. His starched central tab flanked by streamers and adorned with gold ornament, is dominated by the head of a leopard. On the left side of the statue we see the representation of the heir prince, dressed in ceremonial costume and holding a fan.

The king's cartouches are carved on the shoulder and on the belt buckle. The royal titulary appears on the staff of the standard and on the back pillar: Ramses is called "beloved of Amon-Re of Karnak."

The physiognomy represents a young sovereign. The face conforms to the final stage of a Ramesside canon which will henceforth degenerate until the collapse of the New Kingdom. Royal statues bearing standards of deities were associated with the festivals which were celebrated in the temples. During this time the sacred bark and emblems of the god partook in a procession. The king, who was meant to direct the festival in person, eternalized the moment by means of these standard-bearing statues, placed at the entrance of temples. This type of statue is attested since the time of Tuthmosis IV, and found wide use in the 19th dynasty. However, the attitude is known from the Middle Kingdom, with the statue of Amenemhat III, holding scepters (see no. 103).

Bibliography: PM II, p. 142; Legrain, Statues et Statuettes II (CG), no. 42150; pp. 15–16, pl. 13; Corteggiani, no. 89; C. Chadefaud, Les statues porte-enseignes de l'Égypte ancienne, Paris 1982, p. 66. Cf. also: H. Satzinger, Der Heilige Stab als Kraftquelle des Königs, in: Jahrbuch der kunsthistorischen Sammlungen in Wien 77, 1981, pp. 9–43.

some adversary of Egypt since the time of Akhenaten. A peace treaty was signed between the two powers in year 21 of Ramses II following the Battle of Kadesh in year 5.

The second figure is a Bedouin Shasu from Syria with wrists held fast in a handcuff. His characteristic appearance consists of a small beard which connects to his moustache, a ribbed cap with plain headband, composite dress made of a kilt, tunic and a Syrian robe, as well as a circular pendant. The Shasu are attested since the Eighteenth Dynasty and appear in great numbers in the reliefs of Ramesside temples. They were semi-nomadic Bedouin, an important part of the population of Syria and Palestine.

The central captive, with elbows bound up at shoulder height, is the traditional Asiatic, specifically a Syrian prince, recognizable by his sharp beard terminating in two points along the cheek, and the thick mass of black hair. A dark skull-cap with two tassels is held in place by a long fillet with black polka dots. A cape is wrapped around his robe.

The fourth prisoner is a Nubian with kinky red hair. He wears a decorated collar and a short kilt over a long plaited robe with dotted fringe and belt. The fifth and final captive, to the left, is a tattooed Libyan with hands bound in front of his body. He is immediately recognizable by his fringed hairstyle with side-lock, and his pointed beard. He wears a long, close-fitting decorated garment over a kilt with a gridwork design. Tied around the necks of all five prisoners are ropes which terminate in either papyrus umbels or lily blossoms.

To complete the list of pharaoh's enemies, we might mention the (missing) "Sea Peoples" whom Ramses III successfully repulsed, and who may be seen in the reliefs on the walls of the palace and temple of Medinet Habu.

On the other side of these tiles, which were produced en masse, are found the incised impressions of manufacturers' marks, similar to those on the faience tiles of King Djoser. They were set into walls by means of mortar which filled the spaces created by small planks of wood.

Bibliography: PM II, p. 524; G. Daressy, in: ASAE 11, 1911, pp. 49–63, pls. 3–4; U. Hölscher/R. Anthes, in: The Excavation of Medinet Habu IV, Oriental Institute Publications LV, pp. 39–46, pls. V and 31, 32; Propyläen Kunstgeschichte 15, pl. LI; R. Giveon, Les Bédouins Shosou des documents égyptiens, Leyden 1971, pl. 13, 1. Cf. J. Osing, in: MDAIK 37, 1981, pp. 389–91, pl. 60.

226

Upper floor, room 39

Tiles of faience with prisoners

Polychrome faience JE 36457 (a, b, d, h)
Max. H. 26 cm; max. W. 7 cm and RT 12.3.24.13
Thebes, Medinet Habu, palace of the mortuary temple of Ramses III; cleared by the Egyptian Antiquities Service in 1910; excavated and restored by the Oriental Institute, University of Chicago in 1927–1933
New Kingdom, 20th dynasty, reign of Ramses III, c. 1193–1162 B.C.

The inlaying of pieces for the decoration of the palace, a common practice at Amarna, continued under the Ramessides. From the Delta to Memphis to Thebes, both residential and ritual (ceremonial) palaces glittered with polychrome faience inlaid into walls, doorframes and columns. Among the favorite subjects chosen were cartouches, floral friezes, *rekhyt*-birds (see the adjacent cases) and numerous bound prisoners.

We have seen that, according to pharaonic dogma, the traditional fate of enemies was always to be represented subjugated by the king of Egypt. Thus bound prisoners are to be found wherever pharaoh appears, and Ramses III's monuments were no exception. Here is a selection of five captives, representing peoples involved in the political world of the New Kingdom, which come from doors and from the window of appearances of Ramses III's ceremonial palace, opening out onto the first court of his funerary temple at Medinet Habu.

The first captive to the right is a Hittite with pale skin, hands tied behind his back, and a striped skull-cap with a dotted rim. He wears a colorful short kilt and a garment tied at the shoulder. Khatti, the Hittite empire in Asia Minor, was a fear-

227

Ground floor, room 14
▷

Ramses IV triumphant

Grey granite JE 37175
H. 104 cm; W. 24.5 cm; L. 43 cm = CG 42152
Karnak, court of the cachette, cleared by G. Legrain in 1904
New Kingdom, 20th dynasty, reign of Ramses VI, ca. 1142 B.C.

227

with its wings, much as it protected Chephren long ago (see no. 31), who was himself identified with the god.

The prisoner, a Libyan chieftain with tortured expression, has hands bound behind him, and a body bent over almost to a right angle. He wears a fringed, striated wig, a side-lock which falls over the right cheek, earrings and a beard (now broken). A long skirt covers part of his body, leaving the left leg free and revealing the penis sheath traditionally worn by Libyans. Between his legs strides pharaoh's lion, included at his master's side in many a hunting and battle scene. The royal titulary winds around the statue's base and back pillar.

The piece lends the sovereign a very stylized portrait, in contrast to the realistically rendered face of the captive. Ramses IV donated the statue to the temple of Amon-Re at Karnak, where it was discovered among the thousands of monuments buried in the court of the cachette (see nos. 105, 133, 201, 225).

Bibliography: PM II, p. 142; Legrain, Statues et Statuettes (CG), II, pp. 17–18, pl. 15; Propyläen Kunstgeschichte 15, pl. 207; Leclant, Les Pharaons II, fig. 182.

228   Ground floor, gallery 15

Ramses VII and Amon

Black basalt   JE 37595
H. 38 cm
Karnak. Purchased at Luxor in 1904
New Kingdom, 20th dynasty, reign of Ramses VII, c. 1130 B.C.

The eight successors of Ramses III, all descended from him, are all named Ramses and one wonders whether the name of their illustrious ancestor had not become a sort of title. It is also because of this repetition of the name that we have come to call the 19th and 20th dynasties the "Ramesside period".

The last sovreigns of this line succeed each other without leaving us much information about the events of their reigns. We get a glimpse of palace intrigues, social unrest, strikes and other difficulties which disturbed this period from the ostraca and papyri found at Deir el-Medina. There we are witnesses to the decline of Egyptian influence parallel to the enfeeblement of the central authority of the state. Few great building projects are inaugurated. At Karnak, work is limited to the construction of the temple of Khonsu. On the west bank of Thebes funerary temples remain unfinished in spite (or perhaps because) of the ambitious scope of their initial projects. On the other hand, the cutting of the tombs in the Valley of the Kings continued with some splendid results. Thus the tomb of Ramses VI was considered to be the most beautiful of all the royal tombs by visitors of the Ptolemaic period who called it the "tomb of Memnon". Nevertheless, the necropolis was already being pillaged in the time of Ramses IX.

The reigns of these Kings are of very unequal length, some being very short. Ramses VII, although he prayed to the god

New Kingdom statuary is rich in subject matter which was previously depicted only in painting or relief sculpture. Here is a three-dimensional reproduction of a very ancient theme: the triumphant king subjugating a prostrated captive.

One dynasty earlier, under Merenptah, a similar statue was carved, showing the king in the process of striking a foe (on display on the ground floor, gallery 15).

The triumphant Ramses stands with pet lion at his feet, an axe in one hand, and the scalp of a Libyan prisoner in the other (despite the fact that the Egyptian empire was disintegrating during his reign). He appears in the same costume as is found in ritual scenes on temple walls for purposes of dedicating offerings before a god; ceremonial beard, official *shendjyt* kilt, sandals, and a coiffure consisting of a round *ibes*-wig with small curls, and a fillet band with frontal uraeus. On top of his head is the Atef crown with ribbed central bundle, two ostrich feathers and double horns.

Walking around the statue, we see the now headless Horus falcon behind the royal crown. The falcon protects the king

228

a god, a position which permits him to participate in the offerings and prayers addressed to the deity in his temple.

On the left side of the statue, there remains half of a cartouche of Ramses VII hastily engraved and on the back pillar, one can discern the beginning of his titulature.

Bibliography: Leclant, Les Pharaons II, fig. 184. For the king's titulature see: K. A. Kitchen, Ramesside Inscriptions VI, Oxford 1983, p. 385 D.

229   Ground floor, gallery 9
Delegation of Officials

Painted sandstone   RT 14.6.24.20
H. 102 cm; W. 117 cm
Thebes, Assassif
New Kingdom, 20th dynasty, 1196–1080 B.C.

These two fragments formed part of a sandstone wall decorated in sunk relief with a processional scene. We see divided into two registers, of which the upper one is only partly preserved, numerous priests with shaven heads and long garments supported by shoulder-straps, and functionaries sporting lengthy wigs and wearing elaborate robes with flared sleeves. Each one carries the insignia of his position: fan, scepter, baton, palette, or papyrus roll.

Of the file of offering bearers who once followed the dignitaries there remains only one at the extreme left; he carries a stand laden with vessels and jewelry. Surviving colors are few, but black-painted areas, as well as traces of ochre and white, are still visible. The style conforms to that of typical Ramesside relief, with elongated physiognomy. The subject at hand concerns the rendering of both homage and tribute to the sovereign, a theme found in countless tombs in the Theban necropolis since the Eighteenth Dynasty.

Bibliography: PM I, 2, p. 627; Ramsès le Grand, no. 24; Le grand pharaon Ramsès II, no. 10.

Osiris at Abydos (stela in the Berlin Museum) asking for a long and prosperous reign, was not granted his wish any more than was his ancestor Ramses IV in the same circumstances. Large size sculpture was on the decline. The few statues which remain demonstrate that the great era of creativity had come to an end. This statuette of Ramses VII is of hasty workmanship and without vigor. The face is heavy, the expression troubled and devoid of interior strength. The wig, composed of parallel strains which form a kind of visor over the brow adorned with the uraeus, and fall in unusually long locks onto the collar bones (which are not marked) is a vestige of a 19th dynasty style. The widely pleated kilt is ornamented with a heavy front panel. The figurine of Amon, roughly hewn, is of poor workmanship. The god holds the *was* sceptre in his left hand and in his right the sign of life. His high headdress is only just recognizable and the pleats of his kilt have not been marked.

Even the type of statue is not new. From the New Kingdom down to the Late Period private statuary made a wide use of this formula where the dedicator is depicted behind a statue of

Praying scribe

Limestone   CG 25029
H. 44 cm; W. 33 cm
Thebes, Valley of the Kings, Tomb of Ramses VI (no. 9)
New Kingdom, 20th dynasty, reign of Ramses IV, c. 1142 B.C.

This limestone plaque is decorated on both sides with drawings and inscriptions in the name of the scribe Amenhotep. The red ochre sketch was redrawn in its final form in black. On the face of the ostracon here visible, the scribe Amenhotep is represented kneeling, with shaven head, wearing a wide kilt with a scalloped front panel. The torso is bare, the stomach is marked by opulent folds and two small folds underline the navel. He raises his graceful hands in a gesture of invocation to Thoth, the god of learning and the patron of scribes. May the god teach him to master himself and to succeed in the ways of the god, that is to say, to become a good scribe. The prayer is written all around the kneeling figure in a cursive hieroglyphic script.
The god whom he invokes replies on the verso of the ostracon where he is represented seated in the company of Seshat, the goddess of writing.

Ostracon with royal head

Fragment of limestone, painted   CG 25144
H. 42 cm; W. 31 cm
Thebes, Valley of the Kings, tomb of Ramses VI (no. 9)
New Kingdom, 20th dynasty, reign of Ramses VI, c. 1142 B.C.

Figured ostraca, very often displaying simple sketches or student's trial pieces, have the advantage of preserving for us the first draft of the artist's design.
Here an artist has traced with his brush on a fragment of limestone the first sketch of a royal portrait in yellow ochre, later corrected in a diluted red ochre. The final drawing was retraced with strokes of carbon black, while the fold of the eyelid and the lips are emphasized in bright red and the planes around the eye, the cheek and the chin are covered with a pale ochre wash.
Despite the breaks in the limestone fragment, the royal profile is perfectly clear. The King wears the *Khepresh* crown decorated with the coiled body of the uraeus which before it was broken off raised its head above the lower edge of the crown. A second serpent, skilfully drawn, adorns the tabs characteristic of this crown, flanked by two horns. The remains of an inscription which no doubt preceded the name of the King, describes him as "Beloved of Osiris".

Bibliography: Daressy, Ostraca (CG), p. 29 and pl. 29; W. H. Peck/J. Ross, Drawings from Ancient Egypt, pl. I.

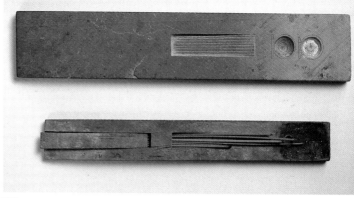

233

Bibliography: Daressy, Ostraca (CG), p. 7 and pl. VI; Propyläen Kunstgeschichte 15, pl. 329; Peck/Ross, Drawings from Ancient Egypt, fig. 49.

232
Upper floor, room 29

Illustrations

Papyrus
JE 31199
L. 55 cm; W. 13 cm
Purchased at Tuna in 1895
New Kingdom, 20th dynasty(?), ca. 1100 B.C.

Two illustrations appear on this fragment of papyrus: lady mouse served by cats, and foxes acting as shepherds.
Drawings in which animals replace humans are often found on papyri and ostraca. Either they illustrate stories, fables or adages, and can even be related to Arab proverbs such as "His protector is his thief," or, they depict parodies intended by role reversal in the animal kingdom to show a topsy-turvy world. In this case they confirm certain social criticisms apparent during troubled times in the literary and artistic milieu.
Our drawings could thus signify that the time has come for the wealthy to serve the humble, or perhaps that the servants serve their masters only to devour them later.
Whatever the correct explanation may be, the drawing is quite amusing. At left we see a cat serving lady mouse who is perched up high upon a stool and dressed in an elegant robe, with a cup in her hand, while another cat adjusts her coiffure. A third cat nurses a baby mouse, while a fourth carries a fan and a vessel. To the right are two foxes acting as shepherds and guarding a recumbent cow or ox. One bears a yoke with two jugs, one of which has been removed by the other fox in order to give the cow a drink.

Bibliography: Smith, Art and Architecture, p. 382–83, fig. 380; Terrace/Fischer, Treasures, no. 34; E. Brunner-Traut, Altägyptische Tiergeschichte und Fabel, Darmstadt 1973, p. 7, 23–29, ill. 3; Corteggiani, no. 88.

233
Upper floor, room 29

Scribes' Palettes

1) Wood
JE 32745
L. 27.6 cm; W. 3.6 cm; thickness 0.8 cm
= CG 69008
Saqqara, found in 1898 by V. Loret
New Kingdom

2) Schist
JE 35762
L. 32.3 cm; W. 6.2 cm; thickness 0.6 cm
= CG 69033
Tell Ruba, found in 1902
New Kingdom or later

Since the birth of writing, the scribe has always been occupied with official documents; he fixes and collects taxes, and keeps track of the accounts; he boasts of "directing everyone's activities", and can be proud of having recorded for the future the literary works of his fellowmen. But for all this, his equipment is of the simplest: reed pens for writing contained in a small case, and two cups for red and black ink; or else a palette combining two hollows for the ink with a slot for the pens. Here are two palettes: the wooden one is a genuine palette showing signs of wear from long usage. Traces of the colors which formerly filled the hollows are still visible and the reed

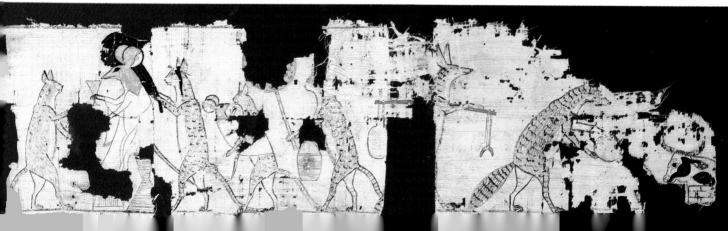

pens are in place in their long slot with a sliding cover. On both sides of the palette are notations concerning a workman's account written in hieratic.

The other palette, made of schist, is a votive model intended for use in the next world. It consists of a plaque in which the two hollows for the ink have been cut, each encircled by a *shen* sign. They held the colors blue and white. A rectangular cavity containing parallel striations imitates the ends of a series of reed pens lying in their box.

Bibliography: Cf.: Naissance de l'Ecriture, Grand Palais, Paris 1982, nos. 290–94; Eggebrecht, Das Alte Ägypten, pp. 347–63.

His palette is composed of simple colors which are preserved in the form of small round cakes. Red and yellow ochre (iron oxides) are products found in a natural state in the desert. Green is obtained from various pulverized copper ores, particularly malachite and chrysolite; blue from azurite or else from a compound of silica, carbonate of calcium, malachite and natron, pulverized after fusion. This same mixture was used in the manufacture of what we call "faience", for beads, amulets and figurines. White was simply powdered chalk.

Bibliography: S.: A. Mekhitarian, Egyptian Painting, Geneva 1954; Leclant, Les Pharaons I, pp. 157–58; T. G. H. James, Egyptian Painting, British Museum 1985, pp. 8–13.

234   Upper floor, room 29
A Painter's equipment

Mortar and pestle in porphyry, Elephantine, 1858	JE 2106 = CG 69053
Schist palette, Tura	JE 92565
Wooden brush, one of a bundle. Unknown provenance	JE 96792
Red ochre, Valley of the Kings	JE 96779
Turquoise blue, Amarna	JE 57327
Blue frit, Giza	JE 57017

Max. L. 24 cm; max. W. 7.5 cm

Examples of equipment emanating from various sources give us a lively picture of the painter's activities.

The small mortar and pestle serve to grind the cakes of pigment which are subsequently diluted with water and an adhesive, such as egg-white or vegetable resin, in small cups or in the hollows of a palette.

The palette with two receptacles has been used to dilute red ochre and lamp-black as we can see from the traces. The hole at one end of the palette was for suspension (see the palette on the shoulder of Hesire, no. 21).

The painter possesses a variety of brushes made from small branches of wood the ends of which have been bruised to liberate the fibres.

235   Upper floor, room 24
Book of the Dead of Pinedjem I

Papyrus   SR 11488
L. 450 cm; W. 37 cm
Thebes, royal cache of Deir el-Bahari; discovered in 1875: cleared in 1881 by the Egyptian Antiquities Service under Maspero
Third Intermediate Period, 21th dynasty, pontificate of Pinedjem I, ca. 1065–1045 B.C.

As the Ramesside period gradually declined, Egyptian sovereignty, to the east or west, was no longer recognized. By the reign of Ramses XI, the actual power in the Thebais rested in the hands of the High Priest of Amon, Herihor, and later, his son Piankhi. In the north, a Delta native named Smendes established a similar power base at Tanis, and proclaimed himself king. This marks the beginning of the Tanite Twenty-first Dynasty, while simultaneously at Thebes the descendants of Herihor maintained military control over their upper Egyptian pontificate. During this time the high priest Pinedjem I, son of Piankhi, married Henuttawy, daughter of the king of Tanis, laid his claim to the throne and became king of Upper Egypt. Robberies and violations of the royal tombs at Thebes continued at such a fierce pace that Pinedjem undertook to rescue the royal mummies; he had them rewrapped and grouped together. Later, under Psusennes II, all attempts to check the vandalism having failed, some of the royal mummies were transferred to a secret cache at Deir el-Bahari (see no. 207). It was here that the mummies of the high priests of Amon and their families were discovered. Hidden between the legs of the mummy of Pinedjem, which had been partially unwrapped, this roll of papyrus had escaped the tomb robbers.

The handwriting is in cursive hieroglyphs: the vignettes are of exceptionally high quality and serve to illustrate the important chapters from the Book of the Dead. The first vignette to the left shows the High Priest Pinedjem in royal attire adoring Osiris, who sits within a naos. His titulary consists of royal cartouches, but they stand under the sign for king, not of the Two Lands, but merely of Upper Egypt. Pinedjem appears again further on offering to Osiris, after which he leaves his tomb and is subsequently introduced by Anubis into the hall

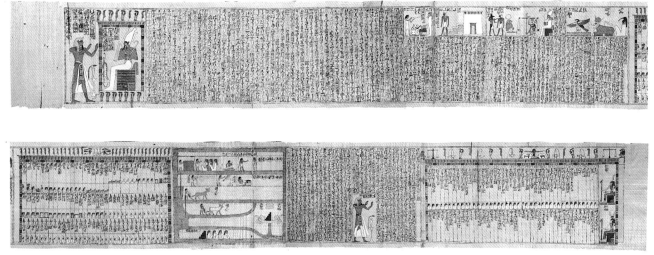

235

of the Two Maats. Here occurred the weighing of his heart in the presence of the baboon of the god Thoth, the falcon-headed Horus, and Osiris. Finally, the god Re rises out of the primordial waters of Nun with Mehet-weret, "the great flood" (see also no. 216), and the ibis-headed Thoth. The representation of the large naos which follows, surmounted by a cavetto cornice and a frieze of Maat-feathers of truth/justice, contains various deities arranged in registers. The final scene shows the Fields of the Blest, who are able to continue living much as they did during their earthly existence.

Bibliography: Maspero, Les Momies Royales de Deir el-Bahari, in: Mémoires publiés par les Membres de la Mission Archéologique Française au Caire I, 1889, p. 570. See also: Budge, The Book of the Dead, London 1898; P. Barguet, Le Livre des Morts des anciens Egyptiens, Paris 1967; E. Hornung, Das Totenbuch der Ägypter, Zurich/Munich 1979.

236

Upper floor, room 29

Am-duat

Papyrus   JE 95656
L. 145 cm; W. 23,5 cm
Deir el-Bahari, tomb of High Priests of Amon, found by Grébaut, 1891
Third Intermediate Period, end of the 21ˢᵗ dynasty, c. 970 B.C.

Following the collections of funerary spells and formulae which evolved from the Pyramid Texts to the Book of the Dead, the Egyptians developed in the New Kingdom a series of homogeneous compositions intended at first solely for the use of the king, but later "democratized" and shared by his subjects. The learned priests taxed their imagination such that the deceased king could enjoy an eternal life just as did Re in heaven and Osiris in the west. The Am-duat ("that which is in the Netherworld") or, more precisely, the Book of the Hidden Chamber, is actually a description of twelve subterranean realms corresponding to the twelve hours of the night, across which the solar bark sailed its nocturnal course in order to reappear in the morning on the eastern horizon. Knowing the names of these realms, and being able to recognize the deities, genii and demons who inhabited them, were all beneficial to the deceased. Illustrations accompany the names and descriptions, and the composition was conceived as a large papyrus unrolled upon the walls of the royal sepulchres at Thebes since the beginning of Dynasty 18. At the end of the New Kingdom, private individuals obtained the right to include papyri, with either the complete or an abridged version of the Am-duat among their funerary equipment.

Thus here is a version of this book in which only the three final hours are illustrated. The hours are divided into three registers. The middle register describes the trajectory of the bark of Re, hauled by divinities and genii, along a subterranean water course. The ram-headed god Re is protected from

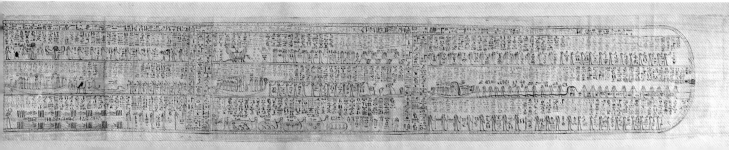

the seventh hour on by the serpent Mehen which surrounds him. The registers above and below represent the banks of this subterranean water course, filled with beneficent genii as well as menacing enemies. The most fearsome of all is the serpent Apophis, who evokes negative force and the peril of nothingness: he is of course vanquished in the course of the journey. During the final hour, the sun is renewed by the primordial deities, that it might once more be reborn. This rejuvenation is achieved through the body of a great serpent. Finally, at the journey's end, the sun is dragged by the beetle, symbol of rebirth, and is reborn unto the day.

This fate could be forever shared by the deceased: his mummy lies at the extreme right of the lower register, waiting to accompany the solar bark in its travels and once again see the light of day.

Bibliography: S. E. Hornung, Ägyptische Unterweltsbücher, Zurich/Munich 1972, pp. 59–194.

237

Upper floor, room 46

Lid of the coffin of Maakare (detail)

Wood, stuccoed, gilded, painted and varnished   JE 26200
Total L. 223 cm; W. 77 cm   = CG 61028
Thebes, royal cache of Deir el-Bahari; discovered in 1875, cleared by the Egyptian Antiquities Service under Maspero in 1881
Third Intermediate Period, 21th dynasty, pontificate of Pinedjem I, ca. 1065–1045 B.C.

Among the daughters of the high priests of Amon at Thebes, there existed princesses sworn to celibacy and devoted exclusively to the service of the god Amon, while retaining all of their royal privileges. They were known by the titles of Divine Votaress and God's wife.

Maakare seems to have been the first of this dynasty of priestesses, who were installed by adoption and came to play an important role in the politics of the Twenty-first Dynasty. She was probably the daughter of the high priest Pinedjem I (see no. 235), and of Queen Henuttawy.

The mummy of Maakare was discovered in the cache of Deir el-Bahari, lying inside two anthropoid coffins and covered by a breast panel with the image of the deceased. The best preserved part of the ensemble was the exterior coffin, whose lid is illustrated here. With its gilding and vivid colors it is doubtless the most attractive coffin of the Late Period.

The oval face retains an extraordinary vivacity with its plain curves, golden sheen and black highlighting. The rounded wig with long strands of hair surrounded by a uraeus diadem is covered by a vulture headdress with colored wings, as well as two uraei, both wearing the white crown. On Maakare's brow were once the vulture's head and two more uraei, but these have been stolen.

The body of the coffin, completely painted, is rich in minute details. Ram-headed winged scarabs, and solar deities seated before winged goddesses who protect the *ba* of the deceased surround the collar and the pendant. The vulture goddess with outstretched wings occupies the center. The lower portion is divided into scenes bordered by the bands of inscription giving Maakare's titulary (central band), and her epithets (lateral bands), which read: "Revered under the gods Re, Ptah-Sokar-Osiris, Horus and Anubis." At the very bottom, a falcon spreads its wings out over the foot case covering the feet of the mummy.

This proliferation of images and symbols compensates in abridged form for the extensive funerary program once represented on the walls of tombs, now reduced merely to uninscribed collective burial caches. The coffin scenes likewise replaced the repertoire of funerary equipment, which was no longer included in the burial.

Inside the coffin of Maakare, beside the mummy was found a deformed mummiform package. Long-accepted romantic opinion held that the Divine Votaress died in childbirth and was buried with her stillborn baby. Modern analysis has revealed, however, that it is the mummy of a pet monkey included in the burial, thus laying all doubt as to Maakare's celibacy to rest.

Bibliography: PM I, 2, p. 600; G. Maspero, Les Momies Royales de Deir el-Bahari, in: Mémoires de la Mission Archéologique française au Caire I, Paris 1889, p. 577, no. 8 and pl. 19; G. Daressy, Cercueils des Cachettes Royales (CG), pp. 82–84, pl. 39.

Anthropoid coffin

Painted wood
L. 203 cm; W. 61 cm
Thebes, Gourna, 1916
Third Intermediate Period, beginning of the 22nd dynasty, reign of Sheshonq I or Osorkon I, c. 925 B.C.

RT 23.11.16.12

The systematic violation of both royal and private burials at the end of the Ramesside era resulted in the eventual disappearance of tombs in favor of caches for final resting-places in the afterlife. The same priests who strove to rescue the royal mummies also made use of caches for their own burials, even if they were merely in simple coffins. Most of the caches were located within temple enclosures, where the clergy was housed.

Since mural paintings were no longer possible, the coffin began to bear all the necessary funerary scenes. The texts gradually gave way to increasingly diverse representations, and a new inconographic repertoire emerged. The coffins are all constructed of wood, completely painted and sometimes even gilded. They all belong to members of the priesthood of Amon.

The owner of this now lidless anthropoid coffin was Djedhoriuefankh, an overseer of altars in the temple of Amon at Thebes. Both interior and exterior are divided into registers showing brightly colored tableaus. The top is reminiscent of the tomb vault decorated in imitation of a tent. A representation of the solar bark fills the upper field, with two uraei and ornamented with papyrus. Below are seated two jackal-deities within a painted naos on either side of the emblem of Isis; each jackal is protected by a winged serpent goddess. Then come the cartouches of Menkheperre on the right, and on the left "the great god, lord of the sky, ruler eternally;" these refer to the deified King Tuthmosis III who continued to be venerated. At the outer edges of the scene are two mourners with human heads and bodies of birds, standing before baskets of offerings. In the central register below, the mummiform Ptah-Sokar sits enthroned receiving offerings from a priest and priestess. Below this scene, a jackal-headed Anubis figure embalms the deceased's body which lies upon a checkered dais; the canopic jars containing the viscera are arranged beneath the bed. In the final register, a priest clothed in a leopard skin censes the mummy, now wrapped in a beaded net with floral garlands. A mourner gracefully crouches at the mummy's feet, tearing her hair as a sign of grief. An offering table is placed in the center of the scene.

The walls of the coffin depict the adoration of the mummy by a priest who brings elaborate floral bouquets. Below this register appear the four sons of Horus, guardians of the viscera.

Bibliography: M. Werbrouck, *Les Pleureuses dans l'Egypte Ancienne,* Brussels 1938, p. 98; A. Niwiński, *Studies on the decoration of the coffins of Amun's priests from Thebes, 21st Dynasty, Theben V, 1,* Mainz 1987, no. 148. Cf. also: LÄ V, 441—444.

239

Upper floor, room 3

The bracelets of the High Priest Pinedjem II

Gold, carnelian, lapis lazuli   JE 26297
Max. Diam. 7 cm; max. L. 15 cm   = CG 52089 and 52090
Thebes, royal cachette of Deir el-Bahari, discovered in 1875 and
cleared in 1881. Bracelets were found on the mummy of Pinedjem in
1886 by Maspero.
Third Intermediate period, 21st dynasty, Pontificate of Pinedjem II, c.
970 B.C.

Rigid bracelets (as opposed to chains) are often overcharged
with decoration. There exist others, however, distinguished
for their elegant simplicity, such as the two bracelets found on
the mummy of the High Priest Pinedjem.
Each bracelet is composed of two symmetrical halves hinged
together on one side with gold wire, the joint being hidden by
a large lapis lazuli bead. The inner face of the bracelet is flat
while the outer side is rounded. It is decorated with stylized
feathers in cloisonné-work filled with carnelian and lapis
lazuli.
The bracelets can be closed over the wrist by a tenon held in
position by a gold pin. Just next to the joint, two small rings
serve as attachment for several pendant tassels: two tassels are
composed of a lapis lazuli pendant suspended at the end of a
gold chain; the others are made of a series of gold and stone
beads intermingled, terminating in a gold flower.

*Bibliography: Vernier, Bijoux et Orfèvreries (CG), pp. 43–44; pl. 11;
Aldred, Jewels, pl. 133.*

240

Upper floor, room 2E

Necklace of Psusennes

Gold, lapis lazuli   JE 85751
H. 64.5 cm; Diam. 30 cm; weight: 6315 gr
Tanis, tomb of Psusennes I, discovered by Montet in 1940
Third Intermediate Period, 21st dynasty, reign of Psusennes I,
1054–1004 B.C.

This sumptuous ornament, which was made up originally of
six rows of rings, now contains only five because some of the
pieces are missing (see the similar necklace made of seven
rows of rings displayed in the same case). Each row consists of
a multitude of gold rings strung on a cord and held firmly
together by a heavy clasp which covers and hides the knotted
ends of the cords. The clasp is decorated on both sides with
the same motif: Underneath a winged scarab, the cartouches
of Psusennes are placed on either side of a papyriform column
(*wadj*) between two friezes of uraei with sundisks on their
heads. On the recto the decoration was embellished with lapis
lazuli inlays still partly preserved; the verso was simply
engraved.
From the clasp are suspended 14 tassels consisting of simple
gold chains which are divided first into two and then into four
smaller chains whose points of junction and whose extremities
are ornamented with small bell-like convolvulus flowers.
In this room one can admire all the marvellous treasures:
masks, jewelry and plate found intact in the 21st and 22nd
dynasty tombs at Tanis (see nos. 241.242). In this new capital,
the necropolis was situated within the sacred temple precincts
(see also in hall 11, the electrum coffin of King Psusennes I).

*Bibliography: P. Montet, Psousennès, La nécropole royale de Tanis,
II, Paris 1951, pp. 136–37, no. 483, pl. 108; A. Wilkinson, Ancient
Egyptian Jewelry, 1970, pl. 68; Ramsès le Grand, no. 68; Götter Pha-
raonen, no. 62; Le grand pharaon Ramsès II, no. 32.*

240

241

Golden vessels of Psusennes

Cup	JE 85897
H. 3 cm; Diam. 16 cm	
Vase	JE 85896
H. 7.6 cm; Diam. 9 cm	
Ladle	JE 85898
H. 4.7 cm; Diam. 10.9 cm; L. 30 cm	

Tanis, tomb of Psusennes, discovered by P. Montet in 1940
Third Intermediate Period, 21st dynasty, reign of Psusennes I, 1054–1004 B.C.

The extraordinary discovery of the royal tombs at Tanis within the enclosure wall of the temple, brought to light in the intact tomb of Psusennes I a large selection of sacred vases celebrated for their elegance.

These three objects chosen from the funerary equipment of Psusennes give an idea of the high quality of artistic work at Tanis. The cup is in the form of a corolla with 16 gadroons whose center is shaped as a rosette. An inscription in the name of Psusennes and his daughter Isetemkheb is engraved around the rim.

The small vase with 24 gadroons formed by a process of hammering is decorated under the rim with four vertically engraved cartouches; the two on the right are those of Psusennes, those on the left of Queen Henuttawy, the royal mother.

The elegant object used for serving liquids is a ladle composed of a round bowl with a long spout, whose handle ends in a duck's head turned backwards to form a loop. On the flat surface of the handle two columns of inscription repeat the name of Psusennes and of Queen Mutnedjmet, his wife.

Bibliography: Montet, Psousennès, pp. 101–103, nos. 393, 401, 403 and pls. 69–70; Corteggiani, no. 94.

242

242

Cult vessels from Tanis

Patera	JE 85904
Silver and gold	
H. 3.6 cm; Diam. 17 cm	
Pitcher	JE 86098
Gold	
H. 20 cm; Diam. 7.7 cm	

Tanis, tomb of Psusennes, discovered by P. Montet in 1940
Third Intermediate Period, 21st dynasty, reigns of Psusennes and Amenemope, 1054–985 B.C.

Besides the royal funerary equipment, the tomb of Psusennes contained that of his general Wendebaunded and of his successors Amenemope and Sheshonq II (see his silver coffin and falcon mask in gallery 10 on the first floor).

The silver patera in the name of Psusennes is an admirable example of craftsmanship with a very original decoration: 8 flowers and 8 buds are arranged around a central boss in gold forming a rosette at the bottom of the bowl. Twenty wavy lines radiate from this center-piece towards the rim where they curve back to rejoin their neighbours. The movable gold handle is held in place by the two thick rings of a plaque riveted to the body, whose ends spread out into palmettes. The titulature of Psusennes is engraved under the rim on the side opposite the handle. A similar patera in silver (case 14) and still another decorated with graceful swimmers formed part of the funerary equipment of General Wendebaunded; these were presents from King Psusennes.

The pitcher with its simple lines, wide flat rim and high flared foot is a type which was used ritually at all periods for the purpose of pouring libations to the gods. Under the spout, the name of Amenemope is the only decorative element. This son and successor of Psusennes was buried in one of the rooms of his father's tomb which had been previously prepared for the royal wife Mutnedjmet.

Bibliography: Montet, Psousennès, p. 103 (no. 405) and p. 163 (no. 633), pls. 71 and 128.

wig surmounted by an unguent cone, raises her delicate hands before Re-Horakhty. The falcon-headed god is crowned with a sun-disk surrounded by a uraeus. He holds the *was*-scepter in one hand, and the symbol of life in the other. Between the two figures stands a table of offerings piled high with food and lotus flowers, and flanked both by tall vessels resting on three-legged stands, and lettuces supporting a floral wreath. Five columns of a retrograde hieroglyphic offering formula are written above the table, and on top of that are two recumbent jackals, one on either side of a vase. The whole scene, with blue-painted background, takes place under the sky sign bent in the form of an arch and supported by two *was*-scepters.

Many little stelae similar to this one are known from this period, and are on display in numerous museums. They are touching not only for their simple beauty, but also for their occasional choice of original compositions, such as this necropolis scene. Other examples show a harpist performing before a deity, or the sun-god beneficently projecting a cluster of sunbeams composed of multi-colored lotus blossoms down upon the face of his worshipper.

Bibliography: PM I, 2, p. 801; Propyläen Kunstgeschichte 15, pl. 40; P. Munro, Die spätägyptischen Totenstelen, Glückstadt 1973, p. 7.

243
Stela of Djedamoniuankh

Wood, stuccoed and painted   RT 25.12.24.20
H. 27.6 cm; W. 23 cm; thickness 2.7 cm
Thebes, Deir el-Bahari. Found c. 1880
Third Intermediate Period, 22nd dynasty, ca. 900 B.C.

This little votive monument may be singled out for the beauty of its painting, the excellent preservation of its colors and the originality of the lower register. We see here for the first time a scene in the necropolis which represents neither a procession nor offering bearers. In the solitude of the desert, the slope of the cliff into which the tomb has been cut is painted pink with white specks. The superstructure of a chapel is visible, surmounted by a pyramid and preceded by a staircase. In front are three more structures, each with a door. The two high buildings are provided with domes and cavetto cornices. A crouching woman mourns her dead by tearing her hair. Behind her a sycamore and two date-palms represent the garden in which the *ba* of the deceased hopes to find shade, fresh air and water. An offering table with bread and a basin of water has been set up between the trees; on one of them a crow has begun to peck at the dates.

The principal tableau above depicts a traditional adoration scene. The stela's owner, dressed in a completely transparent pleated robe and adorned with a broad collar and tripartite

244
Amenirdis the Elder

Alabaster with a basalt base   JE 3420
H. 170 cm; W. 44 cm; L. 71 cm   = CG 565
Karnak. Discovered by Mariette in 1858
Late Period, 25th dynasty, reign of Shabaka, 713–698 B.C.

Amenirdis was the daughter of Kashta, King of a Nubian Kingdom which came into being in the 9th century B.C. and whose capital was Napata, situated at the foot of the sacred mountain of Djebel Barkal. Kashta had succeeded in gaining control of Thebes. During the reign of his son and successor Piankhi (Piye), Amenirdis was adopted as successor at Thebes to the Divine Votaress and God's Wife (of Amon) Shepenupet I, the daughter of Osorkon III of the 23rd dynasty whose successors Takelot III and Rudjamon were forced to recognize the Nubian power.

Once established as God's Wife, Amenirdis in turn adopted as her successor Shepenupet II, the daughter of her brother Piankhi who led a victorious campaign against Lower Egypt then occupied by Bochoris of the 24th dynasty, in a first attempt to reunite the country. The union was completed by his brother and successor Shabaka. Amenirdis retained her position in Thebes during both of these reigns.

This statue is the most celebrated of all the statues of Amenirdis, called the Elder. It was found by Mariette in a small

244

base in front of the right foot. Amenirdis is here designated as "beloved of Osiris Neb-Ankh", the form of Osiris to whom the chapel in which the statue stood was dedicated. This flat base rests on a second larger socle of basalt whose inscription contains an invocation to the god Amon-Re of Karnak associated with Montu, the Lord of Thebes. In later times (under Psammetik II) the names of her father Kashta and her brother Shabaka were erased in the last line of this inscription and on the back pillar which contains a dedication to Osiris Neb-Ankh.

Bibliography: PM II, pp. 14−15; Borchardt, Statuen und Statuetten (CG) II, pp. 114−115, pl. 164; Leclant, Les Pharaons III, fig. 117; H. W. Müller, Ägyptische Kunst, pl. 164; Lange/Hirmer, pl. 259; D. Arnold, Moses und Aida, in: Ägypten − Dauer und Wandel, Deutsches Archäologisches Institut Abteilung Kairo, Sonderschrift 18, Mainz 1985, p. 175, pl. 20.

245   Ground floor, gallery 25
A Head of King Taharka
Grey granite   CG 560
H. 36.5 cm; W. 24 cm; thickness 34 cm
Probably from Thebes. Bought at Luxor
Late Period, 25th dynasty, reign of Taharka 690−664 B.C.

245

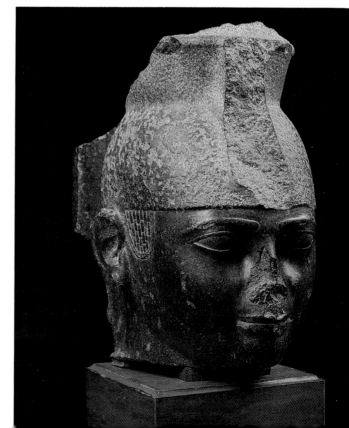

chapel situated inside the enclosure wall of the Montu temple at Karnak and is said to have been the inspiration for the personage of the Princess Amnéris in Aïda, Verdi's famous opera, the scenario of which was written by none other than Mariette himself, who likewise designed the scenery.

Tall and imposing, Amenirdis is depicted here in the attitude and costume traditionally attributed to the Divine Votaress, derived directly from the iconography of the New Kingdom Queens. A heavy wig of stylized ringlets falls in three separate masses on her shoulders and back, surmounted by a vulture whose head is flanked on each side by a uraeus. A diadem encircled by erect uraei originally supported a Hathor crown. Her earrings consist of large rounded studs and she wears a long tightfitting robe, wide decorated bracelets and simpler anklets. Small figures of Amon and Mut are finely engraved on her necklace. Like the Queens, Amenirdis holds in her left hand a flower insignia which falls gracefully on her breast, and in her other hand a *menat* collar.

The grace of the Ramesside Queens has given place here to a massive, monumental style. The charm of the young feminine faces is replaced by the serious expression of a grave but conventional visage in which we can discern no trace of the Nubian origin of the princess. In spite of the excellent workmanship, the statue remains cold.

The cartouches of the God's Wife are inscribed on the flat

Taharka, the son of Piankhi (Piye) and brother of Shabataka whose successor he was designated to be, is without doubt the most important sovereign of the Kushite (Ethiopian) dynasty. He was master of an immense empire which extended from Napata to the Sea. Both in Nubia and in Egypt he built many monuments, pyramids at Nuri and Sedeinga, temples at Sanaam, Djebel Barkal, Kasr Ibrim and elsewhere; he likewise embellished Karnak with a number of edifices, among them the great colonnade in the first court of the temple of Amon. Traces of his activity are to be found throughout Egypt.

In spite of his administrative talents, Taharka, who tried to hold out against the Assyrians, left the country to his successor Tanutamon in a critical situation which ended in the defeat of the Ethiopian and the sack of Thebes by the Assyrian army (664 B.C.). The Kushites withdrew towards the south and in Egypt an indigenous dynasty, which we call the Saïte (from its capital Saïs) took over control.

Taharka is represented here in accordance with the iconography characteristic of the Kushite dynasty, a composite of Ethiopian traits tending towards realism, with the pharaonic idealizing style, enriched by archaic elements borrowed from Old and Middle Kingdom Egyptian art. The characteristics of this Kushite style are admirably illustrated in this portrait. The round cranium is ensconced in a typically Kushite cap probably covered with a veneer of gold and surmounted by the modius which supported a crown. Two uraei are attached to the front of this headdress underneath which the curly hair is visible on the temples and at the back. The face is round with elongated eyes, a rather wide nose and a full mouth.

The coronation name of Taharka is to be seen on what remains of the back pillar.

Bibliography: Borchardt, Statuen und Statuetten (CG) II, p. 108, pl. 94; E. R. Russmann, The Representation of the King in the XXVth Dynasty, Brussels—Brooklyn 1974, no. 9, p. 47 and figs. 8—9; Propyläen Kunstgeschichte 15, pls. 408—9; Corteggiani, no. 100. Cf. also: LÄ VI, 156—167.

◁ 246 ▷

246
Montuemhat

Grey granite   JE 36933
H. 137 cm; W. 32.5 cm; thickness 60 cm   = CG 42236
Karnak, court of the cachette, cleared by Legrain in 1904
Late Period, 25th–26th dynasties, ca. 670 B.C.

Ground floor, room 24

Montuemhat, Fourth Prophet of Amon, Mayor of Thebes and Governor of Upper Egypt came from a priestly family. His father Nesptah was himself mayor and prophet of both Amon and Montu at Thebes.

His career was set against the background of the transition from the Twenty-fifth or Ethiopian Dynasty to the Twenty-sixth (or Saïte). Thus he survived the reign of Taharka before Thebes was sacked by the Assyrians, as well as the subsequent assumption of power by Psammetik I. His immense tomb (no. 34) constructed near the temple of Hatshepsut at Deir el-Bahari indicates both by its location and the splendor of its decoration the unique privileges enjoyed by its owner. Some fifteen statues and a rich epigraphic corpus render Montuemhat one of the better-known individuals of the country.

This almost lifesize statue, discovered in two pieces in the cachette of the temple of Karnak, represents Montuemhat standing in a traditional pose with left leg advanced, the arms hanging down by the sides. He wears a heavy wig which flares out towards the shoulders revealing a plane of curled tresses on either side of the neck. He wears a pleated kilt, a form deriving originally from the Old Kingdom, which was often worn during the Ethiopian period.

The body is powerful. The admirably rendered musculature bespeaks an energy emphasized all the more by the two fists each clenched around a cloth or a short staff. But it is the face which captures our interest. With a forceful physiognomy, the Nubian features of this definitely Egyptian individual are influenced by the iconography of the Ethiopian kings (see the portraits of Taharka and Shabaka in galleries 25 and 30). However, Montuemhat's own features are also present: the narrow eyes, well-defined cheek-bones, pronounced wrinkles, distinct philtrum and frowning mouth. These same features, so idealized on the majority of Montuemhat's other statues, are accentuated to such a point on his black bust (on exhibit immediately to one side) that they render this sculpture the most expressive of the portraits of this period.

On Montuemhat's belt we read, as if on a royal statue, the carved inscription most often accompanying him: fourth prophet of Amon and Prince of the city. The back pillar and the base are amply inscribed with biographical notes citing numerous titles and praising the accomplishments of this individual, accompanied by a threat against those who would divert his offerings. In addition there are offering formulae addressed to the gods Osiris and Anubis, invocations to the gods Atum, Amon-Rê, Montu and Ptah, appeals to the living, to priests and scribes, and a special appeal to the god of the city (called the "Saïte formula").

Bibliography: PM II, p. 151; Legrain, Statues et Statuettes (CG) III, p. 85–87, pl. 44–45; Leclant, Montouemhat, Cairo 1961, p. 3–20, pl. 1–2; Propyläen Kunstgeschichte 15, pl. 216; Götter Pharaonen, no. 69.

247

Block statue of Ankhpakhered

Schist (greywacke)   JE 36993
H. 25 cm
Karnak, court of the cachette, cleared by Legrain in 1904
Late Period, 25th dynasty, ca. 680 B.C.

We have seen (no. 123) that the block statue represents the individual squatting and wrapped in a garment. Even today this is still a favorite pose of the Egyptians. Perhaps the reason for its popularity is that the block statue requires merely a square block of stone. It is compact and difficult to damage. In addition it offers much surface space for inscriptions, prayers and biographical texts. During the Late Period it was placed primarily in temples, thus permitting its owner to participate in temple offerings.

Block statues showing a full-length garment are quite common. Others, however, such as this one, leave the limbs exposed. This statue represents the priest Ankhpakhered, scribe of the offering table in the temple of Amon. His father Herkhabit and his grandfather also served in the Theban clergy. Ankhpakhered lived at the end of Dynasty 25 or the beginning of Dynasty 26, a period with archaizing tendencies which attempted to recreate the glories of the past in renewing the traditions of the earlier times. Sculpture in the round rediscovers idealism.

247

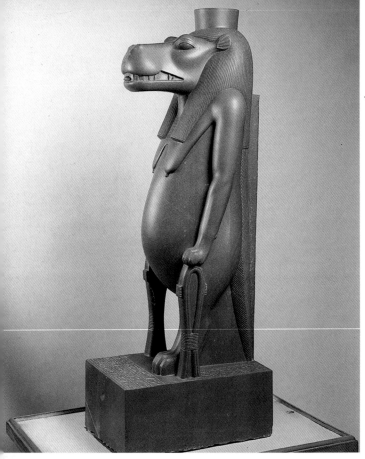

248

◁ 248

The goddess Taweret

Green schist   CG 39194
H. 96 cm; W. 26 cm; profile 38 cm
Karnak; discovered to the north of the temple of Amon-Re in 1874
(by farmers), confiscated and brought to the Museum by A. Mariette
Saïte Period, 26th dynasty, reign of Psammetik I, 664–610 B.C.

This astonishing statuette represents Taweret, "the Great one", goddess of fertility who assisted mothers during childbirth. The piece was dedicated by Pabasa, overseer of priests, who obtained the post of chief steward of the Divine Votaress of Amon, Nitocris.

Of magnificent workmanship and perfectly polished, the statue is that of a hybrid creature: a female hippopotamus with human arms, sagging breasts and rounded belly, standing upon lion's legs and leaning on the magic knot symbolizing protection. The head of the animal is remarkably executed. Her wig is a striated, tripartite affair, on top of which a round base once supported a Hathor crown with plumes, sun-disk and two horns. The rear portion of the wig extends down the animal's back onto a thick appendage which trails off behind in the form of a tail; it is actually the skin of a crocodile with stylized scales.

A few other protective goddesses associated with Taweret, such as Hedjet, "The White One", Ipet, "the Nurse," and Reret, "the Sow", may also assume this generic form. Reret is actually mentioned with Taweret in the inscriptions carved upon the top of the base and on the back pillar of our statue. In this text, the high priest Pabasa beseeches the goddesses to protect the property of the Divine Votaress, Nitocris, and to defend his own estate as well. This property, which Pabasa has been assigned to administer, was ascribed to Nitocris by her father, King Psammetik I. In effect, Nitocris arrived at Thebes furnished with a large dowry in order to be adopted by the God's Wife of Amon, Shepenupet, whose position she was to inherit.

The statue was discovered walled up in a limestone naos whose only opening was a window pierced at the height of the goddess' head. This opening allowed her both to be seen and to listen to the prayers which she would answer in exchange for offerings. The naos, decorated with the image of Taweret receiving sistra from Nitocris, and seven Hathors holding tambourines, was erected in a brick chapel which the Divine Votaress had consecrated to the god Osiris Padedankh ("who-gives-life").

Bibliography: A. Mariette, Monuments Divers, pls. 90–92, p. 28; G. Daressy, Statues des Divinités (CG), p. 284, pl. 55; Roeder, Naos (CG), pp. 106–9, pl. 37; M. Verner, in: Zeitschrift für ägyptische Sprache und Altertumskunde 96, 1969, pp. 52–62; Corteggiani, no. 104; Nofret – Die Schöne, no. 10. Cf.: Vandier, in: La Revue du Louvre 1962, no. 5, pp. 197–204. See also: R. Caminos, in: JEA 50, 1964, pp. 71–101.

Ankhpakhered's face emerges from a flaring wig finely decorated with locks which radiate from a circle carved at the top of the head. It flares out toward the edges of the shoulders, revealing part of the ears, the neck and curled tresses which frame it. The small beard which extends the chin is separate from the rest of the block.

The eyes are fine and narrow, the elegantly extended eyebrows are in relief, the upper eyelids bulging. The mouth is well delineated by the slightly pouting lower lip, the sunken corners of the mouth and the pronounced philtrum.

Ankhpakhered folds his arms upon his knees, and holds a rolled cloth in his right hand. Below the bare torso he wears a long, tight-fitting kilt which forms a flat surface similar to those of block statues, but without hiding the rest of the body; the limbs, sculpted almost in the round, are liberated from the mass.

Framed between the feet and folded arms, the kilt exhibits an offering formula invoking Amon-Rê for the Ka of Ankhpakhered. It also lists his genealogy, continuing onto the base and even around his belt. (Compare the similar but larger block-statue of his colleague Hor, in the next case.)

Bibliography: PM II, p. 152; Hornemann, Types II, pl. 475.

249

Mummy Covering

Gold, stone, faience · JE 35923
H. 145 cm; W. 46 cm · = CG 53668
Sakkara, tomb of Hekaemsaf. Excavations of the Egyptian Antiquities
Service directed by A. Barsanti in 1903
Late Period, 26th dynasty, reign of Amasis, 570–525 B.C.

This beautiful garment covered the mummy of a "Chief of the
royal boats" named Hekaemsaf, in the intact burial chamber
of his tomb discovered by the Antiquities Service in 1903.
The tomb is one of those which were excavated at the bottom
of an immense pit which is still visible at Sakkara to the east
of the pyramid of Unas. In the vaulted burial chamber decorated with extracts from the Pyramid texts, the excavators
found between the limestone sarcophagus and the door the
four canopic jars and a considerable number of models in
pottery and stone: Palettes, boats, pots, plaques, etc.; dispersed on both sides of the door were a total of 401 blue faience *shawabti* figures lying on a wooden platform.
Inside the sarcophagus lined with bitumen was a painted
wooden coffin containing the mummy whose head was
encased in a gilded mask and the body wrapped in a bead garment covered with a linen cloth. Around the mummy were
found a multitude of amulets, figurines of gods, necklaces of
gold, a scarab, rings and beads of stone, while the fingers and
toes of the mummy were entirely sheathed in gold.
The garment was reconstituted at the Museum by Daressy. It
consists of the mask of beaten gold whose eyes are inlaid with
stones and the pleated headdress with dark coloured paste.
The network of gold, lapis lazuli and amazonite beads to
which was attached at the neck a wide *Usekh* collar made up
of 18 rows of beads of the same materials was held together at
each end by a beaten gold falcon's head. Below the collar a
scene composed entirely of elements of beaten gold presents
the goddess Nut, with outspread wings and sun disk on her
head, kneeling above a column of inscription in which she is
invoked by the deceased whose name and titles terminate the
text. Disposed on each side of the inscription are the four
"sons of Horus", protecting genii of the viscera.

*Bibliography: PM III, 2, p. 650; Barsanti, in: ASAE 5, 1904, pp.
75–76, figs. 1–4.*

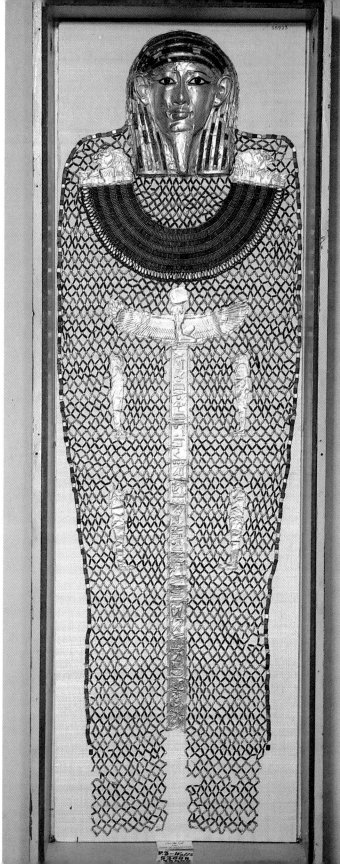

brings up in secrecy, hidden in the marshes of the Delta, so that he may avenge his father and recover the throne of Egypt. As the protecting goddess, par excellence, she is worshipped in many different places in Egypt, for example at Philae and Coptos; but her cult became likewise very widely spread outside the boundaries of the country in Palestine, Phoenicia and Europe. Isis is also the "Great Magician", versed in all kinds of magic formulae and incantations.

Originally a personification of the Throne, as is indicated by her name, Isis very early was represented in human form and appears here as a gracious young woman seated on a throne. She wears the crown characteristic of Hathor with whom she is often associated; as queen, the wife of Osiris the mythical first sovereign of Egypt, she wears the uraeus dominating her long tripartite wig whose tresses fall on her brest and back. Her long tight-fitting robe is moulded to her body, and she holds an *ankh*, the symbol of life, in one of her hands resting on her knees.

Around the base of the statue runs an inscription which begins on the rounded face. It is an invocation for offerings addressed to Isis by the Chief Scribe Psammetik who dedicated the statue to her.

This well proportioned sculpture is of excellent workmanship and marvellously polished.

Bibliography: PM III, p. 670; Daressy, Statues des Divinités (CG), p. 221, pl. 44; Leclant, Les Pharaons III, fig. 133.

250   Ground floor, room 24
The Goddess Isis

Schist (greywacke)   CG 38884
H. 90 cm; W. 20 cm; L. 45 cm
Sakkara, tomb of Psammetik, discovered by Mariette in 1863 to the south of the causeway of Unas
Late Period, end of the 26th dynasty, about 530 B.C.

Isis is the sister-wife of Osiris, god of the dead, and mother of Horus, god of the sky. She is also a member of the Ennead of Heliopolis whose chief god was Atum, the creator. His children Shu (the air) and Tefnut (humidity) were the parents of Geb (the earth) and Nut (the celestial vault) who in turn engendered four children: Osiris, Isis, Seth and Nepthys.
In the myth of Osiris, Isis bewails the death of her spouse, assassinated by his brother Seth (god of evil and confusion); aided by her sister Nepthys, she reassembles the dispersed limbs of Osiris and reconstitutes his body which she, transformed into a falcon, reanimates with the air from the beating of her wings. From their union is born Horus whom she

251   Ground floor, room 24
Hathor and Psammetik

Schist (greywacke)   CG 784
H. 96 cm; W. 29 cm; L. 104 cm
Sakkara, tomb of Psammetik, discovered by Mariette in 1863, south of the causeway of Unas.
Late Period, end of the 26th dynasty, ca. 530 B.C.

The Psammetik who deposited this statue in his tomb along with statues of Isis and of Osiris (nos. 250 and 252), was a high official with important titles: "overseer of seals, governor of the palace."
He is placed here under the protection of the Hathor cow, goddess of joy and life, venerated since the beginning of Egyptian history. Representations of group statues with the king standing or seated under the protection of a theriomorphic or anthropomorphic deity are attested since the Old Kingdom. Private individuals gain this privilege only much later in the New Kingdom, when personal piety strongly manifests itself. This group reminds us immediately of the famous statue of Hathor protecting Amenophis II in the chapel of Tuthmosis III at Deir el-Bahari (see no. 138). The stylized figurine of Psammetik, inserted between the goddess' head and the base of the statue, seems secondary. However, it is admirably integrated into the entire composition. The two figures are in complete harmony whether viewed straight on or from the side.

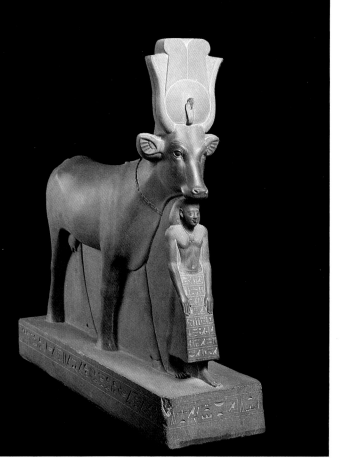

251

252

Psammetik wears a bag wig falling behind the ears. The cylinder seal hanging at his breast is the insignia of his profession. His long kilt with starched frontal section, over which he places his hands in the attitude of prayer, also serves as a base for the inscription listing his name and titles.

On top of her marvellous head, the goddess wears her characteristic crown: the disk with two tall feathers inserted between her horns and dominated by the uraeus. Around her neck is a bead necklace whose counterpoise is that of the *menat* collar, emblem sacred to Hathor. Her four legs appear on both sides of the piece, each time with two sculpted in the round and two carved in relief. Both Hathor and Psammetik advance their left legs.

This sculpture is remarkably executed and has survived in an excellent state of preservation. The exceptional anatomical details of the cow and the fine polish bear witness to the skill of the artists of the Late Period.

Bibliography: PM III, p. 670−71; Borchardt, Statuen und Statuetten III (CG), p. 91−92, pl. 144; Encyclopédie Photo, p. 174−75; Bothmer, Egyptian Sculpture of the Late Period, The Brooklyn Museum, 1960, p. 64−68, 103; Terrace/Fischer, no. 38; Leclant, Les Pharaons III, fig. 132.

252 Osiris
Ground floor, room 24

Schist (greywacke)   CG 38358
H. 89.5 cm; W. 28 cm; L 46,5 cm
Sakkara, Tomb of Psammetik, discovered by Mariette in 1863, south of the causeway of Unas
Late Period, end of the 26th dynasty, about 530 B.C.

Here we have the counterpart of Isis, her spouse Osiris, Lord of Eternity.

Having made his appearance at Busiris, Osiris very soon replaced the earlier divinity of that locality, Anedjty, a divine King. Taking over this aspect of Anedjty, Osiris was considered to be the King of primeval times. As son of Geb and Nut, he was an integral member of the Great Ennead of Heliopolis. After his assassination by his brother Seth, he was resuscitated through the magical powers of his wife Isis. The Falcon, Horus the Elder, a god worshipped throughout the country, reappeared in a new, rejuvenated aspect as the son of Osiris and Isis to become the avenger of his father.

At Memphis Osiris is assimilated to Sokar, a chthonian god already associated with Ptah, from whom he inherits his earliest funerary characteristics. Finally, at Abydos, he is first associated with and later replaces the local god Khentamentiu, the Chief of the "Westerners", and becomes the patron of the dead, lord of the necropolis and guarantor of rebirth in the other world. His cult is disseminated thoughout Egypt. From the end of the 5th dynasty, the dead king who on the one hand tends to be assimilated to the heavenly elements, on the other hand is identified with Osiris.

Sanctuaries and cenotaphs are erected in his honour at Abydos. The nomes, each of which had formerly inherited a part of his body when it was dispersed by Seth after his assassination, take on the character of reliquaries; statues and stelae are dedicated to him in spectacular quantities.

Our statue represents him in his most ordinary form: a mummiform god enveloped in a close-fitting garment, seated on a throne. His *atef* crown, flanked by two ostrich feathers, is adorned with the uraeus. Below his smooth shaven face the divine beard is attached to his chin, and in his hands he holds the insignia of sovereignty, the flail and the crooked sceptre. The usual offering formula addressed to Osiris is inscribed around the base.

In this exquisite statue, especially in the beautifully polished visage, we recognize anew the qualities which we have already noticed in the other two sculpures dedicated by Psammetik. They were found in one of the pits of his tomb where later objects had been added to the original funerary equipment.

Bibliography: PM III, p. 670; Daressy, Statues des Divinités (CG), pp. 96–97, pl. 19; Posener/Sauneron/Yoyotte, Dictionnaire de la civilisation égyptienne, pp. 204–8; LÄ IV, 623–633.

253
The God Ptah

Bronze and electrum   JE 91133
H. 12.2 cm; W. 2.2 cm; L. 2.2 cm
Sakkara. Excavations of Emery in 1964–67
Late Period, 26th dynasty, about 600 B.C.

Ptah is the god originally worshipped in the royal residence at Memphis where he is considered as the patron of artisans. Soon he is promoted to the rank of demiurge and becomes the creator of the universe.

Assimilated to the funerary god Sokar, his neighbour at Memphis whose chthonic aspect he adopts, Ptah is identified with Osiris in his double role of Ptah-Sokar. In the New Kingdom he continues to be honoured as one of the great patrons of the royal house and in Ramesside times he shares with Re-Horakhty and Amon-Re the position of one of the great gods of the Kingdom.

It is at this time that Sekhmet is considered to be his spouse at Memphis, and Nefertum their child.

One of Ptah's most usual epithets is "beautiful of visage", an allusion to his benevolent aspect, perhaps by association with the form of Ptah "who listens to prayers" (see no. 221).

Ptah is an anthropomorphic god in ordinary human form when he is connected with the Memphite god Tatenen (see no. 209), but as a rule he is mummiform, his head covered by a tight-fitting cap, wearing a beard and a wide collar necklace.

253

254

His hands emerge from his mummy garment to hold the *was* sceptre, often combined with a *djed*-pillar and an *ankh*.

It is in this common form that he appears here in a well preserved example of the innumerable bronze statues dedicated to him. The eyes and beard of the god as well as his collar and sceptre are inlaid with electrum (see also the two large sandstone statues of Ptah on the ground floor, gallery 49).

Bibliography: S.: LÄ IV, 1179–1180; M. Sandman-Holmberg, The God Ptah, Lund 1946.

254   Upper floor, room 19
A Lion-Headed Goddess

Bronze   JE 30287
H. 29.8 cm; W. 5.8 cm; L. 13.2 cm   = CG 39128
Sa el-Hagar (Saïs) (?). Came to the Museum in 1893
Late Period, 26th dynasty, about 600 B.C.

The Egyptians always worshipped the lioness as a goddess while at the same time fearing her force and the danger she represented. In the Old Kingdom, the lioness-goddess is considered to be the divine mother of Pharaoh. In the form of a woman with a lion's head she was known by various names in different parts of Egypt such as: Sekhmet "the Powerful" at Memphis; Seshemtet and Bastet in the Delta, and in the south, Matit "The dismemberer", Mehit "The siezer" and Pasht "The mangler", names that reflect the terror which they disseminate.

Assimilated to Hathor "the Lady of the sky", and to the daughter of Re, Tefnut, the lioness-goddess becomes a manifestation of the Eye of Re, that is to say the Far-Away Goddess whose wanderings in the deserts of the south provoke droughts, engender fevers and epidemics and whose fury is capable of destroying the world. According to a late myth, Re sends out scouts to bring her back in order to direct her furious force against the enemies of the sun. When the scouts succeed in appeasing her anger and coaxing her back to Egypt, Re attaches her to his brow in the form of the uraeus (Wadjet) in order that she may burn his adversaries with her flaming breath.

From the Middle Kingdom on these two aspects of the goddess are constantly present: one savage and dangerous, the other tame and protective. In later times the wild lioness-goddess is called Sekhmet, Pasht or Wadjet according to her geographical location, but once appeased becomes the gentle Bastet (no. 255), Hathor or Mut.

These sister lion-headed goddesses are usually crowned with the sundisk and uraeus, and sometimes with the Hathor crown as is the case with our statuette. She held the papyrus-scepter *Wadj*, and the sign of life (broken off). Our goddess is seated on a throne decorated with feathers and the *Sema-tawy* symbol. On the back of the throne a falcon with sundisk is represented hovering under the sky sign and holding in his claws the *shen*-ring and the Maat feather. Below is a kneeling figure wearing the disk and holding in his hands the budding fronds which signify eternity.

Analogous statuettes of the goddess Wadjet are known to have been used as coffins for mummified ichneumon, the enemy of the serpent, that is to say the goddess herself. Thus exorcised, she wards off the dangerous adversary.

Our statue represents the goddess Mut in the form and with the attributes of Wadjet. She can likewise be depicted in human form wearing the double crown. These changes of identity explain the complexity of relationships among these goddesses in the Late Period. The inscription on the base specifies that it is Mut who gives life to a certain Isisirdis.

Bibliography: Daressy, Statues des Divinités (CG), p. 279, pl. 53. Cf. also: LÄ III, 1080–1090; T. G. H. James, in: JEA 68, 1982, pp. 156–65 and Bibliography.

255   Upper floor, room 19
The Goddess Bastet

Bronze   JE 36598
H. 17.3 cm; W. 5.8 cm; L. 12.5 cm
Sakkara, Serapeum. Entered the Museum in 1904
Late Period, 26th dynasty, about 600 B.C.

Bastet, Lady of Bubastis, was originally a lioness-goddess, very early associated with Sekhmet. With time she comes to represent the tame, magnanimous aspect of that goddess's character.

At Heliopolis she is recognized as the daughter of Atum and is assimilated to the "Eye of Re", that is to say the goddess Tefnut. During the Middle Kingdom she is identified with Hathor and later with Mut, both peaceful forms of the Far-Away Goddess (see no. 254).

255

It is in Lower Egypt that she appears particularly in the form of a cat. Cat cemeteries are found throughout Egypt in which the mummified remains of these animals are accompanied by a profusion of bronze statuettes in their likeness.

Our statuette depicts her in this gentle cat form adorned with a wide collar from which hangs a pendant *udjat*-eye amulet. The animal's ears are pierced and no doubt originally held earrings.

On the lyre-shaped base can be seen the inscription of the donor Padiamon to whom Bastet promises life.

Bibliography: Cf.: LÄ I, 628−630; Z. El-Kordy, La Déesse Bastet, Cairo 1968.

256   The Sacred Ibis

Upper floor, room 29

Wood, bronze, gold leaf   JE 71972
H. 24 cm; W. 16 cm; L. 45 cm
Tuna el-Gebel, excavations of Cairo University in 1959
Late Period, 26th dynasty, about 600 B.C.

The Ibis, like the Baboon, was sacred to Thoth, the god of wisdom and learning.

Thoth, a lunar god, is chief of the Ogdoad of Hermopolis (the company of eight primordial gods) among whom he replaced the divine Hare and assimilated to himself the sacred Baboon. The Master of language and inventor of writing, Thoth makes the laws and calculates time. These aptitudes caused him to become the secretary of the gods and the patron of scribes. Since he is supremely skilled in hieroglyphs and all secrets are known to him, Thoth is likewise a magician and consequently a healer. In the Late Period he was assimilated by the Greeks to Hermes under the appellation of "Trismegistus"; at that time he was believed to deliver oracles.

The cult of Thoth was widely dispersed throughout Egypt and the necropoleis overflow with mummified Ibises, particularly at Sakkara and Tuna el-Gebel.

Large numbers of statuettes were dedicated to him by all those

256

257

who honoured or invoked his wisdom. For this reason one often finds a statuette of a scribe reading in a papyrus, squatting at his foot. But this god whose Word created the universe is often found in the company of the goddess Maat, the guarantor of cosmic order, with whom he is closely associated since the Middle Kingdom.

It was no doubt a figurine of this goddess which was placed on the small openwork base facing the Ibis, whose figure is remarkable for its noble attitude.

The body of the sacred bird is of wood covered with gold leaf while his beak, tail and legs are of bronze. The eyes were originally inlaid.

Bibliography: J. Vandier, in: Revue d'Egyptologie 7, 1950, p. 33−35, pl. 4; LÄ VI, 497−523.

257   Ground floor, gallery 30

Naos of Nectanebo (detail)

Pink granite   JE 32018
H. (preserved) 88 cm   = CG 70018
Abydos; small temple to the west of Shunet ez-Zebib; discovered by Mariette around 1860 and brought to the Museum in 1896 by G. Daressy
Late Period, 30th dynasty, reign of Nectanebo I and Nectanebo II, 380−340 B.C.

Under the last indigenous Egyptian dynasty, King Nectanebo I, his son Teos, and the latter's nephew, Nectanebo II, had to repel Persian attempts to reconquer Egypt. Their reigns are marked by a renewed spirit of nationalism, a return to tradition of great ages past, and much artistic and architectural activity. All over Egypt the temples benefited from royal donations. Large monolithic shrines enriched their sanctuaries; some remarkable examples include those of Edfu and Elephantine, still in situ, and the large naos of Saft el Hene (on exhibit here in room 24).

Two shrines dedicated to a small temple at Abydos were discovered in fragments. The one illustrated here, partially restored, was originally a single block of stone with rounded roof. The decoration of the right-hand exterior face bears a double scene betraying an archaistic concern manifested in the pure forms and careful modelling reminiscent of the art of the Twenty-sixth Dynasty. To the left, Nectanebo I, wearing the red crown and a double kilt, advances under the sun-disk with uraei and offers an image of the goddess Maat to Thoth. The latter is represented in the form of a crouching baboon on a high pedestal, crowned with a sun-disk and lunar crescent. In the second scene, to the right, the god Onuris-Shu, crowned by four tall feathers and clothed in a long garment, offers another Maat image to the mummiform deity Osiris-Onnuphris.

Inside the naos, Nectanebo II offers a Maat image to the Abydene divinities and to Hathor, but the relief is poorly preserved.

To judge from the rest of the decorated blocks and statues found at the same site, the little temple, whence derives our naos, was most likely dedicated to Osiris, the principal god of Abydos. The ruins indicate there a structure dating all the way back to the New Kingdom. In the sanctuary of this temple, as in many others in Egypt, the Nectanebos would have donated two granite shrines in order to house statues or divine emblems.

Bibliography: PM V, p. 71; G. Roeder, Naos, (CG), pp. 53–55.

258–259   Ground floor, room 24, at the entrance
Relief sculpture of the Late Period

Limestone
258 Relief of Neferseshem-Psammetik   JE 10978
H. 30 cm; W. 134 cm
Mit Rahina; discovered by Mariette in 1860

259 Relief of Horhotep   JE 46591
H. 29 cm; W. 126 cm
Tell el-Faraᶜin (Buto); discovered by Gauthier in 1920

Late period, 30th dynasty, 4th Century B.C.

A frieze of individuals marching toward the tomb-owner, who in turn receives their offerings makes up the decoration of a series of sculpted fragments topped by a torus moulding. This theme, in use ever since the Old Kingdom, now recurs at the end of pharaonic history following periods of innovation, collapse and archaism, but executed in an altogether new fashion.

The low relief is not flat but is rather carefully modelled. The individuals stand out against the blank background. Even though they take part in a procession, they form quite independent figures, or at least independently composed groups of figures.

In the relief of "presenting gold" (258), four distinct groups are distributed before the scribe of the divine book Neferseshem-Psammetik. The latter remains seated in the classical pose upon a stool with carved bull's legs and holding a staff and rolled napkin. In front of him are written his name and titles. A man identified by the inscription overhead as "scribe of the gold" crouches before his scribal materials. He holds pen and palette and prepares to record the number of gold ornaments received which have been laid out before the deceased on two mats. In the second group, another man, apparently the scribe of gold's assistant, receives a large collar from a woman who also holds a bracelet by her side. Two groups of women follow bearing collars, counterpoises and bracelets. One can distinguish a concern both for high model-

ling which accentuates the full figures of the bodies, and for varying the poses, attitudes and even hairstyles. One woman holds her hand up to her wig; another is bent slightly forward. The second relief (259) contains a procession of offering bearers advancing toward the deceased Horhotep, a high priest associated with Buto. Here each figure is treated separately and the artist has attempted to break the monotony by randomly adding little children waving flowers, or calves with upraised heads. The bearers, with rounded figures and plain faces, wear either long shawls, kilts, or are half-naked. Their offerings consists of flowers and foodstuffs.

While these works of art are thoroughly Egyptian, the passage of some thirty centuries has nevertheless resulted in a certain academism. In spite of the high quality of the relief, these sculptures remain somewhat cold and devoid of vigor.

Bibliography: PM III, 2, p. 852; Terrace/Fischer, no. 40; PM IV, p. 45; H. W. Müller, Ägyptische Kunst, no. 181; Corteggiani, no. 111.

260

Coffin of Petosiris

Pine, glass paste   JE 46592
L. 195 cm
Tuna el-Gebel, tomb of Petosiris. Excavations of the Egyptian Antiquities Service in 1920
Beginning of the Ptolemaic Period, 2nd half of the 4th Century B.C.

This beautiful mummiform coffin belonged to Petosiris, a very important dignitary of the Hermopolite nome during the troubled times which preceded the arrival of the Ptolemies. High priest of Thoth and other deities of the nome, Petosiris's family of priests may be traced back for five generations.

The texts inscribed in his tomb bear witness to the high spiritual sensibilities of Petosiris, who was honored in his day as a sage. This family sepulchre dominates the necropolis of Tuna which stretches out to the west of Hermopolis. It is conceived as a small Ptolemaic temple, its funerary chapel preceded by an elegant columned portico with composite capitals. The interior decoration follows the traditional funerary program, with scenes of agriculture and craftsmanship, treated nonetheless in an original style. The Egyptian "background" has been enhanced by a new aestheticism introduced by the Greeks.

The tomb's substructure, however, remains in the purest Egyptian tradition. The stone sarcophagus encloses two wooden mummiform coffins in order to protect Petosiris' mummy. The burial equipment was robbed in antiquity, but the coffins were left in the sarcophagus; the thieves were apparently content to drag away the mummy in order to strip it of its finery. The interior coffin is the better preserved of the two and has a lid decorated with beautiful inlays. Set into the wood, now blackened by patina are five columns of multicolored glass paste hieroglyphs, topped by the star-filled sign for heaven. The extremely fine detail work gives the impression of gem inlays. Petosiris' name and titles are mentioned, along with the formula from Chapter 42 of the Book of the Dead, in which the deceased obviates the dangers of the nether world by identifying himself with the gods.

Bibliography: PM IV, p. 174; G. Lefèbvre, Petosiris III, Cairo 1924, pl. 58; Corteggiani, no. 112.

260a

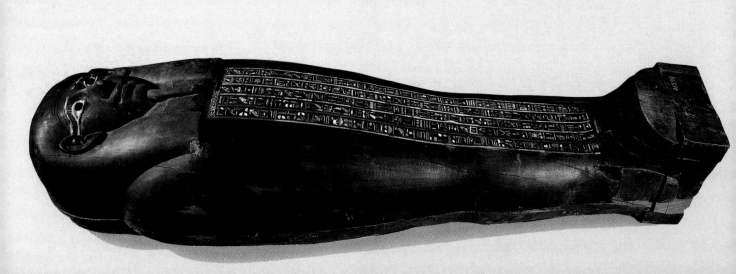

260 b

and bites of scorpions and snakes. It evokes the image of the clandestine childhood of Horus in the marsh, as well as victory over enemies. The magical texts which accompany the representation and continue on the back of the stela can, by virtue of divine protection, prevent threatening dangers or cure stings and bites.

Such stelae were erected in public places, much like healing statues of men or deities, likewise covered with magical texts, and usually representing a stela of the same Horus on crocodiles (see the healing statue of Djed-Hor on display in the same corridor). One need only pour water on it and then drink that water, once it had been imbued with divine power, in order to be protected against reptiles or heal their bites and stings.

Bibliography: PM IV, p. 6; Daressy, Textes et Dessins Magiques (CG), no. 9401, pp. 1−2, pl. I; cf. also LÄ III, 60−61; S. Hodjash, O. Berlev, The Egyptian Reliefs and Stelae in the Pushkin Museum Moscow, Leningrad 1982, p. 243−275.

261
Upper floor, corridor 19
Stela of Horus on crocodiles

Grey schist   CG 9401
H. 44 cm; W. 26 cm; thickness 11 cm
Alexandria; discovered before 1880
Ptolemaic Period, ca. 300−150 B.C.

The Horus child with mask of Bes above his head stands on two crocodiles and grasps dangerous animals such as snakes, a scorpion, an oryx and a lion. He is flanked by divine emblems: the lotus of Nefertum to his left and the papyrus crowned by a falcon to his right.

This type of stela was a powerful talisman against the stings

The Demotic Tale of Setne Khaemwas

Papyrus
L. 102 cm; W. 29.5 cm
Thebes, Deir el-Medina, found in the tomb of a Coptic monk. Bought by Mariette for the Museum in 1865
Ptolemaic period, 3rd century B.C.

JE 95581
= CG 30646 B

A cursive script more closely ligatured and more quickly written than the administrative hieratic from which it derived, made its appearance in the northern part of Egypt towards the middle of the 7th century B.C. Herodotus calls it "demotic" meaning "of the people".

This new cursive script was the vehicle used to express in writing a new phase of the Egyptian language, which like the script in which it was written is also called "Demotic". Both in grammar and in vocabulary it differs considerably from the preceding phase which we call Neo-Egyptian. During almost a millennium it was the only cursive script in general use, hieratic having been relegated to the redaction of religious texts and hieroglyphic being limited to inscriptions on stone.

In order to illustrate this writing which, used at first only for administrative and juridical texts quickly took over other sectors of public life including: letters, accounts, scholarly works, literature, history and even royal decrees (as on the Rosetta stone), here is a page from a literary papyrus chosen for its calligraphy and for its linguistic qualities.

It is the story of Setne Khaemwas, Priest of Ptah at Memphis, the son of Ramses II (see no. 209). The tale relates his quest for a divine book written by Thoth with his own hand which reveals how it is possible by one magic formula to enchant the sky, the earth, and the infernal regions, the mountains and the seas, to understand the language of the birds and reptiles, and then by a second formula to recover one's own identity.

Setne Khaemwas manages to enter the tomb of the prince and famous magician Naneferkaptah who had taken the book with him in death after having been struck down by the gods for discovering this dangerous secret.

Determined to get hold of this book, Khaemwas accepts the challenge of Naneferkaptah to play a board game for its possession. But having lost three games in succession he is only saved from annihilation by an amulet of Ptah which enables him to escape from the tomb taking the book with him. However he subsequently suffers from a terrible dream in which, having met a seductive young girl, he sacrifices everything he has including his children in order to assuage his desire for her. To rid himself of this nightmare he finally consents to restore the book to the prince's tomb.

This papyrus is divided into pages which are, unusually, numbered. The first two pages are missing but the title was preserved, written in red on the verso "The Tale of Setne", and also in the colophon at the end of the text where it is followed by the beginning of a date: Year 15 Tibi, 1st month of the winter season . . . The indication of the reign is lost.

Besides the menace formulated against anyone who tries to penetrate the secrets of the gods, this story proves that Prince Khaemwas, renowned for his learning and for the restorations which he commanded to be made in the Memphite necropolis, was remembered among the common people as a sage occupied with the search for ancient manuscripts. However, it would seem that popular superstition misjudged his intrusions in the tombs.

Bibliography: W. Spiegelberg, Die Demotischen Denkmäler (CG) II, p. 88, pls. 44–47; G. Maspero, Les Contes Populaires de l'Egypte Ancienne, Paris 1882, pp. 145–82; Griffith, Stories of the High Priests of Memphis, Oxford 1900, pp. 13–20, 67–81; E. Brunner-Traut, Altägyptische Märchen, Düsseldorf–Cologne 1963, pp. 171–92. Cf. also: F. Gomaa, Chaemwese, pp. 70–71.

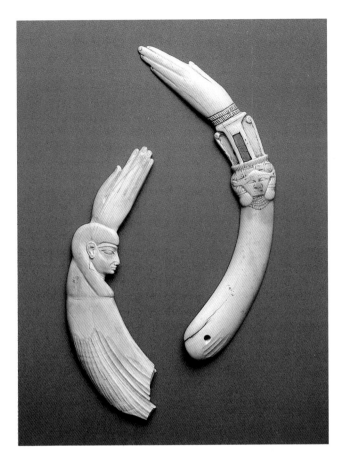

collar supports a structure flanked by two horns. A tapering left hand, adorned at the wrist and with two incised bracelets, elegantly extends the curve of the arm. The hole pierced through the bottom of this arm shows that the clappers were originally attached by means of a string.

Clappers are the oldest musical instruments attested in Egypt. Carved in ivory, wood or bone, they always occur in identical pairs, be it in the form of little curved sticks, or as small plaques, straight or bent, with the interior face curved inward. They were percussion instruments: beating one against the other served since prehistoric times to accompany the dance. Nagada vases often show scenes of dancers with upraised arms, accompanied by the rhythm of clappers.

The small plaques or sticks logically took on the shape of arms terminating in hands, a case of form influenced by function. Tomb equipment of the First Dynasty already contained clappers of this type. The concept of clapping likewise led to a practical design, such as the mallet at the end of each clapper, or more inspired forms such as the head of an Asiatic instead of hands (see room 43 of the ground floor), or simply decorative forms such as clappers with heads of animals.

From the Old Kingdom, mastaba walls include scenes of keeping rhythm during work by means of clappers, but it is more often in dancing scenes that they are used. Dancing calls the goddess Hathor to mind, for she is the mistress of gaiety, and many clappers bear her image. Tucked in between the hand and forearm, or emerging from a papyrus umbel, the head of Hathor, furnished with the ears of the sacred cow, is frequently surmounted by a naos. Priests and priestesses of Hathor owned these instruments and used them to keep rhythm at dances performed in the goddess' honor. In some rare examples, the head of a woman replaces that of Hathor. The use of simple sticks, however, continued both in daily life just as in the official ceremonies and festivals. Often it is Libyans who keep time by beating their sticks during military parades or processions of the sacred bark.

In the Late Period, clappers take the shape of right angles or have handles reduced to the form of bulbs or hollow pine cone halves. This was an innovation on the instrument, now held in pairs in each hand, which later came to be known as the castanet.

Bibliography: H. Hickmann, *Instruments de musique (CG)*, pp. 16−17, pl. 7B; *Nofret − Die Schöne*, nos. 47−48. Cf. also: Ch. Ziegler, *Les instruments de musique égyptiens au Musée du Louvre*, pp. 19−30.

263
Clappers

Upper floor, room 34

Woman's head surmounted by a hand	JE 39765
Ivory	= CG 69234
L. 19 cm; W. 4.5 cm; Diam. 0.7 cm	
Abydos; excavations of Garstang, 1908	
Middle or New Kingdom	

Head of Hathor surmounted by naos and hand	
Ivory of hippopotamus	CG 69235
L. 22 cm; W. 3.5 cm	
Provenance and date unknown	

Although the respective sister pieces of these two isolated clappers are lost, they nevertheless serve to illustrate characteristic types from among the many and varied examples known. The clapper with the broken handle shows a fairly well modelled woman's head surmounted by a right hand complete with fingernails. The other takes the form of a bent arm at the end of which a Hathor head with cow's ears, curled wig and bead

264
Sistrum

Upper floor, room 34

Bronze	JE 53327
H. 31 cm; W. 5 cm; thickness 7 cm	= CG 69316
Provenance unknown	
Graeco-Roman Period	

The sistrum is a musical rattle used in certain rituals, particularly those intended to appease the goddess Hathor. When shaken, it produces a rhythmic sound caused by the loose rods which traverse the frame and are occasionally furnished with rings.

Like the menat collar, the sistrum was also a cult object and a symbol of Hathor par excellence. It is attested in Egypt since the Old Kingdom, and found throughout the long course of Egyptian history in the hands of priests and priestesses. They used it to perform musical rites, whereas the king played it in temple rituals, standing before the gods. Eventually, the queen appears in this role from the New Kingdom on.

One can distinguish two fundamental types of sistrum. One type, called a *sesheshat*, shows a papyrus stalk or simple column for a handle, and a frame consisting of a naos traversed by little rods with rings. Beginning with the Middle Kingdom, a Hathor head supports this edifice. They are found in various materials, precious metals, stone or faience. A monumental stone version of this form may be found in the columns of hypostyles dedicated to Hathor.

The second type, known as arched or bowed, bears the Egyptian name of *sekhem*. An arc crossed by rods sometimes threaded with loose rings crowns the Hathor head in place of a naos. This type first appears in the Middle Kingdom and achieved wide diffusion, even being adopted outside Egypt in the Roman world. Usually of metal, it served as an offering for the sake of placating the angry goddess, and as an instrument for keeping time during dances and processions.

Because the sistrum symbolized the pacifying role of music, it was given in the Late Period a handle fashioned in the image of the god Bes, who appeased the goddess with his music and dance as far back as the beginning of Egyptian history.

Our example combines the two types of sistrum. A Bes figure forms the handle, standing on a base which is flanked by two sphinxes. His tall feathered headdress is based on a frame fit snugly into the handle by means of a tenon. A square abacus supports the doublefaced head of Hathor between two uraei; the latter wear the respective crowns of Upper and Lower Egypt. Above Hathor, the naos which the Late Period texts designate as the monumental gateway housing the *ba* of Hathor, once held a figurine, doubtless a uraeus. It is flanked by two masks of silens borrowed from the Graeco-Roman world.

The rimmed arch is pierced on both sides with three holes, through which the rods pass (one is missing). At the top, a cat, reminiscent of the gentle goddess Bastet (placated form of the malevolent goddess), is surrounded by four kittens, symbolizing fertility, and by a cock, chosen for his waking cry or as a symbol of rebirth.

Bibliography: H. Hickmann, Instruments de musique (CG), pp. 80−81, pl. 46A; Nofret − Die Schöne, no. 45. Cf. also: Ch. Ziegler, Les instruments de musique égyptiens au Musée du Louvre, pp. 31−62; LÄ V, 959−62.

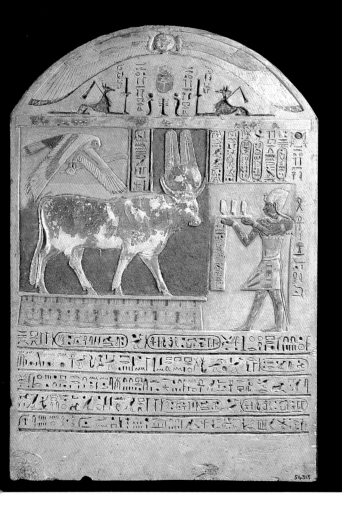

among its splendid burial equipment more than a thousand stelae, the much smaller Bucheum covered a shorter period, from the Thirtieth Dynasty (Nectanebo II) to the Roman period (reign of Diocletian), and could boast but two galleries.

It was in the ruins of the Bucheum that this stela, dated to year 25 of Ptolemy V, was discovered. The stela's lunette above is decorated with the winged sun disk, beneath which a scarab and a *djed* pillar are flanked by emblems, two uraei, and two crouching jackals. The central register, dominated by the sign for heaven, depicts an offering scene in which the Hellenistic King Ptolemy V in pharaonic dress offers the sign of fields to a statue of the Buchis bull. The bull stands upon a completely gilded base, and wears between its horns the headdress of Montu: a sun disk with two uraei and a double feather. It is identified with Rê, and bears the epithets, "living spirit", and "herald of Rê."

Behind the bull, Montu appears in his customary guise as a falcon, as he was venerated at Thebes. Spreading his wings, the falcon holds a fan and *shen*-ring, signifying duration, in its claws. Montu is associated with Rê-Horakhty, and is hailed as the "great god, Lord of the southern On," that is, of Thebes. At the bottom of the stela is a text of five lines, from which we learn that the Buchis in question, which died in year 25 of Ptolemy V and Cleopatra I, was born in year 11 of the same sovereign. It was in Ptolemy's reign that the famous trilingual decree, now known as the Rosetta Stone, was issued, which enabled Champollion to decipher the hieroglyphs in 1822 (the Rosetta Stone is preserved today in the British Museum; see the cast of it in hall 48 of the ground floor).

Bibliography: Corteggiani, no. 115. Cf. E. Otto, Beiträge zur Geschichte der Stierkulte in Ägypten, UGÄA 13, Leipzig 1938, reprint Hildesheim 1964, p. 40—57.

265   Ground floor, room 34
Stela dedicated by Ptolemy V to the bull Buchis

Limestone, painted and gilded   JE 54313
H. 72 cm; W. 50 cm; thickness 14 cm
Armant, Bucheum of Hermonthis. Excavations of the Egypt Exploration Society, 1929—30
Ptolemaic Period, reign of Ptolemy V, year 25, 181 B.C.

The Buchis bull is the sacred animal of the god Montu in the Thebaid, just as the Apis bull was the sacred animal of Ptah at Memphis, and Mnevis the solar bull of Heliopolis.

Just as the enthroned Apis at Memphis enjoyed a royal burial in the Serapeum at Sakkara after a ceremonial life, so did a Bucheum near Hermonthis (Armant) house the mummified bodies of the Buchis bulls. But if the Serapeum was a vast necropolis close to two thousand years old, which revealed

266   Upper floor, room 22
Scarab

Glass paste, wood, gold leaf   RT 15.1.25.44
L. 11 cm; W. 6.5 cm
Provenance unknown; acquired by the Museum in 1925
Graeco-Roman Period

This beautiful blue scarab is veneered to a small piece of gilded wood. It is a naturalistic representation of the coprophagous coleopter (*scarabaeus sacer*) with clearly formed clypeus, free legs and scored wing-case.

The scarab was associated very early on in Egypt with the generative forces of the rising sun and with the concepts of eternal renewal. This little insect, which comes out of the sand backwards dragging its ball of dung behind it, symbolizes the sun's daily journey across the heavens from east to west. This association was reinforced by a play on words: *kheper*, the Egyp-

266

tian word for the scarab, was related to the verb *kheper*, meaning to come into being, to happen, and also to the name of the solar deity *khepri* in his aspect of the rising sun. The scarab beetle sign was used to write all of these different notions, and the god Khepri is often represented with head of a scarab.

Scarabs thus became a potent amulet. They occur frequently, fashioned mostly from glazed steatite or faience, or cut from semi-precious stones, but are fairly rarely found in gold, silver or bronze, possibly because they were subsequently melted down.

From the First Intermediate Period on, stamp seals mounted on a ring or a pendant were well-suited to the form of the scarab, but always retained their amuletic function. On the base of the scarab the Egyptians carved in sunk relief, symbols, wishes or royal names. In the New Kingdom, large historical scarabs were issued in order to herald events such as the political successes of Tuthmosis IV, a hunt, or the marriage of Amenophis III with Tiye, and later with the Hittite princess Gilukhepa, or the construction of a lake for Queen Tiye.

"Heart scarabs", placed upon the breast of the mummy in the position of the heart, are of jasper or green stone, the color of rebirth, or occasionally of black stone. They carry on the base the spell from Chapter 30 of the Book of the Dead: "O my heart, do not bear witness against me in the presence of the tribunal."

Mounted in jewellery, or represented on temple or tomb walls, the scarab always remained the symbol of rebirth.

Bibliography: See.: LÄ V, pp. 968–981; E. Staehelin, Ägyptens heiliger Pillendreher, Basle 1982.

Mummified baby crocodile

Embalmed body of a crocodile, linen bandages   CG 29712
L. 37.5 cm; W. 6.4 cm; thickness 4.5 cm
Thebes, Assassif; acquired by the Museum before 1864
Roman Period, 1st Century A.D.

Mummified fauna were quite common in Egypt, including all sorts of animals thought to represent various divinities. For example, the god Ptah could appear in the form of a sacred bull, Amon as a ram or a goose, Hathor as a cow, and Sobek as a crocodile.

At first the Egyptians only mummified the sacred animals chosen from among the many of their species as earthly representations of a given deity. After a privileged existence within the enclosure wall of the temple, these animals received at their death all the care of an embalming fit for the gods. In the Late Period, the entire species came to be considered sacred, and the Egyptians began to mummify all of them without distinguishing whether they died within or without the temple walls. Some four million ibises buried at Sakkara testify to the longevity of this practice.

The crocodile, sacred animal of Sobek (Greek Suchos), was god of water and fertility since the beginning of Egyptian history. Worshipped originally in the Fayum, Sobek's cult came to expand from the Delta marshes all the way to the desert's edge and the cliffs of Gebel Silsila in Upper Egypt. Sobek himself was eventually considered a primordial god. In the open spaces of his temples, this reptile received the worship of priests and on occasion also of temple visitors. He was glorified with hymns and mummified after his death. The crocodile cemetery discovered near the temple of Kom Ombo revealed a multitude of crocodile mummies of considerable size.

The wrappings of this young crocodile display an arrangement characteristic of the Roman Period: on the top, light and dark bandages intersect to form a geometric pattern. In the position of the eyes are inserted two pieces of plain linen, each marked with a dark iris.

Bibliography: Gaillard/Daressy, La Faune Momifiée (CG), p. 118, pl. 48. See also: C. Andrews, Egyptian Mummies, British Museum, chapter 6.

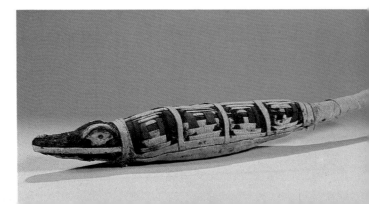

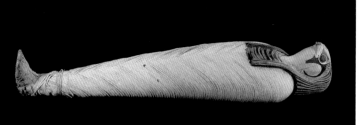

268
Naos with falcon

Wood, stuccoed and painted   RT 18.11.24.46
Total Height 69.5 cm; L. 27 cm; W. 26.5 cm
Provenance unknown
Roman Period, 1st–2nd Centuries A.D.

Judging from its decoration, one might conclude that this attractive little naos painted with vibrant colors held a mummified falcon. It takes the form of a Lower Egyptian shrine crowned with a cavetto cornice. The cover acts as roof to the shrine and bears the image of the falcon equipped with two tall feathers and a sun disk, thus representing one of the forms of the god Re.

The painted decoration consists of a niched palace facade with false door, a winged sun-disk, *khekher* frieze, row of uraei in profile, several scenes of adoration and offerings to Re, and finally the signs for protection and stability. In the central panel (illustrated) a priest accompanied by Nephtys makes offerings before the falcon of Re crowned with a sun-disk. Behind him stands Anubis.

In the Late Period the falcon was worshipped throughout Egypt as Re, Horus or even other deities. Falcons kept in the temples were even used in the ritual of the divine cult. Carefully mummified after their death (cf. no. 267), some were enclosed within beautiful little chests, painted like the present example, then transported in a procession to their tomb. Others were embalmed in groups placed together in painted chests. More common, however, are the falcons buried in more modest coffins housed in simple clay vessels. (See also the falcon mummy [illustrated] on display in room 19 of the upper floor.)

Bibliography: Cf. sarcophagus in Berlin, Inv.-no. 8518: Ägyptisches Museum Berlin, 1967, no. 862. Similar chest in Brooklyn, no. 37.1390 E. See also: Gaillard/Daressy, La Faune Momifiée (CG), nos. 29712–29800.

Bibliography: Edgar, Graeco-Egyptian Coffins (CG), pp. 21–24, pls. 8, 9 and 12; G. Grimm, Die Römischen Mumienmasken aus Ägypten, Wiesbaden 1974, pl. 60, p. 62 and 133 (7, 8). Cf. also: C. Andrews, Egyptian Mummies, British Museum, chapter 4.

269   Upper floor, room 14
Mummy masks

Cloth and painted plaster   CG 33130 and 33131
H. 52 and 51.3 cm; W. 34 and 33 cm; profile 44 and 40 cm
Meir, Nazali Ganoub; acquired by the Museum in 1888
Roman Period, 2nd Century A.D.

The Greeks who settled in Egypt during the Graeco-Roman Period eventually came to adopt Egyptian funerary practices. Embalming the body of the deceased continued up to the 4th Century A.D., but with some Hellenistic modifications. The traditional Egyptian mask gave way to a sort of raised cover furnished with several layers of plastered cloth, upon which the facial features were modelled and enhanced with bright colors. The overall impression was that the head rested upon a cushion. The rendering of the face had by this time lost all of its Egyptian characteristics. The mask extended below the neck as a sort of breast-panel with Hellenistic features.
These two women's masks were part of a typical ensemble from Middle Egypt. A floral wreath in plaster adorns the hair, composed of vegetable fibers once painted black. The eyes are inlaid with glass. The eyebrows, lips, fingernails and wrinkles are painted, as is the jewellery modelled in subtle relief. The red-painted chiton is ornamented with vertical black stripes. A hole pierced between the thumb and index finger indicates that the hand once held some sort of emblem. Two more holes pierced at the bottom of the mask served to attach it to the mummy.
The one element which has remained purely Egyptian is the "cushion", which supports the mask and encloses the head of the mummy. Protective deities are depicted here: Osiris, Isis and Horus, Anubis, Sokar and Nepthys, and at the head, a falcon with outstretched wings.

270   Upper floor, room 14
Portrait of a young lady

Wood, encaustic, waxed and painted   CG 33243
H. 42 cm; W. 23 cm
Hawara, discovered by Petrie in 1888
Roman Period, 2nd Century A.D.

Parallel to the masks in modelled stucco, or those roughly moulded around the deceased's face, there developed in the 1st Century A.D. the practice of covering the face of the mummy with a naturalistic portrait of him. This was painted usually in encaustic, less often in tempera, on a wooden panel which was then inserted among the mummy bandages. They were called "Fayum portraits" because the first examples known derived from the cemeteries of Greek settlements in the Fayum. They are found, however, in many other sites within Egypt. In use up until the beginning of the 4th Century, they disappear in the Coptic period, with the end of the practice of mummification. This young woman's portrait is painted in encaustic on a coated surface. The wax mixed with the pigments allows them to retain their intensity. The shoulders and breast are in three-quarter view, the head fully frontal but slightly tilted to the left. The long face, framed by hair taken up in a bun, is dominated by large eyes, dark eyelids and black eyebrows. Light brushstrokes are visible on the neck and one side of the face. The undeceived mouth underscores the melancholy expression. The jewellery and clothing are rendered by bold brushstrokes, and the overall impression is one of successful naturalism.

Bibliography: Petrie, Hawara, Biahmu and Arsinoe, London 1889, between pl. 10 and 11; Edgar, Graeco-Egyptian Coffins (CG), p. 95, pl. 38; Grimm/Johannes, Kunst der Ptolemäer- und Römerzeit im Ägyptischen Museum Kairo, Mainz 1975, no. 5, pl. E; K. Parlasca, Mumienportraits und verwandte Denkmäler, Wiesbaden 1966.

The Egyptian Museum, Cairo
268 pages with 23 illustrations in black and white and 290 illustrations in colour